W9-BCM-472

Sanctioned Violence
in
Early China

SUNY Series in Chinese Philosophy and Culture
David L. Hall and Roger T. Ames, Editors

Sanctioned Violence
in
Early China

Mark Edward Lewis

STATE UNIVERSITY OF NEW YORK PRESS

Excerpts from "The Wind" and "Sir Fantasy" are reprinted from Burton
Watson, trans. and ed., *Chinese Rhyme-Prose: Prose in the·Fu Form from the
Han and Six Dynasties Periods.* Copyright © 1971, Columbia University Press,
New York. Used by permission.

Published by
State University of New York Press, Albany

© *1990 State University of New York*

All rights reserved

Printed in the United States of America

No part of this book may be used or reproduced
in any manner whatsoever without written permission
except in the case of brief quotations embodied in
critical articles and reviews.

For information, address State University of New York
Press, State University Plaza, Albany, NY 12246

Library of Congress Cataloging-in-Publication Data

Lewis, Mark Edward, 1954–
Sanctioned violence in early China/Mark Edward Lewis.
p. cm.—(SUNY series in Chinese philosophy and culture)
ISBN 0–7914–0076–X.—ISBN 0–7914–0077–8 (pbk.)
1. Violence—China—History. 2. China—Social conditions—To 221
B.C. 3. China—History—Warring States, 403–221 B.C. I. Title.
II. Series.
HN740.Z9V55 1990
303.6'2'0951—dc 19   *88–37052*
                                                   CIP

10 9 8 7 6 5 4 3 2 1

Contents

Preface

This project was first intended to be a study of the role of military institutions, most notably universal military service, in the formation of the Warring States and the first Chinese empires. However, in seeking to trace the historical antecedents of the mass, infantry armies of the fourth and third centuries B.C., I found it impossible to treat warfare in isolation from a whole range of social practices with which it was closely linked in the sources: hunting, vendetta, sacrifice, and blood oaths. Not only were these forms of sanctioned killing equated or closely linked in the *Zuo zhuan*, our only literary source for the seventh through the fifth centuries B.C., but in the following centuries the various elements of this early complex of ritualized violence underwent parallel developments in which what had been the privileged attributes of aristocratic power in the Zhou polity became the universal determinants of hierarchic bonds in the new, autocratic kingdoms. Consequently, the erstwhile study of military institutions grew into a more encompassing examination of the Warring States transition as revealed by changes in the patterns of sanctioned violence. These changes show how the institutional developments of the period entailed a transformation of the basic units of political and kin organization, a re-definition of the nature of authority, a re-creation of the political realm through new forms of ties between men, and a re-imagining of human society and its relations to the natural world.

Given the vast and protean nature of the topic, I have attempted to bring to bear virtually all the surviving literary remains of the Warring States, Qin, and Han periods, as well as relevant evidence preserved in later works. These include historical accounts, philosophy, poetry, myth, commentaries, scientific works, and inscriptional materials. Archeological evidence, both from individual site reports and the synthesizing works of other scholars, has also been incorporated at many points. In light of the range and variety of relevant materials, numerous pieces of evidence and potential lines of argument have doubtless been overlooked, but I trust that scholars will bring these to light in the course of time. This work will have achieved its purpose if it can encourage others to develop more fully the issues which it has raised, or related ones that ought to have been included.

Scholarship is always a collective endeavour, and this book is no exception. The initial stages of its research and writing were guided by Professor Michael Dalby. Later, Professor Ping-ti Ho provided steady assistance in the process of writing, and the earliest version of the work was also read and criticized by Professors David Roy and William McNeill. Revisions of the manuscript were read by Professors Roger Ames and Stephen Owen, both of whom provided valuable suggestions for improvement. My greatest intellectual debts, however, are to the numerous scholars from whose written works I have learned and borrowed so much. I would also like to thank my wife for her invaluable help in preparing the manuscript in all of its many incarnations.

Part of the research for this project was conducted in China and Japan with grants from the Social Science Research Council and the Committee for Scholarly Communication with the People's Republic of China. The writing of the first version was supported by a dissertation writing fellowship from the University of Chicago.

Introduction

The Social Uses of Violence

This book is about violence. Not the deviant, frightening violence of the newspapers but those modes of inflicting harm or taking life which men accept, approve, and even prescribe. These sanctioned forms of violence appear in every human society, sometimes the subject of debate or criticism, sometimes framed with special ceremonies to separate them from mundane affairs, sometimes hidden away from the eyes of polite society, sometimes taken for granted as just another unremarkable aspect of life, but always acting as a constitutive element of the social order. Being universal, variable, and generally a matter of highest concern, sanctioned violence provides a useful key for the comparative study of societies, or for the analysis of changes over time in a single society. This book examines the reorganization and reinterpretation of violence during Warring States China in order to gain a new understanding of the political and social changes that led up to the creation of the first Chinese empire.

Although many aspects of the phenomenon of violence have been studied, there is no systematic exposition of the various uses, either for actual participants or for social analysts, of approved violence. I would suggest at least four such uses: 1) violence as compelling force, as the decisive element of the political order; 2) violence as a definer and creator of social groupings; 3) violence as a marker of significance; 4) violence as an element in myth or in metaphoric thinking.

The use of sanctioned violence as an element of statecraft or a form of legitimate compulsion is well-known in the West, where a major school of modern thought has defined the state through its "monopoly" of force. The most famous formulation of this idea is Max Weber's proposition that a state is a "human community that (successfully) claims the *monopoly of the legitimate use of physical force* within a given territory," but similar ideas figure in the works of thinkers from a wide range of intellectual disciplines and political perspectives.[1] Although other writers have asserted the primacy in politics of the control of language or communal symbols, and like Durkheim defined the state as an "organ of

1

social thought," the identification of the state with the use of violence remains a major strain in Western social thought and certainly represents a central element in the modern political order.[2]

The second role of violence—as a definer of groups—appears in our own society in a form of violence that is decidedly *not* monopolized by the state, the mass slaughter and consumption of animals. In accepting that animals can be killed and eaten, men make the first grand division of the animate world into "us" and "them," and even create a hierarchy of domesticated animals between those which can be routinely killed and eaten and those which would be so treated only in a dire emergency. Within the broad grouping of those beings who should never be killed and eaten, i.e., of men, the world is further divided into those who cannot be killed except in self-defense or for heinous crimes as adjudged in a court of law, and those "outsiders" who in the event of war may be freely slaughtered. Indeed, one of the marks of the modern world as the age of the nation-state is precisely the fact that differences of citizenship mark the primary separation between those who may be killed and those who may not.

The most detailed studies of the uses of patterns of licit violence to distinguish "us" from "them" or "inner" from "outer" appeared in the writings of the British social anthropologists on "stateless" or "acephalous" societies. All crimes in such societies were personal, and it was the duty of the injured party and his kin to repair the loss through receiving compensation or injuring the perpetrator of the crime. However, the possibility and form of redress varied with the relation of the offender to the victim. If the culprit were an immediate relative, a member of a group that shared corporate property, then no compensation was possible and the guilt was symbolically expiated through a sacrifice. If he were a member of a different segmental lineage of the same tribe, then an uncompensated crime initiated a blood feud that could, however, ultimately be settled through mediation. Between different tribes there existed a condition of permanent hostility and intermittent combat that could not be settled; it was a state of perpetual, low-level warfare. Indeed, one scholar has suggested that the agnatic lineage in Nuer society was in fact a code for what were actually territorial units defined by a nested hierarchy of relations of feud and conquest.[3]

In addition to marking social divisions, violence also helps to form groups through uniting individuals in shared hostility to some "outsider." Freud suggested that it was possible for large groups to live together in amity only as long as there were other people "left over" to act as targets of aggression.[4] Even more extreme in his insistence on the social necessity of shared violence is René Girard, who argues that the potentially destructive violence endemic to society can be escaped only by unanimous acts of violence against an outsider or marginal figure; by limiting violence to the sanctioned form of the "sacrifice," society turns its potential annihilation into purgation and a restoration of order.[5] Despite the absurdity of Girard's claims to have presented *the* explanation for sacrifice, religion, myth, and culture, as well as the empirical difficulties involved in applying his universalizing, psychological model to actual cases, the numerous examples of the use of "scapegoats" he has found in ethnographic and literary texts clearly suggest the importance of shared violence in constituting human society and the variety of roles it plays in the creation of culture.

The third major role of sanctioned violence is as a marker, either tangible or abstract, of significance. In the former, the physical death of the sacrificial victim, the martyr, or the war dead charges an action with a seriousness or a compelling power it would otherwise lack; the bodies of the dead give a tangible form to an abstract commitment or belief. In the latter the belief that life is precious leads men to use killing or dying as a measure for value; what men die for is supremely important.

The role of violence as an objective marker of significance through the taking of life was recognized in antiquity by Sallustius.

> . . . prayers divorced from sacrifice are only words, prayers with sacrifices are animated words, the word giving power to the life and the life animation to the word.[6]

The body or life-spirit of a victim charges the accompanying actions or speech with a power they would otherwise lack.

This use of killing to "substantiate" or "animate" words or intent also figures in warfare, as Elaine Scarry has argued at some length. Decisions resulting from wars, rather than arising solely through force or threat, are imposed through the shared conviction of the contestants that they *are* decisive, and this conviction is substantiated through the masses of corpses and wounds produced by the war. The mass of dead and wounded bodies resulting from war's violence acts as a "marker of significance," a "reality-conferring" agent that grants manifest and tangible force to the terms of settlement of the conflict. The compelling power of war parallels that of sacrificial oaths in earlier societies, in which the participants bound themselves to abide by a decision or to validate a pledge through the offering of a sacrifice or the mutilation of their own bodies.[7]

Violence as a marker of significance depends not only on the invocation of physical bodies but on the abstract belief that life is precious and hence a potential measure of value. The ancient Chinese philosopher Mencius, for example, asserted the supreme value of duty and principle by stating that he would give up his life for them.[8] Carl Schmitt argued that the "political" is not defined by any content or function; any common endeavor becomes political when the intensity of commitment is such that the members regard it as legitimate or imperative that participants should sacrifice themselves and kill outsiders for the sake of the cause.[9] In this very German argument, the "political" indicates whatever matters are of greatest concern, but even so eminent and humane a liberal as William James launched his appeal for organized mass altruism with his much-imitated call for a "moral equivalent of war." It is warfare, with its total mobilization and its devotion to the death, that he offered as the standard of commitment by which all social activities were to be measured.

The final function of approved violence is as an element in myth and in metaphoric thinking. Perhaps because of the role of violence as a marker of significance or value, or because it functions as an·extreme case by which men mark out the limits of civilization and humanity, mythology abounds in murders and mutilations of every description. In what has become the primal mythology of Western civilization, the ancient Greek tales of child sacrifice and cannibalism, of savage amazons and frenzied maenads, of man-eating beasts and bestial heroes, and of the murder of parents or spouses all offered a means of depicting the nature and limits of human society. In the systematic play of such oppositions as man and beast, city and wilderness, agriculture and hunting, or woman and man, these stories created an ideal of civilization through meditations on its borderlines and internal divisions. Publically acted out in the tragedies at Athens, these tales of savage violence that negated all social norms became part of the civic order of the *polis*.[10] More recently, the American nation has defined its own ideals of civilization through violent tales of frontiersmen, hunters, and race war with the native Americans.[11]

Tales or metaphors of violence figure prominently not only in meditations on the principles of civilization but also in discussions of the natural world, most notably in attempts to ground human institutions in principles of nature. Perhaps the most famous example of this is the Darwinian "discovery" of a savage struggle for survival in the wild, a discovery that was inspired by the battle for life in newly industrialized England and used to rationalize and justify this society built on competition in economic markets. An even more striking example appears in seventeenth-century England, where the political debate and the understanding of human violence extended into discussions of the principles that regulated matter. Thomas Hobbes's theory of a brutish, violent state of nature was closely associated with his "mechanical" philosophy of nature in which all motion was based on the random collisions of particles. Eager to refute this Hobbesian vision of nature and man, the latitudinarians supported the Newtonian theory of a providentially guided, mathematically regulated universe as a natural sanction for a stable, commercial society under Anglican hegemony.[12]

I have offered this introductory sketch with its all-too-miscellaneous examples simply in order to suggest the kinds of insights that can be gained through the study of sanctioned violence and to show how these insights have actually figured in many aspects of Western social theory and historical analysis. Through knowing what forms of violence were permitted, who could perform them, how these actions were rationalized, and how violence figured in tales and metaphors, one learns about the locus and exercise of authority in a given society, its basic social groupings, to what matters it attributed highest significance, and the manner in which it defined its own civilization and its relation to the natural world. In this way the study of the patterns of violence is potentially as valuable for historical research as is the examination of patterns of the exchange of goods, of kinship ties, or of social hierarchy.

**Sanctioned Violence and the Warring
States Transition**

The Warring States period in China, dated from various years in the fifth century to 221 B.C., is generally regarded as a transitional period between the "feudalism" of the high Zhou state and the creation of a unified Chinese empire by the Qin state. It was a time of unprecedented changes in government, society, economy, and culture. The economic changes included the rise of private ownership of land, the development of water control and iron tools leading to expanding agricultural output, a probable increase in population, a massive upsurge in the scale and diversity of urban centers, the burgeoning of handicraft industries and trade, the increased use of money, and the introduction of hired labor. The social order was transformed by the disappearance of the old aristocracy, the rise of a large class of land-owning peasants, and a substantial increase in the urban classes devoted to trade and handicraft production. Political developments included the creation of a government staffed entirely by appointed, salaried officials, the assertion of direct control over local governments by the court, the promulgation of legal codes, and the comprehensive registration of the population. Among the military innovations were the introduction of cavalry, the invention of the crossbow, the increased use of iron weapons, the rise of mass, infantry armies, and the appearance of commanders who held office through their mastery of the arts of generalship. In the cultural sphere the period is most noted for its competing philosophical schools, which for the first time in China articulated theories of the state, the social order, language, and logic, but it also witnessed significant developments in literary genres, the visual arts, and such diverse sciences as medicine and astronomy.

However, while scholars have agreed on the importance and the revolutionary nature of these collective changes, there is little agreement as to the inner coherence, if any, of the total ensemble. How the various phenomena were related one to the other, which were primary and which secondary, and how to characterize the entire transition remain open questions. Thus, the best overall treatment of the period, Yang Kuan's *Zhanguo shi* [History of the Warring States], provides detailed discussions of each of the developments listed above and many more, yet the only explanatory model offered to link them together is the officially approved theory that this transition marked the change from a slave society to a feudal society dominated by the landlord class.[13] While there were slave-like categories in Shang and Zhou China, the existence of a slave society remains unproven, and there is as yet no evidence whatsoever for the existence of private landlords in the Warring States. Yang Kuan's exposition moves systematically from economic foundations to political superstructure to cultural epiphenomena, but he links them together only through repeated appeals to the interests and actions of a spectral class which has left no trace in the historical record.

The standard one-volume treatment of the period in English, Cho-yun Hsu's *Ancient China in Transition*, focuses on the question of changing social mobility, but it also attempts a general characterization of the transition from Zhou feudalism to the imperial state. For his purposes Hsu adopts Weberian categories and asserts that the basic change was from "communal" to "associative" relations and from "traditional" authority to "rational-legal." The society of the earlier period is described as "familistic," while that of the later is more "individualistic." Related to this general change, he sees the primary change in the political realm as being a shift from emphasis on birth to emphasis on personal character. He also places great stress on the rise of trade and argues that contractual, commercial relations provided the model for basic social relations.[14] Since Max Weber's categories were created to distinguish modern Western society from earlier forms, it is perhaps not surprising that Hsu's "Weberian" account of the Warring States transition sounds exactly like the emergence of modern capitalism. This is clearly inappropriate to Warring States China. While there were dramatic changes in the character and roles of kin groups, it is wrong to describe these as a shift from a "familistic" society to an "individualistic" one; although the word is vague, imperial China was certainly still "familistic." Moreover, Hsu grossly overstates the impact of commerce and of business practices on the social order.

Yang appeals to a fictive landlord class to explain the transition, while Hsu describes it in terms that Weber would apply to the modern, capitalist West and then justifies this through exaggerating the impact of commerce and attributing spurious "rational-legal" principles to the defenders and servants of the imperial state. They are both representative of the general opinion of modern scholars in China and the West in that they assume the necessary priority of changes in the economy over those in other spheres. This tendency of all scholars living under the shadow of nineteenth-century social theory is exacerbated by the fact that the abundant new archeological finds in China, which have the combined appeal of novelty, tangibility, and secure dating, provide far more evidence of changes in technology and urban scale than of those in political organization, social organization, or values. Assertions of the priority of economy, technology, or demography also give scholars the satisfaction of revealing the objective "truth" behind the ideological mask of the native, Chinese tradition, which explained history as a political, social, or moral phenomenon. Nevertheless, the general failure of these scholars to provide coherent arguments that lead from the development of the iron plow to the rise of philosophical schools, or from a putative population explosion to the appearance of the imperial state, suggests that we should try other approaches.

This book is certainly not the first attempt to present an account of the Warring States transition based on the assumption that it was primarily a political and social phenomenon. Various Japanese scholars have made valuable contributions in this field, and they will be cited at the points in my argument where I am in their debt. Nor does it offer a comprehensive account, for several important aspects of the period can only be briefly touched on. However, examining the changing patterns in sanctioned violence provides important insights for a reconsideration of the social and political character of the transition, insights that are particularly useful because of the decisive role played by sanctioned violence in many aspects of the society of the period.

Chapter One focuses on the role of sanctioned violence in the society of Spring and Autumn China, a period named after a chronicle that spans the years from 722 to 481 B.C. This era leads directly into the Warring States period, and a knowledge of its institutions and practices is necessary for an understanding of later developments. In this period China was dominated by a hereditary elite which set itself apart from the general population through the service of its ancestral cults, a service which took the primary forms of sacrifice, warfare, and—as an extension of warfare—hunting. These ritually coded acts of violence that defined the aristocracy, their integration in the ancestral cult, and their common culmination in the presentation of victims and the eating of meat form the topic of the first section, which thus establishes the major forms of sanctioned violence and how they figured in defining the social order.

The next section deals with the question of who was permitted to perform these acts and how this affected the nature of authority. The state of the Spring and Autumn period, schematized in ritual text accounts of "lineage law" (*zong fa* 宗法), resembled the so-called "segmentary" state of anthropological theory in that the lesser or branch lineages of the ruling house reproduced the royal or "ducal" courts on a reduced scale in their own "fiefs." These cadet lineages had their own ancestral temples, where they offered sacrifice to the founders of their particular line. Ritual exchanges of meat from sacrifices at the ducal temples and at these lesser temples formed a basic part of the rituals for the ancestral cult and war. Moreover, the cadet lineages commanded detachments raised from their own fiefs, so that only one section of the state's army was directly controlled by the "duke," while the rest remained under the leaders of the sublineages. These leaders not only conducted their own sacrificial rituals and commanded their own armies, but they also had the hereditary right to offices, including command of the army, which they exercised free of ducal control. Thus the identification of lordship with sacrifices and military action in the Zhou state also betokened a collegiality of leadership in which hereditary officials and lesser lords shared power with the state's ruler.

Because the sublineages formed lesser replicas of the central court, each of them was potentially a state in its own right, and during the Spring and Autumn period effective power in most states passed from the duke to the leading ministerial households, who then began to battle for power among themselves. Moreover, an obsessive concern for personal and lineage honor in a world marked by sociability on a basis of relative equality led to numerous occasions for slights or disputes, which elicited acts of vengeance, feuds, and often civil wars. Although not explicitly approved, these vendettas are so common in the records that they clearly formed part of conventional social practice, and there are even references to books which laid out the principles of vengeance. The frequency of these feuds and their importance in establishing effective power suggest that the significant political divisions in the Spring and Autumn period lay not only between states but also between the sublineages within a state. In many cases it was these warring sublineages who pioneered or developed the new forms of state power that characterized the Warring States.

The final section shows how the "public," non-kin realm in Spring and Autumn China was constituted entirely through blood covenants (*meng* 盟). These covenants, which involved drinking the blood of a sacrificial victim, are a classic example of the "substantiating" role of sacrifice, for they were more binding than a verbal oath (*shi* 誓) without sacrifice. Used to "sanctify" any agreement between non-kin, they were sworn precisely between those who would otherwise engage in battle, including states, sublineages, and the capital populace. As the "mirror image" of combat these covenants likewise demonstrate that the key divisions in society lay between sublineages as well as states. Moreover, they reiterate the crucial role of sacrifice in constituting society, for any people who were not drawn together for shared sacrifice to a common ancestor could only be united through sharing the blood of a common sacrificial victim.

Chapter One thus establishes the forms, uses, and social distribution of sanctioned violence in Spring and Autumn China. It uses these to reveal the concerns and self-image of the elite, the nature of authority, the basic units of society, and the modes of linking men together. It also shows the frequency and importance of both interstate and civil war, for it was out of these struggles that the political institutions of the Warring States emerged.

Chapter Two deals with the mechanism of that emergence. The shift to reliance on infantry armies pioneered by states at the northern and southern frontiers, where the terrain was difficult for chariots, made possible a tremendous increase in the number of men who could be trained and put into the field. In the competition to mobilize ever larger bodies of men, various states began to claim the services of the populations of their rural hinterlands and the lower social classes, which had hitherto played no political role. These reforms involved the allocation of land—gained through the opening of new territories to cultivation or through conquest—in exchange for the payment of taxes and the provision of labor and military service. The process was progressively extended in various states, until it culminated in the reforms of Shang Yang in Qin state, where the entire adult, male population was registered, ranked, and allocated land on the basis of military service. Carrying out these reforms entailed the development of new administrative organs for effective local government throughout the territory of the state, practices for registering and policing large populations, and methods to measure and allocate land. These policies, originally designed for mass mobilization and the control of infantry armies, became the basis for control of the civil population.

This process also entailed a transformation of the basic units of society, including a redefinition of the nature of kin ties and the creation of a new "public" realm outside the networks defined by common descent, shared ancestral cult, and blood covenants. The most important change was the disappearance of the sublineage as a lesser replica of the state. As local administration was introduced to facilitate mass mobilization, the practice of granting fiefs was abandoned; lineages or states that were defeated were partitioned or destroyed by the victors (*fen zu* 分族 or *mie zu* 滅族) and their lands and population reallocated. This process culminated in the victory of the state of Qin, whose ruling house was left as the only lineage with an ancestral temple and an army. In place of the old "lineage law" emerged a kin system based primarily on the individual household, which formed the fundamental unit for registration and the provision of labor services in the new state. This new kin system was marked in the patterns of sanctioned violence in two ways: the principle of collective punishment for families enshrined in the legal codes, and the moral obligation to vengeance for kin articulated in the Confucian ritual texts and commentaries. In addition to providing the engine for the creation of the new state and the destruction of the old social order, the changing pattern of sanctioned violence thus also demonstrates the shift in the nature, range, and social uses of kin groupings.

The final section of Chapter Two deals with the role of changing patterns of sanctioned violence in redefining the ties that constituted the public realm in the Chinese state. The basic mechanism involved was the modification and reinterpretation of the old blood covenant, which had formed the basis of non-kin ties in the Spring and Autumn state. While oaths continued to play a similar role in the Warring States, they were increasingly identified as "bonds" (*yue* 約) rather than covenants. Although sacrifice was still employed, it was de-centered in the ritual, and the writings of the period identify the "bonds" as a form of text, as the basis of written law, and as a ritual in which intent or devotion was more important than the drinking of blood. This de-centering of the physical acts of sacrifice and consumption in order to emphasize the intent or sincerity of the participants was common to the entire Confucian theory of sacrifice articulated in this period.

An important change marked by this shift from "covenants" to "bonds" was the rise of the state's ruler—made possible by his control of the newly mobilized population—to a position of unchallenged supremacy. Through associations with various magical practices and elements of popular marriage ritual, the emphasis on bonds formed part of the "sexualization" of the political in Warring States China, in which the relation of ruler to minister was equated with that of husband to wife. Numerous parables of the period likewise asserted the total devotion of subordinates to the ruler by praising men who died either in attempting revenge or in suicides of protest for those who had recognized their talents and employed them. These parables of "righteous bravery" used tales of violence and death to define the nature and significance of the ties that bound the minister to his lord. This new image of authority, which stressed the absolute power of the prince and total devotion of the official, marked the replacement of the old collegial authority of the Zhou nobility by the ideal of the unchallenged autocrat which characterized both state and family in imperial China.

This discussion of the new forms and relations of authority leads into Chapters Three and Four, which examine changing images and institutions of rule in the Warring States period. One of the most important developments of this period was the appearance of a new form of military commander, a specialist who held office through mastery of military techniques. Associated with these military specialists there appeared a large body of writings that dealt not only with the procedures for commanding an army or defending a city, but also with the principles of warfare and the relation of the army to civil society. In response to these texts many nonmilitary philosophers also began to present discussions of warfare. These new theoretical formulations on warfare and its role in society constituted a major element in the redefinition of the nature of authority and the state. They explicitly rejected the martial ideals of the Spring and Autumn aristocracy, and also divorced combat from the ancestral cult. Instead, they presented combat as an intellectual discipline in which the powers of mind and textual mastery of the commander, along with the unthinking obedience and uniform actions of the troops, guaranteed victory. It was no longer combat itself but the control of men and the manipulation of combat for higher ends that now constituted the essence of war. Moreover, the commander was now understood to be a servant of the new supreme ruler, and battle an element of statecraft or punishment. As in the reinterpretation of sacrifice, the violent act was de-centered or even denied, and the emphasis was shifted to the obedience and hierarchy of the participants, the pattern imposed by the mind of the superior man, and the encompassing power of the cosmically potent ruler.

Chapter Four deals with a variety of rituals associated with this power and its role in assuring the correctness of violence. One aspect of the new ideal of the supreme autocrat was the derivation of authority not primarily from potent ancestors but rather from the direct imitation of Heaven, of which the emperor was the earthly equivalent. Several major physical elements of the emperor's establishment and some associated rituals asserted the cosmic nature of his rule through systematic imitation of the Heavenly patterns of violence. Grandest in scale were the parks where the emperors collected all sorts of plants and beasts and held hunts. In special animal pens and arenas which were lesser models of these parks the emperors also staged combats between beasts, or sometimes of men against beasts. These rituals demonstrated that the emperor's power extended into the natural realm, and also placed human violence and military training—which the hunts were—under the aegis of the Heavenly pattern.

Other major rituals of cosmic violence were based on the calendrical model of the state, in which the actions of the ruler through the year were supposed to parallel the changing actions of Heaven. In this model, rituals of violence were associated with autumn and winter, the killing seasons of the year. One ritual expression of this theory was the cosmic kickball game staged in special stadia in the imperial palace complexes. These games were a form of military training, but they also had a cosmic import, for they acted out the annual cycle which guided the proper use of violence. Another such ritual was the practice of using the pitchpipes that defined the Chinese gamut to "read" the changes in the "ether" that underlay the cycle of the seasons; during the Han this ritual was regarded as being of special importance for military action. There was also a panoply of violent rituals performed at the imperial behest in the New Year season as part of the general purification of the realm. Each of these rituals sought to demonstrate that proper violence in the imperial order was based on the imitation of Heaven.

Chapters Five and Six demonstrate how tales and metaphors of violence were employed in the Warring States and early imperial periods to articulate the new vision of the character of Chinese civilization and its relation to the natural world. Chapter Five deals with what I have called the "social history of violence," actually a set of tales about the origins of warfare, punishments, and perhaps sacrifice. In these stories the introduction of correct, sanctioned violence appears as one element in the creation of human civilization out of a natural state in which men were not separated from animals. The stories of the origins of combat, which evolved out of an earlier set of myths dealing with a cosmic battle between forces of drought and storm, told of the Yellow Emperor and his primal battle with the monstrous Chi You, and they provided mythic prototypes for many of the rituals and institutions of sanctioned violence described in the preceding chapters.

Chapter Six discusses the manner in which the Chinese fashioned a cosmology patterned on their new model of authority, and then used that cosmology to provide a natural sanction for the political order. The new forms of sanctioned violence were central to this cosmology, for the early Chinese identified human violence with the unformed, energetic substrate of matter (qi 氣) and then described the formation of physical objects in terms identical to those used to describe the disposition and manipulation of armies in the field. Combined with the theories and rituals of cosmic violence described in Chapter Four, these usages constituted a comprehensive model in which the proper use of violence in human society exactly paralleled the maintenance of order in the cosmos, and these were in turn paralleled by the "history" of the creation of human civilization out of brute nature. History and cosmology provided a dual sanction for the emergent imperial state, and in both the "social history" and the "natural philosophy" of the new order the ruler's manipulation and control of violence offered the central model for the creation of pattern and hierarchy out of chaos.

Thus, this study will show how the Warring States transition entailed a comprehensive re-creation of human society through changes in the basic units of society, in the nature of the ties that constituted the public realm, and in the role, distribution, and sanction of authority. In the Spring and Autumn period authority derived from service to the ancestral cult. This service was identified with the performance of ritually coded violent acts, and the right to perform these acts was distributed through a series of greater and lesser "courts" based on lineage segmentation. The sublineage constituted the basic unit of elite society and was itself a political entity and a potential state, so the ruler of an actual state was only *primus inter pares* in the collegial authority of the aristocracy. Any "public" ties between non-kin were created through oaths sanctified by the blood of a sacrificial victim. During the Warring States period and early empires, however, authority was derived from the imitation of Heaven by a cosmically potent ruler, an imitation which was identified with bringing order or pattern out of undifferentiated chaos. In legalist practice the primary mechanisms for creating this order in society were universal military service and the penal law, while in Confucian theory hierarchical order was created in the practice of rituals, of which sacrificial rites were the most important. The aristocratic sublineage vanished, and the basic unit of society became the individual household, which was defined through patterns of collective punishment or obligations of vengeance. The public realm, now consisting of the emperor and his servants, was created through sacrificial oaths, which no longer derived power from the sacrifice but rather from the authority of texts and written codes.

Underlying and providing the impetus for all these changes was the constant warfare which dominated the Spring and Autumn and Warring States periods. It was the integrated reforms of service obligations, landholding patterns, and local government carried out by states seeking increased military power that generated the institutional and conceptual changes sketched above. Not only was the Chinese empire established through conquest, but in addition the intellectual and social pre-conditions of its existence were closely linked to the reforms which forged the tools of that conquest. This conclusion will hopefully provide a starting point for new attempts to achieve a more complete understanding of the Warring States transition.

Chapter One

THE WARRIOR ARISTOCRACY

During the seventh and sixth centuries B.C., China was dominated by a warrior aristocracy whose privileged status was marked by its monopoly of ritually directed violence. Sanctioned killing in the forms of sacrifice, warfare, and hunting constituted the central rites of the cults of the ancestors and the state altars, and the performance of these rites set the aristocracy apart from the common people. This aristocracy was in turn divided on the basis of ascriptive kin ties into a hierarchy of lineages, each with its own capital, temple, and military forces. United by kinship and a shared nobility, and identical in their basic organizations and capacities, the senior and cadet lineages in a state enjoyed a proximate equality distinguished only by the ritual ranking of their cults. Originally, the senior lineages were dominant, and interstate wars were the primary form of the ongoing struggle for supremacy and glory, but over the centuries the cadet lineages proved able to expand their power and gradually asserted their dominance in the various states. This competition among lineages led to a world of vendetta and civil war, where alliances both among and within states could be secured only by the religious sanction of sharing the blood of a sacrifice in the ritual of the covenant, and the expansion of the social range and functions of these blood oaths led to a gradual redefinition of the political realm. Thus it was out of the aristocratic pattern of licit violence and the internecine struggles to which it led that the Warring States and the Chinese empire emerged.

The major problem for studying this era is that apart from some of the poems in the *Shi jing* and a few of the later chapters of the *Shang shu*, which cannot be dated with any precision, we have no literary

15

sources written during the period in question. A highly detailed narrative of the years from 722 to 464 B.C., however, appears in the *Zuo zhuan*, a work generally dated to the mid-fourth century B.C. This work is a compilation of historical anecdotes appended to a year-by-year chronicle of events written from the perspective of the state of Lu. It is obviously a multilayered work drawing on many sources and having passed through many hands, but it was compiled in its final form by men working in the Confucian tradition, and it later became one of the "classics" of that school. The judgements and attitudes of the final redactors are consistent with those expressed in the *Lun yu*, and when the stories have a clear "moral," these are in harmony with the positions of the Confucian school. However, the actions and speeches attributed to the historical actors frequently depict a world of institutions and values totally at odds with those of the Warring States Confucians and the other philosophical schools. In many cases these speeches and actions are the objects of criticism, but even the words and deeds of seemingly "positive" characters often suggest a world far removed from that of the Warring States authors, and these traces of an "alien" world offer an intelligible, internally consistent vision of society.

Moreover, in contrast to the philosophical texts of the period, in which historical incidents are cited as adjuncts to an argument, or with the more closely related *Guo yu*, which is "philosophy and rhetoric in a historical setting," the *Zuo zhuan* contains many stories that have no clear moral message, as well as extensive chronicles that offer no more than dated events.[1] The preservation of large amounts of material that serve no moral argument and of speeches and actions that depict a world alien or hostile to Warring States Confucianism suggests that despite heavy reworking, the *Zuo zhuan* is our only detailed repository of information on a social order that was already vanishing by the time that philosophical and historical texts appeared in the late Spring and Autumn period. Because much of the evidence is preserved simply as a target for criticism, and the chronological arrangement of speeches and anecdotes is not necessarily reliable, the text does not allow a detailed study of the process of change in the Zhou socio-political order. Instead, one can at best achieve a schematic contrast of "before" and "after," where the extant text already represents "after," and "before" must be deduced from otherwise unexplainable values and practices appearing in the anecdotes. This reconstruction can also be supplemented by evidence preserved in Warring States philosophical works, the writings of Sima Qian, and many archeological finds.

For expository purposes I have divided the chapter into four sections. The first discusses how the ritual violence of sacrifice, warfare, and hunting in the service of the ancestral cult defined the nobility of the

period. The second shows how a political order defined by lineage segmentation dispersed authority throughout this nobility and produced a
multitude of rivals for honor and power. The third section focuses on
the obsession of the nobility with an honor based on martial prowess
and shows how this led both to constant interstate warfare and a regular
recourse to blood vengeance, vendetta, and civil war. The final section
examines the crucial role of blood oaths in creating new political ties in a
world where internecine struggles were destroying the old ties of shared
kinship and cult.

Warfare and Sacrifice

In the Spring and Autumn period political authority was derived
from the worship of potent ancestral spirits and the gods of locality
through regular offerings made at the altars of the ancestral temple and
the state. The actions that set the rulers apart from the masses were the
"great services" of those altars, and these services were ritually directed
violence in the form of sacrifices, warfare, and hunting. These activities,
symbolically linked through the ceremonial exchange and consumption
of meat, reached their common culmination in the offering up of living
beings at the altars. Thus the noble was above all a warrior and sacrificer, a man who took life in order to feed the spirits who gave him power.

The centrality of violent acts to religious cult and the political
order was axiomatic in the Spring and Autumn period.

> The great services of the state are sacrifice and warfare. In the
> sacrifices one takes the meat from the sacrifices in the ancestral
> temple, and in warfare [before setting out on campaign] one re-
> ceives the meat from the sacrifices at the *she* altar. These are the
> great ceremonies of the spirits.[2]

This passage states explicitly that sacrifice and warfare were the
principal forms of state or public service, and it links them through the
shared ritual consumption of meat. This consumption, in turn, presupposed the killing of sacrificial animals, so the ritualized taking of life
constituted the defining feature of the political realm in Zhou China.

A remonstrance to the duke of Lu supposedly offered in 716 B.C.
not only asserted that warfare and sacrifice were the chief services of the
state, but went further and argued that they were the sole activities
proper to the lords of men.

> When the duke was about to go to Tang to view the fishing, Zang
> He Bo remonstrated, "The prince does not take any animal that is

not of use in the practice of the great services [of state] or whose substance cannot be used to make implements [for sacrifice or battle] . . . Therefore one uses the spring hunt, the summer hunt, the autumn hunt, and the winter hunt, all in the intervals between agricultural labor, to practice the [great] services. Every three years there should be a review of the troops. . . . The lord does not shoot any bird or beast whose flesh is not offered in the sacrificial pots or whose hide, teeth, bones, horns, fur, or feathers are not used on the sacrificial vessels. The creatures which fill the mountains, forest, streams, and marshes and the providing of tools are the business of underlings and the lowly officers; the lord has nothing to do with them."[3]

In this passage lordship is defined exclusively through the performance of ritually coded violence in sacrifices, military action, and the hunt. All other activities are dismissed as the work of "underlings."

The inclusion of the hunt might appear to be at odds with the first passage, which cited only warfare and sacrifice, but as Walter Burkert observed in his study of sacrifice in ancient Greece, "For the ancient world, hunting, sacrifice, and war were symbolically interchangeable."[4] In this period of Chinese history warfare was not clearly separated from hunting, for numerous early texts describe hunts as a form of military ritual or training, and it was not uncommon for a hunt to turn into a campaign or a campaign into a hunt.[5] Writers would often invoke images of the hunt to describe the conduct of battles.[6] Moreover, the hunt and warfare were equated in both linguistic usage and law. The most common terms for "military" or "martial" (wu 武, rong 戎) also applied to hunting, the word "hunting" (lie 獵) could also describe an army's attack, and the same word (huo 獲) applied to what was captured in battle or taken in the hunt. Collective oaths with the force of law were sworn at the beginning of a hunt just as before a battle, and misconduct during a hunt was punished according to military law.[7] Hunting as a form of warfare thus was also one of the "great services."

The identification of sacrifice and warfare/hunting as the central forms of state service is made explicitly only in the Zuo zhuan, but this idea underlies many passages in other Confucian works that generally suppress appeals to the primacy of violence. Thus, in the introduction to his famous periodization of the Zhou decline, Confucius stated:

When all under Heaven has the Way, then rites, music, and punitive expeditions are initiated by the Son of Heaven. When all under Heaven lacks the Way, then rites, music, and punitive expeditions are initiated by the feudal lords.[8]

This passage refers to rites and music rather than simply sacrifice, but given the centrality of sacrifice in the Zhou ritual complex, it clearly echoes the equation of political authority with sacrifice and warfare. This point is made explicitly in another passage attributed to Confucius, where "the Way" itself is identified with sacrifice and warfare.

> Confucius said, "When I engage in war I conquer, and when I sacrifice I obtain good fortune. This could be called obtaining the Way."[9]

The lengthy ode "Closed Temple" is a hymn to the glories of the ruling house of Lu, and its panegyric dwells solely on the wealth and regularity of its sacrifices and the size and conquests of its army. Indeed the two major forms of taxation in the Warring States and early empires were simply transformations of the "feudal" levies for sacrifices and warfare.[10] An account of the proper building of a palace complex stipulates that the ruler should first build the ancestral temple—the locus of sacrifice—then stables and military storehouses—the "locus" of warfare—and last of all the royal dwelling proper.[11] These quotations show that the definition of the political realm through sacrifice and warfare operated not only as an explicit maxim but also as an unspoken assumption underlying ritual practice, poetic conventions, and models of historical evolution.

Evidence from archeology and iconography supports the statements of these literary texts. Bronze metallurgy was the most advanced technology during the Shang, Western Zhou, and Spring and Autumn periods, and the production of bronze artifacts required resources and labor on a scale possible only for those with considerable power. Consequently, the types of artifacts made from bronze clearly demonstrate the concerns and priorities of the ruling elite, and as K. C. Chang has pointed out, bronze was used almost entirely for the manufacture of weapons, ritual paraphernalia associated with sacrifice, and carpenters' tools which were necessary for the construction of chariots.[12] The same priorities are demonstrated in the development of the technique of gold and silver inlay, which appeared first on weapons in the Spring and Autumn period, then on ritual vessels in the early Warring States, and on implements of daily use only in the late Warring States.[13]

The symbolism of royal authority in Zhou China also demonstrates the centrality of sacrifice and warfare. The chief symbols of the monarch were the banner, the ax, and the Nine Bronze Tripods.[14] The first two were aspects of battle: the ax was a weapon which symbolized the king's punishing power, while the banner was the means by which commands were visually signalled. Tripods were vessels in which the meat of sacrifices was cooked, and passages describing the sacred Nine Tripods state that they could cook meat without using fire. Thus political authority was symbolically identified with the waging of war and the performance of sacrifice.

The above evidence clearly demonstrates the primacy of ritually directed violence in the Zhou state, but it explains neither the rationale of linking sacrifice and warfare/hunting together, nor how they served to define the political order. There is evidence to suggest at least two links between sacrifice and warfare in the constitution of authority. First, they were both modes of taking life, and taking life is a vivid expression of power. Second and more important, these activities were recognized as the primary means of serving the ancestors and the gods of locality, a service which consisted of both the physical feeding of these spirits and the "feeding" of their honor. I shall discuss each of these links below.

Earlier scholars have noted that the close linkage of warfare and sacrifice in Zhou China suggests the highly ritualized character of combat in the period, but it also indicates that sacrifice was clearly regarded as a form of bloodshed and killing analogous to warfare. The central act of any sacrificial ceremony was the slaughter and consumption of one or more animals, but the role of bloodshed in these rituals went beyond this. The cereal dishes that accompanied the sacrificial banquet were made with grain from a special field sanctified through the dismemberment and burial of several animals, and even the ice employed in some offerings had to be consecrated with the blood of a sacrifice.[15] Several scholars have argued that the most common character for "sacrifice" (*ji* 祭) was a variant of one character meaning "to kill" and was virtually homophonous with the most common character used to refer to killing (*sha* 殺).[16] In some cases the texts refer explicitly to "killing altar-sacrifice" (*sha yin* 殺禋) or "blood sacrifice" (*xue ji* 血祭).[17] Thus the early Chinese were quite conscious of the centrality of killing to the act of sacrifice.

Moreover, there is evidence from Warring States texts that the Chinese of that period clearly perceived the objects of sacrifice as victims. Stories in the *Zuo zhuan* tell of a barbarian chief who recognized that a cow was lowing to mourn the fate of its sacrificed offspring, and of cocks who mutilated themselves to avoid being sacrificed.[18] The *Mencius* tells of how King Xuan of Qi substituted a sheep for an ox about to be sacrificed because the ox had the "terrified look of an innocent man being led to the place of execution."[19] The *Zhuangzi* repeatedly hailed the good fortune of animals whose imperfections saved them from sacrifice, and scorned the honors that preceded death on the altar.[20]

Not only was sacrifice seen as a form of killing, but the link between taking life and authority was emphasized by the fact that the king and the feudal lords acted as their own sacrificers; they personally performed the sacrifices in their own states.[21] This practice was based on the idea that ancestral spirits would accept sacrifice only from the eldest male descendant of their line, so the heads of the cadet lineages must also have served as the sacrificers in their own temples.[22] Consequently the privilege of personally killing the sacrificial victims offered to the ancestors marked paramount authority in the state and in the subordinate lineages.

However, while the privilege of killing as a sacrificer, hunter, or warrior was a hallmark of power in the Spring and Autumn period, these acts were all justified as elements of ancestor worship, and it was the service of this cult that was the ultimate basis of authority. The cultic role of sacrifice seems clear, but those of hunting and warfare will require some elaboration.

Hunting played at least three roles in the service of the ancestors: 1) it provided animals that were offered up in the temples; 2) hunts were an element of ceremony in several major sacrifices; 3) hunts were identified with combat, which was itself a form of service to the ancestors. Evidence of the third role was provided above, so I will here deal only with the first two.

Organized hunting and fishing expeditions to provide offerings for use in sacrificial rituals or as dried meat for ceremonial banquets are the subject of frequent divination in the oracle bones of the Shang dynasty. The same practices are also mentioned in bronze inscriptions of the Western Zhou and in the poems of the period, both those in the *Shi jing* and the somewhat later poems of the "Stone Drum" inscriptions discovered in the seventh century A.D. Finally, the systematizing ritualist texts of the Warring States period also prescribe the use of seasonal hunts to gather offerings for the sacrificial altars, and they list numerous officials who had charge of preparing this game for use in temple rituals.[23] The role of hunting in providing game for sacrifices is also demonstrated by the fact that the term for whatever was captured in hunt or battle (*huo* 獲) was also a technical term meaning "living beings obtained for sacrifice."[24] Finally, it is probably the use of wild animals in sacrifices that underlay the development of the "animal parks," which will be discussed in detail in Chapter Four. One function of these parks, which first appeared in the Spring and Autumn period, was the training of wild beasts by human handlers, and the use of such animals in sacrifices is portrayed on one of the bronze cowrie shell containers discovered at Shizhaishan in Yunnan.[25]

In addition to providing creatures for offerings, hunts themselves also played a role in some sacrificial ceremonies. When it was devastated by fires in 524 B.C., the state of Zheng held a special sacrifice at the *she* altar to ward off misfortune, and this ceremony included staging a general hunt.[26] Other references to hunts staged as elements of sacrificial ceremonies, including those in the "Stone Drum" inscriptions, also link them to the *she* altar, perhaps because of its strong ties to warfare and punishments.[27] In any case, it is clear that the great, collective hunts were also potentially forms of worship.

Like the collective hunts, military campaigns were also forms of serving the ancestors. This point is explicitly made in a story set in the state of Chu in 555 B.C.

> [Zheng] was going to turn against Jin and raise the Chu army to drive them off, but Zi Kang [chief minister of Chu] did not agree. The king of Chu heard of this and sent his messenger Yang to tell Zi Kang, "The capital populace says that I am master of the state's altars but will not send out the army, and when I die they will not bury me with proper ritual. It has been five years since I ascended to the throne, and the army has not yet gone out. The people say that I am enjoying my leisure and have forgotten the inherited achievements of the previous rulers. May the minister please plan some way to deal with this."[28]

It was as "master of the altars" that the king was obliged to send out his armies. The purpose of sending them out was to defend the "inherited achievements of the ancestors," and the result of failure to do so would be denial of proper rites when he himself became an ancestor. The men of Jin, Chu's great northern rival, also justified warfare as a form of "service to the previous rulers," and in 539 B.C. Shu Xiang supposedly foretold the destruction of the lineage of the ruler of Jin because he and his officers no longer went out on expeditions.[29] To a degree this prophecy reflects a utilitarian recognition of the need for military preparedness, but its stress on regular expeditions and the emphasis on the fate of the lineage clearly link it to the other passages which insist that the purpose of war is to serve the ancestors.

The identification of warfare as a form of religious "service" is also reflected in the highly ceremonial character of military campaigns. Every stage of the campaign was marked by special rituals that linked the actions in the field to the state cults and guaranteed the sacred character of battle. Although some Western scholars have described these as a "ritualistic overlay" covering the pragmatic "reality" of battle, they actually defined the basic nature of warfare in the period. The aristocratic warriors of Zhou China were never allowed to forget that they fought in the service of their ancestors and gods, and that combat was ultimately an element of cult.

Every campaign began at the temples, where the rulers performed a series of rituals to assure the success of the campaign. The state's ruler first sacrificed at the *she* altar and at the ancestral temple, where he announced the campaign to the spirits of the previous rulers. Religious insignia from the *she* and the spirit tablets of the ancestors were then brought out from their temples to accompany the army on its march.[30] The commander of the army received his charge in the ancestral temple and an offering of meat at the *she* altar, and passages from later works say that the ruler also presented him with a weapon, either a bow or an ax, at the ancestral temple.[31] Leaders of participating sublineages likewise sacrificed at the temples of their ancestors and exchanged meat from these sacrifices with the ruler of the state. After the rulers had purified themselves through fasting, the weapons of the army were issued at the ancestral temples.[32] Finally the troops were assembled in their ranks at the *she* altar in a special ceremony (*zhi bing* 治兵), and with the rituals completed, they set out to battle.[33]

While on the march, the army regularly made sacrifices to the major mountains or rivers that they passed. These sacrifices generally took the form of a *lü* (旅), a "travel sacrifice" intended to ward off harm from evil spirits or from the gods of the localities upon whose domains they had trespassed.[34]

When an enemy force was encountered in the field, the day and place of battle would be formally fixed by the two parties, and then the preparations for combat would begin. Many of these were simply questions of physical readiness, such as sharpening weapons, checking chariots, feeding horses, and having the army eat their fill.[35] However, the pre-battle meal is identified by a special name (*ru shi* 蓐食), and it is likely that it was a ceremonial occasion peculiar to the field of battle. This conclusion is supported by the fact that a soon-to-be-defeated commander's recklessness is shown by his remark that he will destroy the enemy first and only then have his meal.[36]

The battle proper was likewise preceded by a series of religious rituals, and these are described in a scene prior to the battle of Yanling in 575 B.C. The king of Chu ascended a sort of crow's nest to observe the opposing Jin army with a defector from that state, and the latter explained what was happening.

> The king said, "They have dispatched men to the left and right; what is this?" "They are summoning the officers." "They have all gathered at the central army." "They are planning together." "They are pitching a tent." "They are reverently divining before [the spirit tablets of] the earlier rulers." "They are striking the tent." "They are going to issue the command [*ming* 命]." "There

is a clamor and a rising of dust." "They are filling in the wells and leveling the cooking-places and then forming ranks." "They are getting on the chariots and those on the left and right [the two warriors on either side of the driver] are picking up their weapons and dismounting again." "They are listening to the solemn declaration [*shi* 誓]." "Will they fight?" "I cannot yet tell." "They have got back on their chariots and those on the right and left have dismounted again." "This is the battle prayer."[37]

Divination and the battle prayer clearly served to invoke the presence of the ancestors and other guardian divinities of the state, and these rituals are mentioned prior to several battles.[38] The systematic destruction of the camp is also a regular feature of the preparation for battle, and it had a strongly ritualistic character. Some argue that it was simply a means of creating a level space on which to arrange the army, but it would have been easier to line up outside the camp. Kierman has suggested that this leveling "had an essentially ceremonial significance comparable to the burning of boats after crossing a river," and this is clearly correct. It was a maxim of the period that the true warrior was the man who had resolved on death, and the leveling of the camp was the tangible expression of this resolution not to return from the battle.[39]

The most significant religious ceremony in the preparations for battle, however, was the "solemn declaration" or "oath" (*shi* 誓). This character signified a solemn statement that invoked the spirits as witnesses to bind a man to act in a certain manner. In Zhou China the commander of an army issued such a declaration before every battle, and the *Shang shu* contains five texts that purport to be examples. Although the declarations attributed to the founders of the Xia and Shang dynasties are fabrications, and it is uncertain that any of the others represents a declaration actually given before an army, these documents show us the basic character of the genre, and their evidence can be corroborated by the text of one *shi* preserved in the *Zuo zhuan*.

The oaths in the *Shang shu* all follow a basic formula. The commander details the crimes of his enemies, asserts that he himself is without particular merit but is following the will of Heaven, tells the members of his army how they are to conduct themselves in the battle, and stipulates the punishments that will befall them if they do not obey and, in some cases, the rewards they will receive if they obey and triumph. The oath in the *Zuo zhuan* follows this pattern.

Zhao Yang [commander of the army supporting the lord of Jin against rebel lineages] declared [*shi*], "The Fan and Zhonghang lineages have gone against the mandate of Heaven, slaughtered the common people, and seek to tyrannize Jin state and slay its lord. Our lord relied on Zheng to protect him, but now Zheng has betrayed him; they cast off the lord and aid his [rebel] servants. But in this battle we follow Heaven's mandate, obey the command of our lord, restore the potency of duty, and eradicate the shame [of our state]. For one who conquers the enemy, if he is a higher minister he will receive a large district and if he is a lower minister a small district; if he is a noble he will receive 100,000 *mou* of land; if he is a farmer, artisan, or merchant he will be permitted to seek service at court; if he is a slave or bound to menial service he will be freed. Should I commit no crime [i.e., win] then the lord will consider [how to reward me]. Should I be guilty [of defeat], then may I be punished by strangulation, may I have only a thin coffin with no outside layers, may it be drawn by an unornamented horse and wagon, and may I not be buried in the graveyard of my lineage."[40]

This declaration differs from those in the *Shang shu* only in that it dwells exclusively on the rewards to be given to the army in the event of success and the punishments to be visited on the commander should he fail. This perhaps reflects the desperation of the situation, which called for drastic measures. In any case, the punishing of defeated commanders was a common practice in the period, and the rest of the oath follows the pattern of the *Shang shu*.[41]

Before every battle the warriors would assemble and be told why the will of Heaven, the imperatives of duty, the honor of the state, and the spirits of the ancestors demanded that this battle be fought. Together with the divination before the tablets of the ancestors, the battle prayer, and the ceremonial command (*ming*), this oath fixed the day's carnage within the political and religious framework. It stipulated the rules of discipline, but did so in a form which bound both the commanders and the warriors to the common service of their ancestors and the gods.

After the battle the immediate task was to dispose of the bodies of the dead. Given the centrality of ancestor worship in the period, securing the corpses for burial was extremely important, and men would fight to retrieve the bodies of their fellows on the field or arrange exchanges after the battle.[42] But the corpses of the enemy might also be collected into a large tomb mound as a monument to bring glory to the ancestral cult. Fan Dang said:

Why doesn't my lord build a collective tomb and gather the Jin corpses into it to make a *jing guan* [京觀, literally a "great display," a large mound with a marker to identify it]? I have heard it said that when you defeat the enemy you must show it to your descendants in order that they not forget the achievements of your military prowess.[43]

The king of Chu rejected this proposal, insisting that such treatment was reserved for the particularly wicked, but even his rejection acknowledges the practice. Other passages in pre-Qin texts also refer to this custom, and one states that the *jing guan* of numberless bones rose up like the hills and mountains.[44]

A victorious army would often use the corpses of the defeated to erect a monument to its victory, like the Greek *tropaion*. These artificial hills would stand as visible and lasting memorials to the victors, and as the passage above suggests, the tumuli were part of the web of practices that linked warfare to ancestor worship and the service of the lineage. The mound was to be left especially for the descendants of the victors, that they might know the prowess and glory of those who came before and seek to extend that glory in their turn.

When the army returned to their own state after the battle, they performed the ceremony of "calling the army to order " (*zhen lü* 振旅) and then the ceremonial drinking (*yin zhi* 飲至) to mark the conclusion of the campaign.[45] Prisoners, the heads or left ears of those slain, and any spoils taken in battle were then presented at the ancestral temples of the state and the cadet lineages.[46] With these ritual offerings the campaign proper ended, although the spoils of battle could also be sent as gifts or tribute to the Zhou king, the hegemon, or a friendly state.[47]

Thus the hunt and the military campaign both culminated in offerings at the temples, and as was noted above, the word for what was taken in battle or hunt had the technical sense of "living beings obtained for sacrifice." All the "great services" converged in the sacrificial service of the altars, and indeed the word translated as "service" (*shi* 事) could in the narrow sense mean "sacrifice," as in the standard phrase *you shi* (有事). When several speakers identified battle as a "great service," and even applied the phrase *you shi* to combat, they were explicitly describing warfare as a form of religious, sacrificial ritual.[48] In this way warfare logically culminated in the offering up of the spoils of battle, and above all in human sacrifice.

Under the Shang dynasty human sacrifice had been a regular institution closely linked to military activities. Excavations have revealed the mass execution of slaves or prisoners to "accompany" the deceased Shang rulers, and the oracle records contain many divinations regarding the sacrifice of members of non-Shang states or tribes. The hundreds of bodies discovered in some royal tombs were probably prisoners taken in warfare, and it is even possible that some campaigns were fought solely for the purpose of obtaining these sacrificial victims. Combat was tied to the service of the cult of the dead, and military success was clearly manifested in the scale of human sacrifice.

Although apparently not as central as it had been to the Shang kings, the practice of human sacrifice continued into the Zhou. A tradition is preserved in many later Zhou works that following his defeat of the Shang army, King Wu sacrificed the Shang king and his two wives, presented the heads of all the slain enemy soldiers at his *she* altar, and then had the heads burnt as an offering at his ancestral temple.[49] The *Zuo zhuan* lists several instances of human sacrifice in order to criticize the practice, but the existence of this polemic—which also appears in the *Mozi*—suggests that in the fourth century human sacrifice was still a common practice. This conclusion is supported by the fact that the king of Qin attempted to ban human sacrifice in 383 B.C.[50] However, the primary evidence for human sacrifice during the Zhou comes from archeological excavations, which show that it continued throughout the dynasty; indeed, more examples have been found from the Warring States period than the Spring and Autumn.[51] Even under the Han dynasty human sacrifice was still practiced in the Dian state on the southwestern frontier, as depicted on the covers of the bronze containers found at Shizhaishan.[52]

The scattered references to human sacrifice in the historical records and even its more frequent appearance at the archeological sites cannot show how often it was performed or how widely accepted. However, there is clear evidence of several regular institutions that were modified versions of human sacrifice. The most important of these was the aforementioned presentation of prisoners at the ancestral temple, the *she*, or some other locus of sacrifice. In several cases the text states explicitly that the prisoners were sacrificed or killed, while in others their ultimate fate was unclear. However, even if the prisoners were finally spared, the symbolism of the practice and the terminology used clearly equated the prisoners with animals taken for sacrifice in the ceremonial hunts, objects captured in battle, and the heaps of heads or ears of the slain.[53] Whether those captured were sacrificed or spared, the ceremonial presentation demonstrated that warfare *logically* culminated in the sacrifice of the enemy, just as the hunt culminated in the sacrificial offering of the game.

A second version of human sacrifice accepted as regular by the speakers in the *Zuo zhuan* and by its redactors was the use of the blood of a prisoner to consecrate newly cast war drums.[54] It is true that in the cases cited in the text no prisoner is ever actually sacrificed, but the speeches and narration show that no one questioned the possibility or probity of the action, and from the evidence of human sacrifice cited above there is no reason to doubt that men were sacrificed in such circumstances.

A final form of human sacrifice was the punishment inflicted upon several major rebels and assassins of rulers, who were rendered into a meat sauce and fed to members of the court or army.[55] Although this was a form of capital punishment, the shared consumption of the criminal evoked the image of sacrifice.[56] Moreover, the etiological myth for this practice, which will be discussed in Chapter Five, clearly demonstrates that it was regarded as a form of sacrifice.

This systematic evocation of human sacrifice in the period reflects the constitution of political authority through the service of the ancestral cult and the altars of the state. The "great services" were ultimately united through their culmination in sacrifice, in the taking of meat at the altars which defined them in the quote with which this section began. Sacrifice was the central religious practice of the period, and the nobility were those who devoted themselves to it. To take life and offer it up on the altars were the defining actions of the political realm, and the rulers of men were those who engaged in hunting and warfare, and then presented the fruits of their prowess to the ancestors and the gods.

The Segmentary Aristocracy

This definition of political authority through the service of the altars in the forms of hunting, warfare, and sacrifice underlay the social order of China in the Spring and Autumn period. Those who participated in these services formed an elite which set itself apart from the general populace through its devotion to ritual performances, and this elite was in turn ranked as king, feudal lords, hereditary ministers, and nobles according to kin ties defined in "lineage law." These ranks were marked in the ritual performances which defined status in this period through the assignment of a graded number or form of various ritual implements or privileges. However, these gradations were based on incremental additions to a fundamental nobility common to all members of the elite on the basis of their kinship and joint participation in the "great services." This idea of a common nobility led to a proximity of status and a sharing of authority which was radically different from the later imperial system.

Moreover, in the "feudal" system based on lineage segmentation, the lords of the individual states were lesser replicas of the Zhou king, and the hereditary ministers lesser replicas of the feudal lords. Each had his own temple for sacrifice and army for warfare, and the authority of king over feudal lord and of feudal lord over minister was based solely *characteristics of Zhou dynasty rule and factors which ultimately destroyed Zhou.*

on relative degree of power and ritual status. Over the course of centuries power gradually shifted from the king to the feudal lords and then from the feudal lords to the ministerial lineages, and the Confucian school and subsequent Chinese writers made this downward shift of authority the fundamental theme in their accounts of Zhou history.[57] This devolution of authority, however, was in fact the direct consequence of the organizing principles of the Zhou elite, the principles of a common nobility and a "segmented" political organization, in which both individual nobles and geographic foci of authority shared common attributes or structure and differed only in degree.[58] This general distribution of power made possible the constant, internecine warfare that finally destroyed the Zhou aristocracy.

The idea of a nobility linked by a common ancestry and devotion to the great services of the state, primarily warfare and sacrifice, is best summed up in a speech attributed to Zi Chan, the reforming minister of Zheng state, who lived in the second half of the sixth century B.C. A member of the court, Kong Zhang, had arrived late at a ceremonial reception for an embassy from Jin and in trying to remain inconspicuous had stood in the wrong position. The emissaries laughed at this *faux pas*, and after the ceremony a minister of Zheng criticized Zi Chan for allowing Zheng to appear ridiculous in the eyes of the visitors. Zi Chan replied:

> Kong Zhang is a descendant of the elder brother of our lord, and his ancestor [Zi Kong] controlled the government of our state. He is a hereditary minister. He has received a charge as an ambassador and traveled throughout the realms of the feudal lords. The capital populace respects him, and the feudal lords know him. He has a position at the court and makes sacrifices in the temple of his branch lineage. In the state he has command of and income from his fief, and in the army he contributes his allotted share of men and equipment. He has his office in the funerals and sacrifices. He receives the meat [from sacrifices at the state's altar] and returns the meat [from sacrifices at the altar of his own lineage]. He assists in the sacrifices at the ancestral temple of our lord, and he already has a fixed, exalted position. His family has held this position for several generations, and for generations they have performed their duties. What have I to be ashamed of if he forgets his place?[59]

In this passage Zi Chan lists the hallmarks of a worthy man: he descends from the ruling lineage, holds hereditary office, participates in the ceremonial of the court, performs the sacrifices in his own temple and assists in those of the state temples, engages in the ritual exchange of meat that

precedes a campaign, and takes part with his followers in military
expeditions. This is an epitome of the nobility based on shared descent
and participation in the great services.

The mention of the ritual exchanges recalls the importance
assigned to meat in the passage with which this chapter began, and the
presentation and consumption of meat indeed played so crucial a role
in the Zhou state that one term for the aristocracy was "the meat
eaters."[60] Those who participated in a sacrifice received some share of
the meat. The Zhou king regularly presented meat from his sacrifices as
a special honor to feudal lords who bore his surname and to descendants
of previous dynasties.[61] Like the Zhou king, the rulers of the feudal
states presented meat to their officers and received meat in return, so
that in fact all ties within the nobility were marked by the giving and
sharing of the meat of sacrifice. This reliance on the "fruits" of sacrifice
to bind men together was a direct expression of the organization of the
state on the basis of kin ties that were constituted through the sacrificial
ancestral cults.

Meat was central not only to carrying out the social role of sacrifice, but also in the second "great service," warfare. The king gave a
ritual present of meat to those of the feudal lords who performed signal
services in the military realm, and consequently the presentation of
meat came to play a fundamental role in the ceremony of designating
the dominant feudal lord as hegemon.[62] Prior to launching any expedition the commander likewise received an offering of meat at the *she*
altar as part of the ceremony of appointment.[63] Hunting, a form of warfare, also culminated in the offering up and communal eating of meat.
So important were these offerings of meat that, according to the
Mencius, Confucius resigned from office simply because the lord of Lu
neglected to give him his share of meat from the solstitial sacrifice.[64] As
the ceremonial culmination of sacrifice, hunting, and even warfare, eating meat was a hallmark of aristocracy and a privilege of all nobles.

In addition to defining men as aristocrats, the performance of the
great services and the closely related ritual consumption of meat also set
them apart from the common people.

> The sons of princes devote themselves to ritual, while the petty
> people use all their physical strength. In devotion to ritual nothing
> is more important than reverence, while in the complete use of
> physical strength nothing is more important than respectful sincer-
> ity. Reverence consists in nourishing the spirits [of the ancestors],
> while sincerity consists in holding to inherited occupations.[65]

This passage posits the division of society into an elite defined by its
devotion to the rituals of ancestor worship and a general populace de-

fined through hereditary occupations. This division also underlies two recurring lists of categories of men that appear in many pre-Qin texts: the listing of the ranks of the nobility and those of the occupational classifications.[66]

The first of these lists the four levels of nobility—king, feudal lord, hereditary minister, and *shi*—and attributes to each level a certain number of some ritual implement, a special appellation, or some type of subordinate. The number, title, and type descend in accord with the level of nobility. Thus the nine tripods were the symbol of monarchy, and each lower level was allowed correspondingly fewer tripods. Other hierarchical ritual attributes included the number of dancers employed in certain rituals, the number of rows of bells allowed in musical performances, the verb used to refer to a man's death, the rank of subordinates, the number of layers permitted for a coffin, the number of ancestral altars, the type and number of animals sacrificed, and the frequency of sacrifices.[67] Although many of these distinctions may have existed only on paper, archeological excavations have shown that some of them, most notably the number of tripods, were actually used to mark the status of a burial.[68] Those which were not related to the material elements of burials would unfortunately leave no trace in the archeological record, but numerous Confucian critiques of nobles who violated the ritual prescriptions suggest that these formulas were still a reality, if a fading one, in the fifth century B.C. These lists of ritual attributes prove that those who "devoted themselves to ritual" were men who held one of the four ranks of nobility, and the archeological evidence confirms that the basic principles sketched in the texts reflect the social reality of the period.

The second list draws together those who are defined through their occupations (*ye* 業). Unlike the lists of the nobility, those dealing with occupations were not fixed. All include the basic categories of merchants, artisans, and peasants, but longer ones also refer to two types of merchants, those who work in orchards or gardens, stable hands, gatherers of wood, herdsmen, seamstresses, menials, and those who collect the produce of mountains and wastes.[69] Several times these people are explicitly identified as those who have an "occupation," and one of the hallmarks of a well-governed state was that these occupations would not be changed. These are clearly the "petty people" who hold to their "hereditary occupations," as contrasted with the nobles who devoted themselves to ritual.

The crucial feature of this model of society is the existence of the hereditary nobility defined in the first list, those men who were set apart from the common people through their focus on the ritual service of the state cults in the forms of sacrifice and warfare. This reflects an organization and interpretation of authority radically different from that of imperial China. The nature of this difference and its significance can best be demonstrated through an analysis of the use and significance of the character *shi* (士). In later social models this term became another occupational category, those who held government office, but in its earlier usages it was a generic term for "nobility" and even "true manhood." This earlier use thus epitomizes the idea of an authority based on noble descent and martial valor.

Although the term *shi* in the narrow sense referred only to the lowest level of the noble hierarchy, there is evidence that it had a broader meaning as a generic term for nobleman. When a hereditary minister (*qing* 卿) went on a mission to the court of the Zhou king, he was introduced in the court with the formula "*shi* + personal name."[70] This shows that the man's office at the court of a cadet lineage did not apply in the court of the king, and without his title he was simply a *shi*, an ordinary noble. A passage preserved in two early ritual texts argues that all levels of the nobility employed the capping ceremony of the *shi* because they were all equal at birth and only distinguished by the subsequent addition of title and office. "The eldest son of the Son of Heaven is a *shi*. None under Heaven is exalted at birth."[71] This idea was expounded at length in a discourse attributed to Confucius, and Han commentators assumed that the rituals for the *shi* were extended to the entire nobility.[72] This broad sense of *shi*, which included all nobles, is also preserved in the compound "minister-nobles" (*qing shi* 卿士) that occurs in several early texts and refers to all who served in the king's court and controlled the affairs of state. In at least one case the *qing shi* are directly contrasted with the "common people", showing that they are indeed identical with "those who devote themselves to ritual," i.e., the nobility.[73]

The principle of hierarchy underlying the graded lists of ritual attributes awarded to the different levels of the aristocracy also suggests a notion of a common "nobility" to which honors or titles were subsequently added. Each higher level was granted more musicians, tripods, coffin layers, or sacrifices, but the lowest level *shi* had some number or form of every attribute. The king was at the top of the nobility and the *shi* at the bottom, but the language and ritual procedures of the period insisted that the two shared a common noble nature, that they were divided in degree and not in kind.

Another facet of the character *shi* that suggests this notion of a shared nobility is its sexual connotations. The character etymologically probably depicted the male sex organ, for in the oracle bones it appears as an element that distinguishes the characters for male cattle and sheep from those for their female counterparts.[74] It preserved this root meaning in later texts where it sometimes meant "man" in opposition to "woman."[75] Thus the original sense was probably something like "man" or "real man," which was easily extended to men of power or nobility. This association of nobility with virility and power suggests that it was at least potentially common to all true men, or at least to all warriors.

Moreover, the focus on killing and on devotion to ancestral cult as the definitions of nobility also marked it as a distinctively "masculine" realm. Through the regular offering of sacrifice to their paternal ancestors, along with the initiation ceremony of "capping," the males created lines of kinship defined and transmitted through religious cult rather than biological generation.[76] This opposition of a masculine kinship based on sacrifice to the "biological" kinship traced through women underlies the argument found in several texts that Zhou, the last ruler of the Shang dynasty, abandoned the sacrifices to his ancestors because of his excessive devotion to women.[77] The way in which this specifically masculine character assigned to the elite's sacrifice/hunting/warfare complex reflected the proximate equality of a shared nobility will become clear in Chapter Two, where it will be shown how in the absolutist state the sexual model for authority became that of the husband's rule over his wife, rather than the shared manhood of warfare and sacrifice.

In addition to the evidence of ritual procedures, terminology, and sexual imagery, there is abundant anecdotal evidence to suggest that all members of the Zhou elite indeed enjoyed a social and ritual proximity that would have been inconceivable in imperial China. Unlike the exalted, unchallenged autocrat of the later Chinese state, the Zhou ruler—whether the king himself or the head of a feudal state—was only "first among equals." Various stories tell of nobles who upbraided the ruler in public and spat at him without being reprimanded or punished, who rejected requests for precious objects, who played board games with the ruler in the midst of his harem, who helped themselves uninvited to food from the ruler's table, or who called on the ruler to share dinner, only to find him out back shooting birds.[78] Being hereditary members of the nobility and rulers in their own domains, the officials and warriors of Zhou China were reduced images of the king or the feudal lords, inferior in rank but not in kind.

This proximity of status based on common descent and service of the ancestral cult was not limited to matters of ritual or sociability; it was built into the very structure of political authority in the Zhou state. Following their conquest of the Shang, the Zhou rulers had been forced to devise a means to control their vast new territories. They had done this by "enfeoffing" relations or allies in walled towns scattered throughout their kingdom and allowing them to act as semi-autonomous "statelets" which owed allegiance to the Zhou king but wielded religious and military authority in their own realms. The kingship itself was transmitted from eldest son to eldest son, forming the so-called "great lineage" (*da zong* 大宗) of the Zhou court. The brothers, younger sons, and allies of the king held hereditary offices in the Zhou court or were enfeoffed in distant cities to act as peripheral foci of Zhou power. The eldest sons of those enfeoffed would inherit the rule of these cities, where they established their own ancestral temples and thus formed a "small lineage" (*xiao zong* 小宗) which replicated the royal line and the royal court in reduced form. The younger sons of these "small lineages" received hereditary offices at the court of the lineage, or they might in turn be enfeoffed in a smaller city within the sphere of influence of the lineage's capital. These lesser fiefs were likewise inherited by primogeniture, and they then established their own ancestral temples and became new "small lineages." Thus the courts of the feudal lords formed a "small lineage" which was a reduced replica of the "great lineage" of the Zhou king, and the hereditary officials of these lords formed a "small lineage" which was a reduced replica of the "great lineage" of the feudal state.[79] This is the political structure that was ritually reproduced in the additive lists of implements and titles that defined the aristocracy.

This structure was also reproduced in the patterns of sanctioned violence that defined political authority. For the performance of sacrifice the king, feudal lords, and hereditary ministers each had an ancestral temple and altars of the earth and soil where they offered up the choicest of their flocks and the booty of their hunts and battles. Each was uniquely empowered as the eldest of his line personally to offer sacrifice to the ancestors in his own lineage, and each also supervised the sacrifices at the *she* and *ji* altars. Each had the privilege of all the ritual appurtenances of nobility for funerals and other rituals, and these were distinguished only in number or scale.

In the realm of warfare this "segmented" pattern of authority—wherein peripheral foci of authority reproduced the administrative, ritual, and military forms of the central government on a reduced level—reappeared in the distribution of command and in the organization of the troops. Even in the early Spring and Autumn period, the actual power of military command lay not in the king or the ruler of the state but in the chief minister (*dangguo* 當國, *guozheng* 國政, *lingyin* 令尹) or in the minister of war (*sima* 司馬). The story cited earlier of the king of Chu who desired to send out the army but was blocked by his chief minister demonstrates this fact, and numerous cases in the *Zuo zhuan* show that such a situation was not exceptional. The most famous case was in the state of Lu, where the three ministerial families who gained control of the state each took command of one of the state's three armies.[80] In another example, Xi Ke of Jin desired to invade Qi to avenge an insult he had received on a mission to that state, but the ruler refused to allow it. However, when the chief minister of Jin retired and yielded his position to Xi Ke, the latter proceeded to invade Qi over the objections of the ruler.[81] As early as the seventh century the "Grand Tutor" in Jin selected the sites of the training hunts and appointed the commanders of the armies, who were generally chosen from among the leading ministerial households. Whoever commanded the central army at the spring hunt would in the next year become chief minister and hence commander-in-chief.[82] These and many other cases show that the titular lords of states neither held supreme command in the army nor had the power to decide who did.[83] Of course these developments were to a degree simply the expression in the military realm of the general rise of the ministerial lineages to dominance, but that rise was made possible by the state's segmentary structure and the distribution of authority throughout the nobility.

Even more important than the division or rotation of the supreme command among the nobility was the fact that each lineage relied on its own fief to provide soldiers, and the army of the state was an amalgam of these locally raised detachments. Bronze inscriptions show that even under the Western Zhou, nobles would provide troops to supplement the royal armies. After the collapse of royal power in the ninth and eighth centuries military power lay in the armies of the feudal states, which were themselves composed of levies (*fu* 賦) from the capital region and the fiefs of the leading lineages.[84] Accounts of campaigns reveal that in the field these levies remained under their own commanders, that major decisions were generally made by group consultation among the leaders, and that the detachments were only loosely bound together so that a commander might lead off his own men without regard for the rest of the army.[85] This constitution of the states' armies through a multitude of private, "lineage" armies also facilitated the innumerable armed feuds and civil wars that characterized society in the late Spring and Autumn period.

Thus the idea of a common nobility that was marked in terminology, ritual, and the patterns of sociability simply reflected the distribution of authority in the segmentary state articulated through the twin principles of "lineage law" and "feudalism." Members of the elite were linked by ascriptive kinship ties and marriage, access to office was gained through inheritance, and the powers of government were dispersed through a multitude of local centers that mimicked the royal court, so the primacy of the ruler remained a matter of degree. Indeed, the subordinates were in many ways stronger than the ruler, who always depended on their local levies to create his armies. As the ties of kinship and shared conquest that had originally united the Zhou state weakened, this segmentary pattern of authority led to a general struggle for power and prestige in which the higher levels steadily lost authority to the lower ones that had direct control of military resources. Since the nobles were by definition warriors, it is scarcely surprising that this struggle took the form of almost continuous warfare, first between feudal states and later between the powerful lineages within the states.

Warfare and Honor

Warfare was the greatest theater for sanctioned violence in the Spring and Autumn period, and it pervaded the life of the nobility. The *Zuo zhuan* lists some 540 interstate wars and more than 130 major civil wars in a span of only 259 years. Moreover, this list of wars is clearly not complete, for the text refers to campaigns which never appear in its pages, and the statistical distribution of wars among the various states clearly reflects limits in the sources employed by the redactors.[86] Years without combat would have been so infrequent that they would scarcely have been noticed, and if one counts the seasonal hunts as forms of warfare, which the Chinese did, then no year went by without military action. Thus the warrior aristocracy lived in a state of constant warfare.

This regularity of warfare is not surprising, since combat was one of the great services of the state and hence a religious duty. The obligation to engage in regular campaigns is demonstrated by the aforementioned plaint of the king of Chu, who faced the opprobrium of the people and the prospect of denial of proper burial for failing to send out the army. This duty to fight was justified by the need to preserve and extend the achievements of the earlier Chu kings, and these "achievements" were clearly Chu's eminence, won through repeated wars, as a leading state and head of the southern league. Warfare was ultimately a matter of prestige or honor, in which the living sought to preserve or augment the glories of their predecessors; it was through its role in defending the state's or lineage's honor that warfare became a fundamental part of the ancestral cult.

Chu's great rival in the north, Jin, also regarded warfare as a means to win eminence among the states and thereby fulfill its obligations to the ancestral spirits. In 633 B.C., the year before Jin's great victory over Chu at Chengpu, a minister of Jin argued in favor of relieving Chu's siege of Song with the argument, "Here is the opportunity to acquire majesty and secure the hegemony."[87] In 597 B.C., prior to the battle of Bi, the commanders of the Jin army had decided to withdraw because Chu was too strong for them, but one commander protested:

> We cannot. Jin became hegemon because of the prowess of its armies and the strength of its officers. Now if we lose the feudal

lords [i.e., the hegemony], this cannot be called strength. If there is an adversary and we do not pursue him, this cannot be called prowess. Rather than lose the hegemony because of this, it would be better to die. If you form an army and go out on expedition and then retire because you hear the enemy is strong, you are not a man. Having received the lord's charge to command the army, you might be willing to end it without your manhood, but I am not.[88]

In 575 B.C., at the battle of Yanling, when several Jin commanders advocated retiring in the face of the Chu army, Fan Wen Zi objected that to retreat would disgrace the "service of the previous rulers."[89] In 570 B.C., the lord of Jin explicitly stated that the reason for engaging in combat was to secure the hegemony. "We assembled the feudal lords for our glory."[90]

These repeated statements that warfare was fought to secure glory or hegemony among the states are supported by Rebecca Byrne's study of the reasons for launching campaigns given in the *Zuo zhuan*.[91] She has shown that virtually all the interstate wars of the period were fought to establish the dominance of one state amongst the others, to carry out the responsibilities that a recognized dominance entailed, to avenge insults to the state or its members, and to eliminate any perceived threat to the state. Thus interstate warfare in the Spring and Autumn period was an ongoing struggle for honor and pre-eminence among the states, and the wars between the ministerial lineages were likewise battles for pre-eminence within the state. In a society that defined its elite through the performance of licit violence and identified manhood with martial prowess, warfare was the ultimate trial of honor.[92]

That warfare was a struggle for honor is shown not only by the statements of participants and the motives of campaigns, but also by the frequency with which "shame" was invoked as a cause of war and the basis of valor. It was assumed in the period that to shame a man or a state was bound to elicit an attack, that men were bound to fight if anyone offended their honor. Thus when the king of Chu asked his ministers if he should humiliate an emissary from Jin, an official replied:

> If you have sufficient military preparations, why shouldn't you? If you shame even a common man you must be prepared to fight, how much more if you shame a state? For this reason the sage kings devoted themselves to diplomatic ritual and never sought to shame anyone.[93]

A few years later Song acceded to a request from Chu because to deny the request would shame Chu and lead them to attack. We saw above how one of the Jin commanders insisted on fighting rather than suffer the shame of retreat, and the idea that honor demanded combat and, if necessary, death appears in other passages.[94] Rebecca Byrne's study indicates that redress for insults or slights was the second most common motive for war, surpassed only by the desire to force another state to acknowledge one's own superiority.

Since defense of one's honor was the primary spur to battle, it is not surprising that various speakers suggested that shame was also the root of military discipline. Only men who had an acute sense of shame would be impelled to risk their lives for the sake of the honor of their state, their lineage, or their person. Thus one man argued that since the Di peoples had no shame, they would be routed if pursued. When criticizing Lord Xiao of Song for refusing to attack the enemy until they had crossed the river and formed their ranks, Zi Yu gave the following account of the conduct of war. "You make clear what is shameful, teach them how to fight, and then seek to kill the enemy."[95] It was the fear of shame that drove men to fight, so instruction in what was shameful was the basis of all military training.

The centrality to warfare of questions of honor is also revealed in the conduct of campaigns. In addition to the numerous rituals which linked their every step to the service of the states' altars, campaigns were also guided by a set of strictures that guaranteed the honorable character of the battle and hence assured the glory of the victors. As we have seen above, an encounter with an enemy in the field obliged an army to fight or suffer dishonor, and in at least one case a commander was executed for withdrawing in the face of an enemy army.[96] Some speakers even went so far as to argue that honor demanded that one attack the enemy army at its strongest point.[97] As combat was a ceremonial trial of strength, states often greeted an invading army with offerings of meat which, as we saw above, established bonds between them as fellow nobles and linked the bloodshed of combat to the sacrificial cults.[98] The day and field of the battle were then formally agreed upon by the two parties, and different terms were applied to distinguish true combats from those which had not been properly arranged.[99] Encounters in the field obliged an army to fight, and every fight had to be properly arranged to allow a genuine test of strength.

Since combat ideally matched the prowess of two prepared foes, the dictates of honor prohibited taking advantage of an adversary's difficulties. Thus if the lord of a state had died, an invading army was supposed to withdraw on the principle that one should not "increase mourning." This principle was so routinely observed that in one case a state successfully secured the departure of an invader by staging a mock funeral.[100] Invaders would also usually leave if a state offered no resistance.[101] These ideas were extended onto the field of battle, as in the famous case of Lord Xiang of Song, who would not attack Chu's army until it had reformed its ranks after crossing a river. In justification, he argued that of old those who commanded an army would not make use of an enemy's difficulties to attack him. Although an adviser criticized his action, with the apparent approval of the "author," elsewhere in the text men state explicitly that to take advantage of a foe's difficulties is cowardly, and this idea accords with the practices of arranging battles, not attacking foes who did not offer resistance, and not beginning a battle until both sides had drummed the signal to advance.[102]

The last and perhaps most striking demonstration of the primary concern for honor on the field of battle was the bouts of formalized provocation (*zhi shi* 致師) that preceded the opening of general hostilities. These were feats of bravado in which one or several chariots would ride out from the host, come dangerously close to the opposing lines, attack some members of the enemy army, and then dash back to their own troops, usually pursued by a substantial force.[103] The textual accounts refer to seeking permission to make a provocation, so these displays appear to have been part of the "formal" preparation for battle. However, since one man who was refused permission proceeded to act on his own accord, they were also personal displays of valor. Both as collective ceremony and personal display they centered attention on the demonstration of courage and prowess, and in this way they epitomized the nature of warfare in this period.

The vindication of honor through force of arms was not restricted to interstate wars, for from the sixth century on ministerial lines came to dominate many of the states, and these lineages likewise fought wars among themselves for supremacy.[104] Moreover, as the official from Chu quoted above remarked, even a "common man" would strike if you shamed him, and indeed in the China of the Spring and Autumn period the nobility regularly wreaked bloody vengeance on anyone who slighted their honor. In contrast with the vengeance systematized by later ritual theorists and written into imperial law, which was justified only in response to the murder of a lord or a family member, revenge in Spring and Autumn China answered any fancied derogation of a man's honor.[105] This vengeance almost always entailed murder and often civil war.

The patterns of vengeance amongst the Zhou nobility reflect in miniature all the features of the social organization of violence discussed thus far. The pre-eminence of warfare as a hallmark of nobility, the obsession with an honor that could be defended only through martial prowess, the general distribution of armed forces through all levels of the aristocracy, and the social and ritual proximity of the nobles with their rulers all figure prominently in the tales of insult, retribution, and civil war. These stories reveal a world in which the casual social intercourse of the nobles provided a fertile ground for quarrels, any perceived slight was answered with force, the segmentation of authority turned appeals to force into wars, and the probability and the severity of reprisals placed great pressure on anyone involved in a quarrel to strike first with full military force in order to avoid falling victim himself to an adversary's assault. It was a world where, as the *Mozi* remarked, men showed that they treasured honor by fighting to the death over a single insulting word, and where elaborate social rituals were gradually erected to minimize the possibility of misunderstandings.[106] It was also a world in which rank was no protection against an avenger's wrath; the *Zuo zhuan* lists thirty-three cases of the murder of rulers and twenty-one of their forcible expulsion from their states, and many of these were the result of acts of vengeance for insults received.

The sorts of insults that could lead to civil war varied from the most trivial to truly mortal offenses. An example of the former is the case of the great strongman Wan of the state of Song. He had been captured in battle with Lu and then returned to Song, and one day while gambling with the lord of Song in the ruler's harem, he chanced to praise the lord of Lu as the only true prince among the feudal lords. Miffed at suffering this aspersion in the presence of his ladies, the ruler observed that since Wan had been captured he no longer respected him. In response to this remark Wan broke his ruler's neck with a single blow, and a second blow to the jaw of an official who ran to the prince's aid shattered it with such force that the flying teeth were lodged in the doorframe. Wan used his own armed followers to set on the throne one of the deceased ruler's sons and waged war on the others.[107] Another ruler was killed for failing to offer some nobles a taste of a rare turtle stew from his table, and a third was driven from his state by nobles whom he had insulted by receiving them while he was still clad in hunting attire.[108]

Graver insults were often related to official functions. Thus when the lord of Zheng at an interstate conference violated the dictates of ritual in his treatment of his chief minister, Zi Si, the latter had the lord assassinated and killed his sons as well.[109] Demotions were also a frequent provocation to vengeance, as in the case of the heir-apparent of Chu, who learned that he was to be replaced by his younger brother and consequently had his father strangled, or the Qin emissary who attacked the superior who had passed him over for the leadership of an important mission to Jin.[110] When Lang Shen was replaced as the spearman for the lord of Jin, a companion suggested that he should commit suicide in disgrace, and when he rejected that notion the friend next proposed vengeance against the responsible official.[111] It seems that any derogation of honor in this period could never be less than mortal.

These cases reveal not only the obsession with honor and the invariable recourse to force to vindicate it, but also the dispersed pattern of prestige and authority in the segmentary state. Several of the quarrels cited above grew out of incidents at the banqueting table or in the prince's private quarters, where nobles came and went with a familiarity inconceivable in later China. Moreover, it is important to note that in those cases where the prince himself felt personally insulted, he generally could do nothing but seek revenge in the same manner as any other noble. The actions, attitudes, and powers of the rulers in these incidents were no different from those of their opponents, and the issues of honor and supremacy were resolved through battle between comparable forces. This identity between rulers and ministers in terms of attitudes and resources is particularly striking in a case in Wei, where the ruler was angered by the fact that his chief minister controlled all the affairs of the court but had no other recourse than to have the minister assassinated.[112]

Of course, such affairs of honor were not limited to incidents involving the rulers of states, although these figure most prominently in the historical records. I earlier cited the case of Xi Ke, who gained command of the Jin army and led it to invade Qi to avenge an insult he had received there. Violent revenge could also be carried out within a lineage, as when Zhao Yang killed a fellow clansman for ignoring his orders.[113] In another case an incident at the dinner table led two sons of the ruler of Qi to launch a civil war against the chief minister and ultimately drive him from the state. In fact, the *Zuo zhuan* depicts a world in which the entire nobility not only went out regularly on state-organized hunts and military expeditions but also lived their private lives surrounded by bands of armed retainers, constantly on guard against insult or attack.[114]

Although vengeance was an ever present threat in the lives of the nobility, it seems to have been particularly prevalent on the field of battle. This is true despite the fact that several speakers explicitly state that one should not use the battlefield, a place of service to the lord or state, to attain private vengeance; perhaps it became an explicit stricture only because of the frequency of its violation.[115] Already loci of violence and the focus of concerns over honor, battlefields and their environs proved fertile grounds for acts of revenge. Men who had quarreled over the choice of weapons at the ancestral temple, who had been slighted in the ceremonial pre-battle meal, who had been demoted, or who had been cheated out of prisoners they had captured in battle all sought recourse to violence to restore their honor, sometimes at the cost of the defeat of their own forces.[116]

These acts of vengeance usually entailed violations of hierarchy and threatened the survival of the state, so they cannot strictly be considered as sanctioned violence like sacrifice, hunting, and interstate warfare. However, they were so frequent that they seem to have been accepted by the nobility as a fact of life, and it appears that few aristocrats would have accepted the possibility of not responding to insults with some form of violence. In addition, there *are* two pieces of evidence which suggest that revenge had indeed taken on some ritualistic and normative aspects. When the ruler of Qi was still crown prince, he had quarreled with Bing Can's father over a piece of land, and after he ascended the throne, he disinterred the corpse of the deceased father and cut off its legs. When Bing Can was finally able to avenge this act by killing the ruler, he formally reported this act to his lineage's ancestral temple before fleeing the country.[117] This action gave the act of revenge a strongly ceremonial character, and indeed linked it to a formal military action which also ended with the reporting of success and the presentation of booty at the ancestral temple.

The "normalization" of vengeance is even more explicit in the case of Yu Pian of Jin state. This man had been punished in front of the entire Jin army by Jia Ji, then commander of the central army, but Jia Ji himself was soon demoted by Yang Hu Fu. When Jia Ji killed Yang Hu Fu for revenge and then fled the state, Yu Pian was given the assignment of escorting the household of the fugitive to the capital. This appointment placed at his mercy the family of the man who had publicly humiliated him, but when urged by his followers to exact his revenge, he quoted a book which stated that neither favors nor insults received from someone could properly be paid back upon his descendants.[118] This reference to a book that dictated the proper principles of reciprocity clearly suggests that the practice of vengeance had some degree of social sanction and regularity.

The cumulative weight of all this evidence shows that honor was supremely important to the aristocracy and that military prowess was absolutely central to their idea of honor. Warfare was one of the two great services of the state, and it was devoted to winning glory for the self and the lineage through victory in battle. In addition, a man's honor could be guaranteed in daily life only if he were ready to fight and conquer whoever slighted him. As the *Mozi* argued in the passage cited above, men demonstrated that they treasured honor and duty by fighting to the death over a single insulting word, so the only honorable man was the warrior.

This equation of manliness with martial prowess was appealed to in the argument of the Jin commander cited earlier, but its most striking formulation occurs in the story of Zi Xi and Zi Nan. These men wooed the same woman, and her father, fearing to offend either, entrusted the decision to the chief minister Zi Chan. Zi Chan discussed the matter with the two suitors, and they agreed to allow the woman to decide. Zi Xi presented himself first, and, clad in his finest clothing, made the correct ritual offerings of jade and silk. Zi Nan followed, but he rode in clad in his warrior's garb, leapt from the chariot, fired in either direction, and then jumped back on the chariot and departed. The woman remarked, "Zi Xi was sincere and fine, but Zi Nan was a man. For a man to be a man and a woman a woman is what we call true order." The spurned Zi Xi sought out his successful rival and attacked him, but in the ensuing battle he himself was wounded.[119]

It is difficult to know exactly how to read this story. The woman's remarks sound almost like a parody of the Confucian doctrine of the rectification of names, and her choice of the warrior over the ritualist inverts the judgement of later Confucianism. However, as I argued earlier, the *Zuo zhuan* often articulates values at odds with those of later Confucianism, and this equation of true manliness with martial prowess not only jibes with many other passages in the *Zuo zhuan* but also with the ideals that appear in many odes in the *Shi jing* and in the "Stone Drum" inscriptions.[120] Indeed, in the *Shi jing* the character *ren* (仁), which in Confucian philosophy came to express an ideal of humanity based on tender compassion or benevolence, apparently simply described physical handsomeness or valor, and it was applied to a stalwart hunter of no moral worth.[121] Thus the equation of true manliness with martial prowess probably reflects the standard judgement of the Spring and Autumn nobility.

Blood Covenants

The preceding sections have revealed an elite defined through sacrifice and warfare, drawn together through kin ties established by the cult of the ancestors and the ritual exchanges of meat, but riven by a segmentary division of authority among men who were devoted to an honor defined by heroism and martial prowess. Interstate wars, interlineage conflicts, and vendettas launched to avenge slighted honor generated incessant conflicts that broke down the old hierarchies of ritual and lineage law and replaced them with an increasingly savage struggle for dominance through armed force. In the conflicts of the Spring and Autumn period, the primary means devised to create new ties among men no longer tightly bound by the old Zhou order was the blood covenant (*meng* 盟). The practice of sealing these covenants through the collective drinking of the blood of a sacrificial victim became fundamental to the political and social order in the early Eastern Zhou period, and it developed increasing importance and new functions through the seventh and sixth centuries. In the beginning it was employed to forge large coalitions of states under the dominance of a hegemon, and these coalitions replaced the Zhou monarchy as the primary link between increasingly independent states. Over the course of the centuries, as the power of ministerial lineages grew and the feudal states were riven by internal conflicts, the covenants also came to play the key role in forming alliances between several lineages, between lineages and alien states, and between the various contestants for supremacy in the state and the capital populace. In short, the sacrifices of covenants gradually replaced those of the ancestral cult as the primary mode of constituting a political order, and this order thus began to detach itself from kin structures. In the changing role of the covenant we can see how under the pressure of internecine conflict one of the primary institutions of the old order, sacrifice, began to evolve into one of the bases of the new.

The fundamental importance of covenants to the Eastern Zhou state is suggested by the sheer frequency of their occurrence in the historical records. The concordance to the commentaries on the *Chun qiu* lists 637 references to covenants, and although a single ceremony is often mentioned many times, there were still several hundred instances recorded over a period of less than three centuries.[122] Moreover, various accounts written during the Warring States, Qin, and early Han periods present the covenant as the basis of the political order of the Eastern Zhou, or even the entire Zhou period. These accounts usually associate the covenant with the reliance on military force that characterized the hegemons of the Eastern Zhou, and they argue that reliance on covenants represented a decline from the charismatic rule of the ancient sage-kings. A story in the *Lü Shih chun qiu* thus portrays the Zhou founders as basing their power on force and blood-smeared covenants, and it criticizes them for "relying on sacrifices and blood oaths in order to create trust."[123] The *Huainanzi* lists the principles and practices that underlay social order in the successive dynasties of antiquity.

> Shen Nong made no commands and the people followed him. Yu made commands but used no punishments. The Xia never went back on their word. The Shang used oaths [*shi* 誓], and the Zhou used sacrificial covenants.[124]

This list is clearly not only in the order of descending chronology but also descending propriety and efficacy. The Han dynasty writer Huan Tan traced a similar descent with a more explicitly moralizing language.

Those without commands and punishments are called *huang*. Those who make commands but do not punish are called *di*. Those who reward the good and punish the wicked and bring the feudal lords to serve in their court are called "kings". Those who raise up armies and bind men with sacrificial covenants are called hegemons.[125]

That the use of blood covenants was linked to the hegemons of the Spring and Autumn period and represented a decline from the morally potent rule of antiquity became the characteristic doctrine of the Confucian school.[126]

Although enmeshed in a vision of history that idealized a mythic antiquity, the idea that covenants emerged in the Zhou and that their rise to prominence reflected a decline in royal power and an increasing reliance on force is both accurate and insightful. While they did not rule without commands or force, the Shang and Western Zhou monarchs had commanded great prestige as intercessors with the gods and had wielded a considerable military power that gave them clear superiority over other nobles and tribal chieftains. Although there is evidence of some covenant-like ceremonies under the Shang and literary references to their use in the early Western Zhou, it was in the struggles of competing states and lineages during the Eastern Zhou that the covenant came to play a decisive role.[127] Even the Confucian texts that regarded them as a sign of moral decay acknowledged their fundamental importance to the political order that emerged from the decline of the monarchy, and they described covenants as one of the "great services" of the state.[128]

Covenants were forms of oaths in which all parties pledged to uphold a certain set of rules or pursue a certain course of action, but they were distinguished from ordinary oaths through the killing of a sacrificial animal and the drinking of its blood. This ceremony invoked the presence of the gods and ancestors as witnesses who would punish any breach or nonobservance.[129] Some Confucian writers state that only after the first of the hegemons, Lord Huan of Qi, did men begin to use sacrifices to sanctify oaths, but various texts including the *Shi jing* refer to blood covenants as early as the Western Zhou, and the records of Lord Huan's activities show that he also used sacrifices.[130] In only one case, in 541 B.C., was a covenant sealed without a sacrifice, and that was only allowed after a special petition because it was simply the renewal of an old covenant.[131] Without the sacralizing power of a sacrifice there could be no covenant.

The clearest evidence of the sharp distinction between oaths with and without sacrifice, and the unique role of the former in creating bonds between men, appears in two stories dealing with the reception of emissaries. One describes how an embassy from the state of Chu to the state of Jin had to cross over Zheng. When they reached the border of Zheng, they were met by a delegation from that state and swore an oath to do no harm within its borders. This was a standard practice of diplomatic protocol that was prescribed in ritual texts. However, in another case of receiving an embassy passing through a state, an attending official faked evidence of the sealing of a covenant—a sacrifice buried with the text of an oath—and then reported this evidence to the king. The use of a covenant demonstrated the formation of ties with another state and indicated that the head of the group that had received the embassy, the heir apparent, was planning a rebellion. As a result he was executed.[132] This contrast demonstrates that the difference between an oath and a covenant was quite clear to the men of the period and that this difference was of the highest significance. The blood of the sacrifice marked a supremely solemn and binding agreement, and it was used to forge political ties between men.

The procedure of sealing a covenant can be reconstructed from scattered references in the sources and confirmed by the archeological excavations of numerous blood covenants at Houma.[133] The participants in the covenant first purified themselves through fasting, erected an altar, and then dug a pit in front of it.[134] They sacrificed an animal, cut off its left ear, placed this in one vessel, and caught its blood in another. The archeological evidence reveals that these sacrifices generally employed a sheep, and the significance of this will be discussed in Chapter Five. Since it was the custom to cut off the left ear of an enemy killed in battle and, according to the *Zhou li*, of animals killed in ceremonial hunts, the disposition of its body clearly equated the sacrificial animal with a vanquished enemy or captured prey. This equation was sometimes heightened through the use of human blood. Blood was then sprinkled on the altar to summon the spirits, and the text of the covenant was read. This text included a list of the participants, the terms of the oath, and sometimes a curse upon those who violated the covenant. Each of the participants then smeared some blood on his lips while another held the left ear of the animal.[135] After the reading of the text and the smearing of the blood, the sacrificial animal and one copy of the oath, also smeared with blood, were buried in the pit. Other copies of the text were given to the participants, and these were stored in special archives.[136] Every convenant had a master (*zhu* 主) who directed the proceedings and was charged with enforcing the terms of the oath. The master of the covenant had the honor of drinking the first draught of blood, and the task of holding the left ear, which resulted in drinking last, became a sign of inferior status.[137]

Athough the text of the oath sometimes included a curse on those who violated its terms, it was a common practice to perform a separate ceremony called a "malediction" (*zu* 詛) following the covenant. This served the purpose of calling down the vengeance of the spirits and ancestors on any who transgressed the oath.[138]

The sealing of covenants extended the sanctions of religion to those interpersonal ties which were not secured through sacrificial duties to common ancestors.[139] In this capacity, the ritual first came to prominence with the decline of the monarchy, when it was used to secure alliances between the increasingly independent states and became the mechanism for establishing the great leagues centered on the hegemons.[140] The flight of the Zhou dynasty to its eastern capital, Loyang, in 770 B.C. marked the definitive end of the political and military dominance of the royal house. When the southern state of Chu began to expand into the valley of the Yellow River and claimed the royal title in 704 B.C., the feudal lords of the Zhou state lacked any means to organize resistance. In response to this threat, Lord Huan of Qi and his chief minister Guan Zhong assembled the rulers of the central states in 681 B.C. at Beixing, and Lord Huan became the "hegemon" (*ba* 霸) of this league of states. In 678 B.C., the league sealed the first recorded multi-state "joint covenant" (*tong meng* 同盟), and in the *Zuo zhuan* the hegemon is routinely called the "master of the covenant."[141] In 656 B.C., Lord Huan led an army of the allied states and defeated Chu. Chu in response organized a league based on a covenant in 633 B.C. For a century and a half the struggle between these two alliances, the northern one generally controlled by Jin and the southern by Chu, dominated the political and military history of China. In 546 and 541 B.C., an assembly of fourteen states dominated by the newly ascendant ministerial houses sealed general covenants to end interstate combat, but these both ended in failure.

In addition to the formation of the great leagues, covenants were used by states to end hostilities, pledge amicable relations, and fix boundaries.[142] The most complete covenant preserved was sealed by a victorious army of several states with the defeated state of Zheng, and it may serve as a model of the content and format of these interstate treaties.

> All those who participate in this covenant agree not to hoard grain, not to monopolize profit, not to protect conspirators, not to harbor criminals, to give assistance in the event of civil war or insurrection, to have the same friends and enemies, and to support the royal house.
>
> If anyone violates these commands, may the guardians of reverence and covenants, the spirits of the great mountains and rivers, the collected heavenly spirits and spirits who receive sacri-

fice, the former kings and former lords, and the ancestors of the seven surnames and twelve states destroy him so that his people desert him, he loses rank and clan, and his state and family are extinguished.[143]

In this interstate covenant of 562 B.C. we already see great concern over internal insurrection and civil war, and during this period covenants were increasingly used to create or reinforce bonds between parties competing for power *within* a given state. Covenants were often sealed between lineages or families conspiring to arrange the selection of a particular prince as heir apparent, to seize the throne, or to destroy an enemy who seemed on the verge of seizing it himself. In some cases, such "private" covenants were likewise sealed between the current ruler of a state and parties whose support was essential to maintain his rule.[144] Covenants also came to play a general role in guaranteeing pledges between individuals and to give religious authority to testimony in legal cases.[145] Thus, over the course of the Spring and Autumn period, these ceremonies came to accompany virtually any collective or public action in which men sought to join themselves together or pledge their good faith and loyalty.

One innovation in the use of the covenant that had a tremendous impact on the development of the Chinese state in this period was the increasing tendency to use covenants to secure the support or allegiance of the capital populace (*guo ren* 國人). As rulers and ministerial lineages battled for dominance, they had increasing recourse to the potential power of the inhabitants of the capital cities who were mobilized for military service or mob action. These inhabitants were the "citizens" of the states of the Eastern Zhou, which at the beginning of the period were city-states that governed directly only their own capitals and the nearby towns.[146] The *guo ren* consisted of the lowest level of the nobility—the *shi*—as well as merchants and artisans. The former were a primary constituent of the army, and the entire population could expel the lord, overthrow the government, and set up new rulers. Consequently it became a maxim that the outrage of the populace was like a raging fire, and the texts often explain that a certain decision was made "in order to quiet the capital populace."[147] The capital's inhabitants thus came to play a decisive role in the internecine struggles between the various lineages of the nobility and often decided the succession to the throne, so ambitious men sought to win their favor through conspicuous exemplary conduct or public charity.[148] In times of crisis the entire populace could be assembled in order to decide the policy of the state.[149] Because of the importance of these men to the political order of the state, many who hoped to seize power, had seized power, or had recovered the throne after temporarily losing it would seal a blood covenant with the capital populace.[150] Thus in addition to providing the mechanism for new modes of elite political organization, the blood covenant also furnished the means of drawing new social groups into the political order and of binding them to the emerging rulers of late Spring and Autumn China. We shall see in the next chapter the crucial role of this development in the Warring States transition.

The archeological finds at Houma cited above have provided some new insights into the developing role of the covenant at the end of the Spring and Autumn period. At this site Chinese archeologists have excavated more than 300 pits that contain fragments of the texts of covenants and the remains of sacrifices. All the texts refer to a single political struggle that, according to the most likely theory, took place in the years 496–495 B.C. That men involved in a life-and-death struggle for power should have devoted the time and energy to perform this vast number of ceremonies in the span of a few years suggests the tremendous importance attached to covenants in the political realm.

Perhaps even more significant than the frequency of the covenants was their content. The participants in the covenants in all cases were the members of the Zhao clan that had temporarily seized power and their allies. While a few texts pronounced a ban on seizing the property of enemy lineages or households that had fled the state, and one appears to have been a formal address or prayer by the puppet lord of Jin, the vast bulk of the texts deals entirely with bans or collective death sentences placed on various enemy lineages or households. Some of these list only a single lineage or household, while others list as many as nine lineages and twenty-one households, even in some cases giving lists of specific relatives such as paternal grandfathers, uncles, and brothers. The most frequent form of text begins with a reference to the "covenant of Jia," a polite term used in lieu of the taboo personal name of the master of this covenant, but others do not mention him, and these are generally presumed to be covenants by former enemies or neutrals who hoped to join the party that was then in power by pledging to help destroy their enemies.

These Houma covenants thus reflect one of the major developments of the Spring and Autumn period, the war to the death between major lineages, which culminated with the destruction of a lineage (*mie zu* 滅族) or its partition (*fen zu* 分族). In the world of the Zhou nobility the lineages were the fundamental units of political organization, each possessing land, offices, military capacity, a dependent population, and an ancestral temple. They became the leading actors in the internecine wars that dominated the sixth and fifth centuries, and when one of them was defeated, the other lineages divided its land and dependents and obliterated its temple.[151] In addition to enforcing the expulsion or extermination of enemy lineages, the Houma covenants also refer several times to the partition of lineages, so they reveal some of the concrete detail underlying the formulas of the literary texts.

Moreover, in their bans on individual households and the listing of their members they reveal a transitional phase in the political history of the family in China, the gradual disappearance of the kin group as a state-like unit and its replacement by the individual household as a unit of economic production and the provision of service. This shift was marked, as will be discussed in the next chapter, by the shift in the meaning of *mie zu* from a political event approximating the destruction of a state to a form of collective punishment that fixed the legal limits of the individual family.

The Houma documents reveal the culmination of the use of covenants to establish new political alliances and a new public realm in the wake of the breakdown of the old "lineage law." In one of the many civil wars that plagued Jin in this period and led to its ultimate division, one party and its would-be adherents sealed collective covenants which drew up itemized lists of the enemies who were to be driven from the state and killed if they returned. In the midst of general breakdown, men were seeking to reconstitute the state through binding all of its members together with covenants that ostracized all others who would not join. In this inclusion of new elements into the public realm, the redefinition of the bonds between ruler and ruled, and the occasional focus on kin units defined by the individual household, we can see some intimations of the Warring States transition that forms the subject of the next chapter.

Conclusion

The Eastern Zhou states were dominated by an aristocracy that defined itself through performance of the "great services," which consisted of offering sacrifice at the altars of the ancestral temple and the state, and winning booty and glory through ceremonial hunts and equally ceremonial combats. All these activities culminated in presentations at the altars, and the distribution and consumption of the meat from these ceremonies served both to define the elite and link it together in networks of exchange.

This aristocracy was in turn divided into a hierarchy of lineages through the principles of "lineage law," but the lower-level lineages were simply reduced replicas of the royal house and the feudal lords, each with its own capital, ancestral temple, *she* altar, dependent population, and military forces. Because this segmentary pattern of authority gave each lineage a base of power independent of its titular lord, and all nobles were ascriptive kin, the lower levels of the Zhou nobility were able to enjoy a proximity of status and a casual sociability with their rulers which was radically different from that of courtiers in imperial China. They were also able to compete with their putative superiors and their fellows in a general struggle for supremacy.

The battles which constituted one element of the "great services" were primarily means of gaining glory for the lineage and the self, so the nobles of the Spring and Autumn period lived a life devoted to the winning of prestige through heroism and martial prowess. This was true not only in wars between states but also in the struggles between lineages for supremacy within the state, and in the constant vendettas and acts of bloody vengeance provoked by the obsessive concern with honor and prowess. The pursuit of honor for the lineage and the individual noble led the Zhou aristocracy into a deepening spiral of civil war and mutual annihilation that ended in the destruction of much of the nobility and the creation of the new political and social forms that characterized the Warring States period.

One innovation that appeared in the Spring and Autumn period itself as a new means of reconstituting the political order was the blood covenant. First used by the most powerful of the feudal states to forge leagues and impose their own authority as the "master of the covenant" or hegemon, these sacrificial oaths were gradually applied to any situation in which men sought to forge new coalitions and impose binding ties on their fellows. In this way these instruments of interstate diplomacy came to provide the means for organizing conspiracy, insurrection, and civil war. They were also employed to draw new social elements, most notably the members of the capital populace, into active service in the political struggles of the day. As civil wars and the increasingly frequent destruction of states and lineages tore apart the old order of feudalism and lineage law, the blood covenant came to play an ever more important role as the sole means of binding men together for collective action. The culmination of this process is vividly demonstrated in the large number of covenants unearthed at Houma.

In the Introduction I suggested that the patterns of sanctioned violence could cast light on the nature and distribution of authority, on the fundamental divisions of a society, on what its people held to be of deepest significance, and perhaps on how men understood their own civilization and its relation to the natural world. For the Eastern Zhou state we have found that authority was explicitly identified with the performance of the ritually guided violence of sacrifice and warfare, that this authority was distributed throughout the aristocracy on the basis of ascriptive kin ties, that the matter of highest significance was honor, that the fundamental unit of elite society was the lineage, and that ritual violence granted authority and structured society through its culmination in the service of the spirits, both ancestral and local. Sanctioned violence and the authority which it defined were both ultimately expressions of the cultic service which linked men to the world of ancestors and gods.

When the social order defined through differential relations to common ancestors and the ritual service of the altars began to crumble together with the monarchy, new political ties were constituted through the presumptive power of blood sacrifice to substantiate words and thus make oaths sacred and binding. With the accelerating disintegration of that order in the incessant wars and vendettas of the late Spring and Autumn period, the use of blood sacrifice to sanction pledges became the dominant form of binding men together in a political order and imposing obedience to the dictates of the new rulers. In this development we see the beginnings of the new patterns of sanctioned violence and authority that characterized the Warring States period.

Chapter Two

THE WARRING STATE

The constant wars of the Zhou noble lineages gradually led to the creation of ever larger territorial units through the conquest of alien states and the extension of central government control into the countryside. These were called "warring states" because they devoted themselves to warfare, they were created through the progressive extension of military service, and the registration and mobilization of their populations for battle remained fundamental to their existence as states.[1] They kept every form of violence that had defined the political order of the Zhou nobility—warfare, sacrifice, blood oaths, and vengeance—but these were reorganized and reinterpreted as constitutive elements of the new order. Whereas under the nobility the actual performance of ritually sanctioned violence had been the hallmark of authority, in the Warring States all men engaged in licit violence, while authority was associated with its manipulation and control. Instead of being a means of defending honor, sanctioned violence served to establish or reinforce the authoritarian, hierarchic bonds that constituted the new social structure. In place of the lineage as the primary unit of both politics and elite kinship, the state secured control of military force, while the kin groups were reduced to the individual households that provided both taxes and labor service. These kin units were in turn defined through patterns of sacrifice, vengeance, and collective punishments. The ultimate sanction of segmentary, aristocratic rule in the ancestral cults was replaced by forms of sanctioned violence and authority that were justified through the imitation of the "patterns of Heaven" by a single, cosmically potent ruler. Finally, this new organization and interpretation of violence

53

allowed the Warring States Chinese to develop a new understanding of the structure of human society and of the natural world. The remainder of this book will deal with each element of this transformation.

This chapter will focus specifically on the means by which the political order was recreated through the changing patterns of military service, and how modified forms of the old, aristocratic patterns of violence were used to establish fixed hierarchies and secure social control in the emerging territorial states. With the rise of universal military service, warfare and the army became a mechanism for hierarchically organizing and controlling the entire population. Blood oaths gradually became emotive "bonds" that formed the basis of legal codes and established the absolute supremacy of rulers over ruled. Sacrifice became a "theatrical" performance in which men defined their social roles by acting them out in choreographed ceremonies. Vengeance, which had been the root of feud and civil war among the aristocracy, was celebrated as a "debt of blood" that defined and hallowed ties of kinship and service. In this way, patterns of approved killing and collective violence created or reinforced each of the social relationships that made up the new order.

Warfare and the Warring State

The history of the development of military organization and its relations to the social, economic, and political changes during the Warring States period would require a large monograph to itself.[2] The present study will examine only how warfare was transformed from a hallmark of the aristocracy focused on the battle for honor into a universal practice that bound men together in a new form of state. The basis of this change was the progressive extension of military service so that what had been a privilege of the urban aristocracy became the duty of the rural peasantry. This process culminated in universal military service and the complete identification of the people with the army.

As was discussed in the preceding chapter, the Zhou conquerors had attempted to control their vast new territories through "enfeoffing" relatives and allies in walled towns throughout their kingdom. These members of the original Zhou coalition and their descendants formed the nobility and at least part of the capital populace, and they monopolized government office, military service, and all the privileges of authority. The elite elements of the indigenous peoples were probably incorporated into the capital populace, while the peasants in the countryside were either awarded to the conquerors as dependents or allowed to live under their traditional elders or chieftains. The early Zhou armies had been based on chariots manned by members of the aristocracy, who were accompanied by foot soldiers drawn from the capital populace or from the dependent populations of the cadet lineages.[3] However, these armies were small and the number of peasants or artisans required few, so in the Western Zhou and early Spring and Autumn period military service remained a prerogative of the nobility and the urban populace, while people who lived any distance from the capitals played no role in the armies.[4]

According to received accounts, the process of expanding military service and identifying the army with the people began with Guan Zhong and his policy of "lodging the army amidst the people" (*yu bing yu min* 寓兵於民) in Qi state in the early seventh century. Although all the records of this reform date from the Warring States period, several centuries after the time of Guan Zhong, their accounts limit his extension of military service to the capital, and the geographic range of Qi's effective power also does not go beyond the capital region.[5] Since the division between the capitals and the rural hinterlands had begun to break down as early as the seventh century, this archaism suggests that the surviving records were at least based on older documents, although they have doubtless been reworked to suit the needs and preconceptions of Warring States redactors.

The most detailed account of Guan Zhong's reform appears in the Warring States compendium that bears his name.

"If my lord desires to rapidly have his will under Heaven and subdue the feudal lords, then your military service must have that in which to hide and your government have that in which to lodge. . . . Set up regulations within [the capital] and lodge the military statutes therein. . . . Divide the capital of Qi into three parts to create three armies. Select worthy men to be the heads of neighborhoods; let the districts organize columns and squads with company commanders to direct them. Moreover, use hunting to assign rewards and punishments, so the common people will master military service." "Good!" said Lord Huan.

Master Guan thereupon instituted each group of five families as a *gui*, and a *gui* had a senior. Ten *gui* made a neighborhood, and a neighborhood had a supervisor. Four neighborhoods made a *lian*, and a *lian* had a senior. Ten *lian* made a district, and a district had a "goodman". He used these to make the military regulations. Thus five families made a *gui*, and five men [one from each family] made a [military] squad of five [*wu* 伍] commanded by the senior of the *gui*. Ten *gui* made a neighborhood, and these fifty men made a small regiment commanded by the supervisor. [and so on up the hierarchy]. . . . Therefore the soldiers and squads were fixed in their neighborhoods, while the divisions and armies were fixed at the outskirts of the town. [i.e., when the army was mobilized the squads would be assembled in their neighborhoods, and the full army then gathered outside the walls.][6]

Members of these units were also to be responsible for mutual surveillance. They were instructed both to recommend those among their neighbors who were worthy of office or suitable for military command and also to denounce any who behaved badly or committed crimes. Failure in these duties would result in collective punishment for the entire unit.

Dividing up the population into a hierarchy of units in which each higher level encompassed a fixed number of lower level units is a trait of Warring States administrative theory and almost certainly does not reflect seventh-century practice. Likewise, both the identity of units of civil government with those of army mobilization and the duty of mutual surveillance within these units were later developments. However, the fact that general mobilization is restricted to the three districts of the capital and not imposed on the hypothetical administrative units of the outer regions (*bi* 鄙) does hint at some basis in seventh-century fact. At any rate, it is certain that the organization of the army into infantry units based on multiples of five began in the eighth or seventh century, and it is not impossible that Qi's initial hegemony was based on expanding its military power through a more systematic introduction of this practice.[7] However, at this early stage the extension of the base of state service did not go far beyond the capital's walls.

According to surviving records, the first state to draw the population of the hinterland into military service was Jin. In 645 B.C. Lord Hui of Jin was captured by Qin and much of his army destroyed. To help Jin recover from this disaster and secure Lord Hui's position on the throne his supporters initiated several emergency reforms.

> Zi Jin instructed him, "Assemble the capital populace in court and reward them in the prince's name. Then proclaim to them the lord's words, 'Even if I should return I would only disgrace the altars. Divine [an appropriate day] to install my son.'" The populace wept. Thereupon Jin created the *yuan* [爰] fields.
>
> Lu Sheng [Zi Jin] said, "The prince does not sorrow for his own death but worries only about his servants. This is the height of benevolence. What should we do for our prince?" The populace asked, "What should we do?" [Lu Sheng] replied, "Make new levies of troops and preparation [of arms] to assist the heir. Then the feudal lords will hear that we have lost a prince but gained a new one, that the assembled servants are in harmony, and that we

have increased our armored soldiers. Our friends will be encouraged and our enemies terrified. This might be of benefit." The populace was delighted, so Jin created the *zhou* [州] troops.[8]

The exact natures of the *yuan* fields and the *zhou* troops have elicited considerable debate over the centuries. The earliest commentators noted that the character *yuan* was homophonous with the characters 轅, 咺, and 換, all of which had the meaning of "to exchange" or "switch." On the basis of this meaning they appealed to a system described in the *Zhou li* in which every three years people would exchange land in order that good and bad land might be shared equally.[9] The Qing scholar Yu Yue (1821–1907 A.D.), however, noted that the *yuan* fields were created as a form of reward to the people and a means of strengthening Jin state; they had no connection with the ideal of equity in the system described in the *Zhou li*.[10] Moreover, the verb applied to the fields is *zuo*, which indicates that this was a new institution and not the restoration of an old one. In the light of these criticisms, but unwilling to abandon the old gloss of *yuan* as "to exchange," many modern scholars have argued that what took place here was the abandonment of the old system of exchanging fields.[11] However, since the link of the reform to exchanging fields depended entirely on this gloss of the character, it seems self-defeating to argue that the content was the opposite of the name.

In the *Shuo wen* the character *yuan* is glossed by the character *yin* (引), which means "to pull" or "obtain." As Duan Yucai (1735–1815 A.D.) noted in his commentary, this gloss was based on the fact that *yuan* was used interchangeably with *yuan* (援), which meant "to pull," "lay hold of," or "assist." Duan pointed out that the graph represents a hand drawing something up or placing something down. In this way it is closely related in form and meaning to the character that immediately precedes it in the dictionary, *shou* (受), which meant "to receive" or "to grant."[12] Not only were these two characters closely related in form and meaning but they could also sometimes be used interchangeably.[13] Thus the *yuan* fields were probably simply an early form of the Warring States "*shou* fields."

Shou field was the standard term for land received from the state, and although it was often applied to the romanticized well-field system, it also appeared as a technical term in the Qin code for the fixed allotment of land received from the state.[14] This link with the Qin land system is not trivial, for in his brief description of the land reform in Qin state Ban Gu said that Shang Yang "instituted *yuan* fields."[15] Since Shang Yang came from Wei, a successor state of Jin, the link is quite plausible.[16]

The identification of the *yuan* fields as the earliest form of state-allocated land fits precisely with their role in the historical narrative. Prior to the creation of the fields, Lord Hui's emissary had declared his intention to reward the people, and the allocation of land was one of the most common forms of reward, although it had hitherto been reserved for the aristocracy. Moreover, these fields were linked to the organization of a new form of military levy, as were the later *shou* fields.

The narrative of the *Zuo zhuan* clearly states that the creation of the *zhou* troops was a means of "increasing armored soldiers," but an understanding of the social significance of this reform requires an examination of the word *zhou*. A passage in the *Guanzi* says that a *zhou* was the same as a *shu* (述), and other sources state that *shu* was an alternative name for a *sui* (遂), the basic unit of the subject populations who lived outside the capital.[17] Two stories in the *Zuo zhuan* also show that the inhabitants of the *zhou* were indigenous peoples or those who had been conquered in war.

> Earlier the lord [of Wei] ascended the city wall, and when he looked out he saw the *zhou* of the Rong [a non-Zhou people]. He asked about it and was told [what it was]. The lord said, "I have a Ji surname [a descendant of the Zhou house]. What business do the Rong have there?" He destroyed their town.[18]

In this story the *zhou* is the unit of the conquered, non-Zhou people, and they are prohibited from living in the vicinity of the capital.

The second story deals with Chu's disposition of the conquered people of Chen. Originally Chu had absorbed Chen as a dependent district (*xian* 縣), but when criticized for cutting off Chen's sacrifices, Chu agreed to restore the state. However, as a precaution they "took one man from each *xiang* [鄉, the administrative unit of the inhabitants of the capital] back to Chu and established Xia *zhou*."[19] Here again the *zhou* was the unit of a conquered people and was explicitly contrasted with the *xiang*, the unit of the elite in the capital. Thus, the creation of *zhou* troops marked a major shift in the Chinese world. For the first time, in order to increase its military power, a Zhou state began to incorporate the subject peoples and farmers of the hinterland into the state structure by having them perform military service. In return these people probably received grants of state land.

This was an emergency measure, but ten years later, when Prince Chong Er returned to Jin and became Lord Wen, he trebled the size of Jin's armies within two years, a move which would not have been possible if the military levies from the countryside did not continue to be used. Similar reforms soon followed in other states. Between 594 and 590 the state of Lu first "taxed fields" and "created the *qiu* [丘] armored troops."[20] The *qiu* was also a unit of population, and from the place names in which it appears, it seems to have been associated with key strategic areas between states, hence areas which were distant from the capital.[21] At any rate, the use of the word *zuo* shows clearly that elements of the population that had not previously provided military service were now being drawn into the army. Moreover, the levying of a tax on land indicates that the state had begun to allot land to individual households, which were then obliged to provide sums of grain or cash and perhaps military service. Since these reforms were explicitly introduced to deal with invasions from Qi, there is no doubt that they entailed expanding the base of the military levy.

Between 543 and 539 B.C. Zi Chan reordered the fields of Zheng into a grid with irrigation channels, levied a tax on land, organized rural households into units of five, and created a *qiu* levy.[22] The opening of new land through irrigation and the levying of a tax on it suggests the institution of some form of land allotment. Since the five-man squad was the basic unit of military organization, the grouping of households into units of five likewise indicates that the populace of the hinterland was being drawn into military service. Finally, the introduction of a "*qiu* levy" clearly echoes the "*qiu* troops" of Lu and shows that Zheng was also expanding military recruitment into the countryside. This introduction of the *qiu* levy was vehemently opposed by the inhabitants of the capital, who were losing their privileged position in the state.

The state of Chu carried out a major reorganization of its military levies and taxes in 548 B.C. This included not only a general survey of land and a redistribution of fields through the introduction of irrigation channels, but also an examination of mountain forests, salt ponds, fish ponds, and marshes.[23] This comprehensive scrutiny of all the material and human resources of the state shows that Chu was also extending its tax and service base not only into the countryside but throughout the entire realm.

The result of this general extension of military service in the first half of the sixth century was a substantial increase in the size of armies. In earlier battles between the most powerful states, such as the battle of Chengpu between Jin and Chu in 632 B.C. or the battle of An between Jin and Qi in 589 B.C., the armies had each mustered only 800 chariots. In 530 B.C., the king of Chu boasted that his four greatest cities could each provide a thousand chariots, and in the following year Jin carried out a general mobilization for a hunt that put an army of 4,000 chariots into the field.[24] This means that in half a century the military levies of the larger states had increased by a factor of five, a result that was particularly impressive because the king of Chu's remark suggests that much of the levy still came from the vicinity of major cities.

While the Zhou states were abandoning the old separation be-

tween a military aristocracy based in cities and a subject rural population, a revolution was taking place in the sphere of military organization
and tactics that would complete the destruction of the old warrior nobility. It was in the middle of the sixth century B.C. that the Zhou states
first introduced armies composed entirely of infantry. While foot soldiers had initially played a subsidiary role in the armies of the Zhou
confederacy, the Rong and Di peoples of north China, who lived primarily in mountainous regions, had long relied solely on infantry.[25] Because they frequently came into conflict with the Di and the Rong, the
states of Zheng and Jin had a long familiarity with the use of infantry
armies. In 541 B.C., because he was fighting the Di on terrain unsuitable for chariots, the commander of the Jin army ordered his troops to
abandon their chariots. He then assembled them as an infantry army,
regrouping the three-man chariot squads into five-man infantry squads,
and executed those who objected to this reduction in their status.[26]

Over the next two centuries mass infantry armies composed of
peasant levies, complemented by the mounted cavalry that appeared in
the fourth century, completely supplanted the chariot armies of the aristocracy. There were several factors responsible for this change. First, in
the second half of the sixth century the states of Wu and Yue in south-
eastern China became dominant powers in the Chinese heartland, and
the armies of these states relied entirely on infantry. Second, soldiers in
an infantry army required fewer specialized military skills and far less
expensive equipment than the chariot-based nobility, so with the new
sources of manpower made available by the extension of levies into the
countryside, states and lineages could rapidly create armies of infantry
that dwarfed the old chariot armies. Finally, archeological evidence has
revealed a set of technological innovations—the invention of the crossbow, the development of lamellar armor, the improvement and general
propagation of the sword, the increasing use of iron weapons—that
made the infantry army a truly formidable force.[27] In the internecine
wars of the late Spring and Autumn period, where the result of defeat
was often destruction, any state that did not recruit as many men as
possible and arm them with the latest weaponry was soon swallowed up
by a rival that did.

The simultaneous extension of recruitment into the subject, rural
population and the general introduction of infantry led to a tremendous
increase in the size of armies. Although no precise figures are available,
a seventh-century army would not have far exceeded 10,000 men, and
even the greatly expanded chariot armies of the third quarter of the
sixth century would have had only about 50,000 soldiers. Warring States
texts, however, record armies as large as 600,000 men, and although the
figures are not absolutely reliable, an approximate ten-fold increase in

the size of armies in the field seems plausible.[28] This massive increase meant that any state or lineage that hoped to survive had to recruit soldiers from an ever larger base, and this could be achieved only by continuing the process of socially extending military service to the lower levels of the population and geographically extending it to wider ranges of the hinterland.

The old city-states, which could not field such large numbers of men, became obsolete. Defeated states were absorbed by their conquerors as "dependent districts" (*xian* 縣), and their land was then allocated to the population in exchange for military services and taxes.[29] In addition to conquest, the expanding territorial states also derived land for allotment by opening up wastes through the clearing of forests and the introduction of water control, drainage, and irrigation.[30] By the Warring States period all of the old Zhou realm and the southern regions had been divided up amongst seven large states that directly controlled much of their territories and mobilized their populations to serve on the field of battle.

The process of enlarging the state structure through the progressive incorporation of the rural population culminated in the reforms of Shang Yang carried out in the state of Qin in the years following 359 B.C. Because of their significance in Chinese history these reforms have generated a massive secondary literature, but no description of them in pre-Qin literary sources has survived, and the Han accounts amount to only a handful of sentences.[31] The discovery of over 1,000 Qin dynasty bamboo strips at Shuihudi in 1975 produced an abundance of new materials, but these have not changed the basic outlines of our understanding of Shang Yang's reforms nor, as of now, resolved many of the scholarly disputes that have developed over the years on the details of the various institutions.[32] Consequently, only the broad outlines of the reforms will be discussed here.

The basic account is that in the *Shi ji*.

He commanded that the people be divided into tens and fives and that they supervise each other and be mutually liable. Anyone who failed to report criminal activity would be chopped in two at the waist, while those who reported it would receive the same reward as that for obtaining the head of an enemy. Anyone who actively hid a criminal would be treated the same as one who surrendered to an enemy [executed and all property confiscated].

Any family that had more than two adult males who did not divide the household would pay a double military tax.

Those who had achievements in the army would in proportion receive an increase in rank [in the twenty rank hierarchy in which the entire populace was rated]. Those who engaged in private quarrels would be punished with a severity in accord with the gravity of their quarrel.

Those who devoted themselves to the fundamental enterprises and through their farming and weaving contributed much grain and cloth would be remitted [from tax and corvee], while those who worked for peripheral profits [in trade and crafts] and those who were idle or poor would be confiscated as slaves.

Those in the royal family who had no military merit would not be listed in the registers of [royal] relatives.

He made clear the exalted and lowly through the orders of titles and ranks. Each according to his degree would receive fields and dwellings, and [the number of] male and female slaves and [type of] clothing would accord with the rank of the family. Those who achieved merit would be exalted, while those without merit, even if rich, would receive no distinction. . . .

And he commanded that among the people fathers, sons, and siblings should not rest together in the same house. He collected the small *xiang* towns together into large *xian* and established officials for them. There was a total of thirty-one *xian*.

For the fields he opened up the *qian* [阡] and *mo* [陌] and set up boundaries. He equalized the military levies and land tax and standardized the measures of capacity, weight, and length.[33]

The basic features of these reforms follow the pattern set by the institutions discussed earlier. A uniform administration was established for the entire population, which was organized into units of five for the purposes of mutual surveillance and military recruitment.[34] The people were responsible for enforcing the laws within their units and were also held mutually liable for the performance of their units in battle.[35] Through these units the Qin government achieved the total identity of civil administration and military organization towards which earlier reforms had tended and which had become the ideal of legalist administrative theory.

This identification of the social order with the army was strengthened through the institution of ranks of military merit. Such ranks were employed in other states, but nowhere so systematically as in Qin.[36] Anyone who gained merit in battle by slaying enemies or commanding victorious units was rewarded with promotion in a twenty-rank hierarchy. Depending on their standing, they would receive stipulated amounts of land, numbers of dwellings, and quotas of slaves. Moreover, these ranks could be used to remit penalties for violations of the law or to redeem relatives from penal bondage. Ranks were not hereditary, but if a man died heroically in battle his descendants received the number of ranks he would have gained.[37] The hierarchy of military merit fixed by these ranks was intended to be the only measure of honor and distinction in Qin society, so that all social rank and status would directly reflect military performance.

In addition to organizing the whole population into units of military service which served as the primary means of civil control, and then ranking all subjects according to military performance, Qin also made *xian*, which were units of military administration, the basis of local government as well. The word *xian* had originally referred to the area outside of a walled city inhabited by dependent populations who provided service to nobles, but in the late Spring and Autumn period they became the primary locus of military recruitment, and lineages or states established them in areas of strategic importance.[38] It was through their role as units of military recruitment and administration that the *xian* and the *jun* (郡), originally a sub-unit of the *xian*, became the basic units of local, civil government.

The final major reform associated with the extension of military service throughout the state of Qin was the construction of *qian* and *mo*. As the cumulative research of modern scholars has shown, these were a network of paths built under Shang Yang as part of his reforms in Qin, and they formed a rectangular grid over the agricultural fields. Because they were evenly spaced, they divided the countryside into equal-sized blocks of land.[39]

According to one source, this grid covered the state of Qin, and a recent study using large-scale topographical maps to examine the patterns of fields in China has shown that throughout much of the north, particularly the former areas of Qin and Jin, roads and footpaths form a striking pattern of rectilinear layouts, everywhere oriented north-south and east-west.[40] Regularity on this scale would be impossible without state intervention, so this evidence offers dramatic, visual testimony to the impact of the reforms of Shang Yang and the earlier Warring States reformers on the Chinese countryside.

This reshaping of the countryside was an integral part of the extension of military service and the attempt to identify the social order with the army. Shang Yang argued that agriculture was the basis of society and the root of all wealth, and his ideal state was a land of small-scale farmers guided by a severe, detailed code of laws. By dividing the land into equal blocks, he was able to allocate to each family sufficient land to be worked by a single adult male. In this way the state could obtain the maximum amount of land in cultivation and the highest possible number of adult males liable for military service and taxes.[41] Moreover, since those who earned high rank received additional land and servants, the systematic partition of the land provided a fixed unit for standardized rewards. It thus served to facilitate the control and mobilization of the population, and to stabilize the units of rewards and punishment that fixed the hierarchy based on ranks of military merit.

The reforms of Shang Yang marked the culmination of the process of breaking down the social and institutional barriers between city and hinterland through the extension of military service. The entire countryside was divided into a rectangular grid, the entire population into military units, the administration into military districts, and then the individual households of the population were "mapped" onto the grid in accord with merits earned in battle or through agriculture.

The completion of these reforms marked the end not only of the Zhou nobility but also of the armed lineages which had been the fundamental unit of aristocratic society. These politicized kin groups had been based in the old semi-independent city-states, where they used their military and cultic power to extract sustenance from the rural villages under their control. With the absorption of the cities into the territorial states, the dispersal of military service throughout the countryside, the division of land among the peasantry in exchange for taxes paid directly to the state, and the disappearance of the ancestral cult centered on the Zhou royal house, the noble lineages had lost the bases of their power and indeed the very preconditions of their existence. Along with the noble lineage, the peasant village as a unit in the fiscal organization of the state had also vanished in the new patterns of land distribution and the extraction of service from individual households. All disposition of military power and claims to service and tribute were now concentrated in the hands of the rulers of the territorial states, while the only significant unit for the definition of kin ties or the offering of service and taxation was the household. Whereas previously political organization and elite kin structures had been identical, they were now separated into a state order (*guo* 國) under a single, absolute prince and a kin realm composed of individual households (*jia* 家), each ruled by its own unchallenged *paterfamilias*.[42]

The political institutions and social order established by Shang Yang expressed a vision of the state epitomized in the *Shang Jun shu*.

> The means by which a ruler encourages his people are offices and rank; the means by which a state arises are agriculture and war.[43]

Underlying this vision was the assumption that those who fought in battle and those who engaged in agriculture were one and the same: the "men of service in farming and warfare" (*geng zhan zhi shi* 耕戰之士).[44] This reflects the historical fact that the infantry armies were formed largely through the recruitment of the peasantry and that the territorial states were created through the incorporation of the rural hinterland. The rulers of these states had been able to destroy the old nobility and establish themselves as absolute masters through their newly developed capacity to command the service of the agricultural population. For the theoreticians of the territorial princes, the state was defined by those who made their rule possible, the mass of peasantry who provided their taxes and served in their armies. The new "great services" of the state were not warfare and sacrifice but warfare and agriculture, and their fruits were now offered not on the altars of the ancestors but at the feet of the absolute monarch.

Only the legalist thinkers insisted that the people should devote themselves solely to agriculture and warfare, and denied all honor or social position to other endeavors, but there is considerable evidence for the identification of the army with the rural population by the other schools. First, the idea that the weapons of war were identical with or originally based on the implements of agriculture appears in many texts.[45]

Second, one major Warring States theory of government common to many schools argued that the actions of the ruler and the state should follow the seasons of the year, furthering reproduction and growth in 月令 the spring and summer, and taking life in the fall and winter.[46] Exponents of this theory argued that punishments and military activity should be confined to the autumn and winter. Although it expressed theories of the seasonal cycle of *yin* and *yang* and the ruler's "imitation of Heaven," this idea also followed logically from the knowledge or belief that those who fought and killed were the same as those who sowed and cultivated. The division of the year into seasons of growth devoted to agriculture and seasons of death devoted to warfare and punishments reflected the two aspects of the "men of service in agriculture and warfare." In the earlier society of the aristocracy, when one element of the population was solely devoted to violence, every season had its hunts and battles, but when the whole society went to war, then warfare and agriculture rose and fell in a cycle of complementary opposition.

The famous and often quoted passage in the *Dao de jing* that described weapons as "implements of famine" (*xiong qi* 凶器) adapted the identification of weapons and agricultural tools to the calendrical model of military action. As "implements of famine," weapons were the complementary opposites of the implements of growth and harvest. Each was a tool of the "men of service in agriculture and warfare," but they were tools that marked their opposed roles as bringers of life or death.

Third, arguments presented by both the Confucians and the legalists against the claims of the military theorists to gain victory through

deceit and the manipulation of the enemy (see Chapter Three) also presupposed the identity of the entire people and the army. The most thor-
ough presentation of this argument appears in Xun Kuang's chapter on
the military.

> The king said, "I would like to inquire regarding the essen-
> tials of the military." Prince Linwu [who represents the position of
> the military theorists] replied, "Above obtain the seasons of
> Heaven and below the benefits of Earth. Observe the changes and
> movements of the enemy, set out after he [has committed himself],
> and arrive before him. This is the fundamental art of using an
> army." Master Sun Qing [Xun Kuang] replied, "It is not so.
> According to what I have heard, the ancient Way of using an army
> in offensive war consists solely of uniting the people. . . . If the
> officers and people do not love and adhere [to the ruler], then even
> Kings Tang and Wu could not inevitably triumph. Therefore he
> who is skilled in causing the people to adhere is skilled in using
> troops. The essentials of using troops consist solely in skill in caus-
> ing the people to adhere."
>
> Prince Linwu said, "It is not so. That which troops exalt is
> seizing benefits, and what they perform is change and deception.
> He who is skilled at using troops suddenly appears out of mists
> and darkness, and none know whence he comes. Sun [Wu] and
> Wu [Qi] used this Way, and none in the world could match them.
> What need had they of the adherence of the people?" Master Sun
> Qing said, "It is not so. The Way I follow is the army of the be-
> nevolent man, and of him who aspires to be king. What you exalt
> is expedient assessments, deliberation, and the seizing of benefits.
> What you practice is snatching away through attack, changes, and
> deception. This is the business of the feudal lords. The army of the
> benevolent man cannot be deceived. Those who can be deceived
> are the idle and the neglectful, or those states where superiors and
> subordinates are at odds. The ruler and his servants treat each
> other in a sly and deceitful manner, and are torn apart. So for one
> Jie [evil tyrant] to deceive another Jie is like a clever and skillful
> operator having a stroke of luck. For Jie to deceive Yao [a sage-
> king] is like throwing an egg against a rock or stirring boiling water
> with your finger. He will be like a man consumed in fire or
> drowned in water."[47]

This argument that the key to victory lies in the Way of the true ruler
because a united people cannot be defeated assumes that those who
engage in warfare *are* the people, and that the unity of the people is

tantamount to the unity of the army. That which created a society created an army, and no specifically military skills or techniques were needed. When Xun Kuang argued that "he who is skilled in causing the people to adhere is skilled in using troops," he dissolved all distinctions between the people and the troops, and between the Way of the military commander and the Way of the ruler. This same position was taken by the legalist philosophers, who insisted that wars were won and lost through proper administration of the state, and that all military arts and maneuvers gained nothing.[48]

This philosophical assumption of the identity of the people and the army reflected the realities of the Warring States era, in which the great territorial states had created themselves through the systematic expansion of the base of military service until it included the entire adult population. The "warring states" were just that, for they were states built through the institutions of military recruitment and control. In these states warfare was no longer the means by which an aristocracy defined its authority, but rather the primary institution used by the rulers of states to organize, rank, and control their subjects.

Oaths and Sacrifice

In the states created through universal military service, blood oaths took on a new nature and functions. In the previous chapter we saw how the social role of these oaths had steadily expanded until they became the primary mode of establishing political ties between men, and this continued into the Warring States period. However, the manner in which they were employed and understood radically changed. The two primary features of this change were: 1) the denial or de-centering of the importance of the sacrifice and an emphasis on the intent of the participants and the written text of the oath, and 2) the heightened one-sidedness of the oath, which increasingly bound servants to masters rather than jointly binding leaders and followers in the common service of the spirits. We have already seen the beginnings of the second feature in the Spring and Autumn period, where the use of covenants to secure the obedience of the capital populace and the attempts at Houma to bind the people to the new ruler both signal a shift from covenants as alliances of proximate equals towards their use as a means of establishing control over a subject population.

The de-centering of the sacrifice in blood oaths also began in the Spring and Autumn period with a new characterization of the role of the hegemon. This "master of the covenant" had originally been a warlord and collector of tribute, but over time many Chinese assigned him a normative and regulating function among the states. According to these men the hegemon had to use his power to maintain the political status quo, to suppress expansionist states, and to preserve or restore states menaced by hostile neighbors.[49] These correlate activities of crushing the strong and rebellious while preserving the weak and obedient reflect the notion of "virtuous potency" (de 德) that was evolving in this period, and indeed several speakers describe such actions as expressions of the hegemon's "potency."[50] Not only did this belief in the hegemon as a wielder of potency cast him in the role of a monarch, but two speakers argued that the hegemon's potency and not the blood covenant secured the mutual trust that guaranteed adherence to the league.[51]

The belief that the appropriate actions and moral potency of the ruler rather than the divine sanctions of sacrifice bound men to obedience were marked by the appearance of a new term for oaths: "bonds" (yue 約). These bonds were used in the same circumstances as the old blood covenants and even employed similar rituals, but they also exhibited several new features that reveal changes in the political order. These new features were: 1) bonds were *texts* and the basis of codified, written law; 2) bonds took on a broader, philosophical meaning which applied to any consciously formed ties between men; 3) bonds were linked through certain elements of marriage ritual and popular magic to the new sexual imagery of the political realm, in which the rule of husband over wife was regarded as the paradigm of all authority; 4) bonds created personal ties between servant and master based on the exchange of total devotion in return for recognition.

The Warring States Chinese employed bonds for the same purposes that their ancestors had used covenants. First, they formed alliances between two or more independent states. The "horizontal" and "vertical" alliances that defined Warring States diplomatic structure were simply multi-state bonds, and like the earlier leagues they had a master (zhu) or "senior" (zhang 長) who directed their concerted actions.[52]

Bonds, like the oaths (shi) discussed in Chapter One, were also proclaimed to stipulate the rules to be observed and the punishments to be imposed when an army assembled for battle. The biographies of Sun Wu and Sima Rangju both consist of single stories in which they execute favorites of the king for violating the army's bonds.[53] That these accounts of the prototypes of the Warring States military commander should focus entirely on the bonds shows their fundamental importance in the new forms of military organization. The military treatise attributed to Wu Qi identified the bonds as one of the five features to which the general must pay attention, and "making clear" and enforcing the army's bonds remained one of the chief hallmarks of the true commander into the period of the Three Kingdoms (220–280 A.D.).[54]

The rubric "bonds" also applied to personal oaths sworn by men to bind themselves to the service of a particular lord or the completion of a specific task. These private bonds included agreements between families or lineages registered with the government.[55] In the commercial sphere bonds played the role of contracts written to record and impose obligations in important transactions. Perhaps the best known example of such a private bond is the famous first-century B.C. "Contract for a Youth" (tong yue 童約) by Wang Bao. Although it is a literary work and not a true legal document, it reflects the actual practices of the period, as revealed in the Han "grave purchase agreements" discovered by antiquarians and in archeological excavations in this century.[56]

In addition to performing the same functions, bonds were often performed together with blood covenants in a single ceremony. The Shi ji and later histories tell of several bonds sanctioned with blood covenants, and of covenants that included a bond.[57] It is also quite possible that unmentioned ceremonial drinking of blood accompanied many of the other bonds. This frequent pairing and the identity of function suggest the possibility that the shift from blood covenants to bonds was primarily a change in nomenclature.

Despite this unquestionable continuity and close relationship, the shift involved far more than a new name. First, bonds were specifically written documents, and their authority was tied to the increasing prestige of writing as a form of control. In the cases in which a bond was linked to a covenant, the bond always specified the content of the vow, and in one case the text of the bond is quoted.[58] The Zhou li refers to the texts of all covenants as bonds and mentions archives in which they were stored.[59] Moreover, a fragment of the lost Warring States Huang-Lao text Yi Wenzi states that when a general went out on campaign the bond was read to the army.[60]

As written texts, the bonds served as the basis of the new codes of law that began to appear in China in the second half of the sixth century B.C. The Zhuangzi links "setting aside laws" and "destroying bonds" as necessary correlates, and the Qin reformer Shang Yang punished men for "violating the bonds."[61] Already in the Warring States period bonds were thus identified as a form of written law. In the Qin-Han interregnum, bonds provided the legal basis for binding agreements, most notably the bond between the rebel generals that whoever first entered the pass would become king of the Qin region.[62]

However, the most famous example of the use of bonds to create legal codes took place at the beginning of the Han dynasty. When Liu Bang occupied the Qin capital, he proclaimed a bond which specified in three regulations the punishments for criminal offences. Although this simple code proved unworkable, and Liu Bang's chief minister Xiao He

basis of new codes of law

later restored much of the old Qin code, this work was also described as "making laws, regulations, and bonds." When Cao Can succeeded Xiao He as chief minister, he made no changes in the laws or regulations, a policy that Sima Qian describes as "uniformly respecting the bonds of Xiao He."[63] In addition, bonds established such basic rules of the dynasty as primogeniture and the principle that only men of the Liu surname could be given the title "king."[64] Ji An opposed a major reform of the Han law code by arguing that such an action would "tangle and alter the bonds of Emperor Gao [Liu Bang]."[65] This argument shows that the empire's laws were regarded as an extension of, or identical with, a bond proclaimed by the founder of the dynasty. The legal independence of generals in the field and the separation of military law from that of civil society, which will be discussed in Chapter Three, were also based on the separate bonds that created an army.[66]

This identification of bonds as the basis of law became widespread even at the local level and among the lower strata of society. In several cases officials who introduced irrigation to an area proclaimed bonds stipulating the regulations for the use of water.[67] When the "Red Eyebrow" peasant rebels formed themselves into an army, their leaders established laws through a bond modeled on that of Liu Bang.[68] In the collapse of civil order at the end of the Han dynasty, many families formed themselves into armed self-defense coalitions and built fortified camps, and several of these groups established laws for themselves in the form of bonds.[69] Even individual families, especially among the merchants, instituted "family bonds" which dictated the behavior of their members and the control of family property.[70] Given the tremendous importance of the appearance of legal codes in China, their identification with bonds indicates a crucial difference between the latter and blood covenants.[71]

The second new aspect of bonds was their role in general theories of the constitution of human society through ties consciously created by rulers. If the bond was originally the text of an oath, then it was the same as a *shi*, which likewise signified the words of a covenant. Indeed, the *Shuo wen jie zi* states, "'Oath' (*shi*) means a 'bond' (*yue shu* 約束)," and the two characters were frequently joined in a synonym compound.[72] So the two characters could act as synonyms meaning "the words or text of an oath."

However, the term "bond" also developed a much wider meaning. As the institution of bonds became the primary mode of establishing political ties and obligations, ritualists and philosophers increasingly used the word as a verb to signify any deliberate creation of links between men or objects. This usage extended the blood oath from its defined social functions to a model or prototype of all social ties. In this more general, verbal sense it often appeared in the compound *yue xin*

(約信) "to bind trust," i.e., to establish relations of good faith and mutual trust between men. Thus the standard formulation of the distinction between oath and covenant states:

> When they bind trust [*yue xin*] it is called an "oath," and in the presence of a sacrifice it is called a "covenant."[73]

Yue in this general sense also appears several times in the *Lun yu* as the defining function or characteristic of ritual.[74] Since in Confucius's thought "ritual" referred to the rules and principles that ideally guided all human action and made possible a human existence, the definition of the role of ritual as "*yue*" suggests that the institution of bonds was becoming synonymous with the possibility of a human community. In this role they were often identified with the power of the ruler to hold men together.

The encompassing sense of *yue* as the general term for all consciously created human ties also figures in several appeals to the previous existence or possibility of a "natural" society in which men assumed the good faith of their fellows without institutionalized pledges. Thus a passage in the *Lü Shi chun qiu* says:

> In ancient times worthy masters employed any means in seeking as servants men who had the Way, and men who had the Way and desired to serve would do anything to seek out a worthy master. Only when they found one another were they happy. Without planning they were like relatives, and without bonds they trusted one another.[75]

Warring States Confucians often linked bonds, perhaps because of their association with legal codes, to the rule of force and guile characteristic of the hegemons, and they contrasted this negatively with the moral rule of the true king.[76] The *Zhuangzi* argued that bonds were like glue or ropes used to hold an object together, but the true sage did not divide things and thus had no need to bind them back together.[77] In all these passages *yue* has the sense of any bonds consciously formed between men.

In his discussion of the "rectification of names" Xun Kuang identified bonds as the basis of all social ties and linked this with their linguistic nature. He argued that the pinnacle of government could be attained only through holding the "bonds of names" and later elaborated:

> Names have no fixed suitability, so you must bind them by command. When the bonds are fixed and customs established,

then we call them suitable, and that which differs from the bonds is called unsuitable.

Names have no fixed content, so you must bind them by command. When the bonds are fixed and customs established, then we may call them "[content-]full names".[78]

Language, the basis of the very possibility of human sociability, became feasible only when words had fixed, common meanings, and these were established by the bonds imposed by the ruler to hold men together in a community of shared definitions.

The third aspect of bonds that distinguished them from the earlier covenants was their ties to certain ceremonial and magic practices related to mating. Through these associations they were linked with the general reconstitution of the political realm through the personal, absolute submission of servants to a master, ties that were consciously identified with those binding a wife to her husband.

The character *yue* has not yet been identified in the oracle bone and bronze inscriptions, and it rarely occurs in early Zhou literature. In the *Shi jing* it appears three times, and it means simply "to tie together" (boards) or "to wrap" (the wheel-naves of chariots).[79] The *Shuo wen jie zi* glosses it as "to tie up a bundle" (*chan shu* 纏束).[80] Although it is possible that a verb meaning "to tie together" was applied by metaphor to the "tying" together of men, there is evidence of a practice that directly links the tying of bundles to the formation of human bonds and sheds light on the political use of the word "bond."

More than a dozen lyrics in the *Shi jing* link the breaking off, gathering, and binding together of certain plants with the joining together, either illicitly or in marriage, of men and women.[81] The Han commentator Zheng Xuan noted this linkage and explained it as a metaphor.

> The manner in which men and women rely on ritual to be united is like the manner in which firewood and fodder rely on human labor before they become bundles.[82]

In the early decades of the nineteenth century, Hu Chenggong (1776–1832 A.D.) noted the frequency of this linkage and suggested that some presentation of firewood, fodder, or bundled shrubs had originally been part of the rituals of betrothal or marriage.[83] In our own century, apparently independently, the French sinologist Marcel Granet also noted the frequent link of tying bundles to courtship, and his work was extended by Matsumoto Masaaki.[84] Itō Seiji found references in early imperial and medieval Chinese literature, as well as evidence from the customs of minority peoples in modern China, to show that collecting and binding firewood or certain types of reeds was sometimes part of marriage ritual and sometimes part of a sexual magic used to secure illicit liaisons.[85] Moreover, the *Lie xian zhuan* and the "Demonography" discovered amongst the bamboo strips at Shuihudi also record examples of picking and manipulating plants to work sexual magic.[86] This same "Demonography", moreover, reveals how the notion of "binding" (*jie* 結, a character closely related to *yue*) oneself to another through written documents was linked to both legal practice in Qin times and the use of oaths and spells to magically obligate ("spell-bind") demons and men.[87] Finally, at least two quotations regarding the political "bonds" show that they were still associated with physical bundles in the minds of Warring States Chinese thinkers.[88] This evidence all suggests that the term "bonds" had originated in certain ceremonial or magical acts thought to have the power to control or obligate the spirits and men, that these rites were linked to the commanding power of written language embodied in legal codes, and that they played a particularly important role in the sexual binding together of men and women.

In support of this hypothesis there is abundant evidence that the Warring States Chinese identified the ties between lord and minister, or ruler and subject, with those between spouses or lovers. The best-known examples of this phenomenon come from the realm of literature. Commentators in the Warring States and Han period routinely explained the love poetry in the *Shi jing* as political allegories in which the sexual longings of lovers represent the yearning of officials for a good ruler, or of the ruler for men to serve him. In the *Li sao* the poet depicts the official and the king as estranged lovers. The first part of the poem presents the poet as a woman who must compete with courtesans for the king's favors, and the second part portrays him as a man seeking his beloved, who is none other than the king.

Various homilies also paired women with those in political service in a manner that clearly suggested that the two figures were analogous. Thus Yu Rang justified mutilating himself and sacrificing his own life to avenge a fallen lord by saying, "A noble man [*shi*] dies for one who recognizes him, just as a beautiful woman adorns herself for the one who pleases her."[89] A related homily attributed to the Wei reformer Li Ke says, "If a family is poor then it seeks a good wife. If a state is chaotic it seeks a good minister."[90] Once again, the minister's role is equated with that of the wife and political ties identified with those in the sexual realm or household.

Various "historical" accounts also show how the roles of political servants and women were treated as equivalent. The story of Confucius's resignation preserved in the *Lun yu* tells how the state of Qi sent dancing girls to the lord of Lu, and when the lord allowed himself to be distracted from his duties, Confucius resigned and departed.[91] In other texts sending women to supplant a minister was presented as a means of attacking a state.[92] Women and ministers were mutually exclusive because they stood in an identical relation to the ruler; if one occupied the slot, then the other had to be removed.

Nor were dancing girls the only women who threatened the relations of ministers with their masters. Among the accusations levelled at King Zhou of the Shang was that he listened only to the advice of his favorite wives, while ignoring the remonstrances of sages and virtuous officials.[93] Indeed, in the *Shi ji*'s account of King Wu's speech preceding the battle of Mu Ford, the first charge against King Zhou was uxoriousness. The deadly seriousness with which the "threat" of women was taken reflects the fact that in a political realm constituted by personal "bonds," the wife or concubine became the rival of the official.

Related parables in the *Shi ji* point out the same opposition between women and retainers. In one such story the prince of Mengchang criticized his father, who was then chief minister of Qi, because the women of his harem were better fed and clothed than his retainers. It was because of his devotion to women that he could not attract good retainers, and Qi did not grow stronger.[94]

Another story pertains to the prince of Pingyuan. One of his concubines, looking out from an upper story, observed a hunchbacked cripple and laughed at his twisted body and odd gait. The offended hunchback went to the prince and pointed out that his ability to attract retainers was due to the fact that he "exalted men of honor and humbled concubines." He then demanded the head of the concubine who had laughed at him. The prince laughingly agreed, but when the hunchback left, he mocked the man who had demanded the life of a concubine to atone for a single laugh. Because his refusal to execute the woman demonstrated that he "loved sex and humbled men of honor," most of his retainers soon left him, and only after he killed the concubine and presented her head to the hunchback did they return.[95]

This equation of officials with wives and concubines appeared not only in poetry, commentary, homily, and story, but even in political theory. It was a commonplace of early Chinese political thought that the household was a microcosm of and a training ground for the political realm. The emperor was the father of his people, and the father was the emperor of his household. This suggests that the rule of the *paterfamilias* over his wives and children was the prototype of all political power. Xun Shuang (128–190 A.D.) presented this idea thus:

> I have heard that only after there are husbands and wives are there fathers and sons; only after there are fathers and sons are there

rulers and ministers; only after there are rulers and ministers are there superiors and subordinates; only after there are superiors and subordinates are there ritual and decorum. . . . Husbands and wives are the beginning of human relations, the origin of the king's transformation [of his subjects].[96]

The political realm derives from the household, so all political relations originate in the family, and the family begins with the husband and wife. Consequently the relation of husband and wife is the source of and model for all political authority.

These equations of ministers or retainers with wives or concubines and the tales of their jealous struggles for the favors of the ruler often strike Western readers as merely bizarre, if not demented.[97] However, this identification of political ties with sexual ones both highlights one of the fundamental tensions of the Chinese empire and reveals a basic feature of its formation.

The fundamental tension to which I refer is the one between the inner and outer courts. The inner court of the Han, the boy emperors controlled by their mothers in the Northern Wei, and the eunuch domination of the late Han, Tang, and Ming are all cases in which the court women or their adjuncts supplanted the "men of honor" of the official court. Hence these strange stories of the jealousy and mutual exclusion of concubines and ministers could be regarded as "charter myths" of the imperial Chinese court.

The basic feature of the formation of the Chinese empire revealed by the equation of political servants with wives was the crucial role played by personal ties between servant and master based on the exchange of loyalty and devotion in return for recognition. These ties involved the total subservience and the complete devotion of the official to the ruler, and it was to express these new ideals that the image of the official as wife or concubine was invoked. In contrast with the nobility of Zhou China, those who filled the courts of the Warring States and the early empires were total dependents who obtained office and status as acts of grace from their ruler, and they were expected to repay this grace with an unswerving devotion unto death. The bonds, as legally binding oath, general model of the formation of personal ties, and emotive markers of complete submission and devotion, were the explicit forms of these ties.

The importance of these personal ties of obedience and devotion in the re-creation of the Chinese political order during the Warring States period has been demonstrated by several Japanese scholars, most notably Masubuchi Tatsuo in his classic study of the origins of the Chinese empire.[98] Beginning with a schematized model of Zhou society in which ascriptive kin ties had defined the relations of the Zhou elite, and village custom had controlled the common people's statuses and roles, Masubuchi traced the gradual emergence of elective, "artificial" ties of service or comradeship between individuals. This process began when certain individuals lost their fixed positions in the old social order and hence became eligible for recruitment to the service of others on an individual basis. Defeated rebels, younger sons of rulers and their followers who fled a state to avoid death at the hands of the heir, members of destroyed lineages or states, younger offspring of cadet lineages who had no place in the kin hierarchy, ambitious elements of the capital populace, and even brigands formed a pool of warriors and political agents whose recruitment could strengthen lineages against their rivals.

In fact, even before the appearance of these "free" elements amongst the elite, there is evidence of the early roots of personalist ties in the late Western Zhou. The farming village was originally a discrete unit for the provision of taxes or service, and early bronzes often measure the populations or territory granted to meritorious nobles in numbers of villages. However, one late Western Zhou bronze refers to a village where several families had switched loyalties to another lord and were forced to return to their original master, while a second one records the transfer of the services of five men in one village from one master to another.[99] This suggests that villagers were able to transfer loyalty from one lord to another and that personal ties might already have begun to replace duties as kinsman or villager by the end of the Western Zhou. The *Guo yu* tells how King Xuan of the Western Zhou (r. 827–780 B.C.), the ambitious monarch who attempted to restore royal power after the Gong He Bo interregnum, attempted a general census of the population but was blocked by the nobility, and this might well reflect some tradition handed down from the time when nobles first began to compete for the services of individual villagers.[100] At a somewhat later date the individual household replaced the village team as the unit for weaving, and this likewise suggests the switch from collective duties to individual ties and responsibilities.[101]

The first record of competition to recruit "free" members of the nobility dates from the struggle for the succession to Lord Huan of Qi (d. 643 B.C.). At that time one of his sons exhausted his family's wealth trying to recruit warriors for his cause.[102] Younger sons of the lords of Jin generally fled that state to avoid execution at the hands of the heir, and the future Lord Wen was accompanied by a number of men who gave up their posts in the state to follow him, showing that personal ties were, in places, beginning to supplant ties to lineage and office.[103] The recruitment of these "free" warriors played an increasingly important role in the intensifying interlineage battles that led to the partition of Jin and the usurpation of the Tian clan in Qi.[104] The attempts to secure the support of the capital populace described in Chapter One were part of the same phenomenon.

In the Warring States period this struggle to recruit followers became a general social trend. Leading political figures, such as the famous "Four Princes," competed in recruiting small armies of followers, who, in exchange for rank and sustenance, devoted themselves to their masters. Men of letters and would-be reformers traveled from state to state, seeking a prince who would employ them and implement their policies. Many of these wandering scholars or warriors joined together to form schools or bands, or, in the case of the Mohists, philosophical schools that also functioned as military units. This pattern of exchanging service and devotion for office and payment laid the basis for the so-called "bureaucratic" government that developed in the period, and the life-giving "potency" of the ruler or hegemon, previously identified with his sparing those who submitted, now referred to the rewards and salaries he distributed to his followers.[105]

This constitution of the political realm through the exchange of service for recognition, office, and material rewards led to the development of a new elite ethic in which men were celebrated for their devotion unto death to whoever "recognized them" (*zhi ji* 知己). The new form of loyalty was summed up in the statement of Yu Rang.

> A noble man dies for the one who recognizes him, just as a beautiful woman adorns herself for the one who pleases her. Zhi Bo recognized me, and if I must die in order to avenge Zhi Bo then my upper and lower souls will have nothing of which to be ashamed.

Later in the same chapter, Yu Rang, who had not bothered to avenge two lineages he had previously served, justified the need to avenge Zhi Bo thus:

> When I served the Fan and Zhonghang lineages they treated me as one of the mass, so I repaid them as befitted one of the mass. But Zhi Bo treated me as a noble man of the state, so I repaid him as befits a noble man of the state.[106]

This reply states explicitly that the loyalty and reciprocity enjoined on a retainer were proportional to the recognition and honor received. It articulates the exchange of the servant's devotion for the honor bestowed by the lord that typified the new political relations, and it marks the extent of that devotion by insisting on the need to seek vengeance at the expense of one's own life.

Yu Rang's statement became a familiar homily in China, and the *Shi ji* contains a chapter devoted entirely to men who sacrificed their lives trying to avenge the death or disgrace of a lord who had honored them. In cases where no vengeance was possible, then followers could express their devotion by mass suicide.[107] Other people, although criticized for their actions, demonstrated this loyalty by sacrificing their sons, or even feeding a son to a ruler.[108] It was these new personal bonds between ruler and subordinate, consciously created and imposing absolute obligations, that received explicit, legal form in the bonds.[109] Hence bonds were the ritual basis of the ruler's authority over his officials, just as they underlay the army regulations and legal codes through which the ruler commanded the common people. The entire political edifice of the warring state was created through these modified blood covenants.

It is now possible briefly to summarize the changes in the character of political ties and the political uses of violence revealed by the "shift" from covenant to bond. Both terms named the same practice, but the first specified the consecration of the oath through the drinking of the blood of sacrifice, while the latter pointed to the text of the oath and evoked rituals of marriage or binding through spells. This new focus suggested the fundamental importance of the intent or will of the participants, the compelling and unequal character of the relationship, and the strong element of devotion implicit in the act. In contrast to the centrality of the sacrifice and the spirits in the covenant, the bond decentered the actual act of taking life and emphasized the moral and emotional basis of human ties, as well as their hierarchic and authoritarian character.

These features of the shift from covenant to bond parallel the new theory of sacrifice developed in the ritual and philosophical texts of the Warring States Confucians. Although various aspects of this theory are scattered through many texts, its clearest expression appeared in Xun Kuang's discussion of sacrifice in his chapter on ritual.

Xun Kuang defined sacrifice as the ritual that gives proper form to reverence and as the "reverent service of the spirits." Sacrifice stemmed from the accumulation of human intentions and longings, and in order to give proper expression to these feelings, the former kings established fixed forms for the sacrifices, which were "the height of the hierarchical duties of treating one's superiors as superiors and one's parents as parents." The role of sacrifice was to create and enforce the proper hierarchical relations among men through serving the three "roots" of sacrificial ritual: Heaven and Earth, ancestors, and rulers. Although it appeared as the service of the spirits, sacrifice was actually the Way of man, for through serving the dead one learned the service of the living.[110]

In this way the sacrifices to the ancestors, just like the blood oath of the covenant, were reinterpreted as forms of making a statement, fixing emotions, and defining roles. They were expressions of human intent and feeling that were given a heightened emphasis and a commanding force through being acted out in the form of ceremony. As Marcel Granet noted, in the official religion that arose in imperial China the old ceremonies of the nobility in which one physically shared a meal with the ancestors in the guise of their grandsons were replaced by a moral, political cult which was primarily symbolic in character.[111] The sacrifices to the ancestors became theatrical microcosms in which men acted out and thereby created the proper hierarchical relations within the family and, by extension, in the larger political order. The meaning of the sacrifices lay in the hierarchical relations defined by them, the roles people assumed in them, and the feelings of duty and devotion fostered by those roles. The true role of sacrifice, as Xun Kuang stressed, was learning how to serve.

There is a strange story in the *Lü Shi chun qiu* that appears to be a meditation on the relations of sacrifice, eating, cannibalism, and devotion. In 660 B.C. the Di tribes completed their conquest of the state of Wei by devouring its lord. A noble of Wei who had been sent on a diplomatic mission returned to find his lord entirely eaten, except for the liver, which had been left behind. He gave the report on his mission to the liver, declared to Heaven that he would be a cover for the remains of his lord, cut open his own stomach and emptied out its contents, and then placed the lord's liver in his stomach. It was because of this action, the narrator asserts, that Lord Huan of Qi decided to restore the state of Wei, and because of this "self-sacrifice to follow his lord" the ancestral sacrifices of Wei were re-established.[112]

Although the exact purport of this story is obscure, it clearly celebrates the devotion to the death that was a hallmark of the new political ties, while offering a symbolic refutation of the old ties of sacrifice and warfare that underlay the "great services" of the Zhou ancestral cult. The eating of the lord of Wei reflects the barbarism of the invaders and the excesses of combat, but it also echoes the Zhou practice of offering up the spoils of combat as sacrifice. This improper sacrifice of the lord of Wei cut off the sacrifices to his ancestors, but these sacrifices were restored by the emissary's sacrifice of himself. The emissary's sacrifice itself, however, was a bizarre transformation of the original cannibalism, for he emptied out his stomach and "ingested" his lord's liver. Thus this act of self-sacrifice is a literal inversion or negation of eating, a "consumption" in which the man gave himself up rather than taking into himself. The true role of sacrifice had been lost in the original, overly literal "sacrificial" meal of the barbarians, but it was restored through the emissary's self-destruction motivated by devotion and service. Denouncing the idea of sacrifice as a triumphant culmina-

tion of battle and asserting the centrality of reverence and devotion, this
story could act as a parable of the new, Confucian theory of sacrifice.

Vengeance and Collective Punishments

Chapter One showed how vengeance was an ever-present specter
and an often-present reality in the lives of the nobility, how it was central to their pursuit of honor, and how it played a major role in the
internecine wars of the period. Vengeance remained a major element in
the social and moral order of China during the Warring States and the
early empires, but its uses and their rationalization changed in a manner
much like that of blood oaths and sacrifice. Vengeance, like sacrifice,
became a form of service to a superior and a means of defining or maintaining proper relations in the political realm or the family, so that the
range and degree of the "debt" of vengeance served to define the major
social relations that constituted the new social order. In the same way,
the legalist state legally defined the significant social relations of its subjects through the range of collective punishments which implicated a
man's family, neighbors, or colleagues.

We have already seen one form of the new, "moralized"
vengeance in the obligation to avenge a slain or disgraced master. The
debt of vengeance to a superior who had recognized and employed a
man served to mark the extent of devotion incumbent upon one who
had been "bound" to service. This ethic of vengeance was closely related to and perhaps derived from that of another kind of righteous
avenger that appeared in the Warring States period, the "bravo" or
"wandering swordsman" (*you xia* 游俠).[113] These wandering fighters
constituted a major segment of those who traveled from state to state
seeking employment with the territorial princes and the leading officials,
most notably the famous "Four Princes" who surrounded themselves
with thousands of armed retainers and became virtually the "patron
saints" of the ethic of vengeance (see below). So numerous were these
you xia that Han Fei routinely paired them with the scholars (*ru* 儒) as
the two primary groups who weakened states through seeking employment at court rather than engaging in agriculture and serving in the
army.[114] These men cultivated an ethic of righting wrongs, of never
going back on their word, and of willingly going to their deaths in the
name of keeping faith, so they were in many ways the chief embodiments of both the ethic of service marked by the bonds and the moralized form of vengeance.[115] Indeed, it is not unlikely that the ideal of
devotion to the death and avenging one's lord at all costs first developed
amongst the fighting men recruited as retainers by the great lineages.

However, the highest claims for vengeance as a moral obligation and a fundamental element of human relations appear in the writings of the Confucian school, most notably the *Gongyang zhuan*.[116] This work, which was probably written down in the early Western Han but embodies earlier traditions, is a commentary on the *Chun qiu*. Unlike the *Zuo zhuan*, which is also appended to the *Chun qiu* but consists primarily of independent narrative, the *Gongyang* is a genuine commentary devoted to the detailed analysis of the *Chun qiu*'s text. It is written in a dry "question-and-answer" style and devoted primarily to explaining how the choice of a particular word or the decision to include or omit a certain event reflects the moral judgements of Confucius, the putative author of the text. However, scattered throughout the terse disquisitions on the technical uses of various words are a handful of dramatic narratives which stand out in sharp contrast to the bulk of the text, and many of these deal with the role of vengeance.

One such story tells of the chief minister of Jin, Zhao Dun. One entry stated that he killed his lord, and then his name was mentioned again in a later passage. The author of the *Gongyang* notes that it is the practice of the *Chun qiu* never again to mention the names of those who kill their lords, and he poses the question of why Zhao Dun has been excepted. He replies that the actual assassin was Zhao Chuan, but the official historian of Jin wrote that Zhao Dun killed his lord, and when Zhao Dun protested his innocence the historian replied:

> Someone assassinated your prince and when you returned to the country [Zhao Dun had earlier fled Jin to avoid being killed by the lord.] you did not punish the criminal. If this is not killing your prince then what is it?[117]

Here the obligation to avenge a murdered lord is treated as so absolute that to fail to do so was tantamount to killing him oneself.

Nor does the belief in the subordinate's moral obligation to vengeance appear only secondhand in the words of an unnamed historian of Jin. At one point the author of the *Gongyang* asks why the *Chun qiu* mentions the death of a lord but not his interment. He replies that mention of the funerary ritual was deliberately suppressed because the lord had been murdered and the assassins were unpunished.

> If a prince is murdered and the villains not punished, the *Chun qiu* does not write of the interment. It holds that he had no sons or retainers. Master Chenzi said, "If a prince is killed and his retainers do not punish the villain, then they are not retainers. If [the sons] do not avenge him then they are not sons. Interment is the service of the living [to the dead]. The *Chun qiu* does not write of

interment if a prince is murdered and the villains not punished, because it holds that he has no ties to servants or sons."[118]

This passage states explicitly that the obligation to avenge is one of the basic elements of the bond between lord and retainer or father and son, and the man who fails to perform that obligation dissolves the ties that linked him to the deceased. Vengeance here appears as the violent aspect of the obligations of burial and mourning through which the Chinese defined their degrees of relatedness to others.[119]

Apart from its insistence on the duty to avenge as an indispensable aspect of familial and political bonds, the *Gongyang* also asserted the moral obligation of vengeance in interstate affairs, and it marked the distinction between the family and the state through differences in the nature of this obligation in the two spheres.

The most extended discussion of the duty of vengeance among states takes the form of a commentary on the sentence ". . . the lord of Ji greatly left (*da qu* 大去) his state."

> What does "greatly left" mean? It means [his state was] destroyed. Who destroyed it? Qi destroyed it. Why does it not say, "Qi destroyed it"? It is tabooed for the sake of Lord Xiang. The *Chun qiu* observes taboos for the worthy. What is worthy about Lord Xiang? He was avenging an offence. What offence? His distant ancestor Lord Ai was boiled at the Zhou court because the [then] lord of Ji slandered him. In acting for this reason Lord Xiang's devotion to serving his ancestors was total. What does "total" mean? When Lord Xiang was about to seek vengeance upon Ji he divined, and the prognostication said, "You will lose half your army." "Even if I die for it, this would not be inauspicious."
>
> How many generations is a "distant ancestor"? Nine generations. After nine generations should one still avenge an offence? Even after a hundred generations one still should. . . .
>
> Can the cadet lineage of a hereditary minister also do so? No. Why can a state? The lords of a state are a single body. The shame of the previous lords is the shame of the present lord. The shame of the present lord is the shame of the previous lords. How can the lords of a state be a single body? The lords of a state regard the state as their body, so they are a single body.
>
> The present state of Ji had committed no crime. Is this not simply [venting] anger? No. If of old there had been an illuminated Son of Heaven, then the lord of Ji would certainly have been executed and there would be no Ji. The fact that the lord of Ji

was not executed and that until today Ji still exists means that there has been no illuminated Son of Heaven.

Of old the feudal lords had the duty of assembling, and they had the Way of attending court and of diplomatic missions. In their speech they had to refer to their ancestral lords in greeting one another. But Qi and Ji had nothing to say in such circumstances. They could not stand together under the same Heaven. Therefore in eliminating the lord of Ji he had to eliminate Ji.

If there had been an illuminated Son of Heaven, could Lord Xiang have acted in this manner? He could not. If he could not, then why did Lord Xiang do this? He did it because above there was no Son of Heaven and below there was no hegemon.[120]

I have quoted this passage at length because it makes several major points. First, it posits that avenging an ancestor is a moral obligation and a supremely worthy act. Ordinarily the author of the *Gongyang* treats the destruction of a state as a reprehensible deed and calls it "the great evil," so the fact that destroying a state to avenge a wrong is saluted as the mark of a "worthy" shows the degree to which he exalted the claims of vengeance.[121] This is especially striking in the case of Lord Xiang, for this "worthy" committed incest with his younger sister before her marriage and ultimately killed her husband in order to resume the liaison.[122]

Second, this vengeance is interpreted as a form of service to the ancestors, and the degree of devotion is marked by a statement of Lord Xiang that he would willingly sacrifice himself to achieve revenge. This linkage of self-sacrifice with vengeance and their occasional substitution also appeared in the story of Yu Rang cited above, and it forms a recurring motif throughout the stories of righteous avengers.

Third, the passage explicitly contrasts the obligation for vengeance of the state with that of cadet lineages and, by extension, any family. The state is in theory eternal; consequently, the duty of vengeance does not vanish along with the generation that experienced the offense. Any wrong ever suffered by a state is a permanent and personal affront to whomever rules that state. By contrast, the obligation of a son or retainer would not last beyond his own lifetime. When the author of the *Gongyang* stated that the duty of vengeance was fundamental to the existence of ties of kinship and service, he posited a model of society in which all human relationships contained a "debt" of violence. This passage extends that model to a higher plane where the debt of vengeance transcends particularist, "private" ties and serves to define a "public" realm.

Fourth, in its discussion of the rituals of interstate relations, the passage suggests one explanation for linking the obligation of vengeance to physical separation, which is the central focus of discussions of revenge in the ritual texts (see below). Men presented themselves and were recognized by others as members of families or states. Any unrequited offense removed the bases of ordinary social commerce or conviviality between members of the offended and offending groups. As a result they could not act as members of a single society; they could not live "under the same Heaven."[123]

Finally, the passage stipulates that the duty of vengeance existed only where there was no proper ruler. In an ideal society the sovereign would punish all offenders and thereby relieve sons and retainers of the task of personally punishing their enemies. This dictum links vengeance with legal punishments as two means of performing a common function, and it played a major role in Han legal thought in the modified form in which it appeared in the case of Wu Zixu.

The story of how Wu Zixu's father and elder brother were unjustly slain by the king of Chu, of how Wu Zixu escaped to Wu state, gained the favor of the king, and helped to destroy Chu, and of how he ultimately fell from favor with the king's successor and was executed appears in many texts.[124] However, the account in the *Gongyang* is unique in its exclusive concentration on the motif of vengeance and in its portrayal and interpretation of moralized revenge. First, the *Gongyang* inserts an episode found nowhere else in which King Helu of Wu is so impressed with Wu Zixu's merits that he offers to raise an army in order to assist him to gain revenge. Wu Zixu demurred:

I have heard it said that serving a prince is like serving one's father. I would not damage your majesty's rectitude in order to pay back the wrong done my father.

At the end of the story the author of the *Gongyang* repeats this statement and argues that it was because Wu Zixu adopted this attitude that he was able to attain revenge.[125] The point of the demurral is that Wu Zixu would not use the king's power in order to serve his family; he would not violate the "public" order in the name of "private" duties. Only when the misconduct of Chu allowed him to destroy that state in his role as minister did he attain revenge.

This point is underscored by the omission of the famous scene in which Wu Zixu whipped the tomb of the deceased king of Chu or, in another version, had the corpse disinterred and whipped. Just as it denies that the revenge of Lord Xiang was the mere venting of anger, so the *Gongyang* insists that what is at stake in the story of Wu Zixu is justice and not the release of emotions.

This insistence that proper vengeance is a matter of justice and not passion also underlies the famous maxim that ends the account of Wu Zixu.

When the father does not receive a [just] execution the son ought to avenge him. If the father receives a just execution and the son avenges him, this is the Way of "pushing against the blade" [i.e., the vengeance will simply draw vengeance back on itself]. It avenges the grievance but does not eliminate the harm.[126]

Like the stipulation that the vengeance of Lord Xiang was only meritorious because no discerning Son of Heaven had punished the crime of Ji, this passage insists that vengeance was a part of law, or rather that legal and private retribution were two violent elements, sometimes interchangeable, of a single web of reciprocity that held together human society.[127] In the *Gongyang* the ties of kinship and service that bound men together demanded that deaths be repaid. Ideally the ruler would do justice, but in a less-than-perfect world the obligation to pay back the wrong fell upon those who were tied to the dead man, and the degree of obligation was determined by their closeness to him. This close identification of vengeance with punishment and the idea that one could substitute for the other was very important in early China and helps to account for the links of the practice of vengeance with the institution of collective punishment (see below).

The pattern of thought suggested by the scattered comments in the *Gongyang* was directly articulated in the Confucian ritual texts. Makino Tatsumi has collected the relevant passages and analyzed their differences in detail, but the texts share certain fundamental ideas.[128] First, they all agree that vengeance was a moral obligation. Second, they all argue that the degree of obligation hinged upon the relationship between the victim and the avenger; the closer the relationship the greater the obligation. These two principles are identical with those of Sima Qian's chapter on assassins and with the judgements of the *Gongyang*.

The ritual texts are distinctive in suggesting an objective scale to measure the degree of obligation. They stipulate an avenger's duty in terms of the physical distance beyond which he is not obliged to go in order to find and slay his enemy. Thus one passage in the *Li ji* says:

One should not bear the same Heaven as the murderer of one's father. One should never turn aside one's weapon if one encounters the murderer of a brother. One should not dwell in the same state with the murderer of a friend.

The killer of a father had to be hunted down wherever he went, the killer of a brother had to be be killed wherever encountered, even if it were in the market or court where the use of weapons was strictly prohibited, while the killer of a friend could be left in peace if he fled the state. Another passage in the same work says:

> Zi Gong asked Confucius, "How should one live without having avenged a father or mother?" The master replied, "Sleep on straw with your shield as a pillow and do not take office. Do not share the same Heaven [with the murderer]. Even if you meet him in the market or court strike without turning aside your weapon." "Might I ask how one should live without having avenged a brother?" "If you take office it should not be in the same state. If you are sent on a mission at the command of your prince, do not attack if you meet him on the way." "Might I ask how one should live if one has not avenged an uncle or cousin?" "Do not be the leader [in seeking revenge]. If the one in charge is capable then follow behind him with your weapon."[129]

Here the avenger of a parent had to fulfill the conditions of mourning until he had killed the enemy, a principle that once again identifies vengeance as an element of funerary ritual. He had to search for his enemy everywhere and kill him instantly, no matter where they met. The avenger of a brother was freed from some of the restrictions of mourning so long as the murderer was in another state, and he could not wreak vengeance while traveling in the service of his lord. The avenger of an uncle or cousin was not close enough to the victim to take a leading role, but he had to help his kin if they were worthy.

The Han texts convert these strictures into simple equations for converting degree of closeness in terms of kinship into extent of geographic separation. Thus the *Bohutong* says:

> One cannot live under the same Heaven with the murderer of a father. One cannot live in the same state with the murderer of a brother. One cannot serve in the same court with the murderer of a friend. One cannot live in the same neighborhood with the murderer of a member of one's lineage.[130]

The *Zhou li* follows the same pattern, but it inserts the formulas of separation into a structure of state enforcement by translating the range of the avenger's obligation into the distance to which the offender was exiled. Since a son could not live under the same Heaven with his father's killer, the hypothetical official in charge of harmonizing conflicts known as the "conciliator" would exile the murderer beyond the four seas. Since a brother could not live in the same state, the conciliator would exile the murderer beyond a thousand *li*. This passage also provided a table for matching the closeness of kin ties with those of political or social bonds. A father was equated with a prince, a brother with a teacher or elder, and an uncle or cousin with a master or friend.[131] Thus, although this text tends to assign the execution of justice to the state, it still defines that justice according to the model of a society defined by interpersonal bonds measured according to the "debt" of vengeance.

The Confucian school identified proper vengeance as a highly moral act that was obligatory to uphold or validate the personal ties that created human society. The problem of reconciling this moral demand for vengeance with the claims of law remained one of the central dilemmas of legal theory and practice throughout the history of the Chinese empire. This tension is expressed clearly in the meditations on vengeance of the Eastern Han scholar, Xun Yue (148–209 A.D.). He began by noting that revenge was an ancient form of "rectitude," but it could not be allowed freely. He then argued that one must "establish [laws]" (*zhi* 制) according to the demands of rectitude but make specific decisions (*duan* 斷) according to law. In this way, he claimed, "rectitude and law can stand together." Should the murderer fail to observe the rule of avoidance stipulated in the ritual formulas, then the avenger should be free to kill him, but if he observed the rule and the avenger still killed him, then the life of the latter should be forfeit. In this way Xun Yue defended the claim of imperial law to ultimate authority, but still found within the regime of law a defined place for the social and familial virtues expressed in the act of vengeance.[132] In debates during the Tang dynasty the opposition traced by Xun Yue in terms of "rectitude" and "law" appeared in the guise of a tension between the claims of "ritual," which viewed revenge as a basic moral teaching, and "law," which forbade the taking of human life.[133] But what concerns us here is not the specifics of this debate but the fact that the violence of revenge was considered to be a fundamental constituent of the Confucian moral order and closely identified with the violence of legal punishments.

Evidence that vengeance was basic to the moral order appears not only in ritual texts, commentaries, and the judgements of historians but also in tales of a more popular nature. Among the stories of Warring States and early imperial China one common motif was that of the "avenging ghost."[134] Texts show that as early as the fourth century B.C. some Chinese believed that "ghosts with a grievance" (*yuan hun* 冤魂) might return and carry out revenge on their murderer or those who failed to offer sacrifice.[135] In early imperial China these stories became so common that they virtually constituted an independent literary genre.

Such stories were not restricted to popular tales of the fantastic. Even though some literati expressed scepticism regarding tales of avenging ghosts, the stories were accepted to such a degree that they were repeatedly offered in the orthodox, dynastic histories as factual events with genuine explanatory power.[136] Alvin Cohen has studied the use of such tales in the dynastic histories from the *Shi ji* to the *Xin Tang shu* and found ninety-seven cases in which tales of avenging ghosts were recounted. Excluding multiple references to single stories, he found sixty-four distinct accounts of ghosts returning to avenge the wrongs done them. Although this is not a high number given the volume of the histories examined, it is sufficient to show that they were not random episodes expressing the quirks of individual authors but rather a carefully and consciously used motif based on generally accepted ideas.

Since the aggrieved spirits sought out their own revenge, these stories do not entail the ideas of reciprocity and a society constituted through bonds marked by the obligation of violence. However, the belief that Heaven itself, whether as a deified cosmos or a personified deity, enforced its justice through supporting personal vengeance in the world of men certainly lent a divine sanction to the obligations for revenge of kin and retainers.

This rationalization and celebration of vengeance in history, philosophy, and popular tales was not a purely literary phenomenon; revenge in early imperial China involved the spilling of blood as well as ink. The courtly bias of the historical records of the period obscures much of popular sentiment and practice, but the frequency of violent revenge and its general social approval appear clearly through the numerous scattered references in the dynastic histories and related works.

From various Han histories Makino Tatsumi collected more than sixty cases of murder or attempted murder which were described as acts of vengeance. In addition, there are numerous references to individuals steeped in the ethic of the "wandering swordsmen" who routinely helped people seek revenge. In many cases the avengers gathered numerous "retainers" (*ke* 客) to assist them, and the frequency and facility with which this was carried out indicates that throughout China there were many bravoes, brigands, and unemployed adventurers who made a living, at least in part, through the regular practice of violent revenge. At certain times in major cities these professional avengers formed large associations that linked up with officials through bribery and intimidation to exert tremendous influence on the conduct of government and daily life.[137]

So prevalent was vengeance in Han society that it became a topic of discussion at court. Thus in a memorial presented in the Western Han, Bao Xuan (d. 3 A.D.) listed the major causes of unnatural deaths among the people, and along with rapacious officials, bandits, plagues, and famine he included the reciprocal slaughter of those seeking revenge.[138] In a memorial submitted to the founder of the Eastern Han, Huan Tan (24 B.C. – 56 A.D.) argued:

> If the bad are executed or harmed, then the good receive blessings. But now when people kill or harm one another, even after they have submitted to law they privately harbor resentments and [thoughts of] vengeance. Descendants avenge one another, the later growing more outraged than the earlier, until whole families are destroyed and their hereditary occupations ruined. And it is customary to call such people heroic and sturdy, so that even the cowardly and weak devote themselves to such behavior. This is to let the people regulate themselves and to no longer have legal prohibitions.[139]

Vengeance had become so common that Huan Tan feared that it might entirely supplant the penal laws of the state, and this fear was not restricted to a single man or period.

> When the Han's ancestor [Liu Bang] relied on the sword [to found the dynasty] the teachings of men of arms flourished. The laws were broad and distant [not detailed], and the rites of civilization concise and summary. They inherited the violent brilliance of the "Four Princes" [famous for gathering retainers. Here they appear as the models for the spirit and ethic of the "wandering swordsmen."], so people harbored thoughts of bullying their superiors. They regarded death lightly and emphasized fighting spirit, and any wrong or favor would invariably be repaid. The laws came from "private" courts, and power shifted to commoners. The practices of the "swordsmen" became their customs.[140]

Revenge, associated with the "swordsmen" and the private realm of the family, threatened to set up an alternative law to that of the dynasty.

The reference here to the Four Princes and the practices of the "swordsmen" merits some attention. As I suggested above, it is quite likely that the ethic of moralized vengeance was first developed amongst the wandering fighters who sought service with the leading notables at court. As Sima Qian noted in the introduction to his chapter on the *you xia*, in times of strife and civil war these men had gained position at the court of princes, but in other times they lived amidst the streets and alleys of the common people.[141] Thus during the chaos of the Qin-Han interregnum they would have flourished, but following the establishment of the Han they survived only as common avengers and popular bandits. Consequently, it is not unlikely that the frequent recourse to vengeance amongst the common people of Han times owed more to the model of the *you xia* than to the moral strictures of the Confucians. Indeed, it is possible that the Confucians themselves were ratifying a popular ethic that had developed in the milieu of the "swordsmen" in the Warring States period.

Even though systematic revenge was so common that some men feared it was becoming a "private" law in opposition to the "public" law of the empire, records from the Han indicate that many, perhaps most, officials approved of vengeance and regularly condoned it in practice. The most obvious expression of this approval was the frequent refusal of local officials to arrest those guilty of murder for the sake of revenge. In other cases officials released avengers who had already been arrested, and although some of these officials had to go into hiding for failing to execute the law, many of them continued in office, a fact that suggests the tremendous leeway for independent action still possessed by local officials under the Han.[142]

Frequently officials even granted avengers special privileges, such as an exemption from corvee, or recommended them for office.[143] Moreover, both officials and the authors of the histories repeatedly described avengers as models of "rectitude" and treated them as moral exemplars.[144] Nor was this praise for vengeance as exemplary limited to the pages of books, for several officials sponsored the erection in public places of illustrated memorial tablets that celebrated the rectitude and filiality of various avengers, and one such illustration of a filial avenger has survived in the famous Eastern Han wall murals at the Wu family shrines.[145] Official support of vengeance reached such a degree that for a period in the Eastern Han the releasing of avengers was regarded as a fixed legal precedent with the full force of law.[146] The subsequent Wei dynasty formally recognized the legal right of kin to seek vengeance, except in cases where a general pardon had been issued or the original killing was accidental.[147]

The evidence in the biographies clearly shows that revenge, like any other murder, was a crime punishable by death and that the repeated releasing and honoring of avengers was a result not of court policy but of the local officials' belief that the "rectitude" of the canonical texts was more important than the laws of the imperial code. However, the central court itself also encouraged the practice of private revenge through its repeated pardons. Biographies tell of men who killed someone to obtain vengeance, went into hiding, and then returned to their old lives when a pardon was issued.[148] Those who described the formation of associations of professional avengers blamed this "routinization" of revenge, among other causes, on the repeated pardons that gave imperial sanction to such activities.[149]

Finally, the law itself contained elements that echoed and fortified the moralized theory of revenge. Vengeance was not the only violent aspect of social reciprocity in Warring States China and the early empires. One of the most striking features of Qin law, which survived in a reduced form into the Han, was "mutual implication" (*lian zuo* 連坐), in which punishment for certain serious crimes did not end with the individual but was extended to his family, neighbors, and in the case of an official to his immediate superiors, subordinates, or the man who had recommended him for office.[150] These social ties defined by the lines of extended liability to punishment were roughly the same as those defined by obligations of vengeance, suggesting an official definition of meaningful social ties through the shared violence of punishment that paralleled the role of vengeance in Confucian ritual theory. Among the significant ties were those between official colleagues and those between neighbors in the units of collective responsibility, but probably the most important were the ties of kinship. In the range of those included in the punishment of "destruction of the lineage" (*mie zu* 滅族) the Qin and Han governments marked out the limits of kinship that they regarded as socially or legally significant.[151]

As the preceding chapter showed, in the Spring and Autumn period *mie zu* referred to a political event resembling the destruction of a state and was an outgrowth of the internecine wars amongst the nobility, but in Qin and Han law it had become a legal and political tool in the government's effort to delimit, register, and control individual households. We have already seen an anticipation of this new pattern in the Houma covenants, where individual "families" (*jia* 家) of the enemy party in interlineage wars were banned, and these bans included lists of what degrees of relatives were to be included. Another important mechanism for the transition to "family liability" was the practice of holding as hostages the families of soldiers and the younger sons of powerful families.[152] Any disobedience or violation of the laws led to the execution of these kin. In the fifth century, quite likely basing themselves on Mohist military practices, states began to collect household registers, and with the gradual widening of military service, the range of "hostages" came to include the entire population.[153] Hence it is not surprising that the non-kin units of mutual responsibility were based on the units of the military levy, for the institution probably originated in military practices.

The collective punishment of families also reflected the changing relations between the family and the state. In the early Zhou, surnames were granted only to aristocratic families, and they alone participated in the rituals of ancestor worship that could define and maintain a lineage over time. Associated with the interlinked reforms of land holding and military service that created the "warring state," the individual peasant household became the primary unit for the exaction of service and taxes, and the registration of individual households became one of the state's major tasks. The evidence of the beginnings of this process preserved in Zhou bronzes was discussed earlier, and by the late Warring States period the individual households of the entire free population had become the basic units of the state structure and the focus of imperial control. The principle of collective liability for punishment on the basis of households was the legal expression of this new institutional order, just as the obligation to avenge immediate relatives was its moral expression in Confucian ritualist theory.

Although the suggestion of a close association between the active obligation of vengeance and the passive burden of collective guilt might seem forced, the two were not opposed in such a clear-cut fashion. First, the practice of vengeance itself included the notion of collective responsibility. The memorial of Huan Tan cited above described how reciprocal vengeance among the people often led to the destruction of entire families. In several cases an avenger did not kill the actual offender, but rather his wife and children or one of his relatives. In other cases a relative of the offender voluntarily presented himself or herself to the avengers in the hope of preserving the life of the threatened kinsman. Consequently, in many texts the parties seeking vengeance are described as the "avenging family."[154] Since the obligation to avenge was based on the ties of kinship, the roles of avenger and victim were played by the collective kin unit rather than isolated individuals.

Second, collective legal liability was to a degree simply the state's mode of participation in a society constituted through the reciprocal blood debts marked by vengeance. As both the biographies and court memorials show, in many cases the targets of revenge were officials who had performed legal executions. In a world where a man's kin were obliged to avenge him, anyone who killed a man had best destroy his family too, and the state could not entirely exempt itself from this rule.

Finally, the practice of collective responsibility was not only a means of terrifying the people through the enormity of the punishment that any crime would entail, but also a method of securing their participation in mutual surveillance. If members of families or neighbors reported the crimes of those with whom they were linked, they not only escaped punishment but could also receive rewards.[155] In this way the centralized autocracy sought to control a large population with a relatively small number of officials, but it had the paradoxical effect, as noted in the book attributed to Shang Yang, that governing the state depended on the active participation of the entire population.

> In regulating the state, if the judgements are made in the families then it attains the kingship; if they are made among the officials then it will be merely strong; if they are made by the ruler it will be weak. . . . If a criminal is invariably denounced, then the people pass judgement in their minds. If when the prince gives a command the people respond, so that the method of enforcing the law takes shape in the families and is simply carried out by the officials, then the judgements over affairs are made in the families. Therefore, with a true king reward and punishments are decided in the people's minds, and the means of enforcing the law are decided in the families. . . . If it is regulated then the people judge; if it is chaotic then the prince judges. Those who regulate states deem it valuable that inferiors pass judgements. Therefore if judgements are made at the level of a unit of ten towns, then the state will be weak; if they are made at the level of five towns, then it will be strong; if they are made by the families then everything will be in abundance. . . . Therefore in a state which has the Way those who regulate affairs do not listen to the prince and the people do not follow the officials.[156]

This extraordinary passage, which read out of context sounds like an appeal for democracy or anarchy, expresses the ideal of the authoritarian, legalist state. Through the institutions of collective responsibility and mutual surveillance the legalists sought to fashion a people who would of their own accord enforce the legal dictates of their masters. In such a political system the people would judge and punish their fellows, or more precisely, they would judge and punish those to whom they were bound through ties of kinship or common membership in the local units of collective responsibility. In the state advocated by Shang Yang a man would judge and punish those people whom he would avenge in the world of the *Gongyang*.

Societies in which human relationships are measured and affirmed by the "debt of vengeance" that people owe one another are not uncommon in historical and anthropological literature, and the collective responsibility of kin is a general trait of primitive law. However, such practices are characteristic of "primitive" societies, generally those that lack a central government claiming the monopoly of force. In China the theory and practice of social integration through the obligation of vengeance and collective responsibility developed along with a powerful state and an elaborate legal system, and they were systematically worked out by the social philosophers of the Warring States. On the one hand this led to a conflict and tension between the claims of personal vengeance embedded in the family or the ethic of service, and the opposing claim to a monopoly of punishment by the agents of the state. On the other hand it led to a mutual influence in which the ties of reciprocal obligation underlying the claims of "socialized" vengeance were embedded in the legal code. The former resulted in various legal strategies to incorporate limited forms of vengeance into the law of the land, while the latter resulted in the establishment of the principle of collective responsibility as an enduring feature of the Chinese legal system. But both of these results reflected the significance attributed by the Warring States Chinese to the bonds of service to elders and superiors, a significance which was marked through the obligation to kill or die.

Conclusion

The new form of state that emerged in China in the late Eastern Zhou was created through the systematic extension of military service among the rural peasantry and the lower levels of the urban populace. Under the increasing pressure of civil wars, the lineages of the Zhou nobility were forced to recruit the services of larger and larger numbers of the common people, but in doing so they undercut the monopoly of sanctioned violence that had defined them as nobles and constituted their authority. In the emerging territorial states authority consisted of the ability to control and mobilize the peasants who filled the ranks of the new infantry armies, and this control was secured through the allocation of land in exchange for service and taxes, the introduction of mutual responsibility, and the use of military districts as the basic units of civil administration. The institutions that forged the new mass armies became the basis of a new political order, and those rulers who could command the common people escaped from the old collegial authority of the nobility and became supreme, unchallenged autocrats.

The creation of the new territorial state entailed the destruction of the Zhou nobility and the armed lineage which had been its basic unit of social organization. In place of the fusion of kin and political structures through the mechanism of the ancestral cult that had characterized the Zhou state, the new order separated the political structure based on territorial states from the kin system now organized around the individual household. Both these realms exhibited an increasingly author-itarian character based on the unchallenged authority in their own realms of the territorial prince and the *paterfamilias*.

The increasingly autocratic character of rule in the states created through the formation of mass armies was marked in the transformation of the nature of oaths. These oaths, which had emerged as the primary means of joining together non-kin in the Spring and Autumn period, had originally commanded men through the sacred power of blood sac-rifice. However, the Warring States elite interpreted religious rituals and ideas in moralizing or "humanistic" terms, and as part of this trend the authority of oaths was located in the "moral potency" of the ruler and the power of written language. These oaths were used to establish the rules of military discipline which were the foundation stone of the "warring state," and they also became the basis of the legal codes which articulated the total power of the new rulers.[157] The bonds forged by oaths were also central to the new forms of personal subordination and dependency that tied those who obtained service at court to the ruler. In this role they were identified with various ritual and magical practices used to compel actions through a "spell-binding" power, practices that were linked to the law but were particularly prominent in sexual unions. Oaths thus became part of the general "sexual re-imagining" of the political realm, in which the male collegiality of shared combat and sacrifice was replaced by the domination of husband over wife as the model of authority.

The same de-centering of the sacrificial act and the power of spirits marked the Confucian theory of sacrifice as a mode of defining hierar-chical roles and instructing men in the duties of service. The power of sacrifice no longer stemmed from the physical feeding of potent spirits, but rather from the moral instruction of the participants and the potency of the superior man who guided them.

Vengeance, like blood oaths and sacrifice, became a means of creating bonds of service and devotion. What had been a matter of honor and a cause of civil war among the nobility became a "debt" of bloodshed that marked the hierarchical ties between men. This moralized vengeance probably first emerged in the ethic of the "wander-ing swordsmen" who sought service as armed retainers in the courts of the leading nobles where they showed their devotion by their willingness to kill or die for their lord. These actions provided a model in which devotion to superiors was marked by the obligation to avenge them. Through the dual character of the "swordsmen," who served as either courtiers or popular bandits and avengers depending on the times, this ethic became generally disseminated throughout society. It was particu-larly elaborated by the Confucians, who saw in it a clear demonstration of the total devotion to elders or superiors that they espoused in the family and in political service. Both fictional tales of avenging ghosts and the accounts of vengeance in the Han histories suggest that this ideal of vengeance as a moral obligation did in fact become common throughout Chinese society, although it remained in uneasy tension with the claims of law.

Just as the violent debt of revenge marked social ties in Warring States society and in Confucian ritual theory, so the shared obligations of collective liability and mutual surveillance defined significant social ties in legalist administrative practice. These institutions evolved out of the criminal bans passed on lineages and families in the late Spring and Autumn civil wars, out of the practice of using the families of soldiers and men in government service as hostages for their good behavior, and out of the ethic of vengeance which charged all social ties with a "debt" of violence. Under this system every one of the ties that defined the territorial state—those between neighbors in their units of military service, among colleagues in their offices at court, and above all within the families who were the basic units of taxation and service—was strengthened through joint liability for criminal actions and mutual responsibility to pass judgement upon one another.

In this way the forms of violence that had defined the Zhou aristocracy also defined the social order in the "warring states" and early empires. Every one of the significant human ties that created the social and political order of Warring States China was defined or marked by its forms of sanctioned violence. However, whereas the performance of ritually-sanctioned violence had set the aristocracy apart from the common people and created their authority, in the new state the universal performance of violence defined those hierarchic relations that bound men in their places. As participants in military service, sacrifice, blood oaths, vengeance, and punishments, the common people of Warring States China obtained not authority but discipline and obedience. While all men now engaged in violence, the authority it had once conferred lay elsewhere.

Chapter Three

THE ART OF COMMAND

The form of authority most closely related to the new organization of sanctioned violence was military command. In the Warring States transition the role of an army's commander was completely transformed, and the new art of generalship both reflected and helped to shape the new modes of political authority in the territorial states. Generalship, as John Keegan has shown so brilliantly, is a culturally based activity whose variations can tell us much about the society of a particular place and era, and the theory and practice of generalship is particularly revealing in a society like Warring States China, where the state had been created through military organization.[1] For convenience I will base this exposition of the art of military command on four features that reflected the new modes of authority in China: 1) command as a mastery of written texts, 2) command as a mental effort that organized or co-ordinated the actions of masses, 3) command as the discovery or creation of pattern in the chaos of battle, 4) command and its relations to political authority and the social order.

An essential prerequisite to the new art of command was the development of a distinctive military specialization in which armies were led by full-time, professional officers who held their positions through the mastery of military techniques that were recognized as a distinctive branch of knowledge. In the Spring and Autumn period there was no difference between those who commanded the state and those who commanded the army; the leading ministers or heads of lineages took command, and there was no education for generals apart from the normal military training received by every noble. However, with the rise of mass armies, which required elaborate administration and organization,

97

and the development of new weapons, which needed careful co-ordination, a specialized officer corps based on expertise and education became essential.[2] Biographical accounts of commanders and the development of specifically military texts both show that some degree of specialization first appeared in the late sixth century, and that by the end of the fourth century there were both generals who were exclusively commanders of armies in the field and technical military treatises clearly intended for a specialized audience.[3] By the middle of the Warring States period the military commander had thus become a distinctive social type and the exponent of a special set of theories, techniques, and administrative practices. In these roles he offered a model for many new aspects of authority in the Warring States.

The Commander and Texts

One major aspect of the development of military specialization in China was the elaboration in written texts of a distinctive body of ideas and techniques pertaining to warfare. During the Warring States period, philosophers and military specialists created a large corpus of writings analyzing the principles of combat and the role of war in the social order.[4] Even before one considers the contents of these texts, it is important to note that their very existence already suggests a radical reformulation of the nature of warfare. In place of the old idea of combat as an arena of heroism where men battled for glory through skill with the chariot and the bow, the existence of military texts and doctrines implies that battle was a form of wisdom or an art, a mental skill that could be verbally formulated and taught. In the writings of the military specialists the key to warfare lay in the man who perceived, calculated, and decided, while those who actually carried arms and spilled blood were reduced to secondary roles. This emphasis on mental skills based on textual knowledge as the key to power was also part of the general Warring States political transition, in which competing schools of thinkers sought to gain office through the wisdom or policies articulated in texts they had written or studied. Since military treatises were among the first books associated with specific schools to appear, they played a leading role in this reformulation of power.[5]

That the emerging military specialists consciously viewed their "textual" vision of warfare as a denial of the chivalric warfare of the old nobility is revealed in a body of tales in which a non-heroic figure with no combat skills gains victory over a great warrior through the possession of a military treatise. These treatises, moreover, were often divinely or magically revealed, and this suggests that the military theorists thought of their doctrines as an esoteric wisdom that expressed divine patterns inherent in the cosmos.

The "prototype" of these tales, although perhaps not the first to appear or to be written down, told of how the Yellow Emperor defeated the invincible beast/warrior Chi You through the power of a treatise given him by the Queen Mother of the West or an unnamed Celestial Woman.

> The Yellow Emperor fought with Chi You nine times and nine times he was defeated. He returned to Mt. Tai and for three nights stayed in the darkness of a fog. There appeared a woman with the head of a human and the body of a bird. The Yellow Emperor bowed his head and then prostrated himself. He lay on the ground and did not dare to get up. The woman said, "I am the black [or "white"] maiden. What do you desire to ask?" The Yellow Emperor replied, "I desire invincibility." He then received a military treatise.[6]

Although the quoted fragment ends here, we know from other sources that the Yellow Emperor was then able to defeat Chi You.

The Yellow Emperor was, by Han times, the first of the mythic sage rulers who created Chinese civilization, and his conquest of Chi You was the theme of a large number of tales and rituals in Warring States and early imperial China. As will be discussed in Chapter Five, these stories and rituals frequently dealt with the origins of warfare and punishments, and with the role of the correct use of violence in creating a human society. Since the tales developed in the Warring States period, their understanding of "correct" violence reflected the new patterns of sanctioned killing that underlay the rise of territorial states. One of the primary features of this new pattern of violence was the belief that warfare was an intellectual discipline based on textual mastery, so the sage-king who had created proper warfare was also the first recipient of a military treatise and hence the originator of warfare rooted in text-based skills. When the Chinese began to compose encyclopedias of the origins of things, the editors stated it as a simple matter of fact that military treatises began with the Yellow Emperor, and all later military writings were "transmissions" of this primal revelation.[7]

Although the story of the Yellow Emperor won recognition as the prototype of tales of revealed military treatises, the first one set down in a surviving text was the story of Zhang Liang, the principle strategist and military adviser of the founder of the Han dynasty. Zhang Liang's family had for generations served as ministers in the state of Han, and as a youth he studied rituals. When Qin completed its conquest of the empire, Zhang Liang went into hiding after organizing an unsuccessful assassination attempt against Qin Shihuang. One day while strolling along an embankment, he encountered an old man who deliberately dropped his sandal over the side and ordered Zhang Liang to fetch it. Zhang Liang suppressed his initial inclination to strike the old man, and out of consideration for his great age he retrieved the sandal. The old man then commanded him to replace it on his foot. Zhang Liang again forebore any angry response, knelt down, and put the sandal on the old man's foot. Then the old man laughed and walked away, but after going a short distance he turned and said to Zhang Liang, "You could be taught, young man. Meet me here at dawn in five days." When Zhang Liang kept the appointment the old man had already arrived, and he scolded Zhang Liang for being too late and told him to come earlier five days hence. He repeated this procedure twice, and after being fully satisfied with Zhang Liang's sincere devotion the old man gave him the *Tai Gong bingfa*. With the stratagems and principles in this military text he helped Liu Bang defeat the unconquerable warrior Xiang Yu and establish the Han dynasty.[8]

This story is clearly linked to the tale of the revelation of the military treatise to the Yellow Emperor. In both cases a figure of no martial prowess or heroic inclinations defeats a warrior of matchless physical power through the divine bestowal of a military book.[9] The account insists on Zhang Liang's weakness and lack of bellicosity and shows that these traits were essential to his success. First, it makes a special point that as a youth he studied "ritual," which by the late Warring States period was consciously opposed to reliance on rewards and punishments or brute force. Again, it states that because Zhang Liang was repeatedly ill, he could not command an army in the field but acted solely as a strategic adviser. Consequently, the biography states that when it came time for Liu Bang to reward his followers, Zhang Liang "had no combat achievements."[10] Finally, the account of the obtaining of the treatise makes it clear that Zhang Liang received it because he was able docilely to accept repeated, deliberate insults and evince proper respect for the aged. It was because he could not be provoked to fight that he could gain the secret of victory in battle.

The story also resembles the tale of the Yellow Emperor in its "Taoist" colorings. Zhang Liang received the text from a spirit or divinity who turned out to be a yellow stone. The Tang dynasty commentator Sima Zhen states that the Wind Monarch, a servant of the Yellow Emperor and reputed author of a military treatise, had become Master Lao, who had in turn become this yellow stone. Moreover, Zhang Liang practiced such Taoist techniques as abstention from eating grain, controlling his breathing, and levitation. At one point he sought to retire from the world to follow Master Red Pine, an immortal who figured in various early Chinese texts.[11] Thus, the story of Zhang Liang clearly had a Taoist provenance and was linked by the Chinese with the Yellow

Emperor. This common grounding in Taoism or Huang-Lao thought was significant, for these schools shared with the military treatises both a common vocabulary and many basic ideas.[12]

A third tale of a revealed text pertains to Su Qin, the great rhetorician and architect of the "vertical" alliance against Qin. When Su Qin first presented his theories at the courts of the warring kings, he met with universal rejection and returned home a failure, scorned and ridiculed by his own family. That evening he retired to his room, and in a box he found the *Yin fu* of Tai Gong and studied it without pause for an entire year. When he had mastered it, he set out once again and this time was able to persuade the rulers of six states to join in an alliance against Qin. He became the chief minister of all six states and for some years dominated the Chinese political scene.[13]

The links of this account to stories of revealed, magically potent military treatises are not obvious at first reading, but upon closer examination they become clear. First, the book which Su Qin discovered was attributed to Tai Gong. In the legends of the period Tai Gong figured as the military strategist whose assistance enabled King Wu to defeat the Shang, and along with the Yellow Emperor he was the transmitter of the secret wisdom of military strategy to the world. Several Warring States military treatises were attributed to Tai Gong, and the Chinese commentators identify the book found by Su Qin as a military one. More significantly, the magic book obtained by Zhang Liang was also attributed to Tai Gong, a shared origin that clearly linked the two stories.[14]

More problematic is the fact that Su Qin never used this text in battle but only to devise stratagems of persuasion. In terms of the military thought of this period, however, such a distinction between grand strategy and rhetorical persuasion, on the one hand, and combat, on the other, was not crucial. Several pre-Qin or early imperial texts explicitly assimilated the arts of the rhetorician and the military commander. These texts, most notably the *Zhanguo ce* and the *Guiguzi*, identified the procedures of the commander with those devices by which a debater masked his true plans, lured his adversary into revealing his intentions, and struck unexpectedly where no defense had been prepared. This is particularly significant because the author of the *Guiguzi* was Su Qin's putative teacher. More importantly, Su Qin himself explicitly identified persuasion and diplomacy as superior forms of warfare in his lengthy critique of reliance on military force.[15]

Finally, the account in the *Zhanguo ce* of Su Qin's discovery of the treatise, when linked with the various persuasions attributed to him, suggests that what the text revealed to him was the proper use of warfare, and this understanding underlay his later success. In the one persuasion attributed to Su Qin prior to his discovery, he sketched the geographic advantages and military power of Qin, stated that war was universal and inevitable, and then tried to convince the king of Qin to conquer the other states through sheer force of arms and become emperor. This persuasion failed completely. After mastering the text he argued for a system of alliances to check the possibility of a war of conquest, dissuaded various rulers from attack, urged princes not to claim the title of emperor, and delivered an extended persuasion on the superiority of seeking power without recourse to the hazards and waste of combat. The story, through the contrast of "before" and "after," dramatized the difference between the correct and incorrect uses of armed power, between one who used brute force and one who conquered through foresight, stratagem, and maneuver. This contrast expresses one of the basic principles of the military philosophy of the period, so what Su Qin learned from the revealed text of Tai Gong was clearly a form of military wisdom.

One final story of a revealed military treatise is not datable to the Warring States or the early Han, but due to its close ties to the above tales and its setting in the Warring States period, it still merits examination here. According to the account of his life in the *Shi ji*, Sun Bin was a descendant of the great strategist Sun Wu and studied military practices with Pang Juan. The latter became a general for the state of Wei, but because he knew himself to be inferior to his old classmate he had Sun Bin invited to Wei and then contrived a legal pretext to have Sun's legs chopped off and his face tattooed. Sun Bin managed to communicate with an emissary from Qi, his home state, and was secretly carried back there. He impressed the lord of Qi with his military acumen and was appointed a tutor. When the lord of Qi decided to send an army against Wei, he desired to appoint Sun Bin commander, but the latter declined on the grounds that his physical mutilation rendered him unfit for the office. However, he was carried along in a supply wagon, and his advice enabled the army of Qi to defeat Wei and slay his nemesis, Pang Juan.[16]

In the popular story-telling tradition, however, this tale became embroidered with various elements from the legends of potent, divinely revealed texts. According to this version Sun Bin and Pang Juan studied under the author of the *Guiguzi*, the old teacher of Su Qin. This figure appeared as a master of esoteric lore who had dealings with immortals, spirits, and deities. He secretly gave Sun Bin a copy of the military treatise of his ancestor Sun Wu, and the younger Sun committed this to memory. After Pang Juan had departed and become commander of Wei's armies, Master Mo learned of the transmission of Sun Wu's text, and he then sought to obtain a position in Wei for Sun Bin by revealing that he had received the secrets of Sun Wu's military treatise. When Pang Juan learned that his old schoolmate and rival held in his memory this supremely potent text, he had Sun Bin invited to Wei in hopes of tricking him into divulging it. After Sun Bin's arrival in Wei, the story follows the account in the *Shi ji.*[17]

It is impossible to know when this version first appeared. Dramatic and largely fictional accounts of many historical figures, such as Su Qin, were known in the Warring States period, and fragments of these appear in various texts.[18] Although it has not survived in any early written work, the tale of Sun Bin may stem from such a source, but it is probably later. At any rate it is clearly tied to the other stories through the motif of the "magical" revelation of a military text which granted its possessor victory. Moreover, Sun Bin's mutilation rendered him the very embodiment of physical helplessness, so this story offers the clearest and most extreme development of the recurrent motif of the conqueror as a man of no martial prowess.

These stories are a form of "charter myth" for the new understanding of warfare. The potency of *texts* shows that warfare was a matter of the mind and that the true warrior was the man who understood the principles or techniques of war and could apply them in battle. The fact that these texts were revealed shows that the principles of warfare expressed or reflected the fundamental patterns of the divine order, a theme that will be explored further in Chapter Four and Chapter Six. Finally, the systematic denial of belligerence or physical prowess on the part of the conqueror constituted a critique of the warrior aristocracy's heroic vision of war. The art of battle no longer consisted in the skills of driving a chariot or handling weapons, but in assessing the terrain and the enemy, organizing multitudes, and devising stratagems. As the master of texts and techniques, it was the commander who now determined the outcome of the battle.

These stories also tie the new organization of warfare to the general reorganization of political power. The claiming of authority on the basis of a special wisdom, increasingly frequently transmitted in texts, was characteristic of many of the men who sought service in the courts of the territorial princes. Zhang Liang, Su Qin, and Sun Bin all used their revealed wisdom to gain service with a ruler or would-be ruler, so they were typical of the new ministers and retainers who were linked to the ruler through bonds and in return owed him total devotion. The shared nobility which had characterized rulers and warriors in the Spring and Autumn period was supplanted in the military realm by the ties of absolute dependence that bound the servants of the territorial princes to their new masters.

The Commander and the Army

Warfare that could be explicated in texts was a warfare of the mind, and the new theory and practice of battle centered on the question of how the ideas of the commander could be realized in the flux of combat. One major element of this problem was the relation of the commander to his troops, and the military treatises constantly insisted that the commander's will had to guide all actions while the troops were reduced to passive objects of manipulation. This idea was expressed in a variety of ways: 1) insistence that the army must be unified as a single body, along with consideration of the methods for attaining this; 2) discussion of the use of organization and training to turn previously autonomous fighting men into standardized, predictable, functionally differentiated members of a co-ordinated whole in which the integrated squad and not the individual soldier was the lowest independent tactical unit, and each unit gained meaning solely through its place in the larger formation; 3) analysis of combat as a duel of two opposing minds; 4) holding commanders entirely responsible in law for the performance of their armies; 5) a rhetoric for the description of battles that reduced the soldiery to the status of natural objects, children, or animals; 6) a transformed sexual imagery of warfare, in which the celebration of masculine courage and strength was replaced by the model of feminine obedience and compliance; 7) systematic criticism and punishment of any attempts at individual initiative or heroism. These changes collectively constituted a reformulation of warfare as a collective enterprise that aimed at forging large numbers of men into an integrated body in which each part was subservient to the whole, and the whole was immediately responsive to the commander's will. It was no longer killing in the service of the ancestors, but rather the organization and control of men in the service of the territorial prince that gave meaning to warfare. As a figure who imparted order and purpose through his ability to direct the actions of masses of men, the military commander exemplified yet another aspect of the new pattern of authority in the territorial state.

Various passages in the military treatises explicitly argued that the commander had to be the mind or active agent, and the troops were extensions of his will. The *Sun Bin bingfa* says, "The troops are arrows and the commander the bow."[19] Other texts argued that the commander was the trunk of the body and the troops its limbs, that the commander was the mind and the troops the body, or that the commander and the troops had to have a single mind.[20] The army had to be rendered totally responsive to the commander's will, so that the skill and wisdom that brought victory could be translated into action on the field.

The transformation of the army into an artificial body guided by the mind of the commander presupposed the forging of the multitude of individuals who composed the army into a seamless unity. The *Wuzi* tells a parable of a condemned man armed with a sword being hunted by a thousand men. Because the criminal was a unity, whereas the pursuers were divided, and because he knew that he had to fight or die while they might each hope to escape alive simply by avoiding any encounter, the fugitive would triumph. It then argued that the aim of the commander was to turn a 50,000 man army into one "condemned bandit."[21] The "Way," which is the first of the "five factors" that determined victory in the *Sunzi*, was defined as that which "causes the people and their ruler to have the same ideas and intentions. As a result they will die or live together with him and not fear danger." Another passage in the same work argues that the commander's banners, drums, and bells united the ears and eyes of the army, and that this unity overrode individual courage or cowardice.[22]

The ideal of total unity in which all the members of an army became a single body under the control of the commander's will was developed most systematically in the *Wei Liaozi*. This goal was to be achieved, on the one hand, through the rigorous enforcement of regulations, and, on the other hand through the commander's sharing of the material conditions of his troops. Through regulations the men of the army could overcome their fear of death and act in total obedience to the commander's will. "Commands," as the text says, "are the mind of the army." This unquestioning obedience would create an absolute unity, and unity rendered the army invincible. Any division, hesitation, or individual initiative would fragment the army and had to be eliminated through unvarying enforcement of regulations. At the same time that regulations and training made men pliant extensions of the commander's will, the general had to drink, eat, and sleep in the same manner as his troops, and then only after their needs had been met. In this way the commander "made himself a model" and "made himself the same as them" so that he and the army became "a single body."[23]

The *Sunzi* takes another approach to this idea when it argues that the commander had to block up the eyes and ears of his men to deprive them of knowledge and consciousness. In this way they would act solely according to his will, and he would become "like one driving a flock of sheep; he drives them to go and then to return, and none know where they are going." "Therefore for the man who is skilled at using troops, it is like leading a single man about by the hand; he cannot but follow."[24] The *Wuzi* offers a similar discussion in which the commander's drums and bells overawe the army's ears, his banners overawe their eyes, and his commands and punishments overawe their minds. "When the commander directs all will obey, and when the commander points all will advance to their deaths."[25] Just as in the *Sunzi*, the commander was to obliterate the senses and minds of his troops so that they would perceive and think only what he directed. This insistence on the absence of thought or reflection on the part of any save the commander also suggests one reason why the military treatises repeatedly denounced any reliance on divination in the field.[26] The commander alone was to think and decide, and any appeal to outside authority threatened the total unity of thought and will that made the army strong.

Since the soldiers were to have no minds of their own, their courage or will to fight was simply an expression of the severity of regulations and their fear of the commander.[27] This tendency to deny any independent volition or courage to the soldiers also led several of the treatises to argue that the commander had to place his troops in a situation in which they had no choice but to fight or die.[28] Nor were these purely theoretical injunctions, for various accounts of battles and campaigns in the late Warring States period and the Qin-Han interregnum show that the commanders consciously employed stratagems, including maneuvering the army into positions where retreat was impossible, to elicit a psychology of desperation in which the troops had no choice but to fight.[29] These practices cast doubt on the ability of the states of the period to mobilize the minds as well as the bodies of their people, but they are also extensions of the identification of the general as the sole actor in military affairs and the reduction of the soldiers to a passive role.

Perhaps the most extreme expression of the tendency to describe the army as a single body guided by the general appears in the *Sun Bin bingfa*.

The commander must have social rectitude. If he does not, he will not be severe, and if he is not severe he will not inspire awe. If he does not inspire awe, then the troops will not [be willing to] die. Therefore social rectitude is the head of the army. The commander must be beneficent. If he is not beneficent then the army will not conquer, and if they do not conquer they will achieve nothing. Therefore beneficence is the belly of the army. The commander must have virtuous potency. If he does not have potency then he will have no strength, and if he has no strength then the army will gain no benefit. Therefore virtuous potency is the hands of the army. The commander must be trustworthy. If he is not trustworthy then his commands will not be carried out, and if his commands are not carried out then the army will not be united. If they are not united then they will have no fame ["name"]. Therefore trustworthiness is the feet of the army. The commander must know [the decisive moment for] victory. If he does not know victory. . . [text missing. Apparently refers to the lack of decisiveness if he does not "know victory".] . . . then the army will be without. . . [text missing] . . . Therefore decisiveness is the tail of the army.[30]

The army's strength, unity, willingness to die, and ability to conquer were all explained as attributes of the commander's virtues and powers, and then each of these virtues was identified as one part of the collective body of the army. The ideal army here was a single strong body, but this body was simply a transformation of the character and skill of the commander.

This repeated emphasis on the army as a collective body entailed a new attitude to the discipline and utilization of the individual soldier. Amongst the Zhou nobility, military training had centered on the martial skills of the individual soldier, and practice in group maneuver had consisted in little more than learning how to co-ordinate a line of chariots so that their wheels did not interlock, and they did not block the line of archery fire of their fellows.[31] In the mass infantry armies, however, the individual chariot was replaced by the squad of five men as the smallest independent tactical unit, and the active manipulation of the formations made up of these squads became the essence of the commander's art and the key to victory in battle. The focus of military training was no longer skill but discipline, not the instruction and development of the individual's abilities but the perfection of a system to which individuals were forced to conform. In this way, just as in seventeenth-century Europe, military discipline became a model for new methods of maintaining social order.[32]

As was described in Chapter Two, the five-man squad (*wu* 伍) had become the basic unit of infantry organization by the eighth or seventh century B.C. The significance of the number five was discussed in a variety of early texts. These discussions were based on various numerological theories, which ultimately merged into the theory of the "five phases" as a general model for all non-binary combinations. Several texts note that "five" (*wu* 五) represents the combination of "two" and "three", the lowest even number and the lowest plural odd, and as such it became the paradigm for all combinations of unlikes and the lowest number of men that could form a discrete column (*lie* 列).[33]

As "five" was considered the prototype of combinations of unlikes, various texts state that *wu* meant to "mix" or "combine." In several early military treatises, most notably the *Sima fa* and the *Sunzi*, this idea of combining was linked with the idea of the "five weapons" to produce the argument that the purpose of the five-man squad was the combination of weapons in order to produce an integrated fighting unit. The basic division of weapons was into long and short in accord with the range of their utility, so lances and bows were the long weapons and swords or halberds the short ones. These weapons were combined in a single squad so that the long weapons could strike the enemy at a distance, while the short ones could come into play if the adversary was able to come close enough to engage in hand-to-hand combat. Thus the *Sima fa* argues, "weapons must be mixed . . . if weapons are not mixed they will not be beneficial." "If all the five weapons are correct, then the long ones will protect the short, and the short will protect the long. If they are used in sequence you can fight a long time, and if they are used together you will be strong."[34] Other texts discuss how the various weapons were to be arranged in accord with the needs of the situation or even, as an expression of the calendrical model of warfare, according to the seasons of the year.[35] That this combination of bows, lances, and swords in a single squad of five was actually employed in the field has been confirmed by the famous battle scenes depicted on the late Warring States bronze water basins discovered at Shanbiaozhen.[36]

/ As a result of this combination of weapons, the individual fighter with his weapon was no longer a meaningful tactical unit. Only when deployed and manipulated in squads could the soldiers of a Warring States army employ their weapons to good effect. However, the five-man squads were themselves only the basic units for the larger units of twenty-five men, and these in turn were units for the formations and maneuvers carried out by the entire army in the field.[37] The military treatises and references to armies in philosophical texts both repeatedly insisted that any breaks or disorder in these formations (*zhen* 陣) led to defeat and that the strength of an army lay in the solidity of its ranks. "In the formations of a conquering army the coward will die in the line."[38] Consequently the focus of training lay on getting men to move and act in unison and remain in the formations imposed by their officers.

> In all warfare, it is not the formations that are difficult but rather causing men to be able to make formations. It is not causing men to be able to make formations that is the most difficult, but rather making men obedient. It is not knowing how that is difficult; doing it is difficult.[39]

The decisive problem of military action was to get men to act obediently and automatically in their formations; only then could the full panoply of weapons be brought to bear in a useful fashion and the maneuvers conceived by the commander be carried out. The repeated emphasis on the unity of the army or the army as a single body reflected the fact that the new infantry armies depended on collective action in fixed units to be effective.

Since the soldiers acted entirely in squads and the army solely in formations, the actions or perceptions of the individual soldier were fragments of a larger order that became intelligible only at the level of the squad, while the actions of the squad had sense and purpose only at the level of the twenty-five-man unit, and those of the twenty-five-man unit at the level of the larger formation. Information moved up a hierarchy of officers from the lowest unit to the next and so on up to the general, and commands moved in the opposite direction, so that increasing authority was marked by the possession of an ever broader range of information and the command of an ever greater number of units. In this way the individual performance or experience of combat was secondary to the encompassing order of the squad in which it was organized, but this higher order was itself only part of a still larger, more encompassing arrangement. This hierarchy of widening pattern and increasing information culminated in the commander, who alone was sufficiently elevated to perceive and guide the army as a totality. All pattern and meaning on the field of battle ultimately lodged in the mind of the commander, which thus alone acted as the mind of the army.[40]

This new form of military organization and the concomitant image of the army as a collective body under a single will led the creators of China's military doctrines to attribute decisive influence to the skill of the commander and describe combat as a duel of two minds. Thus the *Sunzi* lists the commander but not the troops as one of the five factors which determined victory, and it later asserts:

> The commander is the side-guard [the pole mounted on the side of a chariot to keep it from overturning] of the state. If the side-guard is intact the state is strong, but if it has any flaw then the state will be weak.[41]

The *Liu tao* goes even further and calls the commander the "life" or "fate" of the army.[42]

As a result of the identification of the fate of the army with the skill of its commander, battle could be represented as the mental struggle for mastery between two men, as in the aforementioned equation of military campaigns with debates in court. Repeatedly the commander was presented as the key to victory or defeat and the prime object of attack. The *Wuzi* says that the essential in all battles is to know the enemy commander, for from knowledge of the commander one may know how the army will perform.[43] The *Sunzi* argues that the most effective way to defeat the enemy is to "attack his deliberations," to attack the knowledge and plans of the commander.[44] The *Wei Liaozi* argues, "The means by which one knows victory is to match one's commander against the enemy. The commander and the enemy are like a hanging scale [granting victory to whichever side is 'heavier']."[45]

This exaltation of the commander as the essence of the army is also reflected in a literary trope repeatedly used to describe victory in battle. Rather than referring to defeating the enemy or his army, the most common phrase speaks of "toppling an army and capturing [or 'killing'] the commander," and in several cases the authors speak only of "killing the commander" or "capturing the commander." These tropes either pair the commander with the army as co-ordinate aspects of military force, or metonymically substitute him for the entire army.[46]

Since the commander was uniquely responsible for the army, he received both the credit for victory and the blame for defeat. One of the most striking examples of the former appears in the *Zhanguo ce*. Gong-shu Cuo led the army of Wei to victory against the combined forces of Han and Zhao, and he captured the enemy general. When the lord of Wei sought to reward him for his achievement, however, he declined. He explained that the troops had not broken and run because of the lingering effects of the instruction given by his predecessor, Wu Qi. The troops had not become confused or lost because two of his officers had studied the terrain in advance. The troops had obeyed orders because the lord had demonstrated that he kept faith in his rewards and punishments. The commander's sole achievement had been to recognize the enemy's vulnerability and then tirelessly to beat his drum to drive the troops forward. The ruler agreed with this analysis and rewarded the descendants of Wu Qi, the two officers, and Gongshu Cuo.[47] Even seeking to disclaim any credit for the victory, he could do so only by attributing victory to a former commander, his subordinate officers, or the state's ruler. The thought that the troops played a significant role in the victory occurred neither to Gongshu Cuo nor to the lord of Wei.

Blaming the commander for the failures of his men is also common in the military treatises. Thus the *Sunzi* lists six disasters that can befall an army and then says, "These six are not disasters from Heaven or Earth; they are the errors of the commander."[48] The *Sima fa* not only argues that the commander is responsible for any defeat, but that if he desires to fight again, he must swear an oath that he will stand in the front ranks and not return from battle.[49] According to the *Wei Liaozi*, a commander was held legally liable for the defeat of his army, and officers were responsible for any failures of their troops.[50]

As a corollary to assigning sole agency and responsibility to the commander and his officers, the rhetoric of the military treatises tends to identify soldiers with various mindless natural objects or with animals. Sometimes they are compared to logs or stones which are rolled by the commander, and sometimes they assume the guise of flowing water, the storm, or of beasts, objects that have their own dynamism but lack calculation or deliberation. Thus a passage regarding the "sage commander" in the *Heguanzi* variously describes armies as arrows, thunder, lightning, or flowing water.[51] At different points the *Sunzi* describes the commander's manipulation of his troops as "unleashing pent-up water over a high cliff," "rolling logs and stones," "rolling round stones over a high cliff," or "driving a herd of sheep."[52] The *Wei Liaozi* says that an army can be heavy like mountains, forests, or rivers, yet light like a flame. It crushes the foe like a stone wall or swirls over him like clouds; it moves like wind and rain, like an arrow shot from a crossbow, or like a whirlwind. The attack of the army is like a hawk or like water plunging into a chasm. Victorious troops are compared to water, supremely yielding and weak yet able to level mountains because they move in unison. To drain the army's strength by overly long marches is like "cutting off the source of a river." Defeated troops scatter "like water."[53] The *Sun Bin bingfa* also compares a properly commanded army to flowing water or to stones being rolled.[54]

In a related figure of speech the general is sometimes told to regard his soldiers as infants or small children whose lives depend totally on his actions.[55] All these metaphors reduce the soldiers to passive objects impelled by the general's will or mindless creatures guided by his intelligence. In this way they reflect the pattern of mass armies described above, in which information and intelligibility decline as one moves down the hierarchy of units, so that the individual soldier is both totally ignorant of the scheme or purport of the battle, and also completely meaningless as a unit of action or maneuver. Pattern and sense reside entirely in the collectivity, so only the commander can know the whole and act on it as a thinking being.

The equation of soldiers with brute beasts or infants suggests another aspect of the new nature of warfare in the mass armies, the transformation of the sexual imagery of the soldier. Under the warrior nobility the general term for the aristocracy expressed its male character, the fundamental rituals of ancestral sacrifice defined a masculine lineage, and martial prowess had been the definition of manhood. The development of mass armies in the Warring States period, however, was accompanied by a form of sexual reversal, the feminization of combat. To a degree this change was simply one aspect of the more general "reimagining" of authority in terms of the rule of husband over wife that was described in Chapter Two. However, there were also aspects that were distinctive to the military realm.

First, one hallmark of the new mode of combat was the military treatise, and the primal revelation to the Yellow Emperor had been made by a woman.[56] This clearly suggests that the Chinese thought of the new mode of combat as in some sense a "feminine" wisdom. It was feminine in its denial of the martial ethic of the warrior nobility, its associations with guile and deceit (see below), its strong links with the Taoist theory of the superior strength of the weak and the yielding, and its claims to be an esoteric, hidden wisdom.

Not only were the new arts of the commander feminine, but the soldier in the field was also identified with women through the insistence on weakness and obedience as the virtues of the man in the ranks. Sun Wu was the prototype of the new commander and putative author of the first and greatest of the military treatises, but his biography in the *Shi ji* consists of a single parable in which he forges the harem of the king of Wu into an army.[57] This story, among other lessons, uses the figures of women soldiers to show that the ideal combatant was not the bold warrior but the one who submitted totally to the discipline of his/her unit and the will of the commander.

Another link of combat to the feminine in the new theories of warfare stemmed from the calendrical model of combat associated with the rise of the *yin/yang* theory of the annual cycle. In this model, warfare was restricted to autumn and winter, the seasons of death, but also the period of the year when the feminine *yin* was in the ascendant, so the appearance of warfare was associated with the decline of the masculine and the rise of the feminine.

The disappearance of the fighting man as an actor on the field of battle, his absorption by the commander, and his transformation into an inanimate object, an animal, a child, or a woman all implied the denial of the ideal of the heroic, individual warrior that had animated the Zhou nobility. However, warriors and the ethic of individual heroism did not entirely vanish from the accounts of warfare in the military treatises, since they appeared as objects of criticism for carrying out reckless individual actions that threatened the harmony and obedience of the fighting men. The celebration of individual courage implicit in the heroic ideal challenged the unity of the army's collective body, so the centrality of the commmander entailed the negation of the warrior.

This denial of personal heroism took many forms. One argument, which will be discussed below, asserted that the true commander would not need to fight in order to subdue the enemy. Combat was an inferior form of warfare and a sign of failure. But the military texts also included explicit criticisms of heroism. The author of the *Wuzi* argued that Qin's soldiers could be defeated because their individual bellicosity caused the army to scatter easily.[58] The *Sun Bin bingfa* states that one could not gain victory through weapons or courage but only through the commander's knowledge of the Way of combat.[59] The *Sunzi* argued that one of the uses of banners, bells, and drums was to prevent the courageous from advancing on their own, a fault placed on the same level as that of the flight of cowards. Its list of the five types of men who posed a danger to the commander includes those who out of heroism are resolved on death, those of bellicose temperament who are readily provoked to battle, and those who out of excessive concern with personal integrity and honor can be goaded by insults to do battle. Its list of the six disasters that can befall an army includes the cases in which soldiers were more powerful and bellicose than their commanders, and in which officers were inclined to do battle on their own accord.[60]

The most frequent attacks on heroism appear in the *Wei Liaozi*. Early in the text, in a passage arguing that all proper military action must be based on the establishment of regulations, the author states:

> Of old the infantry had their detachments and the chariots their columns. When they beat the drums and waved the banners the first to mount [the walls] were invariably the powerful warriors of the state, so the first to die were also invariably the powerful warriors of the state. To lose one hundred of your men to kill a single enemy is to harm yourself in order to strengthen the foe.[61]

This explicitly attacked heroism as a form of self-destructive recklessness, and it associated such action with the armies of the past. A later passage denounced the aristocratic practice of provoking the enemy to battle through displays of individual daring and argued that such actions reduce the enemy's energy but cannot achieve victory. Still other passages criticized a general who would seek to demonstrate his own courage by recklessly attacking without proper preparation, and insisted that troops must always move in order and not be allowed to "struggle to be first." The text also stipulated that any moves not signalled by the banners and drums of the commander had to be punished by death, and it told the story of a man who boldly sprang out ahead of his fellows, killed two of the enemy, returned with them to his own lines, and was executed for his trouble.[62]

In several of these passages the target of criticism is not simply heroism in general but specifically the practices of the Zhou nobility in the field of battle. A few other passages in the military treatises also suggest criticisms of the aristocratic warfare of the Spring and Autumn period and hence imply attacks on the heroic ideal. Thus, the aforementioned criticisms of divination prior to a battle not only underscore the unquestioned authority of the general but also suggest the inadequacies of the noble warriors who regularly divined before a battle. Another example of such an implied criticism is the passage in the *Sunzi* which located in the ancestral temple the mathematical analysis of the relative strengths of opposing forces carried out prior to a campaign. In this way the author of the text symbolically supplanted the service of the ancestors, which was the organizing principle and justification of the old "heroic" warfare, with the calculating rationality of the new commander.[63]

The implacable opposition between the commander and the warrior is perhaps best expressed in a brief fable regarding Wu Qi.

Wu Qi was about to do battle, and his advisers presented him a sword. He said, "The commander only controls the banners and drums. In the face of difficulties he resolves all doubts. To command the troops and direct their blades, this is the role of the commander. To wield a single sword is not his role."[64]

Here the weapons of combat are explicitly rejected in the name of the banners and the drums, those embodiments of the commander's art through which the collective actions of the combatants were co-ordinated and given shape. Thus the very tools of the commander's craft demonstrated that his role was to integrate, to organize, and control. His authority lay not in killing but in creating order and pattern through a comprehensive knowledge of the field of battle and his complete control of the men-at-arms.

The Commander and Battle

The means by which the commander could conquer without a sword also formed one of the major themes of the treatises, and these discussions all centered on his ability to perceive an intelligible order in the uncertainty and flux of battle, and through this discovery of pattern to guide the unfolding of the campaign to the desired result. In his ability to perceive pattern in apparent chaos and then bring out that pattern in the service of his state, the general once again exemplified an aspect of the new forms of authority, that of the sage who benefited humanity through bringing hidden order and stability out of apparent chaos and flux. For the sake of this exposition, the actions of the commander on campaign will be divided into two aspects that roughly correspond to the realms of strategy and tactics: calculation before launching a campaign or encountering a foe, and evaluation and decision in the flux of battle. The first involved a variety of calculations to decide whether or under what circumstances victory could be obtained and allowed a general to decide where and when to give battle. The second entailed constant assessment of the dynamic tendencies of changing terrain and formations and then selecting the key moments for decisive action.

The calculations before battle are discussed in the greatest detail in the *Sunzi*. The first section of this work is entitled "Calculations," and it argues that by comparing the opposing sides in terms of a variety of factors—the degree of harmony between the rulers and their people, the correctness of the season, the skills of the commanders, and the advantages of terrain—one could know even before the campaign began who would win and who would lose. Before setting out on campaign the commander was to calculate arithmetically the respective advantages of the two sides in terms of these factors, and the side which obtained the higher total in the final tally would triumph.[65] As was noted above, this calculation took place in the ancestral temple, but rather than seeking the support of spirits, the new-style commander sought to impose his own "spirit" on the apparent obscurity of the imminent campaign through the technical analysis of those factors that the emergent "science" of combat held to be decisive.

The belief that victory could be mathematically calculated appears in another passage in the *Sunzi*.

The Earth [as the generator of objects] produces units, units produce measure, measure produces number, number produces relative weighing [i.e., with fixed units and numbers objects can be measured or "weighed" against one another], and relative weighing produces victory. A victorious army is like the weighing of pounds against ounces, while a defeated army is like the weighing of ounces against pounds.[66]

Because these preliminary reckonings were based on the calculation of relative advantage, they could not guarantee victory. Instead, the skilled commander could only avoid battle under unfavorable circumstances, guarantee that he would not be beaten, and wait until some mistake on the part of his adversary gave him the opening he required. Therefore the author argues, "Victory can be known, but it cannot be created."[67] Since he would only fight when victory was assured, the finest commander would not be renowned for his military skills.

If you win in combat and the world says, "Skillful," this is not the highest skill. You do not use great strength to lift the finest strand of fur, nor acuity of vision to see the sun and the moon, nor sharpness of hearing to hear thunder. Of old those who were called skillful in combat were those who defeated the easily defeated. Therefore the victory of him who is skilled in battle will win no fame for wisdom nor merit for courage. . . . Therefore he who is skilled in battle establishes himself in a position where he cannot be defeated, and does not let slip [the opportunity] to defeat the enemy. For this reason the victorious army first conquers and only then seeks to fight; the defeated army first fights and only then seeks to conquer.[68]

The true commander first assured himself of victory through calculation and maneuver and only then gave battle, so combat became the working out of forces and processes already thought through in the mind of the commander. As a result, action on the field of battle became a secondary phenomenon of no significance to the final outcome, and the combatants became shadow figures or puppets whose actions followed a script that had already been composed. In this way the theory of strategy in the *Sunzi* extended into the preparation for a campaign the same mastery of information and total control of pattern that ideally characterized the relation of the commander to his own troops, but on campaign this mastery and control had to be based on sage-like perceptions and calculations rather than simple regulations and training.

The *Sunzi* carried this displacement or de-centering of battle one step further by arguing that the highest victory was won when no battle took place.

Master Sun said, "Of all methods for using armies, the best is [to conquer] an intact state; to smash the state is second best. It is best [to capture] an army intact; to smash the army is second best. . . . Therefore to win all of your battles is not the highest skill. To bring the enemy's army to submit without combat is the highest skill. Therefore the best is to attack his stratagems and deliberations, the next best is to attack his system of alliances, the next best is to attack his army, and the worst is to attack his cities. . . . Therefore he who is skilled in the use of armies brings the enemy's army to submit and does not engage in combat."[69]

The principle that the true commander conquered without fighting or worked out the victory in his mind before giving battle appears in most of the military treatises and epitomized the new art of command.[70] It went beyond the mere denunciation of heroism and martial valor found in the discussions of training and formations, and instead proclaimed their complete disappearance from the realm of warfare. In this new ideal of battle all combatants were to be absorbed through training and regulations into the "collective body" at the disposal of the commander, and the struggle for victory became an intellectual duel between two figures. Ascendancy in war derived from proper discipline in the camp and correct calculation in the ancestral temple, and the carnage on the field of battle became a means by which the superior commander revealed the accuracy of his calculations to those who lacked sufficient insight to follow his reckonings without a demonstration. Battle was no longer the testing ground of prowess or honor for the glory of the lineage, but rather a blackboard on which the sage commander gave lessons to his less-gifted peers.

Although victory without battle was the highest achievement, in the event of a clash of arms the military treatises also provided a theory of tactics. The key terms in their analysis were "power of circumstances" (*shi* 勢), "dispositions" (*xing* 形), "expedient assessments" (*quan* 權), and the "pivots" (*ji* 機).[71] *Shi* meant "conditions" or "circumstances" in the dynamic sense. It indicated not a static arrangement or scene, but a fluid, dynamic configuration and its inherent tendency or inertia. In the military context *shi* referred to the power imparted to an army by the circumstances of the campaign: the lay of the land, the spirit of the troops, the condition of the enemy, and the dispositions of the two armies. Thus the *Sunzi* says that the means by which moving water can carry off boulders is *shi*. Water is weak and formless, while boulders are massive and immobile, but in the "circumstances" of moving rapidly in a channel water can sweep a boulder away. The power is not in the water itself but in the dynamism of the specific situation, and through the use of *shi* the commander could give his troops the "power of round boulders avalanching down a precipitous mountainside."[72]

The *shi* of a battle lay in those variable and dynamic factors over and above the number and strength of the troops, and it was through the manipulation of these factors that the commander could impose his cognitive powers on the field of battle. Thus the *Sun Bin bingfa* says, "Master Sun said, 'Military victory lies in the selection of suitable troops, courage lies in proper regulations, and skill lies in the *shi*.'" It also argues that skill in battle consists in "making the *shi* beneficial and taking advantage of the land."[73] The *Sunzi* explicitly states that the manipulation of *shi* overrode all questions of the individual courage or prowess of the soldiers.

> Number is the means by which one regulates chaos, *shi* is the means by which one makes the cowardly brave, and dispositions are the means by which one makes the weak strong.

> Therefore one skilled in war seeks [victory] through the *shi* and does not demand it of his men. He selects the men and exploits the *shi*.[74]

Here the manipulation of *shi* achieved in battle what training and the enforcement of regulations accomplished in the army, the imposition on the "outer" world of patterns first worked out in the mind of the commander.

The ability to manipulate *shi* had several elements. First, the commander had to assess the season, the terrain, and the foe. These were originally part of the calculation and manipulation that preceded or ideally supplanted the actual battle, but once in the field the commander's mental ability manifested itself through his powers of "expedient assessment" (*quan* 權). This word etymologically signified a horizontal balance and had the verbal meaning of "to weigh" or "to judge." Perhaps through extension it also came to mean that which was expedient to the moment as opposed to unchanging principle. In the military treatises it carried both these meanings and signified the commander's capacity to judge or assess the balance of forces and the dynamic tendencies in a given situation at a given moment and to select the appropriate action. Because of its root sense as a horizontal balance, *quan* often had the narrower meaning of an assessment or judgement based on the weighing of two opposed factors, such as "fear and shame" or "many and few," that would affect the conduct of battle.[75] The sense of "expedient" or "answering to the needs of the moment" is shown in various passages which associate *quan* with "change" (*bian* 變) or with the "extraordinary" (*qi* 奇).[76]

The situation examined through "expedient assessment" was to be analyzed into various polarities such as normative and extraordinary, empty and full, hard and yielding, far and near, many and few, or orderly and chaotic. The key to tactical success lay in the matching of opposites or complementaries one against the other.

> The concentrated overcomes the dispersed; the full overcomes the empty; those on the quickest path overcome those who follow the main road; the many overcome the few and the rested the weary.

The commander ascertained which of these "poles" characterized his opponent and then matched him with its correlate: concentrated where the foe was dispersed, taking short cuts where he followed the main roads, and sending fresh troops against weary ones.[77]

This reading of polarities and the matching of correlates was "expedient assessment," and its use distinguished the true commander from the incompetent in the new tactical doctrine. The *Sima fa* flatly proclaimed, "All war is expedient assessment."[78] The *Sun Bin bingfa* said, "The Way of military action has four [aspects]: formations, power of circumstances, changes, and expedient assessment."[79] The *Wei Liaozi* devoted separate sections to the expedient assessments of attack, those of defense, and those of warfare. It argued that expedient assessments were the means by which a commander obtained complete victory, and it used the phrase "attack through expedient assessment" to describe the methods of the good commander in contrast with the fool who left victory to chance. The phrase "bereft of expedient assessment" indicated total helplessness and defeat.[80]

The *Sunzi* briefly discussed the relationship between the prior strategic calculations and a commander's actions in the field, and this passage is particularly valuable because it links "calculations," "powers of circumstance," and "expedient assessments."

> If the calculations indicate benefit, then announce it. After that you manipulate the power of circumstances in order to assist it on the outside [in the field]. The phrase "power of circumstances" means to handle the expedient assessments in accord with the benefit [calculated].[81]

The calculations were performed within the temple and determined whether a war would be won or lost. This "internal" calculation then had to be assisted by an "outer" performance that manipulated the circumstances over the course of the campaign and on the field of battle. This manipulation was performed through expedient assessments of the changing situation.

Expedient assessment was not limited to intellectual analysis of a given situation; it had to be translated into action in order to take effect. The central act that translated assessment into successful maneuver was the identification of the "pivots" (*ji* 機). This word concretely signified the firing mechanism of the crossbow, but it had the more abstract meaning of a moment of change, or more precisely the moment just before a new development or a shift in direction became visible. These "pivots," which are also translated as "seeds" when applied to processes where an organic metaphor seems more suitable, constituted the nodal points of a situation in flux, and it was a characteristic of the "sage" or "superior man" to recognize them before they became manifest. Thus the "Da zhuan" of the *Yi jing* says:

> The Master said, "To know the pivots, that is divine [*shen* 神] indeed. . . . The pivots are the first, imperceptible beginning of movement, the first trace of good or bad fortune that shows itself. The superior man perceives the pivot and immediately acts. He does not wait for even a day."[82]

In any form of action dealing with a changing situation it was crucial to recognize these pivots of imminent change, to seize the moment of opportunity, and thereby to avail oneself of the natural flow or dynamic of any situation. However, these talents were particularly important in the flux and seeming chaos of battle.

He who listens to the most subtle will be able to hear that which has not yet reached the limit [either "come within the bounds of hearing" or "having reached its extreme and on the point of changing"]. He who looks at the newest will be able to see that which has no form. He who thinks of the most profound will be able to know that which has not yet begun. If you attack when men are frightened, they will be unable to measure [your strength]. If you move when you are in the ascendant, then you will gain their treasures.[83]

This passage posits an ability to seize upon tendencies or processes just before they appear or begin to change direction, and it links this capacity with success in warfare. The same linkage appears in the *Sunzi* in a discussion of the relation of the pivots to the power of circumstances.

When moving water reaches high speed it can toss around boulders. This is the power of circumstances. When the hawk reaches high speed it shatters the prey. This is proper timing. The force of circumstances for one skilled in warfare is like the narrows [of a river, i.e., the maximum of velocity and force], and he times his attack like one who is very close [to the object attacked, i.e., the maximum of precision]. The power of circumstances is like a drawn crossbow, and timing is like releasing the trigger [*ji*].[84]

This links up the ideas of the power of circumstances and the pivot to create a general model of tactical action. The crossbow, as the *Sun Bin bingfa* also argues, is the tangible image of the power of circumstances.[85] A cocked crossbow was a potential power, a force lying latent within the situation, but when unleashed at the correct moment it could kill a man at a great distance, and he would not even know who had slain him. The art of the commander in the midst of battle was to recognize the moment and "pull the trigger."

To recognize an opportunity and seize it was the fundamental act of the commander during a battle in progress, so the military treatises constantly reiterate that the commander must never "doubt" or "hesitate," that any failure to seize the moment of opportunity would lead to disaster.[86] Decisive action at the correct moment was the commander's highest tactical responsibility, for it determined the outcome of the battle.

> The commander raises the drum and lifts up his stick. He gazes on the difficulties and decides the battle. When troops meet and blades cross, if he drums at the correct [point] then he will be rewarded for his achievements and establish his fame. If he drums at the incorrect point, then he will die and the state perish. So rising or falling, security or danger lie at the tip of the commander's drumstick. How could one not treat the commander as crucial?[87]

What began in calculations at the ancestral temple and was extended through the analysis of circumstances in the field culminated in the choosing of the correct moment in the flux of battle to launch the decisive blow. In this way the military treatises enunciated a model of combat wherein the commander imposed his mental powers on each step of the campaign. Just as his regulations and commands forged the army into a collective body wherein each part was subservient to the pattern of the whole, so his sage-like powers of calculation and assessment allowed him to discover the meaningful pattern or order in the flux of the campaign and then use that pattern for his own purposes by skillful maneuver and decisive action at the proper moment. Through the arts of command the organizer of men also became an organizer of events, and the controlling "mind" of the army also brought order to the outer world of battle.

The Commander and the Ruler

The Warring States commander was a master of textual wisdom, an organizer who fashioned men into integrated parts of a co-ordinated whole to which he provided meaning and purpose through his powers of mind, and a sage who discovered the hidden patterns of the world and manipulated them to bring order out of the chaos of battle. However, as an official in the emergent territorial states he was also bound to the ultimate authority of the ruler. Warfare in the military treatises was an extension of statecraft, a means of expanding the power of the prince or preserving the social order through the suppression of rebels and criminals. The displacement of battle to a peripheral role and the ideal of victory without combat made sense only when these were means towards an end, actions in the service of an encompassing, political order no longer defined solely through sacrifice and warfare. That order was embodied in the person of the ruler, so any account of authority in War-

ring States military affairs must include the problem of the relation of
the commander to the ruler, of authority in the army to authority in the
state. This problem was particularly pressing in a society like Warring
States China, for when the army was identified with the people at large,
the command of the army potentially duplicated or supplanted the
ruling of the state.

At one level the relation of the commander to his ruler was simply
that of any official to his ruler, the subordination of lower to higher or
servant to master. However, the unique role of the commander as portrayed in the military treatises created certain anomalies that were not
easily reconciled with the normal roles of subordinate and superior.
First, since the commander was to be the unchallenged and absolute
leader of a force in the field, he was obliged to make frequent decisions
on matters of life and death without any recourse to the distant ruler.
The successful performance of his role required immediate and un-
hesitating reactions to situations in constant flux, and any factor that
blocked his freedom of decision or introduced an element of doubt or
hesitation into his mind could prove disastrous. While other officials
could be simple agents of the ruler's will, his organs of sense or his
limbs, the commander had to be ruler in his own sphere, a lesser sage
in the service of a greater. The reconciliation of these two authorities,
however, was problematic, because the virtues of the commander and
the principles that guided his actions potentially contradicted and undercut the virtues and principles of the ruler.

The roots of this contradiction lay in the theory of combat pro-
pounded by the military thinkers themselves. As was noted above, these
writers described the commander's evaluations and decision making as
the "balancing" (*quan*) of the dynamics of military encounters in terms
of various polar oppositions. The two most important of these were
those of "empty and full" (*xu-shi* 虛實) and "normative and extraordinary" (*zheng-qi* 正奇). The first of these pairs signified relative differen-
tials in numbers, concentration, or power. The "empty" might be a
weak point or gap in the enemy's defenses, or it might be a force of men
who could no longer fight due to lack of organization or of spirit. The
"full" meant just the opposite: a concentration of forces, a strong point,
or troops in proper fighting order and high spirits.

The distinction between "normative" and "extraordinary,"
however, was more subtle and more significant. The "extraordinary"
signified both the techniques of surprise and deception employed by
the commander and, by extension, military action in general. The
"normative" signified what was in accord with universal principle and
hence straightforward and morally correct.[88] As a correlate pair they
had no determinate content, but were rather a generalization or abstrac-

tion of the idea of polarity. The members of any opposed pair could be labeled "normative" and "extraordinary;" what distinguished them was their visibility or predictability. That which was obvious, straight-forward, and predictable was "normative," while that which was other than what it seemed, roundabout, or unexpected was "extraordinary." Of course, something which seemed totally straightforward and predict-able might have some hidden purpose which made it "extraordinary," and a trap or a surprise maneuver might be anticipated, in which case it became predictable and hence "normative." Thus the author of the *Sunzi* wrote:

> In all warfare you attain unity through the normative and conquer with the extraordinary. Therefore one who is skilled in producing extraordinary maneuvers will be endlessly fruitful like Heaven and Earth, and inexhaustible like the rivers. He will reach the end and then begin anew like the sun and moon. He will die and be reborn like the four seasons. There are only five notes, but their changes [i.e., possible combinations] are more than can be heard. There are only five colors, but their changes are more than can be seen. There are only five tastes, but their changes are more than can be tasted. The powers of circumstances available in warfare do not go beyond the extraordinary and the normative, but their changes cannot be exhausted. The extraordinary and the normative give birth to one another, like a cycle without end. Who could exhaust them?[89]

All the manipulations of the power of circumstances were here reduced to the alternation of the normative and the extraordinary, which means that the various polarities in terms of which situations were analyzed all fell within this single, overarching polarity. The extraordi-nary was the opposite of the normative, the formless that lay outside the formed, that which had not yet attacked when an attack took place.

> To respond to forms with forms is normative, but the formless which controls forms is extraordinary. The extraordinary and normative are inexhaustible; this is due to division. . . . Things which are identical cannot overcome one another, therefore one takes what is different as the extraordinary. Stillness is the extra-ordinary of motion, rest is the extraordinary of fatigue, fullness is the extraordinary of hunger, regulation is the extraordinary of chaos, multitude is the extraordinary of isolation. When you attack and these [the attackers] become the normative, then those who have not yet attacked are the extraordinary.[90]

As we saw above, the art of the commander in the field consisted entirely of the analysis and manipulation of these polarities, so the expedient assessment and manipulation of the *zheng* and the *qi* defined the nature of warfare. It was the character of this manipulation that led to the contradiction between the commander and the ruler. The clearest summation of this appears in the *Sunzi*.

> The military is the Way of deceit. Therefore if you are able then evince that you are unable. If you will use [a man] evince that you will not use him. If you are near evince that you are far. If you are far evince that you are near. If he seeks a benefit then tempt him. If he is in disorder then take him. If he is intact and solid then prepare against him. If he is strong then avoid him. Anger and confuse him. Pretend inferiority to make him arrogant. When he is at ease seek to tire him. When he is united seek to divide him. Attack where he has no precautions. Strike where he has not expected it. This is the victory of the military schools.[91]

The word here translated "deceit" (*gui* 詭) also had the sense of deviant or "contrary to the norm," and it was sometimes glossed with the synonym "extraordinary" (*qi*). Thus this passage once again defined military action as the way of the extraordinary, and it identified the manipulation of polarities with deceit. The commander sought to present a picture to his adversary which was the exact inverse of the truth. At the same time he sought to know the truth of his opponent's situation, to take precautions against it, and to strike at his opponent's weaknesses or manipulate his strengths into their opposite weaknesses. Warfare became a match of fraud and deceit in which victory hinged on duping the opponent while penetrating his prevarications. The ultimate level of this duel in the manipulation of circumstances lay in the control of the foe's perceptions; this is what was meant by "victory through attacking an opponent's deliberations." Since knowledge and judgement were the keys to victory in the new mode of warfare, military success lay in falsifying the enemy's knowledge while preserving one's own.

The *Dao de jing*, which either echoed or provided many of the basic ideas and rhetorical tropes of the military treatises, also spoke of conquering a foe through the play of oppositions and the pattern of reversal. Moreover, it asserted that the true Way was in some sense a Way of deception, since it always appeared to be the opposite of the actual case.[92] Although this text did not explicitly argue for victory through deception, it provided a powerful philosophical and rhetorical base for arguing that the path to victory had to be hidden and always ran counter to the precepts of conventional morality and wisdom. The deceit that underlay strategem and maneuver was the root of the contradiction between the commander and his ruler. I have translated *zheng* as "normative" because, in addition to the specifically military usage, it had the broader meaning of "correct" or "properly regulated" and could be synonymous with its homophone *zheng* (政), which meant "to regulate" or "govern." Another sometime homophone of virtually identical meaning (*zheng* 貞, also read *zhen*) could refer to the ruler who attained the highest Way.[93] Thus *zheng* was the characteristic action or virtue of the ruler, and the opposition of the normative and the extraordinary at the higher level expressed the contradiction between the ruler and the commander. This is why the *Dao de jing* and the *Sunzi* both spoke of ruling the state or uniting the army through the normative but conquering in battle through the extraordinary. The army was a social organization whose existence was possible only through those virtues that held together the state, and, as we saw in Chapter Two, it increasingly came to be identified with the state. The prince, whether as the moral exemplar of the Confucians or the distributor of rewards and punishments of the Legalists, could rule only if his commands and rules were trustworthy, so the deceit and treachery that defined the Way of the commander undercut the foundations of the Way of the ruler. Of course the military treatises also insisted that the commander had to be totally trustworthy in applying rewards and punishments to his own men, but the maneuvers, manipulations, and deceptions that constituted his art in the field made any claims to complete reliability impossible. Thus while it asserted that the extraordinary was the basis of all military action, the *Dao de jing* also called "extraordinary" any criminal action punishable by death.[94]

Warring States philosophers presented various solutions to resolve this contradiction between the good faith that was the basis of social existence and the deceit and guile that were the essence of the art of the commander in the field. For purposes of exposition these solutions can be divided into two groups. One group advocated the sequestration of the military into a distinct realm characterized by its own virtues, rituals, clothing, and authority, while the other denied the utility of any deceit and insisted that a properly-governed state would conquer without recourse to the "extraordinary" strategems of the military treatises.

The first position appears in the *Dao de jing* and in the military treatises, with the exception of the *Wuzi*. The *Sunzi*, which insisted on the fundamental importance of deceit in warfare, also argued that the commander in the field could not be controlled by the ruler. Once he had taken command of the army, he was to be master in his own realm and should ignore orders from the state's ruler.[95] The prince could not know all the details and the sudden changes of a military campaign, and the principles that directed action within the state differed from those that guided an army. Consequently, the ruler was not to interfere with a general in the field, and to do so would lead to disaster.

This separation of the army in the field from the state and the independence of the commander were marked by a ceremony described in the military treatises and in various Han texts. The *Liu tao* relates that after divining for an auspicious day and fasting, the ruler met the commander in the ancestral temple.

> The ruler personally took the ax by its head and presented the handle to the commander, and then said, "From here upward to Heaven you shall regulate it." He took a second ax and presented the handle to the commander and said, "From here downward to the [Yellow] Springs [realm of the dead] you shall regulate it. If you see a weakness advance, but if they are strong then stop. Do not take the enemy lightly because of the size of your army. Do not be resolved on death because of the gravity of my charge. . . . Do not sit until the soldiers have sat. Do not eat until they have eaten. Share the cold or the heat with them. If you act like this then the mass of soldiers will fight to the death."
>
> Having received the charge, the commander bowed and replied, "I have heard that a state cannot be ruled from the outside and an army cannot be controlled from the inside. A man of divided mind cannot serve the ruler, and a man whose resolve is in doubt cannot respond to the enemy. Having received your charge, the awesome power of the axes pertains solely to me. I will not dare to return alive. I desire that you grant one more charge to me, and if you do not agree then I will not dare to command. I will not obey your commands but all orders will come from me. When I meet the enemy and decide to fight, I will have an undivided mind. In this way then I will have no Heaven above, no Earth below, no enemy in front, and no prince behind."[96]

In addition to the oral proclamation of the independence of the general in the field, the ceremonial presentation of the axes itself also marked the status of the commander as a ruler in his own domain, for these weapons were symbols of the power to punish, and their bestowal signified that the general wielded legal powers of life and death over his men in the field. As he also held the right to grant them titles and ranks for success in battle, the general exercised those very powers of reward and punishment that defined the ruler in legalist political theory.[97]

The *Dao de jing* and the *Sima fa zhijie* also insisted on a strict division in law and ritual between the army and the state. The former text argued that rituals pertaining to war, just like rituals of mourning, should invert the standard hierarchies of civil society. The latter stipulated that the apparel, language, and rituals of the army had to be distinguished from those of civil society, and that the forms of one sphere could not be permitted to enter the other.[98] These ritual distinctions between the military and the civil spheres highlighted the independence of the commander from the orders of the ruler and reinforced the idea of the army as a separate realm distinguished by its own values and rules of conduct. At the head of the state the ruler had to uphold the normative order of civilized life, while in the army the commander held sway as the official of death and the master of deceit. The ruler presided over the higher sphere, the realm of morality and social order, but this could survive only by nourishing within itself a realm of expedience, treachery, and death.

This separation of the army from civil society did not exist solely in theory, for the historical records indicate that the military camp and the army in the field were in fact legally and ritually separated from the state, and that in the army the orders of the state's ruler often yielded to those of the commander.[99] Although most of the examples of this practice date from the Warring States period, there are instances of the commands of the general taking precedence over those of the Han emperor in a military camp, and Emperor Wu of the Han accepted the separation of the camp from civil society as a fixed legal precedent.

Another line of thought denied the need for, or even the possibility of, a separate military realm with values and hierarchies opposed to those of civil society. This position was associated with the Confucian and Legalist schools, who, despite their many points of conflict, were both defenders of the unquestioned supremacy of a ruler who upheld the social order through proper laws or appropriate rituals. A few thinkers evoked a utopian world under an ideal ruler where violence had no role, but most of them, like Xun Kuang in the passage quoted in Chapter Two, argued that successful military action stemmed from the unified will of the people under a virtuous ruler, and that in a well-governed state there was no need for the deceits and maneuvers of the military thinkers. If the ruler bound the people together through the familial bonds of obedience and affection and the social ties of shame and mutual trust, then they would fight as one man to the death, and none would be able to defeat them. In the "separatist" argument the commander and the army maintained an independent existence within the encompassing social order, but in this second argument the commander disappeared entirely into the figure of the sage-ruler and the army into the social fabric of the state. The authors of the *Sunzi, Sun Bin, Wei Liaozi,* and *Liu tao* all recognized the amoral character of their teachings when they spoke of the "extraordinary" or the "Way of deceit," but they argued that this restricted deviance was necessary for the survival of a higher virtue. In contrast, the defenders of the ideal of an absolute, morally potent ruler dismissed all stratagems, expediency, and deceit as unnecessary aberrations that jeopardized the good faith and mutual trust on which human society and military organization were based. The ruler simply had to hold to his Way, and all else would follow.

Although this theory of proper warfare as a direct extension of the values that created human society was closely associated with the Confucian school, it did not appear in the sayings attributed to Confucius himself. A few passages ascribed to "the Master," however, already suggest the lineaments of a theory of warfare based on a people morally united through the virtue of the ruler. Thus he argued that rites, music, and warfare must all proceed from the Son of Heaven or the state would perish.[100] This proposition, still based on the old social model in which warfare and sacrifice were the two "great services" that defined the state, asserted that military operations must be tied into state ritual and stem directly from the highest ruler. Other passages argued that any warfare had to be based on the "instruction" of the people, a term which certainly included moral instruction.

The Master said, "If a good man will instruct the people for seven years, then they likewise [?] may go to war."

The Master said, "To go to war without instructing the people is to throw them away."

Finally, one passage, though not explicitly dealing with war, suggests a clear judgement on the relative value of a skillful commander and a resolved, united populace.

The Master said, "The commander of a state's army can be carried off, but you cannot carry off the will of even a common man."[101]

This assertion of the invincibility of human resolve and the vulnerability of even the most heavily-guarded individual suggests that the most secure defense is the good will and support of the people.

The *Yanzi chun qiu* clearly articulated the idea that the armed power of the state was based on the virtue of the ruler and secured through the unanimous support of the people. When the lord of Qi planned to invade Lu, Master Yan sought to dissuade him thus:

I have heard it said that when attacking others, if your virtuous potency is sufficient to secure your state and your regulations sufficient to harmonize your people, only then can you raise troops and attack the willfully violent. . . . It would be best to cultivate your regulations and wait until [Lu] is in disorder. Only when the ruler is divided [from his people] and the superiors harbor grudges against their subordinates can you attack them.[102]

Both the justification of war and the means of carrying it out lay in the sphere of social relations. A properly-governed people was the basis of military power, and failures in moral government both justified an attack and guaranteed its success. The virtues of the ruler manifested in government policies led to success on the field of battle just as they did within the walls of the capital. The cunning manipulations of the commander and the separate hierarchies and values of the army were not explicitly condemned in this passage, but through silence they were dismissed as inessential and potentially harmful.

Mencius, the most forthright pacifist in ancient China, tended to reject war as a totally unnecessary evil, and in place of discussions of the role of the military he offered such nostrums as, "If the ruler of a state loves benevolence he will have no enemy [or 'match'] in the world."[103] However, to the extent that he acknowledged the possibility of warfare he followed the "Confucian" position and argued that the virtues of the ruler eliminated any need for a commander or a specifically military wisdom. Thus in the sentence immediately preceding the one quoted above he says, "There are those who say, 'I am skilled in making formations,' or 'I am skilled in making war.' These are great criminals." While dismissing strategists and military professionals as criminals, he made one extended argument on the proper means of warfare.

The seasons of Heaven are not as important as the benefits of Earth. The benefits of Earth are not as important as human harmony. . . . Therefore it is said, "People are not bounded in by the limits of dikes and borders. A state is not secured by the difficult terrain of mountains and rivers. All under Heaven are not overawed by the excellence of weapons and armor." He who attains the Way will have many help him, while he who loses the Way will have few help him. When the paucity of helpers reaches its extreme, then even his relatives turn against him. When the abundance of helpers reaches its extreme, then all under Heaven obey him. If one who is obeyed by all under Heaven attacks one who is abandoned by his own relatives, [how could he lose?] So the noble man will usually not engage in warfare, but if he does he will inevitably triumph.[104]

Mencius here presented the ability of the ruler to secure the support of the people as a form of weapon that guaranteed his victory in a way that no advantages of terrain or military technique could match. Purely military considerations were again rejected and condemned in the name of the powers of the ruler.

Although it is a military treatise, the *Wuzi* also exhibits certain features of the "Confucian" theory of warfare, and indeed this text was traditionally linked to the Confucian school.[105] It divided military action into five categories, and the highest was the army of social rectitude (*yi bing* 義兵) while the two lowest were military action of deceit and expedient assessment, i.e., the modes of combat advocated by most military treatises. It insisted on harmony among the people of the state as the basis of all military actions and suggested that if the ruler could achieve the proper hierarchy within the state, then the formations in the army would already be fixed. The text also stressed the need for ritual and "instruction" before the ruler could employ the army, and it called its ideal army "father and son troops," troops held together by the ties of obedience and affection that united families. Finally, it placed much greater stress on the skills and heroism of the individual soldiers than other military treatises, a fact that reflected the Confucian emphasis on the ruler and the people at the expense of the commander.[106]

The Confucian school's attack on the philosophy of the military treatises culminated in the essay "Yi bing" in the writings of Xun Kuang, the opening section of which was quoted at length in Chapter Two. In this staged debate, which in the manner of some Platonic dialogues rapidly changes into a lecture, a fictive exponent of the military schools insisted that successful warfare depended on a skillful commander who manipulated the circumstances of season, geography, and the enemy's dispositions through his powers of transformation and deception. Against this, Xun Kuang presented the ideal of the army of the true king, which through its complete unity and devotion to the ruler lay beyond the machinations of the skillful commander. This portrayal of the military theorists was a serious distortion, for they always insisted on the necessity of unquestioned good faith and social harmony, goals which could be obtained only through the state's having proper laws and the ruler's having the true Way. However, by eliding the shared insistence on *ultimate* encompassment within a moral order, Xun Kuang highlighted the contrasts and gave dramatic expression to the fundamental point of dispute: the question of the need for a separate sphere of specifically military values and methods.

In denying the need for such a separate realm, Xun Kuang gave the definitive formulation of the nature of warfare under the Confucian sage emperor. When, three centuries later, the devout Confucian Ban Gu wrote an account of the history of warfare in his *Han shu*, he rejected the entire tradition of the military treatises and the related writings of the rhetoricians of alliance. Alone among the Warring States writers on warfare, he claimed, Xun Kuang understood the truth.[107] He alone knew that the highest warfare was not distinguished from the highest statecraft and that under the true king the order and conduct of the army were simply an extension of those of civil society.

As exponents of an all-encompassing state based on a rigorous system of laws, the Legalists were also loath to grant any independent sphere to the methods espoused in the military treatises. For them the army was the primary form of organizing the people, so the techniques that preserved social order also maintained discipline in the army and no separate military arts were needed. Thus the essay "Bing fa" in the *Shang Jun shu* begins:

> All methods of warfare must be based on success in government. Then the people will not quarrel, and if they do not quarrel they will have no private thoughts and take the ruler's thoughts as their own.

And the next chapter begins:

> In all cases of using troops, victory has three stages. When the army has not yet been mobilized then establish laws. When the laws have been established they become customs. When they have become customs then one prepares provisions and implements. . . . Those who rely on numbers are said to be "thatching" [like thatch on a roof, numerous but easily scattered]. Those who rely on equipment are called "artful." Those who rely on the [manipulation of] hearsay and vision are called "deceitful" [*zha* 詐 —the defining virtue of the military Way in the *Sunzi*]. If one relies on any of these three, the army can be taken. Therefore it is said, "The strong are those who make firm their resolve to fight." . . . Therefore it is said, "The differences in troops are produced by the regulations [of the state]." . . . For this reason the strong are inevitably the well-regulated, and the well-regulated are inevitably the strong.[108]

These passages would not look amiss in Xun Kuang's denunciation of the military philosophers and his defense of the Way of the ruler as the key to victory. Both of them share the belief that since the army was identical with the people, those virtues which created civil society created the army, and the principles of proper government were the principles of military command.

The same suspicion of military thinkers appears in the *Han Feizi*.

After attacking the Mohists, Confucians, and the "wandering swords-men," he proceeds:

> Within the borders everyone speaks of troops, and many families store the books of Sun Wu and Wu Qi, but the troops grow weaker. This is because many speak of warfare, but those who wear armor are few. Therefore the enlightened ruler uses their strength and does not listen to their speech. He rewards their meritorious acts and bans that which is of no use. Therefore the people will exert their strength to the death to follow their ruler.[109]

Not only did the military treatises offer useless techniques that threatened the all-important regulations of the state, but they lured the common people away from the universal military service which was the true source of the state's strength. The military philosophers were lumped together with all the competing schools as those who diverted the common people from their true callings of warfare and agriculture, so the writings of Sun Wu, Wu Qi, and the rest did not escape the ban that Qin placed on the private dissemination of the teachings of the "Hundred Schools."[110]

This debate over the relation of the commander to the ruler and of the army to the state was ultimately an outgrowth of the correlated rise of mass armies and military "professionalism." The appearance of military specialists and technical treatises reflected the increasing complexity and sophistication of the methods of organization and combat that accompanied the development of mass, infantry armies. As men came to hold or claim positions of authority on the basis of technical proficiency, they inevitably asserted autonomous authority within their realm of expertise. However, in a society where the entire state had been fashioned on the basis of military mobilization, claims for the autonomy of expertise in the realm of warfare presented a challenge to the authority of the states' rulers and their civil hierarchies. Moreover, for the philosophers who asserted that social order depended on the trustworthiness of the ruler in his rituals or punishments, the claims to autonomy of an art based on manipulation and deceit were clearly unacceptable. This tension is reflected in the history of the Han officer corps, where the powerful, semi-independent commanders of the military elite of the civil war and early decades were gradually supplanted by agents of the court with no military expertise, and military command ultimately became the province of imperial affines and courtiers chosen for their obedience rather than their skill.[111] This triumph of the apologists for autocracy over the claims of expertise initiated both the long-term devaluation of military command in China and the emergent ideal of the literary man who was able when necessary to bring his general intellectual skills to bear on military command.

Conclusion

In association with the rise of territorial states and mass armies, the management of warfare increasingly became the province of organizational and technical specialists. Together with this development there appeared a body of writings which elaborated the tactical doctrines of these emerging military professionals and also formulated a general philosophy of the conduct of battle and the relation of warfare to the political order. As the army was the chief mechanism of state formation and the primary means of social control, the patterns or attributes of command in the army became models or exemplars for authority in the new political order. These attributes included three features: 1) the commander as a master of texts, 2) the commander as an organizer or integrator of men who created social bodies wherein each part had meaning only within the whole, and that meaning was ultimately located in the mind of the leader, 3) the commander as a sage who could discern hidden patterns in chaos and use these patterns to achieve order and success in collective actions.

The ideal of the commander as a master of texts reflected the fact that the new officers rose to positions of authority on the basis of the technical expertise or the skill in commanding men that was expounded in the numerous military treatises. As such it was part of the general process of creating a new bureaucratic state apparatus through the recruitment of servants on the basis of their presumptive skills, and the bearers of these skills were attached to the ruler by ties of dependence created through bonds.

The claims of text-based expertise to underlie military success also presented a conscious critique of the heroic ideal of the declining Zhou nobility, whose warfare had been a theater of prowess and heroism. This critique was expressed most clearly in a body of tales in which weak, immartial, or even crippled men defeated great warriors or powerful armies through the esoteric skills transmitted in revealed military texts. In asserting the primacy of the new techniques of commanding masses of men, these stories explicitly denied the value of the military prowess that had been central to warfare and authority under the old aristocracy.

One major aspect of these new techniques was the forging of large numbers of individual soldiers into a single, collective body with the commander acting as its mind. This was to be achieved through unwavering rigor in the enforcement of regulations and through winning over the men by sharing the conditions of their material existence. The image of the army as a body also reflected the specialization of roles and integration of differentiated parts that characterized the new mass armies. The lowest meaningful military unit was the five-man squad, which combined a variety of long and short weapons. The squad could function as a fighting unit only so long as the weapons were effectively co-ordinated, so the individual fighting man had no role outside the squad. These squads in turn formed parts of larger units of twenty-five men, and these units were combined and manipulated in "formations" which were treated as the key to victory in both military treatises and general philosophical works. Thus the new practice and theory of warfare not only denied the value of individual heroism but also granted the individual soldier a role or purpose only as a co-ordinated element in a larger whole. Since the armies of the period included the entire free adult population and the units in the field were composed of fellow townsmen in civil society, this emphasis on discipline and the subordination of the individual to the group would have played a major role in imposing authoritarian control throughout all levels of society.

The other major aspect of the new art of command was the ability of the general's mind to work out the balances, tendencies, or patterns that lay hidden under the seeming chaos of a campaign, and to use his grasp of this concealed intelligibility to guarantee victory. This mental control of warfare consisted of analyzing the relative strengths and positions of the two sides before setting out, assessing the relative advantages of circumstance and the dispositions in the field, devising "extraordinary" maneuvers and deceits to render the enemy helpless, and striking at the decisive moment to attain victory. This ability to recognize patterns hidden to others and use them to create order out of chaos was one of the central attributes of the sage, and, as will be shown in Chapter Six, generals were regularly described in terms of sagehood.

This final aspect of the new art of command, however, placed the authority of the general at odds with that of the ruler of the state. In order to carry out his role in the field as described in the military treatises, the commander needed freedom from the shackles of both obedience to the ruler and observance of the basic virtues of sincerity and good faith that underlay the social order. Since these virtues were essential to any collective existence, the military commander was lacking in one primary element necessary to the survival of social authority, and consequently he was ultimately dependent on encompassment within a higher moral or legal order which could underwrite his ties to his troops. However, the Confucians and other advocates of the absolute ruler who embodied this order saw in the claims of the military philosophers to a limited autonomy for their realm of deceit and death a challenge to the basic principles of human society. While they accepted the occasional necessity of violence, these advocates of the supremacy of the monarch and social duties could not sanction actions or values that tore up the bonds of obedience and trust which maintained all hierarchies. Their objections are expressed neatly by a modern political observer and moralist.

> Obviously one does not want to inflict death and wounds if it can be avoided, but I cannot feel that mere killing is all-important. We shall all be dead in less than a hundred years, and most of us by the sordid horror known as "natural death". The truly evil thing is to act in such a way that peaceful life becomes impossible. War damages the fabric of civilization not by the destruction it causes . . . nor even by the slaughter of human beings, but by stimulating hatred and dishonesty . . .
>
> What has always seemed to me one of the most shocking deeds of the last war [World War I] was one that did not aim at killing anyone—on the contrary, it probably saved a great many lives. Before launching their big attack at Caporetto, the Germans flooded the Italian army with faked socialist propaganda leaflets in which it was alleged that the German soldiers were ready to shoot their officers and fraternise with their Italian comrades, etc etc. Numbers of Italians were taken in, came over to fraternise with the Germans, and were made prisoner—and, I believe, jeered at for their simple-mindedness. I have heard this defended as a highly humane and intelligent way of making war—which it is if your sole aim is to save as many skins as possible. And yet a trick like that damages the very roots of human solidarity in a way that no mere act of violence could do.[112]

This observation captures perfectly the criticisms of the Confucians and the Legalists. Violence was a regrettable but necessary aspect of life, but the strategems and deceits by which the military philosophers promised to reduce violence wreaked even greater damage on the fabric of human society than any physical brutality. Thus at the same time that the new specialists in the methods of warfare were proclaiming a separate realm of military expertise, moralist and statist thinkers defended the incorporation of sanctioned violence into the social order through the bonds and laws imposed by the ruler, and rationalized the ruler's recourse to violence through appeals to the imitation of Heaven.

Chapter Four

COSMIC VIOLENCE

The Zhou aristocracy had rationalized and justified their patterns of sanctioned violence and political authority as forms of service to the ancestral cult. The new territorial lords, by contrast, defended their use of violence both as a means of upholding the social order through punishments and, above all, as an expression of the divine or natural patterns that informed the cosmos. The simultaneous emergence of absolute, unchallenged monarchs and of a mode of correlative thinking that systematically related the human community to the natual order led to the identification of the actions and powers of the ruler with those of Heaven itself, and these developments included a set of theories, institutions, and rituals that equated the sovereign's use of warfare or punishments with the violence of Heaven and the natural world.[1] These ideas and practices claimed a cosmic sanction for the new political order forged through the development of universal military service, personal bonds of devotion, and the hierarchic ties marked by vengeance and sacrifice. They thus formed a central element in the creation of the absolutist state and in the presentation of the monarch as a semi-divine figure responsible for maintaining the social order.

The attempts to link human violence to the natural order centered on the aforementioned "calendrical" model of statecraft in which warfare, hunting, and punishments were tied to the "killing" seasons of the year. The rulers of early imperial China institutionalized this model in the practice of "watching for the ethers" to detect the shifts in cosmic energy underlying the annual cycle, and in the construction of a ritual calendar based on the alternation of seasons of growth and decline. In addition to the seasonal rituals of violence, the emperors also staged ceremonial games of cosmic kickball that combined military training with a representation of the annual cycle. Yet another element of ritual designed to demonstrate the cosmic character of imperial rule and the ties of human violence to nature was the staging of great hunts or smaller-scale animal combats in specially designed hunting parks and animal pens. Finally, the military training rituals of the tenth month and the beginning of the New Year season included wrestling contests that interlinked feats of strength and sorcery. These matches combined aspects of military training with demonstrations of the control of animals and the forces of nature in the same manner as did the animal combats held in the special pens. In all these rituals and contests the participants were servants, barbarians, criminals, and even beasts, while the emperor and his agents appeared as the human images of Heaven, incorporating violence and death into the overarching patterns of the cycle of calendrical time and the hierarchy of living creatures. Thus the rituals of cosmic violence asserted the same model of authority as did the art of the commander—for the power to rule was identified with drawing individually meaningless parts into a coherent whole—but they tied this image of governance into the very structure of the universe.

The Calendar of Violence

By the third century B.C., virtually all Chinese authors recognized correspondences between the realms of nature and of man, and they consequently insisted that the true ruler must model himself on Heaven or the cosmic Way. This proposition meant different things to writers of the various philosophical schools, but they all shared a common and deep-rooted belief in the intimate linkage of cosmic principles, astral events, and earthly government. This belief was reflected in the close ties of observational astronomy and the calendrical sciences to political power that emerged in Warring States China and lasted into the present century.

The ties between the calendar and political authority in China are both ancient and wide-ranging. The concern of China's rulers with the calendar actually dates back at least to the Shang kings, who divined frequently regarding the appropriate day for sacrifices to various ancestors and gradually developed an elaborate calendar to regularize these offerings. The very first chapter of the *Shang shu* contains the commission of the sage-king Yao to his astronomers to "compute and delineate" the movements of the celestial bodies so that the people might receive their proper seasons, and this suggests that by the Warring States period the establishment of the calendar was regarded as a fundamental duty or privilege of the government. This concern with calen-

dars and the natural cycle was carried into the realm of official historiography, for the oldest surviving history in China is the "Springs and
Autumns," an annual chronicle of the state of Lu from 723 to 468 B.C.
which consists of a season-by-season listing of major political events
along with astronomical phenomena. This work provided a model for
the later imperial dynastic histories, which began with a section of "fundamental records" (ben ji 本紀) that presented the reign of each emper-
or in a chronological sequence subdivided according to year and month,
with relevant astronomical and meteorological events interspersed
among the decrees and memorials. The influence of the calendar as an
image of organization and control had become so great by the late third
century B.C. that when the chief minister of Qin, Lü Buwei, sponsored
the official compilation of a work to explain "all matters pertaining to
Heaven, Earth, and the myriad things" he organized it according to the
divisions of the calendar and called it *The Springs and Autumns of Master Lü* (*Lü Shi chun qiu* 呂氏春秋). Later ritualists adopted the first
section of this work into the "monthly ordinances" which stipulated the
deportment and policies of the emperor for each month of the year, and
this document became the basis for the organization of imperial violence
in accord with the seasons.

The basic principle of these ordinances and the calendrical organization of government was that the actions of the ruler had to accord
with the "activities" of nature characteristic of each season. Official actions pertaining to violence and death, i.e., hunting, punishments, and
warfare, were to be restricted to the killing time of the year, the autumn
and the winter. As was noted in Chapter Two, this theory reflected the
institutional nature of the new states that were based on the levy of
military service and taxes from the peasant population, but it was also
tied to the development of a cosmology based on the alternation of *yin*
and *yang* and the cycle of the "five phases." In these theories autumn
and winter were the seasons when *yin* was in the ascendant, when the
"punishing power" waxed strong, the earth lay still and dormant, and
Heaven itself took life. At this time the ruler, who modeled himself on
Heaven, had also to engage in murder.

> The Son of Heaven in the autumn commands the three lords to
> take select officials and sharp weapons to punish the unrighteous,
> judge legal cases, fix punishments, and hasten the collection of
> taxes, in order to follow the Way of Heaven and assist in the
> autumn killing.[2]

To better correlate the actions of the ruler with the natural cycle
that underlay the change of the seasons, the ritualists of the Han court

employed the technique of "watching for the ethers" (*wang qi* 望氣).
This practice was based on the beliefs that the annual cycle was produced by cyclic alternation within the *qi* (氣), a formless energy that
underlay all physical existence, and that this cycle could be traced
through the mutual interaction between the *qi*, the seasonal winds in
China, and music. The bases for these beliefs are discussed in Chapter
Six, so here it is sufficient to note that wind was regarded as the tangible
form of *qi* and music as a controlled, intelligible wind. Consequently,
shifts in the character of the cosmic *qi* would affect the properties of
musical tones. The twelve tones that defined the Chinese musical gamut
corresponded to the twelve months of the year, and these tones were
defined by a set of twelve pitchpipes of specified lengths. These pitchpipes, in turn, were divided into six *yang* "*lü*" (律) and six *yin* "*lü*" (呂).
The cyclic alternation through the notes of the gamut thus corresponded
to the alternating cycle of *yin* and *yang* that underlay the changes of the
seasons, so the monthly changes in the cosmic *qi* could be traced by the
shifting resonances of the twelve pitchpipes.

The actual technique of "watching for the ethers," which involved
inserting twelve pipes blocked with dirt into the ground in a sealed
chamber and noting when the dirt in each pipe was dislodged by the
"ether" (*qi*) circulating through the earth, has been described in detail
elsewhere and need not concern us here.[3] More central to the subject at
hand is the fact that the Han Chinese regarded this technique as an
aspect of military affairs. Thus Sima Qian justified including a chapter
on the pitchpipes in his great history with the argument that none could
be strong without the military, and that a discussion of the pipes revealed the arts of such ancient sage-conquerors as the Yellow Emperor,
King Tang, and King Wu, as well as military thinkers like Tai Gong, Sun
Wu, and Wu Qi. Although Sima Qian's original chapter was lost, the
current version is a Han replacement that still clearly reflects the ideas
of the period. Its opening passage defends the importance of the pitchpipes through an extended discussion of the principles of warfare and a
sketch of the history of combat.

> When kings regulate state affairs and establish laws, mea-
> sures, and regulations, they act solely in accord with the six pitch-
> pipes. The six pitchpipes are the fundamental root of the myriad
> affairs of state. They are especially important in the use of
> weapons, so they say, "On gazing at the enemy from afar one
> knows the outcome of the battle; on hearing the tone one knows
> victory and defeat." This is the unchanging way of the hundred
> kings.
> When King Wu attacked Zhou, he blew on the pitchpipes

and listened to the tones from the first month until the twelfth. The killing *qi* joined together [i.e., the *qi* of the season and the musical note corresponded], and the sounds exalted the *gong* note. That the same sounds should elicit one another is the natural course of objects; what is remarkable in this?

Weapons are the means by which the sage makes obedient the powerful and savage, brings stability to times of chaos, levels roadblocks and obstructions, and rescues those in mortal danger. When beasts with fangs and horns are attacked they will strike back; how much more so man, who harbors the *qi* of liking, disgust, joy, and anger! If he is joyful then a loving heart arises, but when angry he will have a poisonous sting. These are the basic principles of human nature.

Long ago the Yellow Emperor fought the battle of Zhuolu to settle the disaster of fire; Zhuan Xu had the battle with Gong Gong to settle the disaster of water; Cheng Tang had the battle at Nanchao to extirpate the chaos of Xia. They rose and fell in sequence, the victor governing the affairs of state. This was received from Heaven.

After this, famous warriors successively arose: Jin used Jiu Fan, Qi used Wangzi, and Wu used Sun Wu. They had preternatural comprehension of military covenants and their rewards and punishments never failed. They reduced the rulers and feudal lords to common soldiers and swallowed up the territory of their states. Although they could not match the proclamations and oaths of the Three Dynasties, they were themselves favored and their lords were honored. They were eminent and praised in their own day; how could we not call this glory? . . . Therefore instruction and corporal punishment cannot be abandoned in the household, mutilating punishments cannot be relinquished in the state, and killing expeditions cannot be halted under Heaven. It is simply that in using them some are skillful and some clumsy, in carrying them out some are in accord [with Heaven] and some against it.

Jie of Xia and Zhou of Yin [legendary evil monarchs] wrestled wolves with their bare hands and raced horses with their feet; their courage was not small. They won a hundred battles, and the feudal lords submitted in fear; their power was not light. Er Shi of Qin stationed his army on useless land and lined his soldiers along the entire frontier; his force was not weak. He battled the Xiongnu [in the far north] and blocked the harm done by the Yue [in the far south]; he did not lack power. But his awesomeness was exhausted and his power used up, and the people of his own alleys and side-streets became an enemy state. This disaster arose because in bellicosity he knew no sufficiency, and in delighting in gain he never ceased.[4]

I have quoted this introduction at length because it neatly encapsulates the theory of violence as an expression of the natural order which may be attained in human society through the agency of the cosmically potent sage-emperor. It begins with the bold statement that the pitchpipes provide the standard for all proper government but are of particular importance in military matters, and the rest of the passage is in fact devoted entirely to the defense of warfare and punishments as central to the political order. Since the pitchpipes were significant solely in terms of the calendrical model of government, this argument shows the crucial role of military affairs and sanctioned violence in general to the emergence of this theory.

Having noted the importance of observing *qi* and quoted a popular saying on its use, the author switches to a specific example of proper military action guided by the use of pitchpipes, King Wu's defeat of the Shang and establishment of the Zhou dynasty. The role of the pitchpipes was to choose the correct time for action, and the span involved was one full annual cycle with military action falling correctly in the winter season. In this way the use of the pitchpipes brought military action into harmony with the natural cycle and thereby assured success.

The writer next asserts the necessity and social correctness of violence. He locates the origins of violence in the outer world of nature, as suggested by the model of the beasts, and in the inner nature of human beings, as an expression of the anger experienced by all. After identifying violence as a tool of the sages, he traces it back to the primal battle of the Yellow Emperor at Zhuolu—which will be discussed in detail in Chapter Five—and then shows how it was used by each of the sage-kings in turn. Proceeding to historical times, he lists examples of great commanders who, while falling short of the sages, served their states and won glory for their lords, and he excoriates the naivete of the bookish pedants of his own day who condemn warfare under any circumstances.

Finally, in order to distinguish correct warfare from incorrect, he cites the examples of the legendary evil monarchs of antiquity and of the historical fall of Qin. He begins by pointing out that these rulers were bold warriors who commanded powerful armies, but neither the strength of warriors nor the force of numbers constituted true military prowess. Proper war, according to this author, was the war of the sages, and the hallmark of such war was the imitation of Heaven through the use of the pitchpipes to bring human combat into line with the patterns of nature. By contrast with the sages who fought in the proper seasons, the evil monarchs knew no limits. They fought not only in the seasons of death and punishment but also in those of growth and harvest, so their strength remained unreplenished and was ultimately exhausted. Thus the only systematic discussion of warfare in the *Shi ji*, which is identical in theme if not wording to Sima Qian's original chapter, argued that warfare was necessary and proper to the true ruler, but that it had to accord with the patterns of Heaven as revealed in the annual cycle of nature. This theory of warfare formed a central element in the military thought of the period, for one of the four categories of military treatises in the bibliographic chapter of the *Han shu* was those writings based on "*yin* and *yang.*" The chapter listed sixteen titles under this rubric and its description of them said:

> They set out in accord with the seasons, carry out the punishing virtue [this potent virtue came in the autumn and was sent off at the New Year festival. It marked the autumn and winter as the seasons for warfare, punishments, and any correct killing.] and follow the Dipper to attack. They rely on the assistance of ghosts and spirits.[5]

This is a succinct sketch of the theory of warfare outlined in the chapter on the pitchpipes, although the final sentence suggests some suspicion of this doctrine as a form of superstition. The prominence of this "school" in the Han military writings clearly demonstrates the influence of the idea of a cosmic pattern for human violence in the period.

As was mentioned in the passage quoted, the flux of *qi* could also be read through the observation of visible "vapors" or "emanations."[6] The uses of this technique by commanders in the field will be discussed in Chapter Six, but it is also important to note that it formed a major element in the duty of the Grand Historian (*tai shi* 太史) at court, and that it was again closely linked to attempts to find a cosmic basis and pattern for human violence.

The most extensive discussion of this practice appears in the "Tian guan shu" in the *Shi ji*. This chapter deals primarily with the divination through astronomical observation that was the primary role of the "Grand Historian," but near the end there is a significant section on "watching the vapors" (*wang qi* 望氣). This section describes the *qi* which marked a victorious army, sketches the *qi* which distinguished infantry, engineers, cavalry, and chariots, differentiates the *qi* of various places and peoples, and even attempts a brief description of these vapors:

> Like smoke but not smoke, like a cloud but not a cloud, congealing and scattering, twisting round in a circle . . . like fog but not a fog; it does not wet clothes or hats.

At the beginning of his final summation Sima Qian explained the regular linkage of divination through observing *qi* with that through astronomical phenomena, and he suggested how both of them provided cosmic patterns for human rule.

> From the first appearance of man, when have the rulers of their day not laid out the pattern of the sun, moon, and stars? . . . They looked up to observe the simulacra in Heaven and looked down to imitate the types of the Earth. Heaven has the sun and moon; Earth has *yin* and *yang* [in the flow of *qi*]. Heaven has the five planets; Earth has the five phases. Heaven has its arrayed mansions [*lie xiu* 列宿]; Earth has its provinces and regions. The three luminaries [sun, moon, and stars] are the clear essence of *yin* and *yang*; *qi* is rooted in the earth. And the sage combines them and gives them order.[7]

Qi stood in the same relation to the Earth as the stars and other astral phenomena did to Heaven. Each was the dynamic, moving element in its own region, and as such they were the natural simulacra for human action, linked to society in a great triad of sympathetic resonance. And just as the reading of *qi* through the pitchpipes and observation was primarily of importance in military affairs, so a large share of the divinations described in Sima Qian's astronomical monograph dealt with war and peace. The basic, dynamic patterns of the universe were integrated into a grand vision of a systematically interacting cosmos, in which human violence became a part of the motions of Heaven and the pulsations of Earth. This monograph represents perhaps the largest and most systematic surviving description of the various means by which the observation of natural phenomena could provide guidance for government policy and the use of sanctioned violence.

The bibliographic chapter of the *Han shu* records a large number of books dealing with divination through the observation of astral phenomena and the visible emanations of *qi*, but virtually all of these texts have been lost over the centuries. However, a substantial fragment of one such work was found among the cache of silk manuscripts at Mawangdui. The fragment comprises fifty-seven entries out of an estimated 300, and each entry includes a diagram of the phenomenon in question, its name, a verbal description, and the relevant prognostication. The different natural features covered include comets, individual stars, constellations, clouds, rainbows, and visible vapors of *qi*.[8] This work, like the monograph in the *Shi ji*, thus combines the examination of the patterns of Heaven with those of the emanations of the Earth, and then uses the results of these examinations to provide guidance for action in the world of men. It is particularly valuable for its inclusion of diagrams and the way in which it gives us a fragmentary glimpse of the large body of writings on divination that underlay the few summary chapters that survived through their inclusion in the dynastic histories.

The calendrical or cosmic model of violence did not only appear in the practice of "watching for the ethers," in the writings of the *yin/yang* military theorists, and in the handbooks on divination, but was also built into the Han ritual calendar. The relevant festivals have been discussed at length in Derk Bodde's monograph on Han annual observances, so I will only sketch them briefly here.[9]

The onset of autumn was marked by at least two major rituals pertaining to sanctioned violence: the *chu liu* sacrifice and the great military inspection. In the former the emperor and his officials shot game in staged hunts and offered up the meat at the imperial tombs and the ancestral temple in the capital. The ritual also included some military exercises. Although the various texts refer to different sites, the cumulative evidence suggests that these sacrificial hunts were held in the imperial hunting parks or in the animal pens that were built close to various palaces. These arenas of animal combats and their uses will be discussed in more detail below.

A few weeks after the *chu liu* the Han government staged ritual military reviews. These were held both in the imperial capital and in each commandery throughout the empire, and they formed a central element in the institution of universal military service. No circumstantial accounts of the reviews have survived, but they included an inspection of the assembled troops, performance under the direction of drums and bells of intricate maneuvers through the formations which were central to military practice in the period, and a demonstration of skills in archery, charioteering, and horsemanship. These reviews served to demonstrate the martial potency of the imperial house, to display the skills of the crack troops, and to maintain a minimum level of military skills in the populace at large.

The final major ritual of violence associated with the winter was the competitive hunting that was held irregularly in the ninth and tenth months of the year. These hunts, which will be discussed below, likewise served as demonstrations of imperial power, as a means of military training, and as entertainments for important officials and visiting barbarian dignitaries. They were apparently not formal elements in the fixed ritual calendar, but because of their seasonal nature and ties to the theory of cyclic violence they deserve mention here.

One interesting feature of these forms of ritualized violence was that they re-enacted the old Zhou cultic complex in their interlinking of sacrifice, hunting, and warfare in the service of the ancestral cult. Indeed, many modern scholars have suggested with good reason that the detailed, graphic accounts of Zhou ritual hunts and military exercises in the *Zhou li* actually describe the practices of the late Warring States or Han period. However, there were also several notable differences. First, the hunts of which we have records were primarily elements in the ritual theater of imperial power, and, although they would have served to train elements of the capital armies, the bulk of the Han troops would have taken no part in them. The great military inspections were also more ceremonial than functional, and even in the commanderies they would have been at best an adjunct of more systematic training offered those serving their year-long terms of duty. Second, whereas the hunts and wars of the Zhou nobility, as recorded in the *Zuo zhuan* and systematized in the *Zhou li*, were dispersed throughout the year, the Han military rituals were consciously restricted to the autumn and winter. This reflected both the new theories of cosmic imperium developed in the calendrical model of government and the largely ceremonial character of the hunts and military exercises. Finally, although the animals taken in the *chu liu* sacrificial hunt were offered to the ancestors, both the symbolism of the imperial hunts and their incorporation in the ritual calendar emphasized the character of the ruler as a cosmically potent figure and the earthly embodiment of Heaven, not as a member of a ruling lineage. This shift in emphasis from the ancestral cult to the cult of Heaven was one of the central changes in the rationalization of sanctioned violence and authority between the Zhou and the Han. The cumulative weight of these differences suggests that Han ritual violence was linked to the old Zhou cults solely through a self-conscious archaism introduced by the increasing Confucian domination of court ceremonial, while the actual uses and symbolic significance of these practices had changed radically.

Cosmic Kickball

Another form of military ritual linked to the annual cycle was the game of kickball that was performed in stadia built at all the Han palace complexes. This game was originally a mock battle and a form of military training, but it came to be regarded as a re-enactment of the alternation of *yin* and *yang* that underlay the annual cycle. Because of these various associations the game became a basic element in the rituals of violence that helped to define Han imperial rule.

Liu Xiang (77–6 B.C.) gave a brief account of the game in a bibliographic work written in the last years of the first century B.C.

Kickball deals with the power of circumstances [*shi*, the basic military concept discussed in Chapter Three] in the military. It is a means to train warriors and recognize those who have talents. It is said that it was created by the Yellow Emperor, although some say that it arose in the Warring States period.[10]

These propositions must be examined separately.

First, there is abundant evidence that the game of kickball was a form of military training. In the bibliographic monograph of the *Han shu*, Ban Gu listed a book on kickball and classified it under the military authors.[11] Sima Qian wrote that when He Qubing (145–117 B.C.) was on campaign against the Xiongnu, his men ran out of grain and could barely hold themselves upright, but he still had them dig out a kickball field to continue their training.[12] Moreover, two stories relate that when a Han emperor became overly fond of kickball, his ministers lured him away from the game by substituting the newly-invented chess, which was "similar but not tiring."[13] The fact that chess, which was a simulated war, could substitute for kickball clearly indicates the military character of the latter.

That the game originated during the Warring States period is supported by a statement attributed to Su Qin that all the people of Linzi, the capital of Qi, played kickball.[14] Su Qin lived in Linzi at the end of the fourth century and in the first decades of the third century B.C., so if the attribution has any foundation then the game must have existed in the middle of the Warring States period. In any case the text is undoubtedly composed of Warring States material, so the early development of kickball is not in doubt.

Su Qin's putative statement is also of interest because it associates the people of Linzi's participation in kickball with their love of cock fighting, setting dogs on hares, and gambling. These activities were all characteristic of the reckless youths (*shao nian* 少年) who gave up their days to idle amusements in the marketplaces, but were also willing recruits as avengers, "wandering swordsmen," bandits, or rebels.[15] These associations suggest that even among the common people kickball was associated with violent, proto-military activities, and that it perhaps served to train bandits and rebels as well as imperial soldiers.

The alternative hypothesis of its creation by the Yellow Emperor is also significant. As was noted earlier, this sage was the putative recipient of the primal revelation of military philosophy and the first exemplar of correct warfare in the treatise on the pitchpipes, so it is not surprising that he should be credited with the creation of a military training ritual that, as will be shown below, acted out the annual cycle. Nor is this story unrelated to Su Qin's statement for, as we shall see in the next chapter, many of the tales, rituals, and philosophical doctrines associated with the Yellow Emperor were centered in the state of Qi.

In addition to the simple attribution by Liu Xiang, other texts preserve a tradition that the game of kickball was a ritual commemoration of the Yellow Emperor's victory over Chi You. Until recent years the only evidence of this idea was a statement in the preface to a Japanese work on kickball written in the Tokugawa period. This work said, "Some compared [the ball] to the head of Chi You."[16] However, this isolated statement has found dramatic confirmation in the silk Huang-Lao manuscript discovered at Mawangdui.

> Thereupon [the Yellow Emperor] took out his axes of punishment and mobilized his troops. The Yellow Emperor in person encountered Chi You and slew him. He stripped off his skin and made it into an archery target; he had men shoot at it and rewarded those who had the most hits. He cut off his hair, mounted it in Heaven, and called it "Chi You's Banner" [an astral phenomenon that presaged the coming of war]. He stuffed his stomach and made it into a ball; he had men kick it and rewarded those who scored the most. He fermented his bones and flesh, threw them into a bitter meat stew, and had all the men drink it. Thus the Supreme Emperor [*shang di* 上帝] made his prohibitions.[17]

This passage, which has been dated as early as the fourth century and is certainly no later than the early second century B.C., shows that not only the game of kickball but also the regular archery contests and the practice of pickling and devouring gross malefactors were traced to the Yellow Emperor's victory over Chi You. Since, as will be shown in Chapter Five, this battle was regarded as an archetypal event marking the introduction of organized warfare into human society, it is not surprising that many of the chief rituals pertaining to combat were interpreted as commemorations of the primal conflict. The appearance of kickball among these other rituals clearly demonstrates its military character.

Having established that kickball was a game which combined military training with the ritual celebration of the victory of the Yellow Emperor, it remains to reconstruct the nature of this ceremonial contest. Although no systematic accounts survive, a few fragments describe some aspects of the game. Highly significant among these are references to the fields, for these demonstrate that the game of kickball was a fundamental ritual of imperial authority in Han China. A commentary appended to the account of He Qubing's construction of a field shows that the work on kickball listed in Ban Gu's bibliographic monograph contained a chapter devoted solely to the field. Lu Ji (261–303 A.D.) listed various kickball fields attached to the Han imperial palaces, and since he refers to them as *shi* (室), they were apparently covered buildings.[18] Indeed, the Empress Lü used one as a prison for her rival, the Lady Qi.[19] The subsequent Wei dynasty also had a kickball stadium at its palace in Loyang, and the Wei rulers built a large field at their "travelling palace" in Xuchang.[20] This constant association of fields with imperial palaces shows the ties of the ritual game to the institutions of empire.

Moreover, there is clear evidence that this regular placement of stadia in palace complexes was not simply a means of relieving imperial boredom, for kickball fields and their matches were part of the ritual symbolization of imperial sovereignty. A rhyme-prose on the Wei palace complex at Xuchang says, "To its west there is a field for military training, with nine steps on the left but flat on the right." The following lines make it clear that this was a kickball field. The commentator quotes a passage by Liu Xin (d. 23 A.D.) to the effect that the kickball fields of imperial palaces must have nine raised steps on the left and be flat on the right in order to resemble the state, and that kickball was a simulacrum or double (*xiang* 象) of regulating the state.[21]

The manner in which kickball could be an image of imperial rule is explained in a passage from Li You's (fl. 90–130 A.D.) "Inscription for a Kickball Stadium" that is quoted in the commentary to the next line of the rhyme-prose on the Xuchang palace. The line itself reads, "The two sixes [teams of six men] face each other; the vanguards and wings [military formations] match one another." The commentary then quotes the inscription:

A round ball and square walls; it imitates the [Heavenly] simulacra with a *yin* and a *yang*. Imitating the moon[s] they rush against one another; the two sixes facing one another.

It is an obscure explanation, but all the lines refer to basic Chinese cosmological ideas. The "round ball" and "square walls" evoke the standard description of the universe as a round Heaven over a square Earth. The "simulacra" or "doubles" commonly refer to the various astral bodies and constellations which resonate with and reflect corresponding earthly locales or institutions. These phenomena all have a *yin* and a *yang* in that they pass through an annual cycle based on the successive shift from one to the other. One major exception was the moon—or "moons," for each month was a moon to itself—which passed through a series of monthly cycles that could be mapped onto the solar year only with difficulty. The kickball field had a *yin* and a *yang* in that it was divided into two halves, and *yin* and *yang* were employed as standard, abstract terms for any binary opposition. The movement of the ball from one side of the field to the other would thus have formed a cycle of *yin* and *yang* that corresponded to that of Heaven and Earth.

The reference to "imitating the moons" is explained in the follow-ing line, for "two sixes" form twelve, the approximate number of months or "moons" in the year. Twelve synodic months do not form a full tropical year, and the Chinese inserted intercalary months at two-year or three-year intervals to keep the solar and lunar calendars in agreement, but for most purposes the year was assumed to have twelve months. Moreover, these months were divided into two sixes in the theory of their correspondence to the tones of the Chinese gamut, which as was noted above were divided into six *yin* and six *yang*. Li You's inscription described the kickball game as an extended allegory on the annual cycle of Heaven and Earth as revealed by the pitchpipes, and, as was remarked in the introduction to the *Shi ji*'s chapter on pitchpipes, the cycle traced by their notes was a model for the regulation of the state and was linked primarily to military action. This cosmic imagery ex-plains how a ritual for military training like kickball could also serve as the simulacrum for the governing of the state and become a fun-damental element in the ritual theater of Han imperium.

Imperial Hunts and Animal Combats

Another set of institutions and rituals linked imperial violence to the patterns of nature by consciously extending the range of human war-fare or conflict to the animal kingdom. The idea that human violence was made "natural" by the inclusion of animals was perhaps implicit in the old Zhou identification of hunting as a form of warfare and in the equation, as potential sacrifices, of prey taken in the hunt with prisoners captured in combat. However, while the Zhou had emphasized hunts as actual training and a practical means of securing sacrificial victims, the official hunts of Han China in the great parks were primarily pageants or demonstrations of the all-encompassing range of imperial power, a range which included even beasts and plants. In addition to the great ceremonial hunts held in the parks, smaller scale "hunts" and combats with animals were staged in animal pens located in the Han palace com-plexes. Linked to these ritual combats with animals appeared both stories of sage-rulers who used animals in their armies and arguments that the weapons of men ultimately derived from the horns or fangs of wild beasts, and were direct expressions of human nature. Thus ritual, myth, and accounts of the origins of weapons all suggested that human violence ultimately derived from that of nature and, under the guidance of a sage-ruler, could incorporate the violence of the non-human world into itself.

The major sites of ritualized "natural" violence in Han China were the great imperial parks. These nature preserves were a fundamental part of the early imperial order, and they performed a multitude of functions. They hosted religious rituals, grand imperial banquets, the reception of foreign guests, the great ritual hunts, and even served such mundane purposes as agriculture and pasturage.[22] They contained wild animals, mountains, rivers, exotic flora, and many palaces, and this plenitude of contents was their very *raison d'être*, as is shown in the elaborate poetry devoted to them. In the writing of Sima Xiangru (179–117 B.C.) the imperial park appeared as a microcosm for the subcelestial realm of the Son of Heaven, and in the more exuberant flights of poetry it *became* the entire world.

> Gazing about the expanse of the park
> At the abundance and variety of its creatures,
> One's eyes are dizzied and enraptured
> By the boundless horizons,
> The borderless vistas.
> The sun rises from the eastern ponds
> And sets among the slopes of the west;
> In the southern part of the park,
> Where grasses grow in the dead of winter
> And the waters leap, unbounded by ice,
> Live zebras, yaks, tapirs, and black oxen,
> Water buffalo, elk, and antelope,
> 'Red-crowns' and 'round-heads,'
> Aurochs, elephants, and rhinoceroses.
> In the north, where in the midst of summer
> The ground is cracked and blotched with ice
> And one may walk the frozen streams or wade the rivulets,
> Roam unicorns and boars,
> Wild asses and camels,
> Onagers and mares,
> Swift stallions, donkeys, and mules.
>
> . . .
>
> Peering down into the caves, one cannot spy their end;
> Gazing up at the rafters, one sees them brush the heavens;
> So lofty are the palaces that

Comets stream through their portals
And rainbows twine about their balustrades.
Green dragons slither from the eastern pavilion;
Elephant-carved carriages prance
From the pure hall of the west,
Bringing immortals to dine in the peaceful towers
And bands of fairies to sun themselves
Beneath the southern eaves.[23]

Although they do not match Sima Xiangru's impetuosity or grandeur, other poetic accounts concur that these parks were a necessary attribute of imperium and that their hallmark was the inclusion of all possible forms of topography, mineral wealth, flora, and fauna. This desire to include the widest possible range of natural features expressed the ideal, frequently articulated in the writings and stone inscriptions of the period, that the emperor's rule and the blessings of his potency should reach all beings, even the most lowly or remote.[24] In the diversity of their contents the parks provided the most tangible image of the emperor as a cosmic figure, an earthly simulacrum of the all-embracing Heaven.

As the parks demonstrated the Heaven-like range of the emperor's potency, the great hunts staged within them became earthly images of the celestial violence associated with the annual cycle. The greatest of these was the annual winter hunt, which was a combination of religious ceremony, entertainment, and military exercise in which the emperor demonstrated the awesome, killing aspect of his power. It was the subject of elaborate depiction and furious censure in the major rhyme-prose of the Western and Eastern Han. Combining exuberant descriptions of the scale and diversity of the slaughter with their moralizing lessons, these accounts of the hunts reflect the same concern with the all-encompassing range of the emperor's power as the poems on the parks, but that range was here demonstrated through the extent and variety of the destruction. The hunts had thus become primarily pageants of the encompassing, universal power of the emperor, and sanctions for his use of force through the identification of Han military power with the destructive force of Heaven.

The ritual hunts in the imperial parks were the most grandiose form of natural violence in the Han state, but lesser versions of these cataclysmic battles with beasts took place in special animal pens where wild animals were reared, trained, and pitted in combat against one another or against men. The combats in these pens not only provided another opportunity for training and reiterated the association between human and natural violence, but they also offered a vivid model for the tales that will be discussed below and in Chapter Five of animal warriors and of human fighters who became like beasts. The use of special pens by the Zhou aristocracy to rear wild animals for use in sacrifices was mentioned in Chapter One, and there are many traditions preserved in Warring States texts of the rearing of animals and of combats with animals in antiquity. The *Zhou li* records offices responsible for raising and training wild beasts and birds, and during the Warring States and Han periods several clans traced their surnames to such offices.[25] Later accounts record that the evil monarchs Jie and Zhou both raised tigers; the former unleashed them in the marketplace for sport, while the latter battled them barehanded.[26] The introduction to the *Shi ji*'s monograph on pitchpipes quoted earlier also describes how these tyrants of antiquity wrestled wolves with their bare hands. King Mu of Zhou was likewise reputed to have raised tigers in a special "tiger pen."[27]

However, all these references to rearing wild animals for staged combats in antiquity come from Warring States and Han sources, and it is unclear whether or not such practices actually existed in earlier times. Tales in various cultures of the inclusion of animals in the human realm or of battles in which men conquered and subjected animals often derive from the old cultic or "shamanic" role of animals as the links between the world of men and the realm of the gods and ancestors, so it is possible that these traditions of animal battles in high antiquity, and perhaps the practice in later times of actually staging such combats, ultimately derived from such a source.[28]

The earliest reference to hand-to-hand combats between men and wild animals appears in the *Shi jing*, where one poem describes participants in a hunt stripping themselves and battling tigers barehanded.[29] Several placenames from the Spring and Autumn period clearly refer to wild animal pens, which shows that by this period the Chinese were deliberately rearing wild beasts for sacrifices or staged combats.[30] Confucius once remarked that he would not want to share command of an army with someone who would attack a tiger barehanded, and although this could be interpreted as a rather bizarre figure of speech, the *Mencius* refers explicitly to a man who was famous for battling tigers with his bare hands.[31] Meng Yue, a celebrated strongman from Qi state, was noted for wrestling with bulls.[32] Depictions of hand-to-hand combat with wild beasts also appear amongst the Warring States archeological finds. Some fragments of bronze vessels discovered in a mid-Warring States tomb from the state of Chu show figures grappling barehanded with animals in the midst of hunting scenes.[33] Several late Warring States mirrors depict men with swords attacking tigers, and one of these shows a man with a short sword about to leap from the back of his horse onto a tiger.[34] This cumulative evidence clearly shows that by the Warring States period the Chinese battled animals hand-to-hand as displays of courage during hunts and also reared wild animals for staging combats.

Under the Han these practices were formalized as elements of imperial ritual. The symbolism of the great "competitive hunts" staged in the imperial parks in the ninth and tenth months has been discussed above, and the rhyme-prose on these hunts by Sima Xiangru and Mei Cheng describe how participants captured all varieties of wild beasts with a single sword or their bare hands.[35] In 11 B.C. the Emperor Cheng held a hunt to entertain a delegation from the Xiongnu, and the visitors willingly entered an improvised pen unarmed and captured large numbers of animals.[36] The systematic equation of the violence of men with that of wild animals had become a basic element in the displays of the killing power of the Han rulers.

In addition to the great parks with their hunts and animal combats, demonstrations of the natural sources of human violence also took place in the animal pens. These pens, as we saw above, had appeared no later than the Spring and Autumn period, and the institution was carried forward into the Han. Every Han palace complex contained wild beast pens that were at least large enough to allow for the hunting of the beasts by men on horseback, and the Jianzhang palace built by Emperor Wu contained a tiger pen of "several tens of *li*," along with pens for lions and boars. Moreover, archeological excavations have found the insignia of special officials who were responsible for administering these pens and keeping records of the animals.[37] In these pens the Han emperors staged combats between men and animals for their amusement, and on one occasion the Emperor Yuan took his entire harem to watch animal battles at an imperial tiger pen.[38] Apart from their use for entertainment and the demonstration of the ruler's cosmic power, combat with animals in pens also served religious functions. The most famous example of this was the ritual bullfight, in which a bull was beaten to death by men armed with clubs in order to ensure a good harvest. Many Han tomb reliefs also depict "bull grappling," in which an individual wrestled with a bull, and the strongman Meng Yue mentioned above was famous for his ability to fight bulls.[39]

Although the staging of animal combats was part of the symbolism of imperial power, it was not the exclusive prerogative of the ruling house. At the lowest levels of society, animal combats took the form of the cock-fights and the setting of dogs on hares that were popular entertainments among the village youth. Members of the elite amused themselves with larger-scale combats, as in the case of Liu He, who staged and perhaps participated in battles with boars and tigers while on his way to Changan to become emperor.[40] Although this action figured in the indictment which led to his removal from office, it appears that his sole crime was to stage animal combats during a period of mourning; the activity itself was apparently accepted. Finally, Eastern Han tomb tiles, reliefs, and wall paintings often depict men armed with spears and swords, or in some cases barehanded, fighting one or more animals. Sometimes these illustrations do not show clearly the site of the combats, but others portray walled compounds which were clearly the animal pens mentioned in the literary sources. Other representations depict a pair of animals fighting in these pens, and in at least one case these beasts are being egged on or ridden by human trainers.[41] Since Han tomb art generally depicts the daily life and entertainments of the local elite and their dependents, it seems that the great Han families constructed their own animal pens, where they staged combats in the manner of the imperial house, although on a reduced scale.

One final question concerns the status of those who risked their lives in the parks and pens. Unlike the gladiators of ancient Rome, it does not appear that those who fought were slaves or convicts who were already socially dead. In at least two cases, members of the imperial court who offended the emperor or dowager empress were forced to enter the animal pens as a form of punishment.[42] But battling animals was not invariably an onerous burden or penalty. One of the sons of Emperor Wu, Liu Xu, used to battle barehanded against bears, boars, and other wild beasts simply for sport, and Liu He may well have done the same.[43] Those who participated unarmed or with swords in the hunts and captured wild animals hand-to-hand appear to have done so for sport, and their ability to fight animals in the wilds suggests regular practice in the controlled environment of the pens. The Xiongnu who entered the improvised pen at the hunt in 11 B.C. certainly did so freely, and it is likely that they regarded battling animals as a pleasure or at least a satisfying demonstration of prowess. Thus those who fought in the pens and parks were warriors, barbarians, criminals, or anyone who took pride in his martial abilities. Likewise, animal combats in the lower strata of society were associated with men prone to violence: wastrel youths, "swordsmen," avengers, rebels, criminals, and other marginal figures. The significance of this link between martiality and "bestiality" in the Warring States and early imperial China will be discussed at length in Chapter Five.

Since animals engaged in combat with men in these periods, it is not surprising that there appeared stories in which the Yellow Emperor, the sage creator of proper warfare, formed an army of animal soldiers to fight his enemies.[44] As the tales dealing with the Yellow Emperor form the subject of Chapter Five they will not be discussed in detail here, but it is important to note that the potential equivalence of human soldiers and savage animals was a significant theme in Chinese reflections on warfare in this period.

In addition to the image of animals as "natural" soldiers, various Warring States and Han texts also invoked the "armament" of animals —teeth, claws, and stings—as natural prototypes for human weapons. The introduction to the monograph on pitchpipes quoted earlier defended the use of warfare by pointing out that animals were equipped with natural weapons and invariably fought when threatened. Men likewise had in their fundamental constitution the emotion of anger which would impel them to fight, so they too by nature carried a "poisonous sting." Similar arguments appeared in various texts in a debate over whether human weapons existed as an aspect of nature or were created by culture-hero sages.

> The lord asked, "In what generation did weapons appear?" The Master replied, "This blight has long existed; it was born together with humanity." The lord said, "Didn't Chi You invent weapons?" The Master replied, "No! Chi You was a greedy commoner. . . . How could he invent [any kind of] implement? [Inventing all the basic implements of culture was attributed to the sages, so a common, morally corrupt being could not make inventions.] Bees and scorpions carry poisonous stings, and when they are threatened they will parry to defend themselves. Men are born with joy and anger, so weapons appear together with humanity. The sage uses them to put an end to chaos, while the ordinary man uses them to destroy himself."[45]

This passage insists that weapons cannot have been a cultural innovation because only a sage can make such innovations, and Chi You—the great rebel and mythic creator of weapons who will be discussed in Chapter Five—was clearly not a sage. Weapons consequently had to be a part of the realm of nature, and the author demonstrates this by pointing out animals which are born with "weapons" as part of their bodies. He then elides the fact that men are not born with their weapons by arguing that a propensity to anger is part of man's natural equipment, and anger leads inevitably to violence. Violence was thus part of nature and coeval with man, but only the sage could use it to create order in the world.

The same rhetoric of natural weapons was used by those who insisted that man's use of implements for combat was a cultural innovation, as in this passage from the *Sun Bin bingfa*.

> Sunzi said, "Wild animals have teeth in their maws or horns on their heads or claws and spurs on their feet. When pleased they are

in harmony, but when angry they fight. This is the Way of Heaven and it cannot be suppressed. But those who lack natural weapons [man] make their own defenses. This is a matter for a sage."[46]

Thus even those who insisted that warfare was a human creation and hence the work of a sage still accepted that violent conflict and weapons existed in nature and that the violence of men was analogous to and an extension of this natural combat.

Articulate Chinese of the Warring States period clearly recognized that struggle and conflict existed in nature, and they increasingly linked human violence to these natural prototypes. The received assumption of the Zhou nobility that hunting was a form of warfare led easily to the belief that wild animals were warriors and warriors potentially animals. These ideas perhaps even figured amongst the common people, who often staged battles between fighting cocks or set hounds on hares, but they were particularly important to the elite. In hunts described in the *Shi jing* nobles engaged in hand-to-hand battles with wild beasts as displays of prowess, and later warriors held staged animal combats in specially built animal pens. The grandest versions of these natural battles were the combats undertaken by the warriors, barbarians, and criminals in the imperial animal pens and hunting parks, and in these ritual combats the blending of natural and human violence became part of a pageant in which the all-encompassing power of the Heaven-like emperor extended to "natural" slaughter. Just as the beneficence of the emperor was to reach the beasts and plants, so his powers to mobilize for warfare included the summoning of animals to fight and die.

Feats of Strength and Sorcery

Another form of battle related to both the cyclical violence of the ritual calendar and to animal combats was a form of wrestling known as "matching strength" (*jue li* 角力) or "horn butting" (*jue di* 角抵). Originally used to select or train warriors, it evolved into a form of entertainment that accompanied banquets and festivals, and also served as an element of ritual in various annual observances. By Han times it had become part of an ensemble of entertainments and magical performances that included many forms of staged animal combats. In its evolution from military training to pageant and seasonal ritual in the service of the symbolism of empire, it paralleled the course of the official hunts, kickball games, and animal combats discussed above.

The earliest references to *jue li* appear in two Warring States texts that present three versions of the same story.[47] In this story the spearman of the head of the Zhao lineage engages a reputed strongman in a wrestling match, is defeated, and agrees to yield his post to the victor.

These stories clearly show that wrestling was originally used both to develop and to demonstrate the great physical strength required in battle. Such strength would have been particularly important for the spearman, who was often obliged to dislodge the chariot if it became stuck in the mud.

This origin of the *jue li* in military practices was still remembered in the Han. The various calendars of imperial activities in late Warring States and early Han works all list it together with archery and chariot-eering as an element in the military training rituals that were held in the tenth month.[48] In his monograph on punishments, which was primarily a history of warfare and an account of military practices, Ban Gu described the *jue li* as originally a ritual of military training which had been expanded to become a form of entertainment and used in demonstrations of martial skills. He also noted that the Qin had changed the name to *jue di*, "horn butting."[49] This name first appears in an entry regarding competitions at the Qin court in 208 B.C., and the exact significance of the new nomenclature is not certain. The character *jue* (also read *jiao*) could mean "horn" but also had the broader sense of "to compete" or "to match." In the phrase *jue li* it clearly had the latter sense, but the phrase *jue di* suggested the former. Moreover, there is evidence that actual butting of horns may have played a role in these contests.

As was mentioned above, one form of animal combat in early China that was depicted in tomb reliefs was "bull grappling," in which individual men wrestled with bulls. It is perhaps not coincidental that the best-known practitioner of this "sport," Meng Yue, served the king of Qin, for the importance of battling with bulls in Qin might explain how in that state wrestling became associated with the butting of horns. In any case, there are at least two pieces of evidence which show that human wrestlers in the Han actually put on horns when they fought and thus imitated bulls or goats, and the introduction of this practice probably took place in the Qin as was reflected in the new name for the matches.

One piece of evidence is archeological. A relief in an Eastern Han tomb at Dengfeng portrays a pair of men wearing horns engaged in a wrestling match.[50] There is also one literary account of such matches, although it appears in a post-Han work.

In Qin and Han times they said that Chi You's ears were like swords and the hairs of his temples like lances, and he had horns on his head. When he fought with Xianyuan [the Yellow Emperor] he butted men with his horns, and none could stand against him. Now in Jizhou there is a performance call the "Chi You game." The people divide into groups of two or three, put horns on their heads, and butt each other. The Han had created the "horn-butting game" [*jue di xi* 角抵戲], and this is probably its vestige.[51]

The relation of this passage to the tales of the Yellow Emperor and his battle with Chi You will be discussed in the next chapter, but the text confirms that the common people of China in certain places staged horned wrestling matches, and it traces the practice back to the Han. The tomb relief confirms that such matches did exist in the Han, so the association of wrestling with horn butting and staged animal combats that is suggested by the change in names clearly corresponded with actual practice.

Although originally a simple wrestling match used as military training, the *jue di*, as Ban Gu observed, had been expanded since the Qin into an entertainment and a demonstration of skill. He does not elaborate the changes, but a later work gives a more detailed account. A fragment of the *Han Wu gu shi* preserved in the *Taiping yulan* identifies the *jue di* as a matching of strength in wrestling that originated in the Warring States period. However, it adds the information that it was expanded under the Qin and Han through combination with "barbarian music" and various "extraordinary illusions" so that it came to resemble the battles of "ghosts and spirits."[52] And indeed although as late as the Eastern Han writers still identified *jue di* as a form of wrestling associated with other performances, from the Three Kingdoms period on scholars took the phrase as a generic term for all the competitions, dances, costumed pantomimes, and demonstrations of skill or magic that accompanied banquets or popular festivals.[53]

However, even during the Han the term *jue di* already included far more than ceremonial wrestling matches. Zhang Heng's rhyme-prose describing the western capital states that after a great hunt the emperor visited the arena where he witnessed the *jue di*. In addition to wrestling this included tripod lifting, acrobatics, men disguised as immortals and savage beasts who sang and danced, dancers who simulated a snow-storm while rolling stones to produce the illusion of thunder and lightning, a giant beast that turned into a fairy mountain with bears and tigers fighting on its back, all manner of exotic beasts such as elephants and peacocks, a magic fish that turned into a dragon, men who made turtles dance and commanded snakes, and conjurers who could change their appearance, swallow swords, spit flames, and produce dark clouds. Finally, there were men replicating the feats of "Old Master Huang of Donghai Commandery," who could draw lines on the ground and turn them into rivers, and tame tigers with his magic red dagger and "ax spells."[54] A Jin dynasty work states that this "Old Master Huang" had been able to summon up storms and fogs, create rivers, and command tigers and dragons. The people of the Changan region had used his feats as the basis for various entertainments, and the feats that accompanied the wrestling in the *jue di* were all based on these performances.[55] Although the work is post-Han, its description of the *jue di* entertainments as re-creations of the feats of "Master Huang" agrees with Zhang Heng's account.

It is important to note that these added "extraordinary illusions" were not entirely random. Apart from the lifting of tripods, another feat of strength closely related to the wrestling matches, virtually all the magical feats involved the commanding of storms and of wild beasts. In this they not only corresponded to the powers of "Master Huang" but they were also related to the original "core" meaning of the *jue di* as ceremonial wrestling for military training. As we have seen above, one of the central themes of Han military rituals was the "natural" prototype for military action in animal combat, and this was acted out in the hunting parks and animal pens through battles with animals that demonstrated the emperor's cosmic power to incorporate the natural world in his realm. In the wearing of horns by the participants, the wrestling matches already invoked the image of animal combats, so the inclusion of commanding wild animals and having them fight in the *jue di* "illusions" was a simple extension of this theme. Moreover, as we shall see in Chapter Five, the commanding of storms was also related to ideas about violence in early China, and the entire ceremony of the imperial *jue di* can be explained as a ritual performance of the rivalry between Chi You and the Yellow Emperor. Certainly this was how it was understood by the people of Jizhou, who invoked the figure of Chi You to explain their version of the *jue di*.

Just as other forms of military training such as hunting and kickball had been developed into ritualized pageants that demonstrated the cosmic power of the emperor, so the wrestling matches that had been used to train and select warriors became part of a grand spectacle that celebrated the all-encompassing range of the ruler's potency and the natural sanction for his use of violence. First, the wrestling matches themselves were disguised as bull grappling or animal combats through the addition of horns. Second, the matches were accompanied and their meaning extended by demonstrations of magic feats that commanded wild animals to fight and dance, summoned magical beasts, and invoked the violent power of the storm. Military training became cosmic spectacle, and the power of mighty warriors and beasts was bound into the service of the encompassing imperium.

Conclusion

One of the major consequences of the development of universal military service and the expansion of territorial states was the rise to unquestioned supremacy within the polity of a single, autocratic ruler. With the steady advance of correlative thinking that took place in the same period, it became increasingly common to identify this supreme ruler as the earthly simulacrum of Heaven or the cosmic Way, and to argue that he should base his actions on the imitation of the celestial patterns. In contrast with earlier rulers, who had been the pinnacle of a warrior nobility that claimed authority through the performance of sacrifice and warfare in the service of the ancestral cult, the new ruler claimed power through his ability to imitate the actions of Heaven in the world of men. Consequently, the actual performance of violence that had been central to the Zhou nobility became the sphere of the commoner masses who filled the ranks of the armies, while authority inhered in those who organized the violence and gave it pattern. The military commanders had done this at one level, but they had given order only to a single campaign, the pattern had been that of their own intelligence, and their art had entailed a violation of the basic norms of human society. The ruler, to the contrary, imposed order on the entire world of men and that of physical nature, and the violence of military action and punishments was made part of the annual cycle. The patterns he imposed, moreover, were those of the celestial order itself, and he adhered absolutely to the trustworthiness of law and ritual. In the Heaven-like actions of this semi-divine figure, violence found its proper place in the new state.

The cosmic or natural character of violence in the territorial state was demonstrated in several ways. First, the violence of warfare, hunting, and punishments was built into the ritual calendar of the state and exclusively tied to the killing seasons of the year, the autumn and the winter. Every form of the sanctioned violence that had defined the Zhou nobility had its ritual form under the Han—competitive hunts, military inspections, and the provision of sacrifice for the ancestors through hunts—and these were carried out in the eighth through the tenth months of the Han calendar. At the same time the guidance of the cyclic pulsations of *qi*, as revealed through the pitchpipes and visual observation, and of the patterns of the stars were employed by Han ritualists to bring imperial rituals into accord with the actions of Heaven and Earth and thereby claim a cosmic pattern for the conduct of human violence.

Not only was imperial violence organized through patterning on the annual cycle and the natural designs of Heaven's stars and Earth's *qi*, but it also claimed natural sanction through the incorporation of the spontaneous violence of the beasts. In the great hunts that had once been the primary form of military training and in combats staged in special animal pens the Han rulers conducted a grand pageant in which men and animals met as equal combatants in the field. Together with these ritual battles there appeared stories of animal soldiers who had fought for the sage-kings of antiquity, and accounts of the origins of man's weapons in the natural armament of beasts and the naked emotion of human anger.

Just as hunting was transformed into both an annual ritual of celestial violence and a ceremonial drama of natural combat, so the wrestling matches that had been used to train and select warriors under the Zhou became elaborate ritual performances that demonstrated the cosmic character of imperial rule. Like other imperial ceremonies dealing with the use of violence, they were inserted into the ritual calendar in the killing seasons of the year, in this case the tenth month. With combatants who wore horns they became variations of the bull grappling and the animal combats which demonstrated that the emperor's power extended to and was rooted in the natural world. The accompanying "illusions" in which conjurers led wild beasts to dance or fight, summoned magical creatures, and commanded the powers of the storm all reiterated and intensified the claims to cosmic potency that were acted out in the battles of the "animal" warriors. The savage power of inanimate nature as well as that of beasts was brought into the service of the emperor and offered a demonstration of the celestial origins and character of the violence of the sage-ruler.

Although I have not discussed it in this chapter, the shift to an authority based on cosmic pattern from one based on ancestral service was also marked by the changing emphases of the imperial sacrifical cult. As Lester Bilsky has shown in the only comprehensive study of early Chinese state religion, the major long-term, secular trend in the pattern of state sacrifices between the Western Zhou and the Han was a shift from the predominance of temple sacrifices presented to the ancestors to altar sacrifices given to deities of nature and ultimately to Heaven.[56] This development culminated in the religious reforms of Emperor Wu of the Han, who introduced a range of cults to such cosmic abstractions as the "Grand Unity" and performed the famous *feng* and *shan* sacrifices to Heaven in order to demonstrate the transcendant bases of the emperor's might. While the ancestral cult remained of great significance in Warring States and Han China, it was ultimately supplanted by the direct worship of Heaven as the central state cult, and, as other scholars have shown, sacrifices to Heaven continued to expand in importance as the focus of the political cult over the course of the Han and down through the Tang dynasty.[57]

The ultimate sanction of human violence in early imperial China, as embodied in the institutions and rituals described in this chapter, lay in the claim to be imitating Heaven. This imitation was demonstrated in two primary forms. On the one hand, human violence was linked to the physical processes of nature rooted in the cycles of *qi*, the primal energy underlying all matter. On the other hand, the origins of human violence were located in the natural struggles of the animal world, and the emperor's power to guide the violence of men was extended into control of the violence of the pre-human. In this way the organization and use of sanctioned violence in China became inextricably intertwined with the understanding both of the principles guiding the physical world and the relation of human civilization to the pre-human realm of animal nature. The literate Chinese of the Warring States and early imperial periods constructed both a "history" of the emergence of proper human violence from the savagery of beasts and a "science" that discovered in the principles of matter the prototype of the imperial pattern of sanctioned violence. The rebuilding of the state on the basis of universal military service under a cosmically potent ruler thus entailed a simultaneous reconstruction of the Chinese past and of the natural world, as seen through the prism of the new political order.

Chapter Five

THE SOCIAL HISTORY OF VIOLENCE

During the Eastern Zhou period the Chinese told tales of earlier times to explain the origins and define the nature of their political and social institutions. In the manner of the "charter myths" so common to human societies, these tales of the deeds and creations of ancient sage-kings provided a sacred prototype for the usages and institutions of their own day. In addition, they offered a means of representing a complex social reality, formulating its principles in vivid and dramatic terms, and reflecting on its inherent tensions. Some of these stories were reworked or reinterpreted versions of traditional tales; others were original creations which due to their aptness or power became widely known and frequently cited, but they all came to form a common repertoire of stories that provided both etiologies and models for social action.

One set of stories dealt with the role of violence in human society, and these tales revolved around the figure of the Yellow Emperor (*Huang Di* 黃帝) and his battle with the savage Chi You (蚩尤). They were part of a larger mythology of the creation of the human world by culture-hero sages, who had separated men physically and distinguished them morally from the wild beasts by a series of technological inventions and the introduction of proper social teachings. Among the innovations that created human society, sanctioned violence was both central and particularly problematic. As was shown in the previous chapter, human violence was traced back to the savagery and combats of beasts, so it belonged to the pre-human world of nature, but at the same time it formed the basis of state power and was a fundamental element of the ritual presentation of cosmic imperium. This tension was expressed in the debate cited earlier regarding the origins of weapons. According to

some men, weapons were present in nature in the form of animal arma-
ments, while others maintained that they were the work of sages. Or
perhaps, as the *Sun Bin bingfa* argued, they were both, and it is precisely this mediation of seeming contraries that was performed in the tales
of the Yellow Emperor and Chi You. These presented a history of the
creation of civilization in which violence began with the beast Chi You,
but was then transformed into the basis of the social order through the
innovations of the Yellow Emperor.

In addition to these theoretical meditations on the possibility and
forms of a truly human violence, the stories carried a political message.
As was shown in Chapter Three, Warring States military thought included a systematic critique of individual heroism and martial prowess
in the form of parables of revealed texts, the inversion of the sexual
imagery of combat, and explicit strictures on the supreme importance of
discipline, formations, and maneuver. This same critique, which began
as an attack on the Zhou nobility and was carried forward as a rationalization of the rigorous control of the peasant masses, appeared in the
tales of the Yellow Emperor. As charters for the new order, they were
also justifications of the authoritarian, territorial state.

These tales were themselves based on an earlier set of myths and
shamanic rituals that dealt with a battle between spirits of drought and
storm at the end of the dry winter season. Because the theme of battle
was already present in them, because of the association of the storm
with battle and of thunder with the sound of war drums, and because
winter and warfare became linked in the calendrical model of government, these old myths and rites provided material for reworking into a
meditation on the newly-discovered problem of sanctioned violence. As
the state and the forms of kinship were transformed through unceasing
wars and new military institutions, the exponents and witnesses of this
new order gradually reinterpreted the tales of the battle between
drought and storm as a story of the appearance of violence in the world
of men and its ultimate socialization. While much was added that
reflected the new concerns and practices of the Warring States period,
the stories also preserved many elements from the earlier myths. In
order to make sense of the versions and references preserved in the
Warring States and early imperial texts, it is thus necessary first to work
through the traces of prior forms of the same story organized around
different themes.[1]

In the ultimate versions of the story, the problematic character of
violence in the human world was mythically expressed through the introduction of *two* creators of warfare and punishments. One was a savage beast who created the justice of beasts, with no judicial procedure
or concern for evidence, and the warfare of beasts, in which individuals

battled one another and the strongest conquered. The other was a sage who made both law and warfare expressions of the principles of justice and the patterns of Heaven, and was thereby able to conquer the beast and ultimately make him serve the cause of social order. Reflecting the philosophical tracing of the origins of weapons and violence to the animal realm, the beast was granted priority, and it was his introduction of violence that necessitated the work of the sage. But the Yellow Emperor maintained primacy, and it was his innovations that made violence a constitutive part of the human realm.

Because these tales dealt with the new pattern of sanctioned violence that created the Warring States, they incorporated all the elements that have been discussed in the preceding chapters. The army as a collective entity based on instruction, beast warriors as elements of imperium, revealed military treatises as the key to victory, and the imitation of the patterns of Heaven as the key to proper warfare were all assigned their prototypes in the career of the Yellow Emperor. Thus these tales presented the new military and legal institutions of Warring States China as elements in the creation of humanity itself, as sage revelations that were necessary to separate the world of men from that of the wild beasts.

The Myths of the Sage-Kings

In this discussion the word "myth" refers to any "traditional tale with secondary, partial reference to something of collective importance;" myths are stories which "express dramatically the ideology under which a society lives," that reflect on the elements and tensions that constitute a society, that "justify the rules and traditional practices without which everything within a society would disintegrate."[2]

During the Warring States and early imperial periods, the tales through which the Chinese expressed dramatically their ideology and self-understanding took the form of accounts of ancient history and the emergence of human civilization. The central figures in these stories were the sage-kings, superhuman beings whose wisdom allowed them to recognize the celestial patterns hidden in nature and bring mankind into accord with them. To the sages were attributed all the tools and procedures that formed the Chinese civilization, and the invention of tools, as we saw in the last chapter, became a hallmark of the sage-kings denied to lesser beings.[3]

But the sages were more than prehistoric Edisons. They introduced all those values, institutions, and regular practices that made possible a truly human existence as this was understood during the Warring States period. In the act of yielding the throne to the most capable,

Yao and Shun defined the character of public rule by setting it apart from the claims of kinship and inheritance, as well as providing a rationalization and model for the later practice of changing dynasties.[4] In taming the flood, Yu created an ordered, human geography and provided a mythical prototype for the irrigation and water control projects of the Warring States period.[5] And in his defeat of Chi You, the Yellow Emperor provided a model for the creation of a stable political order based on the proper use of violence.

In reality, the scattered references to the various sage-kings in surviving documents lack the tidy, systematic character suggested here. These figures did not arise together in a pantheon of mutual opposition and complementarity, with the various spheres of the human and natural worlds parceled out among their patron deities. As is now generally agreed, the sage-kings were partially-humanized transformations of earlier, supernatural beings who figured in shamanic rituals, cosmogonic myths, or in tales of the origins of various tribes and clans.[6] The sages arose independently in various regions or among different tribes, and they were drawn into a single "pantheon"—or, rather, a "genealogy"—through the centuries-long process of amalgamation and assimilation that created the Chinese civilization.[7]

In addition to being the products of distinct local cultures, certain sages were promoted as models or patrons by specific philosophical schools. At the end of his chapter on the "Five Emperors," Sima Qian observed that scholars had spoken of the Five Emperors from of old, but the canonical *Shang shu* preserved by the Confucians recorded nothing prior to Yao. While the "myriad schools" spoke of the Yellow Emperor, their writings were "neither proper nor in accord with reason," and even those discussions of the Yellow Emperor attributed to Confucius were not transmitted by the Confucians of Sima Qian's day.[8] Ban Gu observed that the Confucians "traced their ancestry back to Yao and Shun," while the "earlier" sage-kings fell outside the Confucian intellectual genealogy.[9] In similar fashion, the Divine Husbandman (see below) was the patron sage of a school of agrarian primitivists who argued that everyone, including the king and his high ministers, should grow his own crops.[10] Thus the myths of the sages that were transmitted in the Warring States were generally created or adapted as elements in the political or social program of a given school.

The Yellow Emperor, for his part, was intellectually associated with the Huang-Lao (黃老) school of political Taoism and the "scholars of [esoteric] techniques" (*fang shi* 方士).[11] Geographically, he was closely linked with the state of Qi in the northeast. The earliest datable references to him, both in the bronzes and in literary sources, come from that state, and the associated philosophical schools were apparently centered there. Evidence from the monograph by Sima Qian on the *feng* and *shan* sacrifices also links the Yellow Emperor to the official cult of the state of Qin in the west, but this is also ultimately a link with Qi, for the leading families of Qin migrated from the northeast during the Western Zhou.[12]

Though gradually integrated into a single framework through the device of more or less systematic genealogies, the sages retained the traces of their disconnected geographic and philosophical origins in their low degree of mutual exclusion. Because they originally had no relation, they were able to share common attributes, and it was easy for competing adherents to claim the myths of rival sages as their own. Consequently, texts assign the same acts, marriages, and progeny to different sages. However, in spite of the blurring produced by disparate origins, in the Warring States period the major deeds or innovations of the various sages were common knowledge, and members of various philosophical schools recognized and cited for their own purposes the tales of "rival" sages. In addition, more syncretic works or works that were not articulating specific philosophical positions freely incorporated the tales of the whole range of sages. The tales of the sage-kings gradually formed a coherent, meaningful body of myths that articulated the interests, concerns, and dilemmas of the Chinese elite.

Specifically, they constituted a mythology of statecraft; they dealt with the interests and concerns produced by the gradual destruction of the city-based world of the Zhou nobility at the hands of the rising territorial lords. The tales of Yao and Shun dealt with the competing claims of virtue/talent and heredity that became an issue as dependent ministers recruited for their skills and linked to the ruler through hierarchical bonds replaced the nobility that had held office as a hereditary privilege. The myths of Yu and the taming of the flood reflected the transformed relation of the political order to the land in a state that was created through the progressive extension of direct control into the countryside, the mobilization of the agrarian populace, and the allocation of plots of land in exchange for taxes and service. The stories of the Yellow Emperor and his battles offered a dramatic representation of the reorganization and revaluation of political violence in a world where mass, peasant armies under the command of the court were replacing the chariot armies of the warrior aristocracy, and where new forms of law were redefining society. In their reformulations of old cosmogonies and clan myths, the makers and advocates of the new political order discovered the principles of their rule in the origins of humanity.

For the mythology of the sages was nothing less than a history of the emergence of humankind out of a savage nature. Underlying all the tales about the sages was the belief that in the earliest times men had not been clearly distinguished from animals. They lived intermixed with animals in the wilds, went naked or wore animal skins, built nests in trees or dwelt in caves, and ate wild plants or raw meat. The fundamental work of the sages was to separate men from the animals and create a distinctive human world, the world of morality and social existence. This process had three basic aspects: the physical separation of men from animals, the transformation of the material conditions of existence through the invention of tools and technological processes, and the introduction of a specifically human code of conduct. These aspects were united through the overarching image of "separation" or "distinction": physical separation, the distinctions of correct perception, and the social divisions of superior and subordinate that uniquely characterized man. Through the drawing of lines and the introduction of appropriate divisions, the sages created the human world out of physical and moral chaos.

The idea that humanity was created in history through the work of sages was common to all the philosophical schools of the period, but each school defined its own ideal of society through naming different innovations as the crucial ones that set men apart from beasts. Legalist texts such as the *Shang Jun shu*, the *Han Feizi*, and the *Guanzi* described how the sages or former kings distinguished men from animals through the creation of laws and units of measure, and then used the power of the masses to enforce these distinctions on the unruly.[13] The fundamental text of the Mohist school tells of a primal "Humpty Dumpty" world in which each man used the terms of moral judgement in whatever manner he chose. This moral and linguistic chaos shattered the bonds that held men together and reduced the human collectivity to the level of birds and beasts. So the first rulers had to unify the language of moral judgements in order to make human society possible.[14] The major Taoist texts also described a "state of nature" in which men were not separated from the animals, and they attributed the subsequent separation to the work of the former rulers.[15] They opposed the other schools only in that they celebrated the primal unity as the highest state and treated the separation as a decline. One striking passage in the *Zhuangzi* stated that what made a human a human was having the distinction between right and wrong, and then argued that this distinction should be abandoned.[16] Consequently the Taoists denied the title of "sage" to the former kings and reserved that term for their own ideal of the truly wise or perfected man.

Perhaps because they were the school in the Warring States period that assigned the highest importance to the authority of the past and the careers of former rulers, the Confucians presented the most detailed versions of the creation of human society out of an undifferentiated primal unity. A passage from the *Mencius* sketches most clearly the various aspects of the creation of the human world.

In the time of Yao the world was not yet stabilized. Floods ran rampant and inundated the world, grasses and trees grew in profusion, birds and animals multiplied wildly, and the five grains did not grow. These birds and animals pressed close to men, and their tracks crisscrossed throughout the Middle Kingdoms. Yao, in his solitude, worried about this, and he raised up Shun and sent him to rectify it. Shun commanded Yi to take a fire and set the mountains and highlands ablaze, so the animals fled and hid. Yu then channeled the nine rivers and led them, rippling and swirling, to the sea. . . . Hou Ji taught the people husbandry, the planting and reaping of the five grains. The five grains ripened, and the people thrived.

It is the way of men that when they can eat their fill, have warm clothing, live at peace, but have no instruction, then they are like beasts. Among the sages there were those who cared for men, and they sent Qi to be Overseer of the Masses and instruct them in the proper human relations. So fathers and sons had familial affection, lords and servants had duty, husbands and wives were properly distinguished, seniors and juniors had their proper order, and comrades had mutual trust.[17]

Here the three steps of physical separation, technological inventions, and moral instruction were neatly laid out in a point-by-point program of the creation of human society.

One of the most important consequences of this idea of the historical creation of humanity through separation from the animal world was that the fundamental distinctions between men and animals were not biological but technological and, above all, moral. Man was an animal with a particular ensemble of productive skills and a set of social relations, and should he lose the one or the other he would return to his animal state. The passage from *Mencius* quoted above sketched the "ascent of man" as a historical, diachronic process, but in his civilized state he still carried all the stages through which he had passed.

Water and fire have primal energy [*qi*] but no life. Grasses and trees have life but no consciousness. Birds and beasts have consciousness but no duties. Men have primal energy, life, and consciousness, and they also have duties. Hence they are the most exalted beings in the world. They are not as strong as the ox nor as swift as the horse, yet they can exploit the ox and the horse. Why is this? Because men can form groups, and beasts cannot. Why can men form groups? Because they have social divisions [or "categories"]. How can such divisions be made to work? Because of duties.[18]

Man stood at the peak of a pyramid of encompassment, wherein each level contained everything that preceded it and added one new feature. The feature that distinguished man was duty, the performance of the correct hierarchical relations that made possible a social existence. If the sense of duty or knowledge of those relations were lost, then he would revert to the level of the beasts.

Therefore in the study of techniques there is an end, but duty cannot be set aside for an instant. If you carry out duty, then you are a man. If you set it aside then you are a beast.[19]

The humanity of man was not given at birth. As Xun Kuang said (*pace* Plato), "The reason a man is a man is not simply that he has two legs and no feathers; it is because he has distinctions."[20] Since humanity was acquired through education, it could, under certain circumstances, be lost.

Nor was the threat of such a loss simply a theoretical possibility, for the early Chinese lived in a world where men could and did become beasts. Social breakdowns were marked by the disappearance of the physical boundaries between men and animals, and the invasion of wild beasts into the human domain.[21] The legendary evil monarchs of antiquity were nothing but animals, and cruel officials, lesser images of the despots, were likewise savage beasts.

Jie and Zhou cared only for profit and had contempt for the true Way, and therefore they perished. . . . To be a man without duty, to only eat and nothing else, this is to be a chicken or a dog. To battle over food and butt with your horns, with the victor taking command, this is to be a wild beast. To be a chicken, dog, or wild beast and hope that men will honor you is impossible.[22]

Examples of apparent men who were truly beasts were even more common in accounts of the tribes who lived at the edges of the Chinese world. These people often lacked the agriculture, sericulture, and fixed dwellings of the Chinese, and their kinship systems and social hierarchies were not readily comprehended by Chinese observers. As a result they lacked the "duty" and "moral instruction" which were the hallmarks of humanity. Not only did the Chinese regularly tag the characters for their generic and tribal names with animal significs, but Chinese authors stated explicitly that they were "wild beasts." Indeed, given their close ties to the natural world they might even understand the speech of animals.[23] If the central, Chinese states lost the rituals that preserved social order, they would become barbarians and animals themselves.[24] Even the civilized states had "wolf children," human infants whose peculiar howls revealed their wild, animal hearts. If these children were not slain at birth, they would cause the destruction of their lineages.[25]

But the most common category of men who fell into the animal realm, and the one most important to this study, was the warrior. The preceding chapter showed how warriors became animals in ceremonial wrestling matches and staged animal combats in the Han imperial rituals, but this idea had a much wider temporal and spatial range. The animal nature of the great warrior was a commonplace of ancient Indian and Western mythology; he was inhuman both in his strength and speed, and in his abandonment of those norms that constrained human behavior in civil society.[26] The Zhou Chinese likewise identified their fighters with beasts. Soldiers wore tiger skins or draped them on their horses, images of tigers and dragons were painted on chariots, and fierce warriors were described as "tigers".[27] The three thousand elite troops who formed the core of the army that overthrew the Shang dynasty were known as "dashing tigers," and the *Wuzi* used this term as a generic label for any crack troops.

> In an army there must be "dashing tiger" soldiers whose strength makes light of the lifting of tripods, whose speed matches that of war horses, and who can always capture the flags and commanders [of the enemy]. Select and separate out men of this caliber. Cherish and exalt them, for they are known as the "army's fate" [or "life"]. Give title and high position to those who are skilled in the five weapons, able to load a crossbow quickly, and whose will is set on devouring the enemy.[28]

The final phrase about "devouring the enemy" is a standard formula for the conquest of another state, but it also suggests that the savagery of the "tigers" might not have stopped with the defeat of their adversaries. In ancient China, just as in modern, a speaker expressed the highest degree of rage or hatred by saying that even to devour his foe would not suffice.[29] However, there is evidence that in ancient times this was more than a figure of speech. As was noted in Chapter One, perpetrators of heinous crimes were chopped up into a meat stew and eaten.[30] In at least one case, an overly bellicose ruler was overthrown, chopped up, and fed to his son.[31] A barbarian army completed the conquest of the state of Wei by devouring its ruler.[32] Thus the designation of warriors as tigers marked not only their power and speed but also their tendency to slide back into the animal realm, as demonstrated by the supreme bestiality of man eating.

The equation of warriors with beasts was not entirely negative. A tiger was an image of strength, quickness, boldness, and the command of lesser beasts, and this is how the term was used by the Zhou nobility and in the *Wuzi*. However, in the myths of the sage-kings animals were markers of the sub-human world that was to be transcended through the work of the sages, so accounts of the introduction of warfare by the Yellow Emperor had to negate or transform the animal nature of the warrior and create a fully human form of violence. The remainder of this chapter is devoted to the analysis of the myths of the Yellow Emperor's battles and some associated rituals in order to discover the ideals of proper violence that they portrayed.

The Yellow Emperor and his Adversaries

In the Han and Warring States accounts that have come down to us, the Yellow Emperor confronted several adversaries on his way to creating the Chinese polity. Each of these opponents had his own mythic attributes and character, and we can learn much about the nature of the Yellow Emperor and his creations through an examination of the figures he overcame. As the meaning of a word can be discerned through finding the terms which it contradicts or negates, so the significance of a figure in myth is often revealed by the nature of his or her enemies.

The earliest surviving sequential narrative of the career of the Yellow Emperor appears at the beginning of Sima Qian's comprehensive history of China. According to his own account, Sima Qian examined all the relevant texts still extant in his time and also incorporated many oral, local traditions that he had collected during his travels. He then eliminated what appeared to be repetitions of the same events and all incidents that seemed too wild or outlandish. His narrative presents a "true" and "plausible" account of the career of the Yellow Emperor as it appeared to a literate, critical Chinese of the second century B.C. who was devoted neither to the philosophy nor the esoteric practices associated with that sage.

The Yellow Emperor was the son of Shao Dian. His surname was Gongsun and his personal name was Xianyuan. At birth his spirit was magically efficacious, in infancy he could speak, when young he was wise and equable, when he grew up he was quick-witted, and when he reached maturity his perceptions were supremely acute. At that time the lineage of the Divine Husbandman had been in decline for generations. The nobles attacked one another and violently persecuted the common people, and the lineage of the Divine Husbandman could not send punitive expeditions against them. So Xianyuan practiced the use of weapons in order to punish all those who did not attend the ruler's court, and the nobles all served him as retainers.

But Chi You was the most savage of them all, and none could attack him. The Fiery Emperor sought to invade and bully the nobles by force, so they all took refuge with Xianyuan. Xianyuan cultivated his spiritual potency and arrayed his troops. He channelled the five *qi*, planted the five grains, consoled the myriad people, measured the four quarters, and instructed the bears, leopards, and tigers, and with them he battled the Fiery Emperor on the plain of Ban Springs. He fought three battles and finally achieved his goals. Chi You rose up in rebellion, and rejected the Yellow Emperor's charge ["command" or "appointment"]. So the Yellow Emperor levied the armies of the nobles, did battle with Chi You at Zhuolu, and killed Chi You. Then the nobles reverenced Xianyuan as the Son of Heaven, replaced the lineage of the Divine Husbandman with him, and he became the Yellow Emperor.

If any under Heaven did not obey, then the Yellow Emperor led an expedition against them, and when they submitted he departed. He broke through the mountains to open up roads, and never came to rest or dwelt in one place. In the east he reached the sea, and ascended Mt. Fan and Mt. Tai. In the west he reached Kongtong and ascended Cockshead Peak. In the south he reached the Yangzi and ascended Bear Peak and Mt. Xiang. In the north he drove off the Hunzhou people [putative ancestors of the Xiongnu], matched the tallies at Ax Mountain [The commentators disagree as to whether this refers to assembling the nobles at court or receiving a divine sign in confirmation of his rule.], and built a city at the base of Zhuolu. He was always moving without any fixed residence, using only his army as an escort. The titles of his officials were all taken from clouds, so they became a cloud army. He appointed Grand Observers of the Left and Right to oversee the myriad states. The myriad states were in harmony, and there were numerous offerings to the ghosts, spirits, mountains, rivers, and the *feng* and *shan*. He obtained the precious tripods [symbols of sovereignty]. He manipulated the spirit yarrow to lay out the calendar. He raised up the Wind Monarch, the Mighty Shepherd, the Constant Vanguard, and the Great Vastness to direct the people. He followed the divisions of Heaven and Earth [yin and yang and the four seasons], the divinations of the hidden and the clear, the sayings about life and death [methods of immortality], and those about preservation and destruction [military theories]. In their proper seasons he planted the hundred grains, grasses, and trees; through his simple purity he civilized the birds, beasts, reptiles, and insects. On all sides he spread out the sun, moon, stars, water, soil, rocks, metal, and jade. He toiled with mind, body, eyes, and ears. He was sparing in the use of water, fire, and materials. He received the auspicious signs of the virtue of the phase of Earth, so he was called the Yellow Emperor.[33]

Sima Qian intended his work to be an account of the entire history of China, and his first chapter relates the "genesis of the Chinese culture and nation."[34] In his opinion, the history of Chinese civilization began with the career of the Yellow Emperor. But that career did not mark the beginning of all history, for the Chinese of the second century B.C. knew of wonder-working inventors of culture who preceded the Yellow Emperor. Sima Qian's references to the Divine Husbandman above, as well as references to the Husbandman and Fu Xi in his "Monograph on the Feng and Shan Sacrifices," show that he shared this knowledge and regarded it as reliable. But the inventions of these earlier sages, like the division of Heaven and Earth, were prior to the Chinese state or civilization. The historical Chinese culture and polity began with the "invention" or cultural innovation made by the Yellow Emperor, and that innovation was the use of correct violence to establish political authority.

Born into a world where men preyed on each other, and the ruler lacked the means to control them, he learned how to bring order to the world through the use of weapons and the instruction of "warrior" beasts. He ruled as a master of force, striking out wherever disorder appeared and having no capital save his army. The significance of his career lay in his military accomplishments, and the understanding of that significance hinges on recognizing the natures of his defeated adversaries. Sima Qian's account names three opponents: the Divine Husbandman, the Fiery Emperor, and Chi You.[35] In order to reconstruct the meaning of this varied opposition and to recognize the different myths that have been woven together in Sima Qian's narrative, it is necessary systematically to re-examine the accounts of the antagonists in other tales and historical writings.

The Divine Husbandman reveals his nature in his name. The

creator of agriculture, he was the focus of several miraculous tales pertaining to the introduction of cereal crops. First, at the time of his birth, nine wells appeared around him, and when water was drawn from any of them, the others gushed forth.[36] He could summon rain at will and also obtained magic grain that fell from the sky.[37] He planted these divine grains, caused rain to fall on them or watered them from his magic wells, and hence men were able to eat cultivated grains. He was the patron sage of the "school of the tillers," a philosophical school that advocated an egalitarian utopia where all men grew their own food. As will be shown below, his association with this radical critique of the privileges of rulers and of political power in general helps to explain his role as an opponent of the Yellow Emperor.

However, the ties of the Divine Husbandman to the career of the Yellow Emperor are more deep-rooted than his links to a political program, for, as the creator of agriculture, he was responsible for a fundamental change in the role of sanctioned violence by freeing men from the obligation to hunt. Ying Shao (ca. 140–ca. 206 A.D.) wrote of the Divine Husbandman that he "invented the plow, taught men to plant, refined their clothing and diet. . ."[38] This "refining" is not explained, but earlier texts fill out the remark by noting that prior to the Divine Husbandman men ate raw meat and wild fruit, drank blood, and wore the skins of animals.[39] Eating meat, drinking blood, and wearing animal skins were all characteristics of the Zhou nobility, and it is possible that some memories of the warrior aristocracy underlay these Warring States and Han accounts of man in the "state of nature."[40] However, hunting animals for food and clothing also plays a pivotal role in the mythology of violence throughout the world. As Marcel Detienne has written:

> Or, more concisely, it is because, in the order of myth, the activity of hunting constitutes an excellent operator. And this for a series of reasons: as a fundamentally masculine activity in which confrontation with wild animals leads to the spilling of blood at the same time as it provides meat as food, hunting contrasts with farming but is closely linked to war. . . . Situated at the intersection of the powers of life and forces of death, the hunter's space constitutes at once that which is beyond the farmer's fields and their negation. . . . By confronting wild animals, he prepares himself more or less directly to become a warrior initiated into the unshared privilege of men: violent bloodshed.[41]

In the role of the hunt, contrasted with farming but linked to war, we find the place of the Divine Husbandman in the myths of the origins of sanctioned killing. As the premier agriculturist he stands in direct opposition to the figures of the huntsman and warrior. Through his miracles and creations he delivered men from the necessity of the hunt, the eating of flesh, and the drinking of blood, and he thereby made possible a human existence that required no violence whatsoever.[42] Thus it is no accident that the spiritual power of the Divine Husbandman had to wane before the Yellow Emperor's rule through force could begin. Nor is it surprising that the heirs of the Divine Husbandman could not cope with the violence of the rebels, for theirs was the bloodless rule of an agrarian utopia.

This mythic opposition of the creator of agriculture to sanctioned killing in the form of hunting reflects the political program of the philosophical adherents of the Divine Husbandman. The claim that all men should devote themselves to agriculture was an explicit rejection not only of artisanry and trade, but more importantly of any ruling elite that harvested the fruits of taxation rather than those of the fields. This rejection of any government suggests also the repudiation of the punishments and military power that ultimately enforced government authority.

In fact, this repudiation was more than suggested, for early Chinese authors explicitly describe the pacific character of the Husbandman's rule and assert that, in contrast with the Yellow Emperor and later monarchs, he did not kill or punish.[43] The *Lü Shi chun qiu* offers the clearest contrast between the bloodless government of the Divine Husbandman and the practices of subsequent rulers. It describes how the virtuous Bo Yi and Shu Qi heard that the Zhou house was about to attain the Way and went there to observe. They witnessed the Zhou king making sacrifices and burying blood-smeared covenants to secure support in preparation for the coming campaign against the Shang.

> Bo Yi and Shu Qi listened to this, looked at one another and laughed. "How strange! This is not what I call the Way. Long ago the Divine Husbandman held all under Heaven. His seasonal offerings were totally reverent, but he sought no blessings. He treated men with trust and made all correct, but he demanded nothing. He delighted in correctness and thereby made all correct; he delighted in order and thereby made all orderly. He did not achieve his purposes through harming others, nor did he exalt himself through debasing others. Now Zhou sees that Yin [Shang] is deviant and chaotic, and he seeks instantly to make them correct and orderly. So the lord schemes and carries out bribes; he relies on weapons in order to constrain through fear; he carves up sacrifices and swears blood oaths in order to create trust. . . . He kills and assaults in order to seek benefit, and hopes thereby to sum-

mon Yin to his court. This is to exchange rampant violence for chaos."[44]

This passage holds up the Divine Husbandman as a model to condemn those who ruled through sacrifice, blood oaths, and warfare.[45] The critique is aimed explicitly at the Zhou monarchy, but the rulers of the Warring States could not have escaped its condemnation. The Yellow Emperor's replacement of the Divine Husbandman's lineage marked not merely the succession of one dynasty to another, but the mythic introduction of rule through violence. Through sagely historical precedent, it justified the political order of the Warring States period in the face of the denial of the value of monarchy or the propriety of force.[46]

*   *   *

The search for the the Yellow Emperor's second adversary, the Fiery Emperor, leads back to an earlier stratum of myths, in which the image of battle was mythically invoked to describe the triumphant arrival of rain at the end of the dry season, and ritually incorporated in various ceremonies intended to ensure that arrival. Although these tales preceded the shift of attention to the issue of violence, traces of them remain scattered throughout the Warring States and Han texts and rites, so a complete understanding of the myths of the Yellow Emperor must deal with them as well.

The Fiery Emperor, like the Divine Husbandman, suggests his nature in his name. In the Warring States he was identified as the ruler of the phase fire and corresponded to the sun. But his name had a more archaic sense which revealed his original nature. The character which I have translated "fiery" (*yan* 炎) and the character meaning "red" (*chi* 赤), by which this figure was also known, are variants of the same graph. It etymologically represented a human figure standing in flames and referred to a rainmaking ceremony which is known in Zhou texts as "exposing the shaman" or "burning the shaman."[47] Thus the Fiery Emperor was eponymously related to rituals of drought prevention and rain making. He was "fiery" in the sense of an excess of sun and of the homeopathic burning ceremony, and "red" as the color of drought-baked earth.

The Fiery Emperor was ritually and mythically tied to the Yellow Emperor from an early date. The "Monograph on the *Feng* and *Shan* Sacrifices" in the *Shi ji* states that in the last quarter of the fifth century B.C. the state of Qin established an upper altar at Wuyang where they sacrificed to the Yellow Emperor and a lower one where they sacrificed to the Fiery Emperor. Again, when Emperor Wu of the Han sacrificed to the Five Emperors at the base of Mt. Tai, he incorporated the sacrifice to the Fiery Emperor under that to the Yellow Emperor.[48] Moreover, in the Warring States period and the early Western Han there was a widespread tradition that the two were brothers.[49] The tradition of the battle between them, referred to in numerous texts, also constitutes a bond. Finally, the *Lü Shi chun qiu* linked them as wielders of "natural" weapons.

> The ancient sage-kings had "weapons of duty," but there were none who brought an end to the use of weapons. Weapons originated long ago; they appeared together with mankind. Weapons constrain through fear, and what constrains through fear is force. To constrain through force is men's nature, and nature is what is received from Heaven; it cannot be contrived by men. . . . The Yellow and Fiery Emperors used water and fire. . . . Some men say that Chi You created weapons, but Chi You did not create weapons. He only made them sharp [reference to the use of metal for weapons].[50]

This passage links the Fiery and Yellow Emperors as the users of weapons of water and fire. Nor is this an isolated instance, for several texts refer to the "calamities of fire" caused by the Fiery Emperor.[51] These "calamities of fire" recall his links to the sun and droughts, and they suggest that his "weapons of fire" produced a drought that could only be dispelled through the "weapons of water." We see the outlines of an early myth in which two spirits identified respectively with drought and with rainfall engaged in a battle between fire and water to determine the fate of the agricultural season.

And there is, in fact, abundant evidence that the Yellow Emperor was a lord of rain and storm. First, the *Shi ji*'s account of his career mentioned his minister "Wind Monarch" and told how he gave his officials the titles of clouds and had a "cloud army," and these stories appear in other texts as well.[52] Moreover, various texts state that the Yellow Emperor had the face of a dragon, that his imminent attainment of Heaven's Mandate was marked by the appearance of dragons, that the constellation that bore his name had the body of a yellow dragon and ruled thunder and rain, and that he departed on a dragon at the end of his life.[53] Since dragons were identified with clouds and rain, the fact that the Yellow Emperor was, or had the attributes of, a dragon clearly indicates his command of storms and rainfall.

His birth legend also shows his ties to storms. Like the other sages, the Yellow Emperor's birth resulted not from ordinary conception but from divine inspiration by a "spirit progenitor," and the cosmic father of the Yellow Emperor was a bolt of lightning that encircled the North Star.[54] Other texts show in various ways that the Yellow Emperor was also the lord of thunder.[55]

A final piece of evidence linking the Yellow Emperor to storms appears in the third century B.C. text *Han Feizi*.

> Lord Ping [of Jin] asked, "May I hear the clear *jiao* music?" Shi Kuang replied, "No. Long ago the Yellow Emperor gathered the ghosts and spirits on the western summit of Mt. Tai. He rode an ivory chariot pulled by six dragons. Bi Fang ran alongside, while Chi You went in front. The Wind Monarch swept the path, and the Rain Master wetted down the dust. Tigers and wolves were in front, and the ghosts and spirits were behind. The lizards and snakes were beneath, while the phoenix was above. He gathered all the ghosts and spirits, and created the clear *jiao*. Now my lord's virtuous potency is meager, and it is not sufficient to listen to it." Lord Ping said, "I am old and what I most love is music. I wish to hear it." Shi Kuang had no alternative, so he played it. Once, and black clouds rose from the northwest. Twice, and a great wind came, followed by a great rain. It rent the curtains, broke the vessels, and sent the tiles of the portico flying. Lord Ping was terrified and hid between the portico and the rear chamber. The state of Jin then had a great drought which baked [The verb is actually "reddened." It is the alternate form of the character of the Fiery Emperor.] the earth for three years.[56]

In this account not only does the Yellow Emperor command dragons and masters of wind and rain—in addition to Chi You, who will be discussed below—but he is the creator of a potent music that unleashes storms and triggers droughts. Thus the reasons for his pairing with the Fiery Emperor in the mythology of rain and drought are clear.

In addition to storms, the Yellow Emperor was also associated with fog. As a sage he was an inventor of devices or a revealer of meaningful patterns, and many of his major innovations came to him in the fog. Chapter Three included the story of the primal revelation of a military treatise made to him after three days in the darkness of a fog. His discoveries of the compass and of the sacred *He tu* manuscript were also made after extended periods in fog.

> The Yellow Emperor battled Chi You at Zhuolu, and Chi You created a great fog which lasted three days. The soldiers did not know what to do, so the Yellow Emperor ordered the Wind Monarch to imitate the North Star [the Yellow Emperor's spirit

progenitor] and create the "south-pointing chariot" [a proto-compass] in order to distinguish the four directions, and they captured Chi You.

In the time of the Yellow Emperor the sky was filled with a great fog for three days. While wandering about above the Luo River, the Emperor saw a great fish and killed five sacrificial beasts to offer up to it. Then Heaven sent down a great rain for seven days and seven nights. He received an illustrated book which was the *He tu*.[57]

This link of the Yellow Emperor's sagely capacities to the fog is clearly tied to his role as a master of clouds, wind, and rain.

The first story quoted above is also of interest because Chi You's use of fog to attack the Yellow Emperor is the first specific example of a "water weapon." A more extensive account of such weapons appears in the *Shan hai jing*.

Chi You created weapons and attacked the Yellow Emperor, so the Yellow Emperor ordered the Responding Dragon to attack him at Jizhou. The dragon sucked up the waters, but Chi You asked the Wind Monarch and Rain Master to unleash great winds and rain. The Yellow Emperor then called down the celestial woman Bo, and the rain stopped, whereupon he killed Chi You. Bo was unable to ascend again, and wherever she dwelt it did not rain. Shu Jun spoke of this to the Yellow Emperor, who placed her north of the Red River [The character "red" is once again the name of the Fiery Emperor and descriptive of drought-seared earth.]. Shu Jun then performed the *Zu* ceremony [see below] to the fields. Bo sometimes escapes, and those who desire to chase her away command, "Spirit, go back north!" First they clear out the waterways and dredge the gutters and ditches.[58]

From Guo Pu's commentary we know that a ritual against drought associated with this story was still in use in the fourth century A.D., and another passage in the *Shan hai jing* shows the links of this myth to popular rainmaking rituals.[59]

These stories demonstrate that the tales of the use of water weapons by the Yellow Emperor were related to rituals for warding off drought in early imperial China.[60] However, they also pose a problem. In the two examples of water weapons given above, the Yellow Emperor's adversary Chi You produces rain and fog, while the Yellow Emperor halts rain and brings on droughts. This is exactly the opposite of the results predicted by the analysis of the traits of the Fiery Emperor in his opposition to the Yellow Emperor. To resolve this problem we must turn our attention to the figure of Chi You.

*   *   *

The analysis thus far has defined the Yellow Emperor through two oppositions: he was a master of political violence in contrast to the bloodless rule of the Divine Husbandman, and he was a master of storms in contrast to the droughts of the Fiery Emperor. Chi You had characteristics that figured in both of these oppositions, and in both cases he aligned on the side of the Yellow Emperor, for he was a master of weapons and a master of storms.

As with the Divine Husbandman and the Fiery Emperor, the search for the nature of Chi You can begin with his name. Through phonetic and paleographic analysis of the characters of the name, several modern scholars have argued that Chi You was originally a snake or dragon spirit.[61] While I will suggest a different origin of the name below, there is no doubt that Chi You had certain attributes of the dragon. First, as we saw in the stories above, he could command wind and rain. Second, several texts record that Chi You ate sand and rocks, and a passage in the *Huainanzi* states that eating these substances was a defining trait of earthworms and the closely-related dragons.[62] One of these texts also refers to Chi You's "bronze head with iron forehead," which might be derived from the scales of a snake or dragon, although it might also be a reference to the horns which we have already seen in other accounts of Chi You. A description of Chi You preceding the account of the "Chi You game" in Jizhou cited above states explicitly that he could "create fogs and clouds." Finally, Dong Zhongshu (179–104 B.C.) identified Chi You as the recipient of the summer sacrifice for rain, a sacrifice that involved erecting a model of a dragon.[63] Chi You, like the Yellow Emperor, was thus clearly associated with dragons and acted as a master of wind and rain.

Chi You was also a lord of warfare, specifically a "master of weapons." Under that title he received sacrifice from Qin Shihuang (258–210 B.C.) in the state of Qi.[64] Many texts attributed the creation of weapons to Chi You. Others explicitly denied it, as we have seen in two passages quoted earlier, but the existence of these denials clearly shows that the belief was widespread, and even some of those who said he did not create weapons in general granted him credit for the introduction of metal weapons.[65] Indeed, Chi You can be iconographically identified in Han art only through his regular depiction bearing the "five weapons."[66]

Not only was he the mythical creator and patron of weapons, but during the Han he also figured as the tutelary "deity" of warfare, and the very origin of warfare was identified with Chi You. In describing the frequency and ferocity of the warfare from the Qin dynasty's conquest of China to the establishment of the Han, Sima Qian wrote, "From the time of Chi You to the present there has been nothing like it."[67] When Liu Bang, who later founded the Han dynasty, became the Lord of Pei in 209 B.C., he sacrificed to Chi You, and Sima Qian linked this sacrifice with his ability to capture the Qin capital and become the king of Han.[68] In 204 B.C., when Li Yiji tried to persuade the king of Qi to ally with Liu Bang rather than Xiang Yu, he argued:

That the king of Han [Liu Bang] was able to mobilize Shu and Ba, pacify the region of Qin, cross beyond the West River, rescue the troops at Shangdang, capture Jingxing, execute the Lord of Cheng-an, smash Wei Bao, and capture thirty-two cities, this was the work of Chi You's weapons; it was not the strength of man but the blessing of Heaven.[69]

Because of his association with the establishment of the dynasty, the Han rulers instituted regular sacrifices to Chi You in the capital and, after 61 B.C., at the reputed site of his burial. These sacrifices were abolished in 31 B.C., reflecting a program of economies and the general decline of the status of the military in Han China, but as late as 72 A.D. Ma Yan made a sacrifice to Chi You at the armory of Loyang.[70] The military aspect of Chi You also figured in astronomical divination, for he was identified with a comet whose appearance signalled that there would be "royal military expeditions in all directions."[71] Moreover, from the appearances of Chi You in the tomb art of the Eastern Han and his role in popular festivals, it is clear that in his martial aspect he remained a major cultic figure over the course of the Han dynasty.[72]

Thus there were two creators and patrons of warfare in early imperial China, and both of them were lords of the storm. This link between warfare and storms is not unusual; many gods in different cultures share elements of the violence of storms and that of men, e.g., Indra and Thor. In China this link was clearest in the overlapping images of thunder and the drum. One story told how the Yellow Emperor slew the thundering *kui* beast and made it into a drum with which to overawe the world, and it was a common metaphor in Chinese literature that thunder was the drum of Heaven.[73] The drum was, for its part, an instrument of war. Dedicated with the blood of captured enemies, it was beaten in battle to signal commands, to provide a rhythm for movement in unison, and to spur men on to greater valor. So it is not surprising that the creators of warfare in Chinese mythology were originally lords of thunder and the storm.

Although it is unremarkable that the creators of warfare in China were also lords of the storm, it is puzzling that there should be two of them. Chi You was an opponent of the Yellow Emperor, but he shared many of the sage's basic traits, both as a bringer of storms and the introducer of warfare. In contrast with the other adversaries, he relates to the Yellow Emperor not in neat oppositions but as a strange double. The roots of this doubling lie in the role of these twinned adversaries in the sacrificial rituals and the festivals of the New Year season.

The Myths and the New Year Festivals

The New Year season was the center of the ritual calendar in early imperial China, and it was a time rich in festivals.[74] Since it occurred during the second half of the dry season in the monsoon climate of northern China, it was a time of concern over the coming of rain, and as it fell in the winter, it became linked to violence in the calendrical model of government. Thus it is reasonable that the lords of storm and creators of warfare should appear in the mythology and rituals of this season. Chi You figures in the New Year season as a tutelary spirit of the *Zha* (蜡) festival and as the mythological prototype of the exorcist at the *La* (臘). In both of these roles he figured as a guardian of processions and an apotropaic deity who used his weapons to drive off evil spirits. There is no direct evidence of the Yellow Emperor in these rituals, but literary discussions of various elements of the *Zha* ritual and of the exorcist show that in the former Chi You appeared as the servant of the Yellow Emperor, while the latter was identified as a wife or son of the Yellow Emperor and tied to his service. In the New Year rituals the two appear not as adversaries but as master and servant, or as deity and votary. This provides a plausible explanation for the mythic sharing of attributes or doubling of the two figures, and it also reveals the ritual background to the various texts that describe Chi You as a minister of the Yellow Emperor.

The *Zha* was a major festival under the Zhou dynasty, and Han scholars identified it with their own great New Year festival, the *La* (臘). This identification remains disputed, but it is clear that the *Zha* had been one of the central festivals of the New Year season and dealt with the same basic concerns as the better-documented *La*.[75] Following the completion of the harvest by the tenth month, the world entered a period of dormancy and the community a period of relative idleness which was devoted to putting itself in order for the labors that accompanied the return of life in the spring. These preparations would have included such utilitarian concerns as the repair of tools, the dredging of irrigation channels, the preparation of seeds, and so forth, but the festivals were devoted to ritually cleansing the community and restoring it to proper order by sending off the accumulated pollution and evil influences of the past year. It was in the rituals of expulsion and cleansing that Chi You played a major role.

There are several pieces of evidence which show that the *Zha* festival, like the later *La* and the New Year season in general, was concerned with the elimination of pollution and restoration of order. First, a prayer for the *Zha* recorded in the *Li ji* reads:

> O dirt, return to your proper abode. O waters, return to your channels. O insects, do not arise. O wild grasses and trees, return to your wastes.[76]

This invocation summons the various items of the natural world to return to their proper places and seeks to remove dirt from the community and wild plants from the agricultural fields.

A second element of the ritual that invoked the image of removal or sending away was the wearing of white garments by the man who performed the sacrifices. A passage in the *Li ji* explains that this was in order to "send off that which has ended" and "mourn that which is killed."[77] Winter was the season of death and dormancy, and one of the major tasks of the New Year season festivals was to ritually dispose of the dead remnants of the old year in order to prepare for the coming of the new. The sacrificer wore white, the color customarily worn at funerals in China, because the ceremony was a rite of mourning and sending off the "dead." As we shall see below, Chi You was regularly invoked as a guardian of funeral processions, and it was in this capacity that he figured in the *Zha*.

The etymology of the character *zha* likewise demonstrates this aspect of the festival. Definitions in Han dictionaries and the analysis of phonetically-related characters both suggest a focus on the problems of aging, spoilage, and decay.[78] In the *Zhou li* the character was the title of an official with three duties: to dispose of rotting meat or bones with meat still attached (apparently the remains of sacrifices); to guarantee that criminals, people in mourning, and foreigners were not in the capital during major sacrifices; and to arrange for the burial of strangers who died on the road and the disposition of their goods.[79] All these duties were of a piece, for they consisted of the removal of polluting elements and the restoration of proper order or purity. Moreover, his role in funerals also linked him to the "funereal" aspect of the *Zha*. Finally, the duties of this official reveal ties between the *Zha* and the rainmaking ceremonies linked to the Yellow Emperor and Chi You that were discussed above, because the collection and burial of corpses was one element of the Han rituals for seeking rain.[80]

There are several pieces of evidence linking Chi You to this ritual of communal cleansing and the expulsion of evil influences. First, the *Zha* as performed by the Son of Heaven involved sacrifices to eight spirits and was thus also known as the *Eightfold Zha*. Qin Shihuang made sacrifices to eight spirits in the state of Qi, sacrifices which were noted for their antiquity even in the third century B.C., and one of these eight spirits was Chi You.[81] While the fact that the sacrifices were made to eight spirits is merely suggestive, we know from a fragment of a Wei dynasty (220–264 A.D.) anthology preserved in a commentary to the *Shi ji* that the sacrifice to Chi You in Qi was regularly made in the tenth month, the month of the *Zha*.[82] Thus the sacrifice to the eight spirits by Qin Shihuang was held at the time of the *Zha*, which shows that Chi You was one of the deities of the New Year *Zha*.

There is also clear evidence that at the popular level the *Zha* had a riotous, orgiastic character as the peasants celebrated the successful harvest and their momentary escape from the crushing burdens of agricultural toil.[83] This presumably included eating and drinking, music, dancing, and ceremonial masquerades. Since the sacrifice to Chi You was held at this time, it is quite possible that these festivities would have included the "Chi You game," which was part of the public cult of Chi You held at the supposed site of his execution by the Yellow Emperor. At any rate, we know that the *La* festival of the Han included a performance of the *jue di*, the Han ancestor of the "Chi You game."[84] Thus Chi You not only received sacrifice at the *Zha* but also appeared in ritual performances and popular festivities.

The reason for Chi You's appearance in the *Zha* is explained by his role as an apotropaic deity who escorted processions and protected them from the attacks of evil spirits. He performed this role in sacrifices accompanying the seeing-off of travelers on journeys, in funeral ceremonies where he escorted the coffin to the tomb and guarded it there, and as the exorcist in the *La* festival. Since the *Zha* was a ceremony of "sending off" and was ritually equated with funerals, Chi You was invoked as one of its guiding spirits, and it was through this role that he ultimately became the exorcist in the Han *La*, which was either the later equivalent of the same festival or an extension of the same seasonal ritual concerns.

As was seen above, the *Zha* was explicitly identified in the ritual texts as a ceremony of "sending off." In addition, it was linguistically equated with the sacrifice used to send off a traveller (*Zu*), which in Han times was a regular part of the New Year festivals. The Han dictionary

Shuo wen jie zi glossed *Zha* with the character 䐣 *tsag, which was homophonous and interchangeable with the character *zu* (祖 *tsag), the name of the travel sacrifice. Moreover, there is clear evidence of a fixed, annual *Zu* ceremony associated with the *La* and the New Year season. The Eastern Han scholar Ying Shao immediately followed his discussion of the *La* with an account of the *Zu*, stating that it was a regular, annual sacrifice to the god of the road. The Wei dynasty ritual specialist Gao Tanglong (d. 237 A.D.) wrote a memorial dealing with the days on which the ruler should hold the *La* and *Zu* sacrifices, which again shows that the *Zu* was an annual sacrifice celebrated as part of the New Year festivals.[85] Since this *Zu* was homophonous with *Zha*, played the same role, and appeared at the same time in the ritual calendar, it is likely that it was the Han version of the same festival.

There is clear evidence that Chi You played a role in the *Zu*, and this sheds light on his role in the New Year festivals and his relation to the Yellow Emperor. The evidence appears in a prayer for a *Zu* composed or recorded by the Eastern Han scholar Cai Yong (133–192 A.D.).

> In a felicitous year and a good month, an auspicious day and a fortunate hour, may you be very happy when you set out in the light of dawn. The spirit turtle has auspicious cracks, and propitious mists shine brightly. The hexagrams have favorable prognostications, and the three lights appear in the sky. The phoenix calls, "Yong yong." The four stallions are high-spirited. You mount the chariot, and the road opens before you. May the Wind Monarch and the Rain Master wet down the road. May the "sun-catching mirror" seek blessings. May Chi You ward off weapons. May the Green Dragon go alongside. May the White Tiger help you proceed. May the Vermillion Bird lead you. May the *xuanwu* [spirit of the north, a snake wrapped around a turtle] be your companion. May *Gou Chen* [the North Star] reside in the middle and subdue the four quarters. You go to a neighboring land; may you have eternal joy without end.[86]

In this passage Chi You appears as a benevolent deity whose role was to ward off the harm of the weapons he had created. Equally important is the appearance of the Yellow Emperor, in the guise of the North Star, who was his spirit progenitor. Perched in his traditional spot at the center, he rules the four quarters, here identified by the four symbolic creatures. There is a very close resemblance between this passage and the *Han Feizi*'s description quoted above of the Yellow Emperor's procession to Mt. Tai for the performance of the clear *jiao* music. Once again the masters of wind and rain prepare the road, Chi You serves as an escort, a magical creature runs alongside, and the Yellow Emperor sits in the center. The only significant modifications are the addition of the beasts of the four quarters and the traveler himself. It is unclear whether Cai Yong modeled his prayer on the passage in the *Han Feizi* or whether the latter was itself based on mythic tales associated with the *Zu* ceremony already in use in the third century B.C., but in either case Chi You and the Yellow Emperor appear as guardian deities of travel and processions.

The Yellow Emperor also appears in the etiological myths of the *Zu* sacrifice. Han dynasty works state that the god who received the sacrifice in this ceremony was the son of an ancient ruler, most commonly the Yellow Emperor, who had died while traveling.[87] Later texts make the same assertion and suggest that the role of the sacrifice was to assuage the ghosts of all those who had died on the road, received no regular sacrifices, and hence might threaten travelers if not appeased.[88] This explanation links the *Zu* to the *zha* official, whose duties included the disposition of unknown, wayside corpses, and also with the theme of purification and restoration of order of the annual *Zha* festival.

In summation, the role of Chi You in the *Zha* was to guard against evil influences as the community "sent off" the lingering pollutions of the dying year. He was assigned this duty because he played the role in the then homophonous *Zu* ceremony, and this latter had by the Han become a basic element of the New Year rituals. Chi You performed this role under the direction of the Yellow Emperor, who was the patron of the *Zu* through his mythic identification as the father of the god of the sacrifice.

During the *La*, the central New Year ceremony of the Han dynasty, Chi You played an almost identical role, but in this ritual he appeared in the guise of the "exorcist" (*fang xiang shi* 方相氏).[89] The most detailed account of this figure appears in the *Zhou li*.

It is his duty to drape over himself a bearskin with four gold eyes, to wear a black upper garment and a red lower garment, to grasp his lance and lift up his shield, and lead his many assistants in the seasonal exorcisms, searching [the verb used is *suo* 素 *sak. This word is offered as a homophonous gloss for the *Zha* festival in the *Li ji*. Whatever the value of this gloss, it shows that during the late Warring States period both festivals were closely identified with the seeking out and expelling of impurities.] through the chambers and driving out pestilences. At great funerals he goes in advance of the coffin. When they reach the tomb and the coffin is inserted in the burial chamber, he strikes the chamber's four corners with his halberd to expel the Fangliang. . . . The exorcist has four subordinates called the "madmen."[90]

Earlier scholars have identified this figure with Chi You on the basis of a description of the latter that appears in a rhapsody by Zhang Heng (78–139 A.D.).

Then Chi You grasped his lance, shook his shaggy coverlet with its stripings and warded off the improper. Thereby spirit treachery was made known and the Chimei and Fangliang could not come against the imperial procession.[91]

The weapon and shaggy hide roughly correspond to the costume of the exorcist. Chi You's covering appears to be a tiger skin rather than that of a bear, but in Eastern Han tomb art Chi You sometimes looks like a roly-poly bear, as in the Wuliang reliefs and at Tomb no. 1 near Changli, and sometimes has a tiger's head, as at Yinan, so the discrepancy is not crucial. Moreover, the Chimei and Fangliang were two of the types of demons expelled in the great exorcism. These links have led most scholars tentatively to accept the identification.

The case for the identification, however, is considerably stronger than this. First, the exorcist had four eyes, and so did the Chi You spirit that appeared at Jizhou and was celebrated in the horn-butting "Chi You game."[92] Second, in Cai Yong's prayer and the passage in the *Han Feizi* Chi You was called upon to precede the traveler and guard his way, and this was also his role in the poem cited above as well as in another poem in the same anthology. These all reflect his role in the *Zu* ceremony, and Shen Yue (441–513 A.D.) noted that this ceremony was performed before a funeral procession set out.[93] This would indicate that Chi You was summoned to go in front of funeral processions to ward off evil spirits, which is the role assigned to the exorcist in the *Zhou li*. Moreover, excavations of Warring States and Han tombs have revealed several pieces of evidence that Chi You was a guardian of tombs and hence the mythic prototype of the exorcist.

The first body of evidence concerns the role of horned creatures as tomb guardian figures. As described in the *Shu yi ji* and commemorated in the horn-butting game, Chi You had horns on his head, and in his depictions in Han tomb art he has a crossbow "growing" out of his head in an apparent variant of these horns. There is a long tradition in China of invoking horned creatures as apotropaic or guardian spirits generally associated with tombs. The famous *tao tie* design which is so common on Shang ritual bronzes clearly has horns, although its exact function is not certain. In many tombs of the region of Chu state, archeologists have found statues of monstrous, horned creatures that were apparently tomb guardians, and at Changsha, Xinye, and Zhaogu the same function was played by a pair of horns or antlers mounted on a base. These fierce, horned figures continue to appear in tombs down to the Tang dynasty.[94] Thus the horns of Chi You were probably linked to his role as a guardian of tombs.

The most direct evidence of Chi You's role as a tomb guardian, however, comes from the use of his image in Eastern Han funerary art. The most notable example appears in the tomb at Yinan, where he is carved on the northern wall of the front tomb chamber, directly over the doorway leading to the central chamber where the corpse was interred. With his weapons, tiger visage, and horns in the form of a crossbow, he clearly functioned as a tomb guardian to keep evil spirits and perhaps grave robbers from intruding in the inner chambers. Equally notable is the fact that he is surrounded by images of the animals of the four quarters, just as he was in the *Zu* prayer of Cai Yong.[95] Since the *Zu* was performed prior to carrying the corpse to the tomb, these wall illustrations permanently fixed in defense of the corpse the spirit forces marshalled by the ritual to guard it on the way to the tomb. It is also worth noting that the exorcist as described in the *Zhou li* struck the four corners of the tomb chamber with his halberd, and the association of Chi You with the animals of the four quarters might well reflect this ritual performance of a comprehensive exorcism in all four directions. The exorcist's four eyes are also probably related to the same practices and mythic associations.

This cumulative evidence clearly demonstrates that Chi You was the mythic prototype of the exorcist, and his performance of this role derived from his function in the earlier *Zha* and *Zu* ceremonies. However, in the case of these earlier ceremonies we saw that he was identified as a servant of the Yellow Emperor, and in his role as exorcist he was associated with the same sage. Just as Chi You served as a mythic double of the Yellow Emperor in the tales of the battles of fire and water and those of the origins of warfare, so the exorcist appeared as a physical double of the Yellow Emperor, and in one set of myths as his consort or servant.

The most notable physical traits of the exorcist were the bearskin and the four eyes, and these were both features associated with the Yellow Emperor. Numerous early texts record that the Yellow Emperor ruled "Bear Country" and as a result was called "bear."[96] Several scholars have argued that the passage in the *Tian wen* which asks, "Where is the hornless dragon who travels with a bear on its back?" refers to the departure of the Yellow Emperor on the back of a dragon.[97] So the exorcist's bearskin suggests a link to the Yellow Emperor.

There was also a tradition that the Yellow Emperor had four eyes, or four faces, to look in all directions. This was probably related to his common designation as the spirit of the center, with the eyes or faces corresponding to the four quarters.

> Zi Gong said, "In ancient days the Yellow Emperor had four faces. Do you believe it?" Confucius replied, "The Yellow Emperor gathered around him four men and had them rule the four quarters. . . . This is what is meant by 'four faces.'"[98]

In spite of the rationalizing explanation, this passage clearly demonstrates the belief that the Yellow Emperor had four faces. Other texts dating back to the late Warring States testify to the same tradition, and one refers to four eyes.[99] Moreover, even the euhemerist theory of the four ministers associates the Yellow Emperor with the exorcist, who was assisted by the four "madmen." So a figure with four eyes and wearing a bearskin could represent the Yellow Emperor.

In addition there is direct evidence linking the Yellow Emperor to the office of the exorcist. A Tang dynasty account of his career says:

> When the Yellow Emperor was traveling around, his primary wife Lei Zu died on the road. The Emperor sacrificed to her as the spirit of the *Zu*. [This is identical to the account in the Eastern Han *Si min yue ling*, except that here the eponymous Lei Zu is identified as a wife rather than a son.] He ordered his secondary wife Mo Mu (嫫母 *mwag mwag) to guard the roads [or "guard it on the road," referring to the funeral procession of Lei Zu]. He sacrificed to her seasonally, and accordingly made Mo Mu the exorcist [*fang xiang shi* *piwang siang jieg. The commentary explains that this meant 防喪氏 *biwang sang jieg "protector of the funeral." The gloss is ingenious, phonologically consistent, and fits with accounts of the ritual function of the exorcist.].[100]

The text is relatively late, but it is based on earlier materials. The first significant point here is that it links the exorcist with the *Zu* ceremony. Although there is no explicit statement in a Han or pre-Han text that the exorcist participated in the *Zu*, one story suggests that he and the "madmen" did in fact play a role in that ceremony.[101] Moreover, in a detailed study of the various evil spirits that the ancient Chinese feared to encounter on the road and who were consequently the "targets" of the *Zu*, Jiang Shaoyuan has shown that these were closely related to and often identical with those expelled by the exorcist at the Great Exorcism.[102] This indicates the extremely close relationship between the roles of exorcizing evil influences at the New Year and protecting travelers on the road, which makes the common performance of these roles by the exorcist quite plausible. This is yet another argument for the identification of Chi You as the prototype of the exorcist.

Of course this passage states that Mo Mu, not Chi You, was the mythic prototype of the exorcist, but these two figures were closely related. Mo Mu is well attested in pre-Han and Han sources, and these references demonstrate two points. First, she was indeed linked to the Yellow Emperor, probably in a sexual manner.[103] Second, she served as a literary trope to describe the ultimate in physical ugliness.[104] This extreme ugliness proves that the identification of Mo Mu as the exorcist was not a late development. Mo Mu was regularly contrasted with the legendary beauty Xi Shi, but in one passage the latter was contrasted with the "ugly spirit-mask [*qi* 頎 *kieg].*"[105] As is shown in other sources, this "ugly spirit-mask" was the mask worn by the exorcist, and several passages show that ugliness was its defining characteristic.[106] Since the hideousness of which Mo Mu was the mythic embodiment was the defining characteristic of the exorcist, the identification of Mo Mu with the exorcist probably dates back to the Warring States period.[107]

This identification, however, does not invalidate the proposition that Chi You was the prototype of the exorcist, for the ugliness that characterized Mo Mu and defined the exorcist was also a distinguishing feature of Chi You. The first character of his/her name (蚩 *t'ieg) was virtually homophonous with the character meaning "ugly" (醜 *t'iog), and in several texts from the Han and later periods the character *chi* was used with the sense of "ugly" or "vile."[108] Hence Chi You's name quite possibly meant "the ugly prodigy," which would suggest very close ties to Mo Mu indeed.

One further feature of Mo Mu is significant here. Both of the homophonous characters that make up her name were also homophones of the character *wu* (巫 *mwag "shamaness"), and the name Mo Mu probably originally meant "shamaness." So the story of Mo Mu's marriage or intercourse with the Yellow Emperor recalled the ritual encounter of the shamaness, one of whose duties was to make rain, with the god of the storm.[109] Chi You was perhaps the mythic projection of the rainmaking shaman or shamaness, who would also have played the role of the exorcist in the appropriate rituals. This link of shamans to Chi You and the exorcist is not purely speculative, for a passage in the *Xunzi* specifically states that shamans performing exorcisms preceded the king when he went out, and this action was immediately linked to the offering of travel sacrifices when the king went to another state.[110] This shows that in the third century B.C. shamans actually played the role assigned to Chi You in the passage from the *Han Feizi*, the *Zu* prayer, and the Han rhyme-prose. The origin of Chi You as shaman and votary of the rain god would also account for the mythic doubling of the two figures and for the tradition in various later texts that Chi You was the Yellow Emperor's minister.[111]

This emergence of the figures of the Yellow Emperor and Chi You from rainmaking ritual is also supported by the oracle bone inscriptions pertaining to the ritual burning of shamans. As Qiu Xigui has pointed out, the original character for this rite was composed of the elements *huang* (黃), here apparently a representation of some kind of human figure, and the graph for fire.[112] Since *huang* was phonetically close to the word for the burned shaman (*wang* 尪), and the character depicted a man being burned, it is quite possible that the word "yellow" in the emperor's title etymologically meant "rainmaking shaman" or "rainmaking ritual." This admittedly novel etymology finds support in the tradition that King Tang, founder of the Shang dynasty, ended a drought by offering himself as a sacrifice to be burnt, thus substituting the king for the shaman.[113] This close link between the Yellow Emperor and the shamaness would also explain why the asterism that bore the Emperor's name was the celestial simulacrum of the "female ruler" and perhaps account for his ties to the Queen Mother of the West and the Celestial Maiden in the tales of revealed military treatises.[114]

So the figures of the Yellow Emperor and Chi You, like that of the Fiery Emperor, all emerged from rituals used to expel evil influences at the end of the old year and bring on rain at the end of the dry season. As the days grew shorter and the weather colder, vegetation and animal life both subsided, and the rainfall ceased. In order to guarantee the rebirth of spring and the return of the rains, the early Chinese carried out a series of rituals that were accompanied and explained by tales. The death of the world and its rebirth with the resumption of the rains were imagined as a battle between cosmic spirits of storm and drought who were closely linked in cult and mythically identified as brothers as well as rivals. The shamanesses or shamans who conducted the rainmaking magic, and were potentially offered as human sacrifices if rain did not come, took on the physical attributes of their deity in the rituals and hence shared many of his attributes in myth. These same people performed the travel sacrifice and exorcisms when the ruler went out, and they conducted the Great Exorcism at the New Year season. For these purposes they put on various costumes, masks, and other regalia, and they were known for the hideousness of the guises that they put on to frighten off evil spirits. These costumes were either copied from or provided the model for the frightening, horned tomb-guardian beasts who were carved in statues and painted on walls. In such rituals and the tales told to explain them emerged the earliest versions of the Chinese accounts of the creation of violence in the world of men.

The Violence of Beasts and Men

In the Warring States the cultic roots of the tales of the Yellow Emperor were gradually suppressed as part of the general reinterpretation of ancient divinities as historical figures. This "suppression" of the magical, shamanistic roots of these tales, like those of the related myths of Yu, reflected the changing character of official religion and the class basis of cultic practice in Warring States and early imperial China. Among the common people shamanic rituals devoted to a host of anthropomorphic spirits continued to flourish throughout the Zhou and indeed the entire history of imperial China, but elite religion and the state cults focused increasingly on ancestor worship, official sacrifices to abstract natural forces or spirit analogues of the bureaucracy, and the commemorative cults of select moral exemplars. The reinterpretation of ancient cult figures as historical personalities who provided models and sanctions for state power, and the devotion of the state cults entirely to abstract deities such as Heaven, Earth, or the Supreme Unity were part of a general re-creation of the spirit world by the emerging elite of the Warring States. It was the first round in a battle for control of the realm of the spirits that would span the history of imperial China, a battle between the historicizing, philosophical intellect of the literate elite and the protean religious practices of the local, peasant communities.

In this process the tales of cosmic battle between rain and drought were recast as accounts of the origins of warfare and punishments, and they were incorporated into the general mythology of the separation of the human world from that of the animals. These new versions recapitulated the philosophical debates over the origins of weapons, and they incorporated the competing claims of the animal origins of weapons and their creation by sages. They did this through the discovery of two creators of warfare, the beast-like Chi You who actually created weapons and the sage Yellow Emperor who made these implements of death the basis of a human, political order. In different versions of the tale all the various elements of the transformation of sanctioned violence discussed in earlier chapters were given historical precedents—or mythic prototypes—in the innovations of the Yellow Emperor. The New Year rituals also increasingly took on an explicitly military character.[115] So men of the Warring States, Qin, and Han periods knew the Yellow Emperor and Chi You as creators of warfare and punishments.

The doubling of these two figures stems from their old cultic links, but this would not explain why the Warring States Chinese found it necessary, or even possible, to have *two* creators of punishments and warfare. Moreover, the explicit rivalry between Chi You and the Yellow Emperor would appear to be a novel element in the second "layer" of the myths, so it must be explained in light of the manner in which the tales dealt with the specific problem of human violence.

One of the earliest and most important texts for the examination of this problem is the "Lü xing" chapter in the *Shang shu*. This presents a discussion of punishments and legal procedure, and it is prefaced by a mythic history of their origins. This account is another version of the creation of the human world through separation from nature by the achievements of the sages, and at the center of this creation it places the introduction of law and punishments. The term "law" (*fa* 法) in China was synonymous with "punishments" (*xing* 刑), and the latter originally involved physical mutilation or execution. Moreover, from at least the Warring States period, warfare was often interpreted as a form of punishment. Consequently, a myth of the origin of law and punishments in China was also a myth of the origin of warfare, and in this tale their creation was attributed to both Chi You and the Yellow Emperor.[116]

The account does not directly assign the creation of punishments to Chi You, but they appear as a consequence of his actions. The "Lü xing" states that Chi You first created disorder and thereby polluted the moral character of the people so that "there were none who were not robbers and bandits, rapacious villains and traitors, thieves and plunderers, usurpers and killers."[117] The story does not specify how Chi You created disorder, but in light of the accounts of his career in other texts it is almost certain that this refers to his creation of weapons and warfare. However, the text focuses not on the act of creation but on its consequences. Following the introduction of violence, all men became violent; violence appeared as a plague that passed from the "criminal" to the "victim," and soon all men were contaminated.

> Why does the spirit of revenge, wherever it breaks out, constitute such an intolerable menace? Perhaps because the only satisfactory revenge for spilt blood is spilling the blood of the killer; and in the blood feud there is no clear distinction between the act for which the killer is being punished and the punishment itself. Vengeance professes to be an act of reprisal, and every reprisal calls for another reprisal. . . . Vengeance, then, is an interminable, infinitely repetitive process. Every time it turns up in some part of the community, it threatens to involve the whole social body.[118]

This is the result of Chi You's actions, and the social corruption was mirrored in government. The Miao people instituted punishments, but since they made no distinctions and had no legal procedures, their punishments were no different from the crimes, and the result was the same. "The people started to affect one another and overflowed all bounds; they did not keep faith, so all covenants were overthrown." The aggrieved and unjustly punished called upon Heaven, so the Yellow Emperor destroyed the Miao.

Having destroyed the creators of punishments, however, he proceeded to break the connections between Heaven and Earth and then himself had laws and punishments reintroduced.

> Then [the Yellow Emperor] sent down three rulers to devote themselves to achievements for the people. Bo Yi sent down the code of laws and controlled the people through punishments; Yu fixed the waters and land, and controlled the naming of the mountains and rivers; Ji sent down the planting of cereals, and the fields grew fine grains.

This passage presents in brief the creation of the human world through the innovations of the sages, in which the breaking of the primal unity between man and nature is followed immediately by the introduction of punishments, the controlling of the floods, and the revelation of agriculture by the Zhou ancestor Hou Ji. After presenting various exhortations and decrees by the Zhou king, the text then offers a characterization of the nature of laws and punishments:

> It is not that Heaven is not just [or "Without Heaven there is no justice"], but men must have its Mandate. If Heaven's punishments were not perfect [or "the standard"] then the people would have no good government on earth.

In this account the creation of punishments was the central act in the formation of human society, and the two creators of warfare reappeared as creators of punishments—although both actually manifested themselves through the agency of others. However, the two creations were sharply contrasted. Acting under Chi You's impulsion, the Miao created punishments, and all social order collapsed. The Yellow Emperor then instituted punishments through the agency of Bo Yi, and the world of men became stable and tranquil. Paying attention only to the first "creation," Derk Bodde argued that this text shows the early Chinese abhorrence of law and their tendency to give it a purely "secular" or "sociological" origin.[119] In fact, this story attributes the origin of law to Heaven and the sages, and all early Chinese accounts of this subject, except for that of the *Shang Jun shu*, say that law was modeled on the patterns of Heaven and Earth or those in the minds of men. While the Chinese did not speak of law revealed by an omnipotent deity, they believed it was created by superhuman culture heroes under the inspiration of Heaven in accord with divine patterns. As the Huang-Lao text discovered at Mawangdui stated in its opening line, "The Way gave birth to the law."[120] Law was not supernatural, but it was divine. The "Lü xing" condemned law only to the extent that it was purely "human"; "Heaven's punishments" were the precondition of good government and social order. Law itself was not denounced, but it had to be decreed by the holder of Heaven's Mandate, in accord with the eternal principles of the cosmos, and executed with strict, impartial regard for the truth.

Although the text states that the Miao "punished the innocent," "made no distinctions," and "had no testimony," it does not specify how judgement was passed. However, other sources suggest a hypothesis. An alternative tradition in Warring States and Han China regarding the origin of law and punishments assigned their creation to Gao Yao, a minister of Shun. The Han dynasty scholar Wang Chong preserved the story that Gao Yao passed judgements with the aid of a magic, one-horned goat that could distinguish the innocent from the guilty and would butt only the latter.[121] He suggested that this procedure was a piece of deliberate mystification used to secure convictions where neither evidence nor a confession could be obtained, to intimidate potential criminals, and to deny any claims of injustice through the pretense of divine assistance. This was a clear example of justice that made no distinctions and had no testimony.

In fact, there is a considerable body of evidence linking butting and goats to the origins of legal procedure in China. Gao Yao, the creator of punishments under Shun, was reputed to be an ancestor of several of the states whose ruling lineages were surnamed Jiang.[122] The graph of this surname represents a goat and a woman. It was a graphic variant of the character qiang (羌), which represented a man and a goat and was the generic name of a group of tribes that lived to the west and northwest of the Chinese heartland. In its definition of this character the Shuo wen says, "The western barbarians. They are of the goat race."[123] This tradition of their animal ancestry was attested as early as the Shang oracle inscriptions and was also reported in the chapter on the Qiang in the Hou Han shu.[124] Moreover, later texts preserved records that showed goat worship among the Qiang.[125]

The goat was clearly the sacred, totemic animal of the Qiang peoples, and the Jiang surnamed states were supposedly descended from the Qiang. Thus the tradition that Gao Yao, ancestor of the Jiang states, passed judgements with a magical goat may well have some foundation in actual practices. Moreover, the Miao people, who created law according to the "Lü xing," were reputed to be ancestors of the Qiang, and Bo Yi, the agent of the Yellow Emperor who handed down the law, was also a putative ancestor of some of the of Jiang-surnamed states.[126] Finally, as was noted earlier, Chi You was a major cultic figure in Qi, a Jiang-surnamed state, in the local traditions and in Han iconography he had horns, and in one source he was said to have emerged from the "Goat River."[127] In short, all the beings credited or blamed with the introduction of laws in China were tied to the Qiang people or the Jiang surname, and linked to the activity of butting.

While it may be methodologically naive to seek in these myths a direct representation of reality, it is possible that the Qiang employed a sacred goat or a man in a goat's costume in the levying of punishments. And indeed there is evidence of just such a practice in a story from the state of Qi preserved in the canon of the Mohist school.[128] It tells of two ministers who were engaged in a lawsuit which the lord could not settle. In order to resolve the dispute, the lord had them sacrifice a goat and use its blood to swear an oath at the altar of the state. The testimony of the two men was then read, and when the false words were pronounced, the goat sprang up and butted the man who had sworn to them.

This is a clear example of using the butting of a "magical" goat to resolve legal cases. Shiratori Kiyoshi has assembled anecdotal and etymological evidence for the use of such "animal judgements" in early China, and he links them to the practice of the blood covenant that played such an important role in Spring and Autumn law and international relations.[129] Indeed, as was noted in Chapter One, the sacrifices for covenants excavated at Houma almost invariably consisted of sheep, which were not linguistically distinguished from goats. Moreover, as is shown in the final section of this chapter, there was a tradition that the Yellow Emperor's sacrifice of the horned Chi You was the mythological prototype of the covenant, so there were indeed links between these "animal judgements" and covenants.

Such practices provide a model of justice, associated with Chi You through the motif of butting, that stands in marked contrast to the legal procedures and rules of evidence introduced by Bo Yi at the behest of the Yellow Emperor. In contrast to the "human" justice introduced by the sage as the basis of the separation of men from nature, those tales in which butting replaced legal procedure presented, both literally and figuratively, the justice of beasts.

This contrast between human and bestial justice parallels the myths of the origins of punishment to those of the introduction of warfare. As was noted above, the ancient Chinese identified warriors with animals, and Chi You was both a matchless warrior and a beast. In Han tomb art he appeared as a bear or tiger; in popular legend he had horns and hooves; and in Han poetry and descriptions of the exorcist he wore the skins of animals. As the god of battle and the scourge of demons, he epitomized the bestial and demonic character of the warrior.

Although a creator of warfare, the Yellow Emperor was no warrior. In the various accounts of his battles he appears as a commander of armies, a trainer of animal warriors, a recipient of military wisdom in magically-revealed texts, and the creator of the rituals and practices that allowed warfare and punishments to accord with the patterns of Heaven. In short, his battles offered the mythic prototype for all the major innovations in military organization, practice, and philosophy that were described in the first three chapters of this book. He was the putative creator in high antiquity of the pattern of sanctioned violence that emerged in the Warring States. For purposes of exposition I have divided the innovations credited to the Yellow Emperor into three sections: organization, strategy, and normative rituals.[130]

By "organizing" I refer to the Yellow Emperor's role as a creator of armies through the instruction of animals. The *Shi ji* told how he instructed bears, tigers, and other beasts and led them to serve in his army and battle the Fiery Emperor. This became an important action in later accounts of the Yellow Emperor, and the *Liezi* used it as one example in an extended discussion of the relations of men and animals and the nature of the sages.

> Fu Xi, Nu Wa, the Divine Husbandman, and Yu had snake bodies with human faces or the heads of oxen with tiger noses; they had an inhuman appearance yet the spiritual power of the sage. Jie of the Xia, Zhou of the Shang, Lord Huan of Lu, and King Mu of Chu had the seven apertures and in appearance were the same as men, but they had the hearts of beasts. And ordinary men hold only to appearances in seeking the supreme minds; how wrong they are!
>
> When the Yellow Emperor fought with the Fiery Emperor at Fanxuan, he used bears, wolves, and tigers as his vanguard and eagles, pheasants, hawks, and kites as his banners. This is to command beasts through force. Yao had Kui regulate the music; he beat the stones and led the myriad beasts to dance. The *xiao* and *shao* music were completed, and the phoenix came with proper ceremony. This is to lead the beasts through music.
>
> So then how are the hearts of animals different from those of men? Their shapes and sounds are different from men's, so we do not know the way to make contact with them. But the sage is ignorant of nothing and penetrates everything; therefore he is able to lead and command them. The minds of animals have that which

is naturally the same as men's. . . . In high antiquity they lived together with men and walked beside them. In the days of the [Five] Emperors they were first frightened and scattered. In later days they fled and hid in order to avoid harm. . . .

In high antiquity the sages knew completely the states and tendencies of all things, and they understood the sounds of all the species. They gathered them together, instructed and cherished them, just as they did human beings. So first they gathered the ghosts, spirits, and *chimei*, then they reached the people of the eight quarters, and last they assembled the beasts and insects.[131]

Although the community of animals and men was assigned to high antiquity, the model of the sages suggested that the true monarch should include the whole animal kingdom in his realm. As was noted in the discussion of animal combats in Chapter Four, this idea was proclaimed as an ideal in several Warring States texts and in the stone inscriptions of Qin Shihuang. In contrast with the bestiality of Chi You, which turned human warriors into beasts, the teaching of the sage turned beasts into men through bringing them into the community of those united by the laws and potency of the true ruler.

These myths provided the "historical" sanction for the insistence that armies be social bodies constituted by the virtuous potency of the ruler, and they were also the models for the ritual demonstrations of that potency in staged animal combats and the *jue di*. The popular tradition preserved at Jizhou traced the origins of the *jue di* wrestling matches to Chi You, and the accompanying pantomimes and magic acts were probably depictions of the feats of the Yellow Emperor.

As I pointed out in Chapter Four, the performances that followed the wrestling matches dealt almost entirely with commanding animals to dance or fight, summoning up dragons and other magical beasts, and creating storms or thunder. Moreover, these feats were explained as re-creations of the powers of a certain "Old Master Huang" of Donghai Commandery. The Chinese for his name is *Huang Gong* (黃公), which could also be read "Yellow Lord." Thus this mysterious figure shares not only the Yellow Emperor's powers but also his name, and the Donghai Commandery where he originated was in the state of Qi, the old center of the cult of the Yellow Emperor. But the key piece of data linking this "Yellow Lord" to the Yellow Emperor appears in the fourth-century A.D. proto-Taoist work *Baopuzi*. In the chapter "Ascending Mountains" Ge Hong (280–342 A.D.) wrote:

Someone asked, "Those who practice the Way are often in mountains and forests, but there are many tigers and wolves there. How does one avoid them?" The Master Who Cherishes Simplicity replied, "When they entered the mountains, men of ancient days always carried at their waists the Seal of the Ax Talisman of the Yellow Spirit. It is four inches wide and has one hundred and twenty characters on it. If you use it to make seals at each of the four corners of a square of one hundred paces around the place you stay, no tiger or wolf will dare to enter. When in walking you see fresh tiger tracks, if you press the seal in the direction of the tracks the tiger will depart, and if you press it in the opposite direction it will return. If you carry this seal at your waist when walking in the mountains and forests, then you need fear no tigers or wolves."[132]

The fact that the talisman was called "Ax" and could command tigers links it with the tales of the "Yellow Lord," who also used "ax spells" to perform his magic.[133] Moreover, the apocryphal *wei* texts of the Eastern Han clearly identify the "Yellow Spirit," who was the master of this talisman, as the Pole Star, the spirit father and astral double of the Yellow Emperor.[134] This was not an esoteric gloss restricted to a single school, for Ban Gu mentioned the "Yellow Spirit" in a rhyme-prose, and Ying Shao explained that it referred to the Yellow Emperor.[135] Thus the "Ax Talisman" came from the Yellow Emperor, and the Yellow Lord who commanded beasts through his "ax spells" and served as the prototype of the magic acts of the *jue di* can probably be identified with the sage.

The exact nature of their connection is difficult to assess. It is possible that the story of a human "Old Master Huang" was a euhemerization of the original mythic figure or deity who became the "historical" Yellow Emperor. In any case, it is likely that the various pageants and magic acts connected with the *jue di* wrestling matches were part of the mass public "madness" associated with the winter festivals. Originally depictions of the commanding of dragons and storms as part of the ceremonies of drought prevention, they survived as entertainments that had lost their original cultic meaning. However, just as the wrestling matches celebrated the matchless power of the warrior Chi You, so these accompanying magic acts re-enacted, although the men of the Han were perhaps no longer aware of it, the powers of the Yellow Emperor to command the storm and animals, and in a sense they mythically encompassed and absorbed the physical powers of the warrior Chi You. Thus these ritual depictions of the cosmic nature of the Han emperor's use of violence and of the extension of his rule to the beasts were ultimately derived from the cosmic violence of the rainmaking Yellow Emperor, the mythic master of beast warriors. And both the rituals and myths demonstrated the ultimate supremacy of collective violence based on moral unity to the individual violence of the great warrior.

Just as the animal-taming Yellow Emperor was the mythic prototype of the collective and organizational bases of military power, he was also the "first" recipient of a revealed military text and hence the patron sage of strategic wisdom and the art of the commander. In Chapter Three I quoted the story of the revelation of the text and noted that it became accepted that this was the primal revelation of military arts from which all the others were derived. The bibliographic monograph of the *Han shu* attributes one military text to the Yellow Emperor, four to his ministers, and one—in the category of skill with weapons—to Chi You.[136] The Song anthology *Taiping yulan* in addition contains fragments of several military treatises attributed to the Yellow Emperor. A couple of these tell the story of the revelation of the military treatise, and a variant of the story in other texts speaks not of a treatise but of a tally, the sign of the general's charge from the ruler.

> Before the Yellow Emperor began to carry out the role of ruler, there appeared Chi You and his eighty brothers. They had the bodies of beasts, the speech of men, bronze heads, and iron brows. They ate sand and stones, and created weapons such as staves, knives, lances, and bows. They terrorized all under Heaven and slaughtered barbarically; they loved and nurtured nothing. The people desired for the Yellow Emperor to carry out the tasks of the Son of Heaven, but he practiced love and virtuous potency, and could not make forcible prohibitions, so no one could oppose Chi You. The Yellow Emperor looked up to Heaven and sighed, and Heaven sent a Celestial Woman to bestow upon the Yellow Emperor the Spirit Tally of Military Efficacy. With this he conquered Chi You and thereby ordered the eight directions. After Chi You died, all under Heaven again became disordered and without peace, so the Yellow Emperor painted an image of Chi You in order to terrify all under Heaven. Everyone cried, "Chi You has not died." And the myriad states of the eight directions all submitted.[137]

In another version of the same story the Yellow Emperor used the power of the tally to make Chi You his servant and then led him to conquer the world. These stories once again portrayed the Yellow Emperor as the prototype of the commander, who through his powers of office led the beast/warriors to bring order to the world. The use of a "tally" to conquer or command Chi You also recalls the traditions of the "Yellow Lord" in the *jue di*, who likewise used a magic tally to command beasts. It invokes the powers of the general, wielding authority through the charge of the ruler, and also suggests the Taoist milieu in which the philosophies associated with the Yellow Emperor flourished, where tallies patterned on those of the imperial government gave men powers over the spirits.

Whether they speak of texts or tallies, all these stories of the Yellow Emperor located true military potency in the skills and office of the commander, and they showed that this potency could conquer the greatest warrior. In this way they were dramatic versions of the criticisms of heroism and individual initiative that appeared in the military treatises, and celebrations of the superior powers of the commander.

The final element of the new pattern of sanctioned violence that found mythic sanction in the tales of the Yellow Emperor was the modeling of warfare and punishments on the patterns of Heaven or nature. As was noted in Chapter Four, the major forms of this were the staging of animal combats and the calendrical model of government. The Yellow Emperor's role as the model of the commander of beast warriors has already been discussed at length, and he was also given credit for the calendrical model of government, with particular emphasis on its use to guide violence.

As for the association of the Yellow Emperor with the calendrical model of government in general, there are two major pieces of evidence. First, the *Lü Shi chun qiu*, which gave the most systematic and detailed account of the seasonal differentiation of the actions and policies of the ruler and provided the model for the Confucian "Yue ling," described itself explicitly as the Yellow Emperor's teachings.[138] Second, the primary mechanism for tracing the annual cycle in order to guide government policy was "watching for the ethers" by means of the pitchpipes, and in myth these pipes were invented at the behest of the Yellow Emperor.[139]

The evidence for his association with the calendrical pattern for violent actions is even greater. First, as was shown in Chapter Four, the game of kickball that provided military training and also mimicked the annual cycle was a ritual commemoration of the victory of the Yellow Emperor over Chi You. Second, all the military treatises associated with the Yellow Emperor and his officials appear in the *yin/yang* category of military thought, the category of those who "set out in accord with seasons" and "follow the Dipper to attack." These five treatises constitute almost one-third of the books in this category, so there is little doubt of the strong ties of the Yellow Emperor to the use of calendrical patterns and divination in military affairs. Finally, the second section of the silk Huang-Lao manuscript discovered at Mawangdui devotes considerable space to the Yellow Emperor and his ministers, and it repeatedly insists on the necessity of linking military action to the seasons.[140]

Set against the bestial violence of Chi You, the mythic achievement of the Yellow Emperor was to create a truly human violence, a use of force that upheld the social order and did not reduce men to the level of animals. This took place both in the realm of law, where he introduced proper legal procedures and concern for evidence, and in warfare, where he introduced instruction to make the army a collective body, the strategic wisdom of military texts, and the principle of modeling military action on the patterns of Heaven. Politically, these myths defended the claims of monarchy against those who denied the need for rulers with their punishments and armies, and in the early Warring States they asserted the claims of the new states with their mass armies, military specialists, and cosmic rulers against the old warrior aristocracy. After the disappearance of the aristocracy, they defended the police powers of the state against local toughs, avengers, "wandering swordsmen," bandits, and anyone who attempted to set his own prowess and sense of justice against the claims of the holder of Heaven's Mandate.

Myths of Sacrifice and Heaven's Mandate

Behind the idea of sanctioning the violence of warfare and punishments by imitating the pattern of Heaven lay the theory, first formulated by the Zhou dynasts, that the ruler held power by virtue of a "mandate" from Heaven or acted as the agent of Heaven on earth. However, the Zhou theory of a Mandate or Heaven-based power had internal contradictions, because the power to rule that revealed the Mandate was itself won through defeating in battle and killing the preceding king. The Mandate sanctioned the warfare and punishments that followed its winning, but one who would gain it had first to become a rebel and a regicide. In the Warring States period, as the imitation or sanction of Heaven became increasingly important to claims to rule, this dilemma was reflected in a series of myths dealing with dynastic changes and human sacrifice.

In the early decades of this century Marcel Granet collected literary evidence that in ancient China a chief had to kill or drive out the old sovereign before establishing his own dynasty, but that in doing so he polluted himself. In order to expiate his deed, he had to sacrifice a victim—presumably standing in for himself—dismember it, and throw its limbs out of the four gates of the city.[141] In the myths of the Warring States the same problem was confronted, but the usual solution was to offer up the regicide himself in a sacrifice that was declined, or to treat the murder of the previous king as a form of sacrifice.

In her study of a lost text from the *Shang shu*, Sarah Allan has shown how a myth in which the Shang founder achieved his position as king by offering himself as a sacrifice was transformed under the Zhou into a meditation on the problem of regicide involved in the transfer of

Heaven's Mandate. In the later version, the Shang founder's killing of the villainous King Jie triggered a great drought that was ended only when the new king offered himself as a sacrifice. The approval of Heaven expressed by the coming of rain signalled that his murder of the previous king had been expiated. In other tales the onus of regicide was escaped by first offering the throne to some contemporary sage who invariably declined the honor, leaving the erstwhile rebel free to rule in peace.[142]

In yet another set of stories this problem was muted by describing the murder of the rival as a form of sacrifice. In the various accounts of the Yellow Emperor's career, his killing of Chi You led directly to his assumption of the mantle of emperor. In the account of this killing in the Huang-Lao text from Mawangdui, the Yellow Emperor's victory is treated as a sacrificial ritual.[143] In this version of the story, the battle between the Yellow Emperor and Chi You entirely vanishes. Instead, it simply states that the Yellow Emperor took out his axes, "aroused" his troops, and personally encountered and slew Chi You. It then narrates how he divided up the body of Chi You for various purposes, and this dismemberment culminated in cooking the flesh as a meat stew that he fed to his followers. This version clearly portrays the final battle as a "sacrifice" in which the Yellow Emperor, acting as his own sacrificer, killed the horned beast Chi You and then shared him in a communion meal that became the basis of his authority as ruler.

Another version of the same story appearing earlier in the text is identical in its account of the killing of Chi You, but it does not mention his role as the main course in a sacrificial banquet. Instead, it simply states that after killing Chi You, the Yellow Emperor proclaimed a covenant which stated that whoever "went counter to duty or went against the seasons" would meet the same fate as Chi You. This proclamation clearly echoes the passage in the first version which states that the Yellow Emperor "established his prohibitions" by dismembering Chi You and having him eaten. More importantly, a covenant, as was shown in Chapter One, had to have a sacrifice, and one form of the curse invoked on violators was that they should meet the fate of the sacrificial victim.[144] So the proclamation of the Yellow Emperor clearly indicates that Chi You was the sacrificial victim whose blood made the covenant's oath binding.[145]

Another feature common to both accounts is that prior to killing Chi You, the Yellow Emperor withdrew from the war to discuss with his ministers the principles of government and combat. In addition, the first version states that he withdrew for three years "in order to seek [within?] himself." This retirement from the world for purposes of concentration or meditation recalls the period of withdrawal for purification undergone by the ruler in preparation for a major sacrifice, and the number "three" evokes the three days of strict seclusion and fasting that completed the process.[146]

The equation of the Yellow Emperor's withdrawal with the period of preparation for sacrifice becomes much clearer in the later versions of the story that dealt with the revelation of magical tallies or texts.[147] In these stories the Yellow Emperor was enveloped in a fog for three days, precisely the period of strict seclusion, at the end of which he encountered a divine spirit and received the magic "weapon" that allowed him to slay Chi You. The three days of withdrawal in the fog and the resultant epiphany occur at the same juncture, and play the same role, as his withdrawal from the battle for three years and the final decision to take up his axes do in the account in the silk manuscript. However, in the later stories, the period of withdrawal actually culminates in the personal encounter with the spirits that, according to the *Li ji*, was the aim of purification for sacrifice. Consequently, the modifications in the later stories make clearer the underlying structure of the earlier ones, but in both sets of stories the "plot" parallels the sequence of a sacrificial rite.

These stories show that the killing of Chi You was a sacrifice, and they provide a religious foundation for the stories in which the defeated Chi You or his painted image helped the Yellow Emperor conquer the world. As the sacrificial victim, Chi You was both the evil miscreant responsible for pollution and disorder in the world, and also the divine being whose death laid the foundation for a stable, social existence. So these stories of the origins of warfare also suggest the ultimate unity of sacrifice and warfare in the process of dynastic foundation, and they sanction the establishment of royal power on the basis of murder by identifying the killing as a sacrifice. The twin creators of warfare, who were both identical and opposite, here reappear as the prototype of the sacrificer and the sacrificed, who in the logic of the sacrifice must be both identified and distinct.

Although in some versions Chi You was described as a rival monarch, this story does not deal explicitly with the transfer of dynastic authority. However, two other sets of stories preserved in Warring States texts tell of dynasties transferred through a "cannibal" sacrifice. The first deals with the death of the mythic archer Yi. Many stories of this great culture hero tell of his battles against the forces of nature. When ten suns rose in the sky, he shot down nine of them; he captured the "great wind;" he shot the lord of the Yellow River and took his wife; and he killed a variety of strange creatures and monsters in the time of the emperor Yao. However, in the stories that concern us here, he appeared as an outstanding archer and hunter who usurped the throne of the Xia dynasty. Devoting himself solely to hunting, he left the government in the hands of a treacherous chief minister who engaged in illicit relations with Yi's harem, won over the court through bribes, and finally had Yi killed in ambush. Yi was then cooked and fed to his own son.[148]

In several ways this story echoes that of Chi You. Yi was a matchless warrior, and in some texts he was credited with the invention of the bow. In his supernatural aspect, he alternately appeared as a renegade enemy of the natural order and the servant of the sages. In his historical, human form he devoted himself entirely to hunting, a form of warfare, and was ultimately slain and eaten. In contrast to the story of Chi You, or that of Zhou which will be analyzed below, the "sacrifice" of Yi did not lead to an immediate restoration of order, which occurred only after the treacherous minister and his sons were killed. However, since the texts state that the minister "followed Yi's house," i.e., took over his harem and his dynasty, the death and consumption of Yi directly prefigured the restoration of the legitimate Xia. In addition, the evil minister took upon himself the guilt of regicide and thus removed the onus of succession from the Xia.

A final story in which warfare against an arch-renegade culminated in a "sacrifice" dealt with King Zhou of Shang and his defeat at the hands of King Wu. Zhou was the archetypal "evil last monarch": dominated by women, given up to sensual self-indulgence with his "pools of wine and forests of meat," oppressing the people with his taxes, carving open a pregnant woman to examine the fetus, and killing or imprisoning all who remonstrated against him. He was also famous for his great speed and strength and fond of battling with wild animals, and he was a noted devourer of human flesh who fed several feudal lords to his court and even duped King Wen of Zhou into eating his own son.[149]

Several Warring States and early Han texts preserve the tradition that King Zhou and his favorite wives committed suicide when the Shang armies were defeated, and that when King Wu entered the capital, he personally shot their corpses with arrows, stabbed them with his sword, chopped off their heads with his axes, had the heads mounted on his war banners, and then presented the heads at the Zhou ancestral temple.[150] This story of the hacking up of the bodies and their presentation at the ancestral temple already evokes the image of a sacrifice, and a more detailed version of the story preserved in a fragment of the *Shizi* states that King Wu hacked (or "bit") open Zhou's neck, befouled his hands with his blood, lapped up the blood (or "ate him raw"), and "at this moment became like a wild beast."[151] In this text the haste and passion of the "sacrifice" reduce it to the level of cannibalism, which makes even clearer the ties of this story to those of Chi You and Yi.

The identification of the killing and dismemberment of Zhou as a sacrifice is also suggested by the tradition preserved in two places that the overthrow of the Shang was preceded by a drought, in the form of the "ten suns," and followed or accompanied by the coming of rain and a bountiful harvest.[152] Just as in the second version of the story of the self-sacrifice of King Tang, a sacrifice was necessary to expiate the pollution of the regicide, but in this case it was the dead king himself who became the sacrificial offering. Both these stories invoked the image of sacrifice, derived from the old sacrificial myths and practices that underlay them, to sanction claims of bringing order to the worlds of nature and man through the killing of evil dynasts.

Stories of the "sacrifice" of Zhou, whether hidden and ceremonial or overt and bloody, and those of Chi You and Yi all follow the same pattern. In each of them a great malefactor/fierce warrior/evil ruler plunged the world into chaos and then was slain and eaten in a human sacrifice that restored the world. But these world-redeeming sacrifices were also acts of savagery and, in some cases, regicide. Perhaps Chi You was sufficiently "animalized" that his consumption could avoid the stigma of cannibalism, but the cases of Yi and King Zhou admitted no such easy moral escape. The "sacrifice" of Yi was performed by a villain who was himself quickly disposed of by more virtuous elements, but the "scandal" of King Wu's sacrifice of Zhou was more difficult and was never entirely resolved. As Gu Jiegang has argued, Mencius's famous call for the suppression of those sections of the *Shang shu* that cast doubt on the benevolent and peaceful character of King Wu's ascent to power was probably directed at a chapter that included accounts of the dismemberment of King Zhou.[153] The disappearance of the chapter from the canonical *Shang shu* and the fact that all surviving texts except the *Shizi* elide the physical disposition of Zhou's corpse suggest that some suppression actually took place. Nevertheless, even the censored version was so scandalous to the moral sensibilities of later Confucians that they either denounced the conduct of King Wu or denied the veracity of the story.[154]

The problem of rationalizing and ritualizing the forcible overthrow of the legitimate ruler remained a basic issue in the use of violence throughout Chinese history. The theory that each dynasty had its own characteristic "potency" associated with one of the Five Phases, that each phase naturally gave birth to the next, and that the propriety of the transition would be revealed in various natural signs and prodigies offered yet another justification of violence through claims of accord with natural patterns and the imitation of Heaven. The historiographic cliche of the "bad last ruler"—who was the historical version of the evil ancient rulers offered up in sacrifice—and indeed the very practice begun under the Tang of having each dynasty compose the history of its predecessor in order to trace the rise and fall of its ruling virtue, sought to grant moral and historical justification to the change of dynasties. Finally, the rituals of dynastic transition and accession all sought to present the often bloody process of transition as the inevitable expression of natural and moral principles.[155] In these ways imperial China carried forward the legacy of the "sacrificial" transitions of mythic antiquity.

Conclusion

As the fundamental political and social institutions of China were transformed during the Warring States period, the emerging elite sought sanction and precedent for their vision of society through re-imagining the history of Chinese civilization. Perhaps noting the creation of institutions in their own day, they came to realize that the practices that defined their world were not given in nature but had to be created through conscious effort. This recognition was transposed into history through the emergence of a shared conviction that in earliest times men had not been naturally separated from animals, but that the work of this separation had been accomplished by the "former kings," superhuman sages who physically expelled the animals, invented the technologies necessary for civilized existence, and introduced the moral practices and social hierarchies that defined humanity. The various schools presented the innovations of different sages as the key to the creation of human society, but they shared a general mythology in which certain sages were linked to specific innovations and feats, and the ensemble of these creations defined the Warring States elite's understanding of a proper social order.

The sage who created human forms of warfare and punishments was the Yellow Emperor, and in several histories and genealogies he was credited with the creation of Chinese civilization and described as the primal ancestor of the Chinese people. This figure, like many of the sages, had originally been a deity invoked in the religious ceremonies of earlier times. He had been a spirit of the storm invoked by shamans or shamanesses in rainmaking rituals, and the return of the rain at the end of the New Year season had been imagined in the form of a cosmic battle between this lord of the storm and a lord of drought who was linked to him in cult and later identified as his brother. The shamans who were the votaries of this god dressed themselves in animal skins and hideous masks as elements of their ceremonies, and wearing these costumes they staged mock battles to exorcise evil influences and perhaps expel the drought demon.

As the Zhou elite gradually replaced shamanic rituals devoted to anthropomorphic deities with rationalizing philosophy and the cults of more abstract spirits like Heaven and Earth, these ancient gods were employed as the raw material for the emerging "history" of the creation of Chinese civilization. Their feats in myth and story became the technological inventions and political or moral innovations that separated humanity from brute nature. These innovations, not surprisingly, echoed the social programs and institutional changes pioneered by the political reformers or advocated by the philosophical schools in the Warring States. The emerging elite took over the deities of shamanic cults and transformed them into historical exemplars for their own claims to wisdom and authority.[156]

The tales of the Yellow Emperor and his battles were reinterpreted as accounts of the origins of violence in the world of men and its subsequent use by the sages to create a proper political order. In these stories the disguised shamans, or rather the powerful demons and tomb-guarding beasts whom they invoked, became the hideous, bestial Chi You, who created weapons and plunged the world into chaos through his savage, unstoppable violence. In the account of the origins of law, the Yellow Emperor destroyed the original makers of savage punishments and then reinstituted the "punishments of Heaven" that were based on proper legal procedure and the rules of evidence. In his military defeat of Chi You, the Yellow Emperor was credited with the ancient prototypes for all the major innovations in warfare that took place in the Warring States: the creation of armies based on collective action through instruction, the introduction of a combat based on mental skills transmitted through books, the extension of the ruler's potency to the beasts through animal combats, and the modeling of military action on the natural cycle of the year. The defeated Chi You, for his part, became a god of combat and fighters, and he set the pattern for later Chinese history in which mighty warriors who had been defeated in battle, like Xiang Yu and Guan Yu, became the gods of war. In the disposal of Chi You's corpse, the Yellow Emperor was also credited with the creation of several of the major military rituals and of the practice of using blood oaths to secure loyalty. These tales of the Yellow Emperor's defeat and sacrifice of Chi You also formed one element in a set of tales that sought to rationalize the violence of dynastic transition through the imagery of the sacrifice of an evil monster.

In its earliest forms the story of the defeat of bestial but unstoppable fighters through moral instruction, strategic skills, and imitation of the patterns of Heaven was probably a critique of the heroic, martial ethic of the Zhou nobility, men who equated manhood with martial prowess and saw battle as a field for the winning of glory. The military treatises and the legalist texts both contain extended critiques of heroism on the field of battle, and the tales of the Yellow Emperor presented these same critiques in dramatic form. As the aristocracy and their values were forcibly driven from the political stage, the criticisms of heroism and martial prowess were readily transferred to the avengers, "wandering swordsmen," brigands, and rebels who threatened the imperial order. The claims for the indispensability of moral instruction, textual military skills, and the patterns of Heaven were used to rationalize and justify the government's mobilization and control of the peasant populace. In this way the tales of the Yellow Emperor became a charter myth for the absolutist state.

This authoritarian character, indeed, was the very essence of the mythology of the sages. The message that in the beginning men were not separate from beasts, and that humanity had been created *by rulers* through their superhuman powers and perceptions was perhaps the most radical claim to political authority that has ever been made. If men were made men solely by a set of technologies and moral teachings created by former kings and maintained by the present rulers, then subjects were human only through the authority of their masters. Without the controls and institutions imposed by the elite, the common people would be nothing but beasts. In accounts of ancient history, the Warring States elite thus justified their political power as the very definition of humanity, the only barrier or dividing line between civilization and the savage world of the beasts.

Chapter Six

THE NATURAL PHILOSOPHY OF VIOLENCE

At the same time that they were uncovering in high antiquity the precedents for their policies and institutions, members of the Warring States elite were probing into the basic principles of nature, and here too they discovered the image and sanction of their own power. In a classic example of what Marshall Sahlins has described as the "reciprocal dialectic of nature and culture," these thinkers first explained the physical world in terms of their own self-understanding and then "discovered" that their practices and institutions exactly mirrored or expressed the natural order of things. Human values and characteristics were confounded with nature, and the nature thus fashioned in the human image was reapplied to the explanation of man. The result of this dialectic was the articulation of social action in terms of nature and the fashioning of the cosmos on the model of human society. Central to this dialectic was the tracing of the origins of human violence back into the elementary "stuff" that underlay all physical existence, and the description of the creation of human society through the proper use of violence as a process that paralleled the emergence of an orderly universe from primordial chaos.

The key term in the Chinese articulation of the dialectic of nature and culture was *qi* (氣), a primal "stuff" or "configured energy" that constituted or suffused all physical entities and hence was common to inanimate matter, plants, animals, and men. This shared substrate suggested not only that men and the physical world followed common principles, but also that they acted directly upon one another through the medium of *qi*. These ideas probably developed in the context of early Chinese medical theories, which were heavily influenced by emerging political doctrines in the last three centuries B.C.[1] However, the belief in the mutual influence of the natural environment, human physiology, and political action became particularly prominent in reflections on the question of violence, for the primary expressions of *qi* in the human world were anger and aggression. Violent men or fighters were identified with the unthinking impulsions of this "configured energy," while the military theorists and the exponents of celestial patterns for violence all self-consciously identified their methods and policies with the principles that guided *qi* in the world of nature. The socialization of violence projected into high antiquity in the tales of the Yellow Emperor thus appeared in natural philosophy as the transformation of a rampant, chaotic *qi* into an orderly universe.

Qi in Man and Nature

Etymologically the character *qi* apparently depicted vapors rising from cooked grain, and Bernhard Karlgren glossed its early meanings as "air, breath, temperament, disposition, vital principle."[2] The range of definitions is very close to that of the Latin *spiritus*, proceeding from vapors to air to breath (air breathed) to life principle (revealed in breath) to human spirit. For the Chinese, the closest tangible referent or analogy for *qi* was wind, and several scholars have argued that the idea of *qi* was derived by abstraction from observations of the actions and effects of wind.[3] A passage from an early chapter of the *Zhuangzi* most clearly reveals this identification: "The universe exhales its *qi*, and it is named 'wind.'" Or as Ban Gu described it: "The *qi* of Heaven and Earth intermingles to produce the wind." Indeed, the words "wind" and "*qi*" were frequently linked together in a synonym compound.[4]

The early Chinese modeled their "vital principle" on the wind not simply on the analogy of human breath, but also because of the links of the wind to the agricultural cycle. North China's climate features a monsoon pattern, a wind system with clear seasonal changes in direction; during the summer the wind comes from the southeast, but during the winter it blows harsh and cold out of Mongolia and Siberia to the north. From early times men regarded the wind, which brought warmth and growth during the agricultural season and took them away in the fall, as an animating principle. In the oracle bones the Shang identified only two seasons, spring and fall.[5] Although these texts do not show that the seasons were correlated with the alternation of the winds, the early chapters of the *Zhuangzi* contain stories in which the annual cycle appears as an alternation between the north and south winds.[6] The putative author of these chapters, Zhuang Zhou, was an inhabitant of the state of Song, which had been created by the Zhou founders for the descendants of the Shang kings, so these stories may well reflect old Shang traditions from the time when only two seasons were distinguished. However, by the last centuries of the second millenium B.C. the Shang had already distinguished four winds that were correlated with the four directions, and to which sacrifices were made to secure a bountiful harvest.[7] This model, in which the east wind was associated with the spring and the west wind with the fall, served as the pattern for mapping the winds onto the annual cycle throughout Chinese history, and it underlies the order in which the directions are listed in modern China—east, south, west, north.[8]

Because the alternation of the winds accompanied the change of seasons, the wind itself appeared as the fundamental vitalizing force. Thus the most important early medical text, the *Huang Di nei jing*, traced the origins of human energy to the wind.

> The east gives birth to the wind; the wind gives birth to [the phase] wood; wood gives birth to the sour flavor; the sour flavor gives birth to the liver; the liver gives birth to the muscles; the muscles give birth to the heart.[9]

This association with vitality is also shown by the fact that the character for "wind," *feng* (風), also came to mean "sexual arousal" or "being in heat."[10] Consequently, the explanation of hexagram forty-four of the *Yi jing* stated that the wind under Heaven was the image of mating, and a first-century B.C. apocryphal text dealing with the *Yi jing* asserted that when the winds blew in their proper seasons, then the creatures of the world would be able to procreate and grow.[11] In all these passages the wind was the bringer of life.

Qi as wind appeared in human physiology in the form of breath and, by extension, human spirit, for emotions and dispositions were all forms of *qi*.[12] Since wind and the passions or impulses that guided human action were all forms of a common *qi*, they had a direct, reciprocal influence. This influence was most clearly expressed in the belief that the distinctive behavior or temperament characteristic of each region was shaped by, and in turn influenced, the enveloping wind.

> All people have a nature of the five constancies, but their firmness or softness, slowness or speed, and the differences in their sounds [language and music] are all determined by the wind-*qi* of their environment. Therefore we call it "wind." Their likings or disdains, accepting or rejecting, and whether they move or remain

still is inconstant; it follows the emotions and desires of their lord. Therefore we call this "custom." Confucius said, "To move the wind and change customs, nothing is better than music."[13]

The phrase "move the wind and change customs" became a standard trope for changing the behavior of a community, and it is still preserved in the modern compound meaning "customs."[14] Indeed, the compound appeared as early as the *Shi jing*, and in the Eastern Han it figured in the title of a lengthy volume on folkways, Ying Shao's *Comprehensive Meanings of Wind-Customs* (*Fengsu tongyi* 風俗通義). In his preface Ying Shao explained the title thus:

> By "wind" we mean the cold or warmth of the Heavenly *qi*, the difficulty or ease of the Earthly terrain, the excellence or pollution of waters and springs, and the hardness or softness of grasses and trees. By "customs" we mean the way in which creatures with blood imitate these and live.[15]

Here "wind" was used to stand for all environmental influences, and its regular correlate "customs" represented the response of living beings to the impact of their natural surroundings. That the influence of environment on living things passed through their respective *qi* was recognized as early as the fourth century B.C., when Mencius observed, "Where one dwells transforms one's *qi*, just as food transforms one's body."[16] By the early Han this idea had been elaborated into a systematic theory of the impact of the environment on human physique and character through the medium of *qi*.

> Varieties of land each produce according to their type. The *qi* of mountains will produce many males; the *qi* of swamps will produce many females; the *qi* of places with obstructed access will produce many mute people; the *qi* of windy places will produce many deaf people; the *qi* of forests will produce many hunchbacks; the *qi* of woody places will produce many with curved spines; the *qi* of river banks will produce many with dropsy; the *qi* of stony places will produce many strong people; the *qi* of difficult, inaccessible places will produce many goiters; the *qi* of hot places will produce many early deaths; the *qi* of cold places will produce much long life; the *qi* of valleys will produce much paralysis; the *qi* of mounds will produce much madness; the *qi* of low, damp places will produce much benevolence; the *qi* of hills will produce much greed. Light soil produces quickness; heavy soil produces slowness; clear water makes voices soft; dirty water makes voices loud; rapid water

makes men quick and changeable; slow water makes them heavy and stolid; the central soil produces many sages. Each one imitates its *qi*; each one answers to its own kind.[17]

All these passages have described how the spirits and the bodies of men were shaped by the wind or *qi* in which they lived. The influence, however, also went in the other direction, for customs and behavior affected the character of the *qi* and wind around them. This phenomenon was described at length in the rhyme-prose "The Wind," which is questionably attributed to the third-century B.C. author Song Yu.

Thus it is that this cool, fresh hero wind,
Leaping and bounding up and down,
Climbs over the high wall
And enters deep into palace halls.
With a puff of breath it shakes the leaves and flowers,
Wanders among the cassia and pepper trees,
Or soars over the swift waters.
It buffets the mallow flower,
Sweeps the angelica, touches the spikenard,
Glides over the sweet lichens and lights on willow shoots,
Rambling over the hills
And their scattered host of fragrant flowers.
After this, it wanders into the courtyard,
Ascends the jade hall in the north,
Clambers over the gauze curtains,
Passes through the inner apartments,
And so becomes Your Majesty's wind.
When this wind blows on a man,
At once he feels a chill run through him,
And he sighs at its cool freshness.
Clear and gentle,
It cures sickness, dispels drunkenness,
Sharpens the eyes and ears,
Relaxes the body and brings benefit to men.
This is what is called the hero wind of Your Majesty. . . .
The wind of the common people
Comes whirling from the lanes and alleys,
Poking in the rubbish, stirring up the dust,
Fretting and worrying its way along.
It creeps into holes and knocks on doors,
Scatters sand, blows ashes about,

Muddles in dirt and tosses up bits of filth.
It sidles through hovel windows
And slips into cottage rooms.
When this wind blows on a man,
At once he feels confused and downcast.
Pounded by heat, smothered in dampness,
His heart grows sick and heavy,
And he falls ill and breaks out in a fever.
It strikes eyes with blindness.
He stammers and cries out,
Not knowing if he is dead or alive.
This is what is called the lowly wind
Of the common people.[18]

Commentators have suggested that this piece was a thinly-veiled criticism of the king for failing to share his wealth and ease with the common people, but the entire poem is based on the idea that men's lives and their environments acted reciprocally on one another through the medium of the wind. Winds that pass through rich furnishings and comfortable lives carry cool refreshment, while winds that pass through filth and scenes of desperation make men ill. These ideas were later systematically developed into the Chinese theory of environmental influence known as "wind and water" (*feng shui* 風水).

The reciprocal influence of wind and customs implied that men could consciously alter the behavior or nature of the winds in order to assure both improved public morals and bountiful harvests. The primary mechanism for such alteration was music, a form of refined wind.[19] The word *feng*, which meant wind, was also the name of one of the major sections of the *Shi jing*. As Gu Jiegang has shown, all the "poems" in this text were originally performed with music, so *feng* was a form of music.[20] Moreover, there is abundant evidence that the word *feng* also meant "tune," much like the English "air." A passage in the *Shi jing* itself says, "Jifu made a praise-song to present to Shen Bo; its lyric (*shi* 詩) was grand and its tune (*feng* 風) was splendid." Twice the *Shan hai jing* linked "wind" with "music" in a compound, and the commentator explained that "wind" meant "tune." Likewise, in the *Zuo zhuan* the phrase *tu feng* (土風) meant "local tune."[21] The *Zhuangzi* gives the most vivid account of wind as a form of music.

"The Great Clod [universe] exhales its breath and this is named 'wind.' This has not yet arisen, but when it rises then the ten thousand apertures wildly call out. Can you alone not hear their long, drawn-out sound? In the towering mountain forests, the apertures of huge trees of one hundred spans are like noses, like mouths, like ears, like jugs, like cups, like mortars, like deep ponds, like muddy pools. They boom like waves, whistle like arrows, bellow, gasp, shout, scream, moan, and howl. Those in front sing *yuuu*, while those who follow sing *ouuu*. In a light breeze they make small harmonies, but in a wild wind they form a great symphony. And when the savage wind ceases then the massed apertures are empty. Have you alone never seen their shaking and waving?"

Zi You said, "Then the pipes of the earth are those massed apertures, and the pipes of men are bamboos placed together."[22]

Human music was a form of controlled or artificial wind, and wind a form of natural music. Each could directly influence the other.

Since music was wind guided and shaped by man, it was the most direct means to modify the wind and hence improve the influences of the environment. This is what Confucius meant when he spoke of music as the best way to "move the wind and change customs," and music became a technique of proper government, in which the ruler could harmonize the winds in order to guarantee the smooth progression of the annual cycle, the success of agriculture, and the tranquility of the people.

Government imitates music; music follows from harmony and harmony from stability. . . . we cast [musical instruments] in bronze, work them in stone, bind them with thread on wood, bore holes for them in bamboo gourds, and then give them rhythm with drums and perform on them so as to give order to the eight winds.[23]

This use of music to guide the winds was the active form of the technique of using the pitchpipes to trace the alternation of *yin* and *yang* that underlay the cycle of the seasons and the winds. But since music was itself based on the pitchpipes, these were the ultimate key to guiding the winds to secure a beneficial climate, good harvests, and proper public morals. As the *Li ji* stated, "The eight winds follow the pitchpipes and are not treacherous."[24] By altering the winds, the pitchpipes and music not only secured the harvest, but they could also improve the wind-influenced customs and behavior of the people.

Therefore the sage tours the twelve provinces, regards their wind and customs, and learns their natures and dispositions. Thus he lays out the twelve customs, and fixes them through the six pitchpipes and the five tones.[25]

Just as correct music gave proper order to the winds and assured the state's prosperity and the people's obedience, so improper music would have the opposite effect. Through errors or innovations in musical performances the ruler could bring on drought, as in the case of the irregular performance of the clear *jiao* music by Lord Ping of Jin, or pervert the people and bring ruin to the state. In one story in the *Guo yu*, the music master Shi Kuang prophesied the destruction of Jin's ruling lineage because the ruler delighted in the new music, the lascivious music of Zheng and Wei.[26] Another story dealing with Shi Kuang tells how Lord Ling of Wei passed the Pu River on his way to Jin and heard ghostly music from the river. He had his music master learn the tune and proceeded to Jin. When he had the music performed for Lord Ping, Shi Kuang interrupted the performance and explained that it was music that had been composed for the evil King Zhou of the Shang. When the Shang fell, the composer had drowned himself in the Pu River. Hence this was "the music of a perished state," and anyone who played it would destroy his own realm.[27] In these stories music directly expressed the moral failings of those who produced it, and any who listened to corrupted music would be led to reproduce those failings through an "artificial" influence of music that was the human variant of the "natural" influence of the wind.

Perhaps the best-known story about the transmission of personal character and public mores through music was that of Ji Zha and his embassy to Lu in 544 B.C. Because Lu had preserved the Zhou cultural heritage, Ji Zha took advantage of his visit to listen to ancient songs. Simply from the music he was able to distinguish its state of origin and the character of society at the time it was composed.[28] Thus music not only expressed and influenced character or morals, but also preserved a record of their changes over time.

The idea that music could transmit the moral character of its composer or his age hinged on the belief that it was uniquely able to reveal the state of a man's mind or temperament.

As for the sound of bells and drums, if you are angry and strike them they will be martial; if you are worried and strike them they will be sad; if you are happy and strike them they will be joyful. When the mind changes the music will likewise change.[29]

The most famous expression of this idea that music revealed the mind or moral resolve of its performer was the story of Bo Ya and Dong Ziqi, for the latter could immediately recognize the thoughts of the former in his music.[30]

Not only did music immediately depict the mind of its composer or performer, but it was also an expression of his moral nature and potency. When Confucius was surrounded in the state of Kuang, his song of mourning paralyzed the attackers, and the potency of his music demonstrated that he was a sage.[31] The idea that the capacity of music to influence its listeners depended on the potency of its creator suggested that music was not merely a generalized technique of government at the disposal of all, but specifically a tool of the sage ruler who would guide lesser beings through his mastery of true music. In this way the theory of the moral influence of music was incorporated into the ideal of the sage and the belief that his power and perceptions separated men from beasts.

> All tones are produced by the hearts of men, but music is that which totally comprehends moral relations and principles. So those who know only sounds are beasts, those who know tones are the masses, but only the noble man knows music. . . . One examines the music to know government, and the Way of control is thus complete.[32]

The image of the sage commanding through the power of music also appeared in the story, cited in the last chapter, of Yao leading the beasts with his music.

Further evidence of the belief in the relationship of wind, music, the agricultural cycle, social order, and the potency of the sage comes from an examination of the mythical bird *feng huang* (鳳凰), commonly translated "phoenix." The written character for its name was originally identical with that for "wind," and it was in fact an embodiment of the wind, dwelling in the wind-caves and following the cycle of the wind. Moreover, the tones of the pitchpipes were copied from the song of the phoenix, and several musical instruments were supposedly replicas of its body or wings. So this embodiment of wind was also the prototype of music. Again, where the phoenix danced grain grew of its own accord, and the coming of the phoenix was associated with rain. The embodiment of wind and music thus also brought the blessings of a rich harvest. Finally, the appearance of the phoenix in the world of men was a sign of proper government and social order, and it signalled that the ruler had the virtuous potency of the sage.[33] In a single image the phoenix contained the entire complex of wind/*qi* in both its natural and social aspects: wind as the source of vitality, music as refined wind, successful harvests as the result of harmonious wind, social order as the expression of "natural" wind harmonized by music, and the potency of the sage as the ultimate source of proper music and its consequent social harmony.

Gaozong's mourning

Qi and Violence

As applied to human beings, *qi* in its broadest sense meant vital spirit: "Human life is the concentration of *qi*; when it is concentrated they live, but when it disperses they die."[34] More narrowly, it appeared as the energetic drives and emotions that propelled human action, and among these energies and passions it was particularly associated with anger and belligerence. In the writings of the Confucian school *qi* regularly appeared in the phrase "blood and *qi*," where it meant something like "animal energies," but the most common expression of these energies was in fighting or combat. Thus the *Zuo zhuan* stated, "All things that contain blood and *qi* engage in struggle."[35] In the *Lun yu* Confucius asserted:

> There are things against which a man of honor keeps guard. In his youth, before his blood and *qi* have settled, he keeps guard against sex. When he reaches his prime and his blood and *qi* have just grown firm, he keeps guard against fights. When he reaches old age and his blood and *qi* have withered, he keeps guard against acquisitions.[36]

The idea that bellicosity and a tendency to fight characterized *qi* in its fullness also appeared in the writings of other philosophical schools. Thus the legalist *Shang Jun shu* contains the argument that while the resource of the rhetorician lay in his mouth, that of the hermit in his sincerity of purpose, and that of the craftsman in his hands, the resource of the bold warrior lay in his *qi*.[37] The silk Huang-Lao manuscript from Mawangdui says:

> Violent anger is blood and *qi*; battle is the outer flesh. If this violent anger is not released [in battle] it will seep out as an abcess.[38]

This same energetic *qi* that drove men to fight also impelled wild beasts to kill.

> Even before they have achieved their finished form, the young of tigers and leopards have the *qi* to devour cattle.[39]

Even Mencius, best known for his theory of the innate goodness of human nature, associated men's *qi* with the tendency to fight. His famous discussion of the "flood-like *qi*" emerged directly from his reflections on true human courage, on what could properly impel a man to fight, kill, or die.[40] He differed in arguing that truly potent *qi* emerged from righteousness rather than from raw animal spirits, but it still manifested itself in combat.

Nor was this association of the fundamental "stuff" of nature and the essence of human vitality with bellicosity limited to philosophical arguments; it also figured in the linguistic usage of the period. A man who was *hao qi* (好氣), "fond of *qi*," was bellicose, devoted to martial valor, and prone to associate with the violent "wandering swordsmen." One who *shi qi* (使氣), "gave free rein to *qi*," was a man prone to fighting. *Ke qi* (客氣), the "guest *qi*," referred not to politeness, as in modern Chinese, but rather to a sudden inspiration of martial valor in a man not otherwise inclined to combat. This link to anger and bellicosity survives in the modern Chinese phrase *sheng qi* (生氣), "to produce *qi*," which means "to provoke anger" or "become angry."

As the energy that drove men to fight, *qi* was essential to the success of an army and fundamental to the art of the commander. Consequently, all the military treatises placed great stress on *qi* and its manipulation. The *Wei Liaozi* remarked:

The means by which a general wages war is the people; the means by which the people wage war is their *qi*.

At the beginning of the same passage, the author divided victory into three types, and the highest was "victory by the Way," a victory won by destroying the enemy's *qi*.[41] The *Wuzi* listed the "four pivots" of battle, and the highest was the "pivot of *qi*."[42] The *Sun Bin bingfa* began a chapter devoted to techniques for "prolonging *qi*" thus:

In gathering an army and concentrating the masses, the principle task is to excite their *qi*.[43]

The *Sima fa* stated simply, "The Way of warfare consists in arousing their *qi*."[44] All the writers agreed that *qi*, this "fighting spirit" or "morale" that emerged from the elemental dynamism of nature, was the fundamental ingredient to obtaining victory.

But this emphasis on *qi* betokened more than a belief in the primacy of morale or fighting spirit in determining the outcome of battles; it was intimately linked with the denial of heroism that was fundamental to the vision of warfare in the military treatises and the mythology of the Yellow Emperor. In several texts the *qi* of the troops was explicitly contrasted with the mind of the commander, in the same manner as other passages cast the troops in the role of collective body to the general's mind.[45] Just as the mind of the commander had to rule over the *qi* of his troops, so in the individual, as Mencius observed, "The will is the commander of the *qi*, while the *qi* is that which suffuses the body."[46] *Qi* was a surging, formless energy that could not calculate or restrain itself; reflection and analysis were reserved for the army's leader. Noting the decline of men and mores, a third-century B.C. philosopher observed:

> In high antiquity men competed in the Way and virtuous potency. In the middle era they battled with cunning wisdom and plots. Now they battle with *qi* and physical strength.[47]

Not only was *qi* linked with physical strength and bellicosity, but it was explicitly contrasted with the mental acuity and reflective capacities of the commander and with the potency of the sage. It was a "natural," animal fighting spirit that in order to serve the state had to be kept under the sway of the human mind of the commander and the celestial, moral order imposed by the ruler.

This identification of the soldiers' *qi* as naked energy that was contrasted with intellectual or moral capacities also appeared in the *Xunzi*, where it was linked with the opposition between reckless youth and the wisdom of age.

> Blood, *qi*, and muscular strength wither, but wisdom, reflection and [correctness in] taking or rejecting do not wither.[48]

Qi was linked with unthinking youth and physical strength, and opposed to the reflective mental powers. As the *Da Dai li ji* pointed out, energetic youth without the control of old age led to unchecked violence and social collapse.

> Jie of Xia and Zhou of Shang were savage towards all under Heaven. They slaughtered the innocent and massacred the guiltless. They were inauspicious towards Heaven and scattered the families of the people. They avoided the elders of the state and associated with the young and beautiful. The violent and overbearing became their intimates, and flatterers and payers of bribes took office. To speak or act according to law was treated as a crime. They cut off the Way of Heaven and went against the four seasons; ritual and music were not performed, so the youthful wind [*you feng* 幼風] ruled all.[49]

In Chapter Five we saw how the evil rulers were described as animals, and here they suffer the closely related accusation of uncontrolled youth. Ignoring the bonds of morality, ritual, and the patterns of

Heaven, they followed the blind impulsions of their untrained passions and energies. This is the consequence of *qi* not being restrained by human mind or celestial model.

In Warring States and early imperial China the man guided by his *qi*, the man of combat, was a suspect and dangerous figure who fell outside human society.

> Zi Mozi said to Luohuali, "I hear that you are fond of valor." Luohuali said, "That is right. When I hear that there is a valorous warrior in a town, I must go there and kill him." Zi Mozi said, "Under Heaven there is none who does not desire to associate with those who have that of which he is fond in order to eliminate that which he hates. Now you hear that in a town there is a valiant warrior and must go to kill him. This is not fondness of valor; it is hatred of valor."[50]

As Confucius remarked, the noble man does not harm his own kind, so the heroic warrior who could find glory only in destroying his fellows had no place in the world of the Warring States philosophers.[51] Heroism was the expression of a rampant *qi* which, if not checked or guided by some moral authority, obliterated the possibility of order and discrimination.

The most famous articulation of this idea was the story, often depicted in Han tomb art, of the three powerful warriors and the two peaches. These warriors were famous for their strength and courage, and they were unsurpassed in the wrestling of tigers. Confident in their matchless power, they ignored the ritual expressions of respect owed to their ruler, and the king did not dare to punish them. In order to dispose of them, Master Yan gave them two peaches as a reward and asked them to divide them up amongst themselves according to their merits. This led to a quarrel that ended in the deaths of all three warriors. The story was followed by this narrative commentary:

> Lord Jing held the archery competition, but Master Yan prepared the preliminary ritual banquet and awaited him. The lord said, "I am sick of the rituals associated with selecting archers; I [only] desire to obtain the most valorous warriors under Heaven in order to plan for my state." Master Yan replied, "If a noble man has no rituals, he is a commoner; if a commoner has no rituals, he is a beast. If men's courage is great they will assassinate their princes, and if their strength is great they will kill their superiors. That they do not dare to do so is solely due to rituals."[52]

Individual bellicosity and valor, the primary expressions of human qi, negated the possibility of human society and reduced men to the levels of beasts. In the social history of violence this bestiality was overcome through the innovations of the sages; in the natural philosophy of violence the creation of order was imagined in terms of giving form to the rampant chaos of qi, on the model of Heaven's patterns emerging from the undivided primordial chaos.

The Sage Commander

The authors of the military treatises set themselves explicity against the bellicosity and valor that characterized qi, insisting instead on the primary importance of the unity negated by individual heroism.

Whenever men discuss commanders, they always judge them on the basis of valor. But valor is only a small part of a commander's makeup. A valorous man will invariably regard unity as unimportant. One who treats unity as unimportant and does not know its benefits cannot be a commander.[53]

Only when united under the encompassing powers of the general's mind and guided by his commands could the soldiers' qi play its appropriate role.

The lightness or weight of the disposition of the million men of the royal army resides in a single man; this is called the pivot of qi.[54]

Qi was essential to victory, but it had to be shaped by the general's mind into the formations and maneuvers that were decisive in battle. And just as natural qi was guided by the ruler through the power of music, so the military commander directed his men through the use of drums and bells.

The links of music to military action in China were very ancient. There was a tradition that on the eve of their battle with the Shang, the Zhou troops held a great war dance which lasted through the night and thus struck terror into the opposing forces.[55] This dance and the subsequent victory were ritually re-enacted in the wu (武) dance that became one of the major elements of Zhou court musical performances.[56]

During the Warring States such war dances continued, but they were used as elements of military training in which men practiced precise movements in unison to the beat of the drum. Advancing and retreating, assuming square formations and shifting into circles, kneeling and rising, each of these was collectively rehearsed under the guidance of music and chant. The chapter on music in the *Li ji* contains several descriptions of the *wu* dance and the maneuvers it entailed, and these accounts jibe closely with descriptions of military training in the *Zhou li* and the *Wuzi*. Moreover, this and other texts assert that one role of music was to give order to military formations.

> Therefore, listening to the tunes of the *ya* and *song* [categories of court songs], their ambition will be vast. Grasping spears and shields, practicing looking up and down or stretching out and retracting, their appearance will be stalwart. Moving within the fixed limits and bound by the rhythms, their columns will be straight, and they will advance and retreat in unison.[57]

In addition to providing the pattern for collective action in training, music was also the mode of imposing order and communicating commands in the field. According to the highly schematic model of the *Zhou li*, each level of the military hierarchy had its own distinctive drum to signal commands.[58] Drums were used to signal the rhythm of the march and to communicate orders to men who were too far away to hear the voice or see the gestures of their commander. The patterns of music thus formed the nerves through which the commands of the general's mind passed to the collective body of his army, or in the images of natural philosophy they musically gave direction, harmony, and order to the formless *qi* of the troops.

In addition to providing a rhythm for collective action and relaying commands, music was also employed to stir up the *qi* of the troops and horses and thus drive them into battle.

> Xi Ke was wounded by an arrow, and the blood flowed down to his shoes, but he did not stop beating the drum. At last he said, "I am wounded," [and left the battle]. . . . Zhang Hou [Xi Ke's charioteer, who was also seriously wounded] said, "The eyes and ears of the army are on my banners and drum, and in advancing or retreating they follow them. If a single man controls this chariot, he can bring the battle to completion. This being so, how could one on account of a wound cause the ruin of this great service of the prince? When you put on armor and pick up a weapon, then you resolutely go to your death. Although I am wounded, I have not yet died, and I will press on." Holding both reins in his left hand, he held the stick in his right and beat the drum. The horses dashed forward, unable to stop, and the army followed them. The army of Qi was routed.[59]

The single man beating the drum won the victory; the army and horses were impelled forward in unison by their aroused *qi* as though in response to some physical propulsion. Such was the power of the proper manipulation of *qi* through music.

Just as a commander could use the drums to drive his men to victory, so the clever strategist could make use of his opponent's drums to strip the enemy of his fighting spirit.

> The Lord [of Lu] was going to sound the drum but [Cao] Gui said, "Not yet." The men of Qi sounded their drums three times. [The armies would not advance till both sides had sounded their drums. Qi drummed, waited for Lu's reply, drummed again, waited again, and drummed again.] Gui said, "Now", and the army of Qi was routed. . . . Having won, the lord asked the reason for his actions. Gui replied, "War is the *qi* of valor. Sound the drum once and *qi* rises; twice and it wanes; three times and it is exhausted. They were exhausted, and we were full; therefore we won."[60]

Q.E.D. The spirit of the armies and consequent result of the battle shifted in fixed ratio to the sequence and number of the soundings of the drums. The Han dynasty dictionary *Shi ming* offered the definition, "'Martiality' [*wu* 武] means 'to dance' [*wu* 舞]; the movements of an assault are like the drumming out of a dance."[61]

In the same manner that the music of the drum could arouse and direct the *qi* of the combatants at the behest of the commander, so the music of the pitchpipes could "read" the *qi* of the participants and thus predict the outcome of specific engagements. This tactical divination of *qi* through music took several forms.

> The men of Jin heard that there was an army from Chu, but Shi Kuang said, "They will do no harm. I played the northern tune [*bei feng* 北風] several times and also the southern tune [*nan feng* 南風]. The southern tune is not strong and is mostly the sounds of death. Chu will certainly achieve nothing."[62]

The precise technique used is not clear, but it apparently involved the playing of tunes associated with particular geographic areas and using some unspecified aspect of the sound to deduce the *qi* of the army from each area and hence the probable outcome of the battle.

Another method for predicting the results of battle with the pitchpipes involved eliciting a shout from one of the contending hosts and listening to which pipe produced its note in response. The *Tai Gong liu tao* describes how a commander could know the "waxing and waning of an army and the results of a battle" through the use of the twelve pitchpipes.

[On a night when] the *qi* of Heaven [which would interfere] is still and there are no clouds, wind, or rain, a cavalryman with the twelve pipes should approach the enemy camp and shout in order to arouse them. He then listens to the answering clamor and notes which pipe sympathetically responds.[63]

A related practice was described in a fragment of a "military book" preserved in the *Zhou li*. The passage itself simply states that the Grand Musician "grasps the pitchpipes to listen to the sound of the army and proclaim the good or bad fortune," but the commentary provides more detail. It said that on the day the army was to set out, the general received a bow and arrow from the king. The general drew the bow, and the army gave a great shout. The Grand Musician listened with the pitchpipes and divined the results of the battle.[64]

In addition to the use of pipes, the *qi* of an army could also be read through the observation of the visible vapors or emanations described in Chapter Four. A passage in the *Mozi* simply stated that through watching *qi* one could distinguish the great general from the lesser, retreat from advance, and victory from defeat.[65] The passage in the *Liu tao* immediately following the one cited above described how to read the enemy's *qi* through the use of banners (based on the association of *qi* with the wind) and of emanations over the adversary's citadel.[66] And the aforementioned "Tian guan shu" in the *Shi ji* discussed a wide variety of visible emanations associated with various aspects of military campaigns.

Because the art of the commander was identified with the arousing, guiding, reading, and manipulation of *qi*, treatises often described military action as a cosmological process that recapitulated the actions of nature, and the commander appeared as a *daemon* who acted upon his men in the same way that the principles or patterns of Heaven acted upon the *qi* of physical matter. In early Chinese natural philosophy *qi* was the "configurative energy" that served as the unformed substrate of all matter, while *shen* (神) signified the "spirit" or "structive force" that gave form and thereby created objects out of chaos.[67] Moreover, the word commonly used to describe military formations and their manipulation, *xing* (形), meant "form" or "formed object" in cosmological or ontological contexts. Since the potency of the general to shape battle through force of intellect was often described as *shen*, the relation of the commander to his troops recapitulated the processes that created and shaped physical objects, and he thus was cast in the role of a cosmic figure who mimicked or shared in the actions of Heaven and Earth. The troops and their energy or morale corresponded to the unformed substrate of matter, the commander to the principle or spirit that imparted form, and the disposition of the troops to the formed, material objects of the physical world.

This identification of military action with natural processes was not limited to a shared vocabulary. In its opening passages the *Sunzi* argued that there were five factors to be assessed in military actions: the Way, Heaven, Earth, the commander, and the law. Although they have more limited, technical uses—Heaven corresponding to weather and Earth to geography—the first three factors still lie in the realm of "cosmology" rather than military action in a narrow sense. The same text later stated that victory came from the extraordinary, and that one skilled in the extraordinary would be "endlessly fertile like Heaven and Earth, inexhaustible like the rivers and oceans, ending and beginning again like the sun or moon, dying and being reborn like the four seasons."[68] Elsewhere it asserted that "he who is skilled in defense hides beneath the nine Earths [the depths of the earth]; he who is skilled in attack moves above the nine Heavens [the heights of the universe]." The text compared the elusiveness of the skilled commander to the swirling, primeval chaos and then continued:

> Therefore if one is skilled in attack the enemy will not know how to defend himself; if one is skilled in defense the enemy will not know how to attack. Subtle! Subtle! He achieves formlessness. Spirit-like [*shen*]! Spirit-like! He is soundless. Therefore he can be the Ruler of Fate to the enemy.[69]

All of these passages explicitly insisted that the arts of the true commander allowed him to act like Heaven and Earth and to imitate the powers of natural or cosmic processes, and in relation to his troops or the enemy he appeared as a spirit or a god.

The *Sunzi* is in no way exceptional in this attribution of "divine" powers to the commander. Other Warring States military treatises also repeatedly described the commander as a *daemon* whose movements followed the cycles of the seasons or of birth and death, as the officer of death who acted as a third to Heaven and Earth, as the officer of cosmic principle who ruled the myriad objects, as an illuminated master of structive force who perceived without senses and commanded without words, and as a being whose power stemmed from the principles or forces that guided the cosmos. In total harmony with the principles of nature, the true commander became a divine spirit or a sage who participated as an equal with Heaven and Earth.[70]

The inverse side of this vision of warfare, as was noted in Chapter Three, was the casting of the soldiers in the role of material objects, or of mindless but dynamic forces like water or lightning. These metaphors reflected the soldiers' character as the embodiments of unthinking *qi*, which in the natural philosophy of the period was the stuff of brute matter and aimless, chaotic motion. Only in the mind of the commander as transmitted through the medium of music could these random elements find purpose or meaning in the collectivity of the army.

The Socialization of *Qi*

However, just as the art of the commander found its purpose only in the encompassing moral order of the ruler, so the general's manipulation of the violent chaos of human *qi* culminated in a moral state patterned on cosmic principles. This idea was already implicit in the calendrical model of statecraft, in which the actions of the ruler accorded with the cycle of *yin* and *yang* through the medium of *qi*, but it was articulated in the greatest detail in the Huang-Lao manuscript discovered at Mawangdui. This text traced the principles of law and statecraft back into the fundamental rules or regularities that guided the cosmos, and one of its central concerns was military action.

It begins with a proclamation of the cosmological bases of all government.

> The Way produces law. Law measures out gains and losses with its cord [like a carpenter measuring the straightness of wood] and thereby illuminates the crooked and straight. Therefore he who holds to the Way produces the law and does not dare to violate it; the law is established and he does not dare to set it aside. . . . [text missing] . . . able to measure oneself with the cord, and only then see and know the human world without confusion. Empty and without form, its axis is dark and impenetrable, this is the origin of the myriad objects.

Having located the principles of statecraft in the order of the universe and traced the moral law and physical objects back to a common source, the text then asserts the supreme importance of these principles by noting that they determine the fundamental questions of victory and defeat, of life and death.

> . . . Therefore they all emerge from the dark and impenetrable, but some die and live, some are defeated and some achieve success. Disaster and good fortune come from the same Way, but none know from what [their difference] comes.

The choice of these particular questions already suggests the central place of warfare in the scheme of the book, for it is combat that decides victory and defeat, life and death. So the next passage invokes specifically, although in highly abstracted language, the art of the military commander.

> To cut apart and then reunite, to perish and yet survive, who knows its structive force? To die and then return to life, to turn disaster into good fortune, who knows its limits? Seek it back in the formless and thereby know the origin of disaster and good fortune.
>
> . . . The constant regularities of Heaven and Earth are the four seasons, light and dark, birth and death, and soft and hard. The constant occupations of the myriad peoples are agriculture for men and weaving for women. The constant ranks of noble and humble exist so that the capable and the unworthy will not be placed together. The constant Way of nurturing servants is to employ the capable and not go beyond their talents. The constant measure of commanding the people is to do away with bias and establish impartiality. Those who change these constancies or surpass proper measure are controlled with the "extraordinary."[71]

This passage elaborates in detail the fundamental polarity of the "normative" and the "extraordinary" that defined the relation of moral government and military action in many Warring States texts. The established degrees, the fixed measures, and the constant regularities, occupations, and ranks represented the normative order of the state. But paired with this was the "extraordinary," the hallmark of military action, which, as we know from various military treatises, allowed one to be cut apart and yet reunite, to perish and yet survive, to die and then return to life.[72] These military skills of the extraordinary were reserved to punish those who violated the normative order.

The text also discusses specific means to bring warfare into accord with Heaven. Its fundamental maxim was the previously discussed principle that all military action had to accord with the seasons of Heaven. The ruler nourished life in the growing seasons while restricting armies to the seasons of death, and thus military action mirrored the cosmic order.

In addition to according with the seasons of Heaven, the ruler had to follow the Way of men, through action in accord with proper moral standards. This idea was based on the theory that the social order derived from the principles of nature and that one followed Heaven by acting in accord with received moral precepts. One passage argued, "If you attack inappropriately, then you will, contrary to your hopes, attain only disaster." "Martiality" meant attacking appropriate targets in the proper season, and the appropriate targets were those who did not submit or committed crimes.[73]

Another section traces military victories to the establishment of proper laws and titles, the maintenance of social hierarchy, and the enforcement of punishments. It describes a seven-year program in which the ruler first wins the hearts of the people through according with custom and displaying his virtuous potency and beneficence, then issues titles and commands to create hierarchy and discipline, and finally institutes punishments to guarantee the force of law. These policies unite the hearts and minds of the people and make them willing to die for the state, and only then can he launch a campaign.[74] Since the text explicitly stated that laws and standards emerged from the cosmic Way, this once again shows that military success stemmed from accord with cosmic principles.

Yet another version of the "cosmological" aspect of military action derived from the idea that the underlying principle of natural processes was the cycle; everything that reached an extreme would then "reverse" and move in the opposite direction. According to this principle, one accorded with Heaven not simply by ensuring the proper social order and moving with the seasons, but by timing one's strategy with the waxing and waning of the enemy's power.

> But if you pass the limit and act inappropriately, then Heaven will send down disaster. If another is strong enough to defeat Heaven, then carefully avoid him. When Heaven reverses and conquers this other, then you move together with it. First contracting then expanding, you will reach Heaven's limits and not claim for yourself the merit of Heaven.[75]

The pragmatic tactic of avoiding the enemy when and where he was strong and attacking his weaknesses was basic to military philosophy, but here it became a question of moving in tune with the forces of the cosmos and following Heaven's cycle of waxing and waning. Victory came to him who moved with Heaven and patterned his attacks on the cyclic movements of natural process. Such victory was called the "merit of Heaven" because it was won by the power of Heaven rather than the ruler's prowess.

Other sections also elaborate the relation of the ruler's "structive force" to combat. One argues that only by modeling himself on Heaven can the ruler obtain the structive force to shape events in the world.

At the limit of structive force, vision and knowledge will never be confused. The ruler holds to this Way, and in this manner he holds to the limits of Heaven and Earth and manifests himself [or "sees"] together with Heaven. He completely. . . [text missing] . . . within the four limits [east, south, west, and north], and grasps the six handles. . . . The six handles: one is observation, one is discourse, one is motion, one is rotation, one is change, one is transformation. Through observation he knows which states will live and which die. Through discourse he knows the locus of survival and perishing, rising and falling. Through motion he can destroy the strong and raise up the weak. Through rotation he will not lose. . . [text missing] . . . of right and wrong. Through change he will attack those who are to die and nourish those who are to live. Through transformation he will make clear his potency and eliminate those who do harm.[76]

By holding to the cosmic Way the ruler takes on the structive force of Heaven and is thereby able to understand the principles of life and death and to realize these principles on the field of battle. His victory becomes as inevitable as the rising of the sun.

Another section of the work clearly equates the structive force of Heaven as the creator of objects with that of the ruler at war.

The Way is the source of structive force and illumination. These two are located inside proper degree, but manifest themselves outwardly. . . . Located inside proper degree they are still and do not shift. Manifesting themselves outwardly, they move but are not changed. Still and not shifting, moving but not changing, therefore it is called the structive force. Structive force and illumination are the standards of all vision and knowledge. . . .

When an object first . . . [text missing] . . . it establishes itself on Earth and overflows Heaven, so none can see its form. It vastly fills up the limits of Heaven and Earth, so none know its name. Therefore it moves contrary to completion. . . . Therefore it suffers the punishment of contrariety, and disaster will reach its very being. . . .

So he who holds to the Way is able to be empty and still, impartial and correct. Then he manifests. . . [text missing] . . . Then he obtains the truth of names and principles. If chaos accumulates within and balance is lost without, then he will attack. Those who lose their form [or "dispositions". The form of the object in the preceding paragraph here becomes the formations of the army.] within and who wrongly launch expeditions outside [their borders] will be destroyed. Those who go against precept and overflow upward without knowing where to stop will perish.[77]

The Way of Heaven produced the structive force that formed objects according to proper measure, while itself remaining still and unchanging. Any object that exceeded proper measure would "overflow" its bounds and, lacking limits or definition, lose both form and name. As a result it suffered the "punishment" of ceasing to exist.

In the same way, the still and unchanging ruler modeled himself on Heaven and held the structive force of names and principles. States that violated the principles of social order would, just like the objects that exceeded proper measure, overflow their bounds, lose form and name, and be destroyed. The author clearly equates these two processes through using an identical vocabulary of "losing form" (*wang xing* 亡形) and "overflowing upward" (*shang yi* 上溢) to describe the fate of the object and that of the state.

The idea that warfare emerged from the "stuff" of nature and could be socialized only through imitating the actions of Heaven was not limited to the military theorists and Huang-Lao philosophers, for it also informed the calendrical model of government and the Han institution of "watching for the ethers" discussed in Chapter Four. These were both based on the idea that the violence of warfare was the human version of the annual slaughter of vegetation and animal life inflicted by winter. Since the natural philosophy of the period interpreted the annual cycle in terms of the alternation of *yin* and *yang* through the medium of *qi* as mirrored in the cycle of the winds, the calendrical model also traced warfare to origins in *qi*, and correct warfare was based on bringing human *qi* into accord with cosmic *qi* through the proper use of music and the pitchpipes. "Music is produced from the tones; the tones are produced from the pitchpipes; the pitchpipes are produced from the wind."[78] And the winds were the tangible image of *qi*. The pitchpipes gave the state a rudimentary political technology for patterning its manipulation of human *qi* on the cosmic cycle, and they were, as Sima Qian remarked, particularly important in military affairs.

Given their insistence that the moral rule of the sage-king obviated the need for any specifically military wisdom or technology, the Confucians said little about the manipulation of *qi* and its relation to warfare. However, their rejection of military arts was based on the belief that the total unity of the people based on the ruler's moral potency obviated the need for the general's skills, and it is noteworthy that Confucian discussions of the relation of the ruler to the people adopted the same rhetoric as the "natural philosophy of violence" applied to the relations of the commander and the ruler to the army. Although the specific issue of violence was not explicitly discussed, the Confucian school developed a natural philosophy of the state that closely mirrored the theory of the socialization of human violence through the skillful manipulation of *qi*.

The Confucian theory of proper warfare recognized that the people were identical with the army, and it argued that the virtues of the ruler would unite the people and make them invincible in battle. In Warring States Confucian thought the support of the people was equated with the Mandate of Heaven, and Heaven was identified as a moralized nature which reflected the condition of the people, so the strength of the army depended on following the moral principles of Heaven/nature. This theory also assimilated correct military action to following the patterns of nature, and it differed from the military treatises and Huang-Lao texts only in its exclusive emphasis on the moralized character of this "nature."

At first glance it might appear that the Confucian thinkers were at odds with the other schools, for they generally identified the people with, or substituted them for, Heaven. Several of the later chapters of the *Shang shu* and the *Mencius* stated that the perceptions of Heaven are those of the people.[79] The *Mencius* went even further, arguing that a man who knew his own nature knew Heaven and that the Mandate of Heaven was equivalent to the support of the people.[80] This assigning of the role of the Zhou divinity *Tian* to the collective common people was part of the general Confucian project of reinterpreting the ancient Zhou religion and sacrificial cult as a vision of what Herbert Fingarette has described as "the human community as holy rite."[81] We have already seen one aspect of this change in Chapter Two, which showed how the feeding of ancestral spirits was reinterpreted as a ritualized delineation of hierarchical human relationships, and in this Confucian religion of human society it is not surprising that the role of Heaven, conceived as a moralized nature, was taken by the collective body of the people.

However, this theory did not actually contradict those rival schools who identified Heaven with the ruler and the people with natural objects. The true significance of this substitution of the people for Heaven in Warring States political theories and polemics is revealed in the frequent invocations of the doctrine in the *Zuo zhuan*. Throughout the text various speakers criticize the use of sacrificial offerings to secure good fortune for the ruler, and the reliance on natural prodigies or omens to discern the future. The people, they state, are the masters of the spirits, so the spirits of Heaven follow the collective inclinations or desires of the people. In place of seeking support from a deified Heaven, the ruler had to base his political power and prosperity on the support of the people. Rather than attributing prodigies of nature to supernatural spirits, he should recognize that they reflected disturbances in the human realm. One man even argued that the people generated prodigies and natural disasters through the power of their *qi*, linking Confucian notions of the people as Heaven to the theories of the interaction of man with nature through their shared energetic substrate.[82]

These passages reveal that the Confucian identification of Heaven with the people was basically a criticism of belief in a personified Heaven or spirits who could be bought with sacrifices, and who revealed their will in omens and natural prodigies. It substituted the people for Heaven in its role as the basis of political authority—hence Mencius's identification of the Mandate with the support of the people—and as creator of prodigies. It did not, however, assign to the people the role of Heaven as guiding principle or creator of patterns, for as we will see below, these were reserved for the rulers. The people as Heaven manifested themselves in the world not in cosmic pattern or order but in the negation of that order expressed through prodigies, monstrosities, and disasters. Their equivalents or doubles in the natural world were floods, the raining of blood, two-headed calves, and any other freak or abortion of conventional nature that signalled the breakdown of proper order. Although critical of those who saw in natural omens and prodigies the will of supernatural spirits, the Confucians simply substituted the people for these spirits, so the will of the people was identified with the actions of inanimate objects and natural forces, just as in the natural philosophy of violence discussed above. And just as in that philosophy, the people were equated with nature in its chaotic aspect, while the bestowal of order was reserved for the rulers.

The structural parallel between the two theories is shown by their common strategy of reducing the army or the people to the role of children, animals, bodies, or inanimate objects, while attributing mind, design, and purpose to the leader alone. Many examples of this appear in the major Confucian texts. Mencius twice stated that the people would flock to the moral ruler "like water flowing downward with tremendous force," and also compared their granting of allegiance with the spread of fire, with the manner in which animals naturally headed for the wilds, or with a drought-parched field hoping for rain. Other passages argued that the ruler's relation to his people was like that of parents to small children, and that he should treat the people as invalids. Likewise, the famous statement attributed to Confucius, equating the ruler with the wind and the people with bending grass, presented the people as passive objects responding automatically to dynamic control imposed from the outside.[83] Just as the people's turning to a virtuous ruler was identified as a natural, automatic, physical process, so their rejection of an evil ruler was identified with fleeing from water or fire.[84] Xun Kuang, for his part, described the people's relation to the virtuous ruler as that of

water flowing downhill, an echo responding to a voice, a shadow following a body, a horse yoked to a carriage, or of children to a parent. And
his famous metaphor for the state, in which the ruler was a boat and the
people the water, also reduced the people to the status of formless,
insensate, potentially chaotic matter and granted design and purpose
solely to the ruler.[85]

Another trope that portrayed the ruler as the active, thinking
agent and limited the people to passive, automatic responses, was the
Confucian insistence that the people would inevitably take on the moral
character of the ruler. If the ruler were benevolent and righteous, then
the people would be likewise; if he were greedy, calculating, and
vicious, then the people would become corrupt. Only the great man, as
Mencius argued, could criticize or correct the prince, while the common
people would blindly copy him.[86]

In the military treatises, the insistence that the leader took the
initiative while the people passively responded often took the form of a
metaphor in which the commander was the mind and the army the body.
The identical metaphor was regularly invoked by the Confucian philosophers to describe the relation of the ruler to his people. Mencius
stated several times that the ruler was the mind and the people the body.
Likewise, he asserted that the "great men" were those who used their
minds while the petty, common people toiled with their bodies, that
these great men became great because they devoted themselves to their
minds, and that men of rank were those who had the true human virtues
and were the culmination of humanity. The petty people, by contrast,
did not cultivate their minds and hence became like animals.[87] Xun
Kuang likewise insisted that the rule of the sage-king over his people
was like that of the mind over the body, and that the true ruler treated
objects as objects, while the common people were themselves rendered
into objects.[88]

Finally, just as the military theorists spoke of the commander as a
daemon who led his men like Heaven guiding natural processes, so the
Warring States Confucian philosophers spoke of the true ruler as a sage,
a "spirit," or the divine god (*tian di* 天帝) who became a "third with
Heaven and Earth."[89] Thus the Confucian theory of proper warfare as
being identical with the moral government of the sage converged with
the models of the military theorists, the Huang-Lao texts, and the *yin/
yang* thinkers in their shared rhetoric. All spoke of guiding inanimate
objects, mechanical forces, or animals, of minds commanding bodies,
and of the ruler as a cosmically potent figure who led the collective mass
of men like Heaven directing the myriad objects. Although they differed
in their vision of nature, they all modeled their ideals of normative,
sanctioned violence on their understanding of natural processes, and

they imagined the relation of the ruler to the ruled as that of Heaven to formless matter. As the *Guanzi* summarized it:

> The ruler and his servants are in the position of Heaven and Earth, while the common people are the image (*xiang* 象) of the myriad objects. Each stands at his post to await the orders of the ruler. How could the servants and common people each use their own minds to establish private interests?[90]

Conclusion

Most articulate Chinese of the Warring States period traced the origins of human violence and warfare back into the world of nature, primarily in the form of the blind impulsions of *qi*. Consequently, the control and use of violence, both in the immediate conduct of battle and in the incorporation of warfare into the social order, were analyzed and described according to the same terms and categories that were applied to the study of physical processes in the realm of nature. In these theories the penchant of men to fight was linked to the driving energy of *qi*, so fighting men were those who acted under the impulsion of *qi* and consequently threatened the social order. As *qi* in nature was equated with winds and harmonized through the artificial wind of music, so the *qi* of human violence was to be controlled through music in military training and on the field of battle. This music forged the individual soldiers into a collective body and imposed the will of the commander. Through the agency of the pitchpipes the manipulation of music also enabled the ruler to pattern military action on the cycles of cosmic *qi* and thereby bring human violence into accord with the principles of Heaven. Because the guidance of human *qi* was assimilated to the processes of nature, both the military commander and the ruler were described as replicas of, or "thirds to," Heaven and Earth who led their men like cosmic principles guiding the formation and motion of matter.

This natural philosophy of violence was elaborated by members of the intellectual elite of the Warring States period, and it reflected its origins in at least three ways: it was an abstracted depiction of the new order, a critique of the old nobility, and a rationalization of the social role of the elite.

First, as a depiction of the world of Warring States China, the natural philosophy of violence reflected the political history and institutional reforms of the period. The frequency and scale of warfare in these centuries certainly suggested some universal predisposition to violence. Moreover, as the institutions and values of the old warrior aristocracy were forgotten, accounts of their constant warfare, hunts, and vendettas would have appeared as evidence of an underlying barbarism from which civilization emerged.

A theory of universal violence also reflected the institutions of the new order. The social role of sanctioned violence had changed, as was discussed in Chapter Two, from serving as the exclusive privilege and defining trait of the elite to being a universal attribute of all members of society. The depiction of violence as universally inhering in all men was a projection into nature of the social facts of universal military service, sacrifice in every household, and the general obligations of vengeance and collective responsibility for punishments. Like the theoreticians of post-Napoleonic warfare, they discovered the "primordial violence" and "passions" of the common people underneath the social obligation of universal military service.[91]

Second, the new understanding of violence as "natural" formed part of the critique of the Zhou nobility and their idealization of the warrior. This rejection of martial heroism, which figured in legalist writings, the military treatises, and the myths of the Yellow Emperor, appeared in the natural philosophy of the period through the identification of bellicosity with the elemental stuff of matter and blind, unchecked energy. Violence, which had been the hallmark of the aristocracy, became an attribute of the formless, mindless, and inarticulate masses, the very stuff of brute nature, an elemental power that had to be checked, channeled, and guided in order to create the human world.

The natural philosophy of violence also provided a model by which the role of the new rulers derived from celestial principles. The purposeless dynamism of qi, moving but formless and incoherent, always requiring the imposition of some mind or "spirit," was the image of the peasant populace. In his discussion of stereotypes of the peasantry in imperial China, Frederic Wakeman noted that they were portrayed in two paradoxical images: the dull, diligent yeomen toiling productively to produce the wealth of the empire, and the savage, rebellious armies that swept across China in times of rebellion.[92] These two stereotypes were both embodied in the image of peasants as qi, the surging energy that generated all life but became destructive violence if not controlled and guided by educated minds. This twin aspect of the peasantry likewise appeared in the calendrical model of government, in which the farmers followed the cycle of qi that constituted the year, toiling to produce life in the spring and summer, killing in the fall and winter.

With the peasant soldiers cast in the guise of qi, the rulers assumed the role of configuring spirit or mind. They were those who labored with their minds, the bearers of order or pattern (*wen* 文), the drawers of lines and the makers of distinctions. Thus Xun Kuang insisted that the primary role of the ruler was to divide and to rank, and he also asserted that the fundamental role of ritual, the Confucian prototype of all proper action, was to divide.[93]

In the mythology of the sage-kings, which was the mythology of the territorial states and the subsequent empire, the world of man was created through a series of technological inventions and cultural innovations that separated man from the animals. Separation and division were the root of humanity, and it was the sages who created all distinctions. The sages, in turn, were the mythic prototypes of the territorial rulers. Thus the implicit claim of these tales was that rulers created and maintained humanity through their mastery of division and appropriate pattern, a pattern imposed from above on the brute masses. The natural philosophy of violence, likewise, created a model of the world in which the mind or spirit of the ruler created civilization through imposing order on the formless "stuff" and seething energy of the masses. The lords of humankind played the role of Heaven bringing orderly existence out of undifferentiated, primeval chaos, of Yu creating a demarcated, human world out of the rampant, watery obscurity of the flood, or of a greater father and mother who brought life to the people through the gift of division, hierarchy, and limit. Having banished violence to the realm of undifferentiated nature, they claimed authority through their bestowal of intelligible pattern on the brute masses.

Conclusion

The basic elements of the Warring States transition are clearly revealed in the shift from the aristocratic pattern of sanctioned violence in the Zhou city-states to the universal, authoritarian pattern that characterized the territorial states. In this conclusion I will review the major elements of the changes in the patterns of sanctioned violence, and then discuss what they reveal about the inner logic or coherence of the changes in the Warring States period.

Under the Zhou nobility the Chinese polity consisted of a cluster of city-states, in which each capital city was the political base of a lineage. These lineages were the basic units of the Chinese political order, and authority was distributed throughout the entire elite on the basis of the lineages' relative rankings and the place of the individual within his own line. The hallmark of authority was the actual performance of the "great services" of the state—sacrifice, warfare, and hunting—and members of the elite bound themselves together through the shared consumption of sacrificial meals and the swearing of blood oaths. Those in the elite were all warriors, so martial prowess and military glory were their central concerns and indeed the very definition of manhood. Because of the fundamental importance to the Zhou elite of glory won or honor defended in combat, they engaged in a continuous, internecine struggle for supremacy on the field of battle. With the sequential decline of the Zhou monarchs and the hegemons, the growing ambition of the sublineages, and the entrance of non-Zhou states onto the scene, these battles increased dramatically in scale and ferocity over the course of the Spring and Autumn period.

These constant wars were the primary spur to the ensemble of institutional reforms and new modes of linking men together that transformed the social and political order of China in the Warring States period. The destruction of defeated lineages steadily reduced the number of armed, political units in China, until agents of the ruling lines of the surviving states had secured an effective monopoly of armed force within their boundaries. Members of destroyed lines and ambitious men from the peasant or merchant populations provided a pool of "free-floating" talent from which competing lineages recruited supporters to

243

augment their power. These new supporters were totally dependent on their "host" lineages, and they were tied to the latter through blood oaths that formed the prototypes of the hierarchic, personal bonds between ruler and servant that underlay the emerging "bureaucratic" state. These bonds were equated with the ties of marriage in a new sexual imagery of political power which equated the power of a lord over his ministers with that of a husband over his wife. On the basis of these new ties political authority took on an absolute, authoritarian character quite different from the collegial, kinship-based rule of the Zhou nobility.

The emerging states extended their rule into the countryside through the steady expansion of the bases of recruitment for military service. In an interlinked series of reforms, various states allocated land to individual peasant households, or recognized land that peasants had already made their own, in exchange for taxes and military service. At the same time, in order to make up for the relatively small numbers of officials in the service of the states, households were grouped into units of five for purposes of military recruitment, mutual surveillance, and collective responsibility for crimes. These reforms culminated in the state of Qin, where the entire free, adult, male population was registered and ranked on the basis of military service, and the territory of the state divided up into fixed plots of land for purposes of allocation. The various philosophical schools of the period accepted the identity of the population with the army as a fact of life, an aim of policy, or an unspoken assumption. During the late Warring States period this identity of the army with the populace marked the high degree of the state's claims upon its subjects, who were subject to the discipline of military life and also obliged to risk their lives for their rulers. This creation of the state through military recruitment and the emphasis on total obedience in the military thought and training of the period increased further the authoritarian character of rule noted above. The high degree of devotion and obedience marked by the identification of the subject with the soldier had a lasting impact on the nature of the Chinese empire, even though universal military service vanished under the Han.

The other forms of sanctioned violence that had defined the Zhou elite also continued under the Warring States, and, like military service, they were gradually extended throughout the population. However, rather than marking authority, they were employed to define and substantiate the new forms of hierarchical human relationships that constituted the Warring States social and political order. Thus sacrifice was reinterpreted as a form of ritualized drama in which men learned obedience and devotion to their elders and superiors through acting out their social roles in the microcosm of the sacrificial rite. Vengeance became a debt of blood owed to one's immediate kin, thereby defining the limits of the households that were the basis of the new political order, and to one's political superiors, thereby defining the total devotion incumbent upon an official. The range of collective liability for punishments likewise defined the primary groupings that constituted the new order: the household, the neighborhood unit for military recruitment, and the ties of superior to subordinate amongst officials.

Hunting, which amongst the Zhou nobility had been a form of military exercise and a means of providing animals for sacrifice and elite consumption, became a fundamental element in the symbolism of cosmic imperium. The great parks, with their overwhelming variety of flora and fauna, demonstrated that the emperor's rule was universal and extended even to beasts and plants. The ritual hunts staged in these microcosms, and the associated combats in the animal pens, portrayed the "punishing potency" of the emperor and linked that potency to the forces of nature and the cycle of the seasons. Along with the cosmic kickball game and the rituals of military training, these hunts demonstrated the cosmic character of imperial rule through identifying state violence with the violence of nature.

Finally, these new patterns of violence played a major role as themes for reflection in the rationalization and justification of the new order. In the histories of the creation of humanity in high antiquity and in their accounts of the order of the physical universe, the Warring States elite meditated on the origins of violence and its role in the human world. In both these discourses they identified violence with prehuman chaos or bestiality, and then discovered in the achievements of the Yellow Emperor and in the role of Heaven prototypes for their own function in society as creators of pattern through the processes of separation and the making of distinctions. The actual performance of violence that had previously characterized the elite was now assigned to the common people, while authority lay in the appropriate division, manipulation, and intellectual guidance of the otherwise chaotic masses. Now identified with the creation of pattern and the direction of collective actions, authority became tied to textual mastery and mental skills.

In the Introduction I suggested that violence was used to mark authority, define fundamental groups, substantiate matters of highest significance, and reflect on the nature of human society and its relation to the natural world. Applied to the Warring States transition, the study of sanctioned violence has shown the following: 1) authority changed from a collegial, kin-based form marked by the performance of ritual violence to the absolute rule of a single, cosmically potent figure who bound all his officials to him as totally dependent servants; 2) the basic unit of political society changed from the city-based lineage to the territorial state which exercized authority over all the households and land within its boundaries; 3) the "matters of highest concern" substantiated through violence changed from the honor of the individual and lineage derived from the service of the ancestral spirits to the hierarchic bonds that linked men together and preserved order in society; 4) reflection on violence discovered natural and human worlds that avoided chaos only through the imposition of appropriate divisions by bearers, human or spirit, of cosmic principle, and it identified these bearers with the rulers of the state. The core of the Warring States transition was thus the development of the unqestioned supremacy of a single, cosmically potent autocrat who ruled as the image of Heaven on earth, and the reconstitution of the public order around this figure through new forms of interpersonal ties and the extension of military service to the entire population of the state. Patterned on this development, all of society was re-imagined in terms of the hierarchical ties of superior and subordinate, and the absolute character of authority was extended into the family in the role of the unchallenged *paterfamilias* and into the intellectual world in the total dominance of teacher over disciple.

This account of the Warring States transition in terms of changing modes of authority, units of social organization, and forms of interpersonal ties has several advantages over the models cited in the Introduction. First, there is no need to appeal to a purely hypothetical class of landlords, nor to assign primary explanatory power to phenomena, such as the rise of commerce and the role of merchants, which play a peripheral role in the historical records. Second, it provides coherent interlinkages for virtually all the major developments of the period as sketched in the Introduction. Even the major economic changes in the period, such as the rise of a land-owning peasantry and large-scale irrigation, were clearly related to the pressure to expand military service. Analyses which assume the priority of economic or demographic developments, in contrast, can only make sense of the political and social changes by appeals to the aforementioned landlord or merchant classes, or by simply treating all the changes as simultaneous but unrelated. Third, it locates the impetus for the transition directly in the socio-political order, cultural values, and patterns of behavior of the Spring and Autumn elite, revealing both the pressures for change and some of the reasons why change took the particular forms it did. Fourth, it highlights several crucial features of the transition that have been neglected in previous treatments. The shifting territorial range of state control, the pivotal role of military reforms in reconstituting the state through the service of the entire population, the dramatic rise in the power and status of the states' rulers, the new forms of personalist ties of total dependency that underlay the rise of the "bureaucratic" state, and the total re-imagining of the nature of authority have all scarcely been noted in earlier discussions of the period in the Western secondary literature.

Finally, it is an account of the Warring States transition which focuses attention on precisely those features in the development of the Chinese polity and society that characterized the imperial era as a whole. To the extent that the interest in the Warring States period lies its role as the formative era of the empire, it is important to find the origins and nature of those elements which remained significant throughout the history of imperial China. Given the tremendous changes that took place in later Chinese history, the fundamental threads of unity were the imperial mode of governance itself, the state based on extraction of taxes or services from the rural population, and the dominance of the authoritarian, patriarchal household at the local level. This study has made some contribution to understanding the emergence of these features and their interconnections.

While I would not deny the importance of the rise of commerce, the development of iron tools, the flourishing of handicrafts, and the increase in population, their connection to the total ensemble of changes is unclear, and no scholar has yet succeeded in giving a plausible account of their role as causative factors in the political, social, and intellectual changes that remain the primary focus of attention in the study of this period. Nor would I claim to have provided an "explanation" of the Warring States transition; changes of such scale and duration are not to be squeezed into the pages of a single book. What I hope to have accomplished is to have demonstrated the utility of systematic analyses of patterns of violence and at the same time to have focused attention on some of the underlying unities and internal coherence in the wide-ranging ensemble of changes that made the Warring States period a pivotal era in Chinese history.

Notes

Introduction

1. Max Weber, "Politics as a Vocation," in *From Max Weber: Essays in Sociology*, ed. H. H. Gerth and C. Wright Mills, paperback edition (New York: Oxford University Press, 1958), p. 78. A good collection of passages defining the state through its use of force appears in Hannah Arendt, "On Violence," in *Crises of the Republic* (New York: Harcourt Brace Jovanovich, 1972), pp. 107, 113–15, 134–38. Authors quoted include Bodin, Hobbes, Rousseau, Clausewitz, Marx, Engels, Sorel, Fanon, Mao, C. Wright Mills, and Bertrand de Jouvenel. On the manner in which even fundamentally opposed theories of the state agree on the definitive role of force, see also Gianfranco Poggi, *The Development of the Modern State: A Sociological Introduction* (Stanford: Stanford University, 1978), pp. 1–15. This emphasis on the monopoly of force reflects the historical fact that the modern nation-state was created by royal houses who were able to disarm their nobilities and become the sole armed power within their territories. See Bertrand de Jouvenel, *Du Pouvoir* (Paris: Librarie Hachette, 1972), pp. 21–43, 143–288. It has even more ancient roots in the classic Greek idea that heroism and warfare were the hallmark of elites, and the Christian tradition that denied moral value to the state and tended to regard it as, in Augustine's formulation, a larger robber band which, if it were just, could intimidate the weaker robbers through force of arms. See Eric Havelock, "War as a Way of Life in Classical Culture," in *Classical Values and the Modern World*, ed. Etienne Gareau (Ottawa: University of Ottawa, 1972), pp. 19–78; Alexander Passerin d'Entreves, *The Notion of the State: An Introduction to Political Theory* (Oxford: Clarendon Press, 1967), pp. 21–27; W. B. Gallie, *Philosophers of Peace and War* (Cambridge: Cambridge University, 1978), pp. 100–32.

2. For a judicious assessment of the relation of violence to other elements of state power, see Anthony Giddens, *The Nation-State and Violence* (Berkeley: University of California, 1985).

3. On the marking of degrees of kinship and the boundaries of inner and outer in "segmentary lineage systems" through the varying forms of permitted violence, see E. E. Evans-Pritchard, *The Nuer* (Oxford: Clarendon Press, 1940), pp. 150–72; M. Fortes and E. E. Evans-Pritchard, eds., *African Political Systems* (London: Oxford University, 1940), pp. 215–30, 278–79, 283, 291–93; John Middleton and David Tait, eds., *Tribes Without Rulers* (London: Rout-

249

ledge & Kegan Paul, 1958), pp. 19–22, 118, 207; Kathleen Gough, "Nuer Kinship: A Re-examination," in *The Translation of Culture*, ed. T. L. Beidelman (London: Tavistock, 1972), pp. 85–88, 98, 116.

4. Sigmund Freud, *Civilization and its Discontents*, trans. James Strachey (New York: W. W. Norton, 1961), pp. 59–62.

5. René Girard, *La violence et le sacré* (Paris: Grasset, 1972); *Des choses cachées depuis la fondation du monde* (Paris: Grasset, 1978); *Le bouc émissaire* (Paris: Grasset, 1982); *La route antique des hommes pervers* (Paris: Grasset, 1985). For criticisms see Paul Dumouchel, ed., *Violence et vérité* (Paris: Grasset, 1985); Michel Deguy and Jean-Pierre Dupuy, eds., *René Girard et le problème du mal* (Paris: Grasset, 1982); *Berkshire Review* 14 (1979); *Diacritics* 8 (March, 1978); Marcel Detienne, "Pratiques culinaires et esprit de sacrifice," in *La Cuisine du sacrifice en pays grec*, ed. Marcel Detienne and Jean-Pierre Vernant (Paris: Gallimard, 1979), pp. 25–35; Valerio Valeri, *Kingship and Sacrifice: Ritual and Society in Ancient Hawaii*, trans. Paula Wissing (Chicago: University of Chicago, 1985), pp. 67–70; Luc de Heusch, *Le sacrifice dans les religions africaines* (Paris: Gallimard, 1986), pp. 35–37.

6. *Sallustius: Concerning the Gods and the Universe,* trans. Arthur Darby Nock (Cambridge: Cambridge University, 1926), "Text and Translation," p. 29. On the role of sacrifices in the "substantiation" or "animation" of words and ceremonies, see Valeri, *Kingship and Sacrifice*, pp. 52–55, 313.

7. Elaine Scarry, *The Body in Pain: The Making and Unmaking of the World* (New York: Oxford University, 1985), ch. 2, esp. pp. 91–108, 115–17, 121, 127, 132–33. For an extended study of how wars begin and end through changes in perception, see Geoffrey Blainey, *The Causes of War* (New York: Free Press, 1973).

8. *Mengzi zhengyi*, annotated by Jiao Xun, in *Xinbian zhuzi jicheng*, vol. 1 (Taipei: Shijie, 1974), ch. 11, pp. 461–62.

9. Carl Schmitt, *The Concept of the Political*, trans. George Schwab (New Brunswick, New Jersey: Rutgers University, 1976).

10. The manner in which Greek myths defined social norms through meditation on the fundamental oppositions which defined civilization, and the relation of these myths to the tragic theater have been elaborated in the numerous works of Jean-Pierre Vernant, Marcel Detienne, Pierre Vidal-Naquet, and the scholars inspired by their results. For a brief sketch in English see Charles Segal, *Tragedy and Civilization: An Interpretation of Sophocles* (Cambridge, Ma.: Harvard University, 1981), chs. 1–3.

11. Richard Slotkin, *Redemption Through Violence: The Mythology of the American Frontier, 1600–1860* (Middletown, Connecticut: Wesleyan University, 1973); Richard Slotkin, *The Fatal Environment: The Myth of the Frontier in the Age of Industrialization, 1800–1890* (New York: Atheneum, 1985).

12. On the relation of Hobbes's social philosophy to his vision of nature, see T. A. Spragens, Jr., *The Politics of Motion: the World of Thomas Hobbes* (London: Croom Helm, 1973), esp. ch. 6; M. M. Goldsmith, *Hobbes's Science of Politics* (New York: Columbia University, 1966). On the relation of Newtonian science to the social philosophy of the latitudinarians, see Margaret C. Jacob, *The Newtonians and the English Revolution, 1689–1720* (Ithaca, New York: Cornell University, 1976).

13. Yang Kuan, *Zhanguo shi*, 2nd ed. rev. (Shanghai: Renmin, 1980).

14. Cho-yun Hsu, *Ancient China in Transition: An Analysis of Social Mobility, 722–222 B.C.* (Stanford: Stanford University, 1965), esp. pp. 1–2, 175–80.

Chapter One

1. Ronald Egan, "Narratives in *Tso Chuan*," *Harvard Journal of Asiatic Studies* 37.2 (1977), pp. 350–52.

2. *Chun qiu Zuo zhuan zhu*, annotated by Yang Bojun (Beijing: Zhonghua, 1981), Lord Cheng year 13, p. 861.

3. *Zuo zhuan zhu*, Lord Yin year 5, pp. 41–44. I have translated *wu* (物) when linked to "vessels" as "animals." See K. C. Chang, *Art, Myth, and Ritual: The Path to Political Authority in Ancient China* (Cambridge, Ma.: Harvard University, 1983), pp. 63–65; Wang Guowei, *Guantang jilin* (Taipei: Heluo, 1975), ch. 6, p. 13; Yang Shuda, *Jiweiju xiaoxue shulin* (Beijing: Kaogu Yanjiusuo, 1959), pp. 62–63. *Wu* in the sense of animal offerings and *qi* are linked as the emblems of sacrifice in the *Guo yu*, just as they are here. See *Guo yu*, annotated by Shanghai Shifan Daxue Guji Zhengli Xiaozu (Shanghai: Guji, 1978), ch. 18, pp. 559–60.
For a study of the interlinked roles of hunting, sacrifice, and warfare based on an analysis of this passage, see Yang Ximei, "Chun qiu Yin Gong she yu yu Tang shuo boyi," in *Wen shi* 26 (March, 1986), pp. 13–33.

4. Walter Burkert, *Homo Necans: The Anthropology of Ancient Greek Sacrificial Ritual and Myth*, trans. Peter Bing (Berkeley: University of California, 1983), p. 47. On the close ties of hunting and warfare in archaic Greece, see also Emily Vermeule, *Aspects of Death in Early Greek Art and Poetry* (Berkeley: University of California, 1979), pp. 84–94.

5. For theoretical descriptions of the hunt as a form of military ritual or training, see *Li ji jijie*, annotated by Sun Xidan (Shanghai: Shangwu, 1935), ch. 5, p. 39; ch. 12, pp. 99–100; *Zhou li zhengyi*, annotated by Sun Yirang (Shanghai: Zhonghua, 1934), ch. 55, pp. 10a–19b; ch. 34, pp. 7a–b; ch. 56, pp. 1a–17a; *Chun qiu Guliang zhuan zhushu*, annotated by Yang Shixun, in *Shisan jing zhushu*, vol. 7 (Taipei: Yiwen, 1976), Lord Zhao year 8, ch. 17, pp. 7a–b; *Guo yu*, ch. 6, p. 232; *Sima fa zhijie*, annotated by Liu Yin, in *Mingben wujing*

qi shu zhijie, vol. 1 (Taipei: Shi Di Jiaoyu, 1972), ch. 1, pp. 5b–6b; *Guanzi jiaozheng*, annotated by Dai Wang, in *Xinbian zhuzi jicheng*, vol. 5 (Taipei: Shijie, 1974), ch. 8, p. 123; *Wuzi zhijie*, annotated by Liu Yin, in *Mingben wujing qi shu*, vol. 1 (Taipei: Shi Di Jiaoyu, 1972), ch. 1, p. 1b. For historical examples of hunts as training or elements of campaigns, see *Zuo zhuan zhu*, Lord Huan year 4, p. 101; year 6, p. 114; Lord Xi year 27, pp. 445, 447; year 28, pp. 450, 472–73; year 31, p. 478; Lord Wen year 6, pp. 544–45; year 8, p. 568; year 10, p. 577; Lord Xuan year 12, pp. 735–36; Lord Xiang year 13, p. 999; Lord Zhao year 8, p. 1302; year 11, p. 1324; year 12, p. 1338; Lord Ding year 13, p. 1589; Lord Ai year 11, pp. 1658–59; year 14, p. 1682.

6. *Zuo zhuan zhu*, Lord Wen year 17, p. 626; Lord Xiang year 14, p. 1006.

7. On the linguistic equivalences see *Zuo zhuan zhu*, Lord Xiang year 4, pp. 936–39; Lord Xi year 22, p. 399; *Wuzi zhijie*, ch. 1, p. 18a; *Tai Gong liu tao zhijie*, annotated by Liu Yin, in *Mingben wujing qi shu zhijie*, vol. 2 (Taipei: Shi Di Jiaoyu, 1972), ch. 6, p. 64b; *Zuo zhuan zhu*, Lord Yin year 6, p. 49; Lord Xi year 33, pp. 498–500; Lord Zhao year 5, p. 1271; year 10, p. 1318; year 11, p. 1327; Lord Ai year 7, p. 1643; *Zhou li zhengyi*, ch. 8, pp. 14b–16a; *Li ji jijie*, ch. 3, p. 83; Gu Jiegang, "*Yi Zhou shu* 'Shi fu pian' jiaozhu xieding yu pinglun," in *Wen shi* 2 (April, 1963), pp. 14–17.

On the oaths see the passages from the *Zhou li zhengyi* cited in note 5 above. See also *Li ji jijie*, ch. 7, p. 38. On the use of military law during the hunt see *Zuo zhuan zhu*, Lord Wen year 10, pp. 1577–78; *Mao shi zhengyi*, annotated by Kong Yingda, in *Shisan jing zhushu*, vol. 2 (Taipei: Yiwen, 1976), ch. 3.1, p. 17b. The Song dynasty scholar Wang Yinlin (1223–1296 A.D.) first analyzed the evidence pertaining to law contained in this poem. See Wang Yinlin, *Kun xue ji wen* (Taipei: Zhonghua, 1966), vol. 2, ch. 3, p. 10a.

8. *Lun yu zhengyi*, annotated by Liu Baonan and Liu Gongmian, in *Xinbian zhuzi jicheng*, vol. 1 (Taipei: Shijie, 1974), ch. 16, p. 354. In the same text it is stated that the matters in which Confucius was most conscientious and careful were purification for sacrifice, warfare, and guarding against disease. See *Lun yu zhengyi*, ch. 8, p. 141.

In another passage Confucius criticized Lord Ling of Wei as unworthy. When he was asked why Lord Ling did not perish, Confucius replied that he had capable men to handle the reception of foreign emissaries, the service of the ancestral temple, and the army. This list reproduces the pairing of sacrifice and warfare, but it also adds the field of court ritual. See *Lun yu zhengyi*, ch. 17, p. 116.

9. *Li ji jijie*, ch. 7, p. 2.

10. *Mao shi zhengyi*, ch. 20.2, pp. 1a–16b. For the evidence that the taxes of the territorial states were derived from earlier levies used to provide offerings to the ancestors and men for military service, see Miyazaki Ichisada, "Kodai Chūgoku fusei seido," in *Ajia shi kenkyū*, vol. 1 (Kyoto: Dōshōsha, 1957), pp. 67–74.

11. *Li ji jijie*, ch. 2, p. 12. I have here translated the word *ku* (庫) as storehouses for chariots. For this definition see *Shuo wen jie zi zhu*, annotated Duan Yucai (Taipei: Yiwen, 1974), ch. 9b, p. 13b; Katō Jōken, *Kanji no kigen* (Tokyo: Kadokawa, 1972), p. 390. Although by Warring States times it had developed a broader meaning, it also retained the narrower, original sense of a storehouse for chariots and weapons. See *Li ji jijie*, ch. 10, p. 64; *Jing fa*, annotated by Mawangdui Han Mu Boshu Zhengli Xiaozu (Beijing: Wenwu, 1976), p. 78. The immediate linkage with stables in this context shows that here it is to be read in the narrow sense.

12. Chang, *Art, Myth, and Ritual*, p. 108.

13. Yang, *Zhanguo shi*, p. 70.

14. Chang, *Art, Myth, and Ritual*, pp. 95–100.

15. *Guo yu*, ch. 1, pp. 18–20; *Zuo zhuan zhu*, Lord Huan year 14, p. 140; Lord Zhao year 4, pp. 1248–49.

16. Ikeda Suetoshi, *Chūgoku kodai shūkyō shi kenkyū* (Tokyo: Tōkai Daigaku, 1983), pp. 411–18; Guo Moruo, *Jiagu wenzi yanjiu* (Shanghai: Dadong, 1931), vol. 2, "Shi shi," pp. 2–3; Guo Moruo, *Buci tongzuan* (Tokyo: Bunkyodo, 1933), p. 87; Tang Lan, *Guwenzixue daolun*, 2nd ed. enlarged (Ji'nan: Qilu, 1981), p. 169; Tang Lan, *Yinxu wenzi ji* (n.p., n.d. [1974?]), pp. 30–32. The reconstructed pronunciation of *ji* is *tsad, that of *sha* is *sad.

17. *Shang shu zhengyi*, annotated by Kong Yingda, in *Shisan jing zhushu*, vol. 1 (Taipei: Yiwen, 1976), ch. 15, p. 27b; *Zhou li zhengyi*, ch. 33, p. 9b.

18. *Zuo zhuan zhu*, Lord Xi year 29, p. 477; Lord Zhao year 22, p. 1434.

19. *Mengzi zhengyi*, ch. 1, pp. 47–48.

20. *Zhuangzi jijie*, annotated by Wang Xianqian, in *Xinbian zhuzi jicheng*, vol. 4 (Taipei: Shijie, 1974), ch. 4, pp. 81–82; ch. 19, p. 285; ch. 17, pp. 266–67; ch. 32, p. 460. This text's recurring equation of serving a king with being the victim of a sacrifice is also suggestive of the identification of political authority with bloodletting. This same equation appears in *Shizi* (Zhejiang Shuju, Huhailou edition, 1877), ch. 2, pp. 29a–30b.

21. *Mao shi zhengyi*, ch. 9.3, pp. 9a–11b; ch. 20.2, pp. 5b–6b; *Shang shu zhengyi*, ch. 15, pp. 17a–b, 21a–22a, 25a–26a; *Li ji jijie*, ch. 2, p. 45; ch. 3, pp. 83–84; ch. 7, pp. 42–44; ch. 9, pp. 25, 28–29; *Bohutong de lun*, compiled by Ban Gu et al., in *Han Wei congshu*, vol. 1 (Taipei: Xinxing, 1977), appendix, pp. 1a–3b.

22. *Mao shi zhengyi*, ch. 13.3, pp. 4b–16b, esp. pp. 7b, 12a, 14a, pp. 20a–21b; *Li ji jijie*, ch. 9, pp. 23, 26, 28–29; ch. 12, p. 47; *Zuo zhuan zhu*, Lord Xi year 10, p. 334; year 31, p. 487; *Lun yu zhengyi*, ch. 3, p. 41; Sanaka Sō, *Sengoku Sōsho kan shinkō to gijutsu no kankei* (Kyoto: Kogakukan Daigaku, 1977), pp. 6–17.

23. For evidence from oracle bones, see Luo Zhenyu, *Zengding Yinxu shuqi kaoshi*, in *Luo Xuetang Xiansheng quanji sanbian*, vol. 2 (Taipei: Wenhua, 1968), ch. 3, pp. 58a–b; Shang Chengzuo, *Yinqi yicun* (Nanjing: Jinling Daxue, 1933), figure 656; Dong Zuobin et al., *Xiaotun dierben: Yinxu wenzi: yibian*, part 2 (Nanjing: Academia Sinica, 1949), figure 6751. For bronze inscriptions, see Luo Zhenyu, *Sandai ji jinwen cun*, in *Luo Xuetang Xiansheng quanji qibian*, vols. 17–18 (Taipei: Wenhua, 1968), ch. 4, p. 13b, figure 1; ch. 8, p. 52b; Chen Mengjia, "Xi Zhou tongqi duan dai," *Kaogu xuebao* (1956) 3: 120–21, figure 69. For poetry see *Mao shi zhengyi*, ch. 9.4, pp. 7b–10b; ch. 10.1, pp. 1a–3a; ch. 10.3, pp. 1a–10a; ch. 15.1, pp. 1a–2a; ch. 16.2, p. 22b; ch. 19.3, pp. 7b–8b; Akatsuka Kiyoshi, "A New Study of the *Shih-ku Wen*: the Ancient Letters Carved in Ten Drum-Type Stones," *Acta Asiatica* 4 (1963): 80–96; Gilbert Mattos, "The Stone Drums of Ch'in" (Ph.D. diss., University of Washington, 1973). For the ritual texts see *Li ji jijie*, ch. 4, p. 87; ch. 7, p. 38; *Zhou li zhengyi*, ch. 7, pp. 14b, 16a; ch. 8, pp. 1b, 4a, 5b, 7a, 14b, 16a, 17b, 19a, 20a, 21a; ch. 55, p. 15b; ch. 56, pp. 3b, 15a.

24. *Zuo zhuan zhu*, Lord Ding year 9, p. 1572. The chapter of the *Yi Zhou shu* analyzed by Gu Jiegang in the article cited in note 7 also lists examples of animals taken in the hunt as objects of sacrifice.

25. Yi Xuezhong, "Jinning Shizhaishan shier hao mu zhu bei qi shang renwu diaoxiang kaoshi," *Kaogu xuebao* 1987 (4): 426–27.

26. *Zuo zhuan zhu*, Lord Zhao year 18, pp. 1398–99.

27. *Zuo zhuan zhu*, Lord Zhuang year 23, pp. 225–26; Lord Xiang year 24, p. 1090; Akatsuka, "A New Study of the *Shih-ku Wen*," pp. 83–85, 90–91. On the links of the *she* altar to warfare and punishments, see Utsugi Akira, "'Sha ni korosu' ni tsuite—*Shū ri* no sha no seido ni kansuru ichi kōsatsu," in *Chūgoku kodai shi kenkyū* (Tokyo: Yoshikawa Kōbun, 1962), pp. 161–88.

28. *Zuo zhuan zhu*, Lord Xiang year 18, p. 1041.

29. *Zuo zhuan zhu*, Lord Cheng year 16, p. 882; Lord Zhao year 3, p. 1236.

30. *Li ji jijie*, ch. 3, p. 83; ch. 5, pp. 78–79; *Zhou li zhengyi*, ch. 36, pp. 13b–15a; *Zuo zhuan zhu*, Lord Cheng year 16, p. 884.

31. *Zhou li zhengyi*, ch. 45, p. 11a; *Tai Gong liu tao zhijie*, ch. 1, pp. 63b–67a.

32. *Zuo zhuan zhu*, Lord Yin year 11, pp. 72–73; Lord Zhuang year 4, p. 163; Lord Min year 2, p. 265; Lord Xiang year 10, pp. 979–80.

33. This ritual is prescribed for use in the regular hunts in the ritual texts cited in note 5. For performances before battle see *Zuo zhuan zhu*, Lord Zhuang year 8, p. 173; Lord Xi year 23, p. 409; year 27, p. 444 (2); Lord Xuan year 15, p. 763; Lord Xiang year 13, p. 999; year 19, p. 1041; Lord Zhao year 5, p. 1271; year 13, pp. 1353, 1356; *Guliang zhuan zhushu*, Lord Zhuang year 8,

ch. 5, pp. 11a–b. There are also two references to the ceremony under the name *zhi rong* (治戎). See *Zuo zhuan zhu*, Lord Cheng year 3, p. 813; year 16, p. 889. Chu called the ceremony *jing shi* (井師). See *Zuo zhuan zhu*, Lord Zhuang year 4, p. 163; Lord Xuan year 12, p. 722. On setting out from the altar see *Mao shi zhengyi*, ch. 16.2, p. 20a.

34. Lester Bilsky, *The State Religion of Ancient China* (Taipei: The Chinese Association for Folklore, 1976), p. 177.

35. *Zuo zhuan zhu*, Lord Wen year 7, p. 560; Lord Cheng year 16, p. 889; Lord Xiang year 26, p. 1121.

36. *Zuo zhuan zhu*, Lord Cheng year 2, p. 791. The term *ru shi* also appears as the name of a special pre-battle meal in the *Hou Han shu*. The commentator, writing in the seventh century A.D., glosses *ru* (蓐) as *ru* (褥) "bedding," and he says that it meant a meal eaten by the army amidst their bedding before dawn. See Fan Ye, *Hou Han shu* (Beijing: Zhonghua, 1965), ch. 31, p. 1103.

37. *Zuo zhuan zhu*, Lord Cheng year 16, p. 884.

38. *Zuo zhuan zhu*, Lord Xi year 15, pp. 363–65; Lord Xuan year 13, pp. 726–28; Lord Ai year 2, p. 1613; year 9, pp. 1652–54. In Lord Huan year 11, p. 131 a general rejects a proposal to divine, but this shows that the practice was common. On the battle prayer see *Zuo zhuan zhu*, Lord Cheng year 16, p. 889. For a discussion see Frank A. Kierman, Jr., "Phases and Modes of Combat in Early China," in *Chinese Ways in Warfare*, ed. Frank A. Kierman, Jr. (Cambridge, Ma.: Harvard University, 1974), pp. 32–34.

39. On the destruction of the camp see *Zuo zhuan zhu*, Lord Cheng year 16, p. 883; Lord Xiang year 14, p. 1009; year 26, pp. 1121, 1122. On the resolution on death or "integrity to the death" as the hallmark of the warrior, see *Zuo zhuan zhu*, Lord Cheng year 2, p. 791; Lord Xiang year 3, p. 929; Lord Ding year 4, p. 1544; year 14, p. 1595; Lord Ai year 16, p. 1700; *Shi ji*, ch. 70, p. 2289; *Tai Gong liu tao zhijie*, ch. 3, p. 65b; *Jing fa*, p. 12; *Guanzi jiaozheng*, ch. 3, p. 40; *Wuzi zhijie*, ch. 2, p. 20a; *Wei Liaozi zhijie*, annotated by Liu Yin, in *Mingben wujing qi shu zhijie*, vol. 2 (Taipei: Shi Di Jiaoyu, 1972), ch. 2, p. 40b; ch. 5, pp. 14a, 17a; *Lü Shi chun qiu jishi*, annotated by Chen Qiyou (Shanghai: Xuelin, 1984), ch. 8, p. 441; ch. 15, p. 917; *Zhanguo ce*, compiled by Liu Xiang (Shanghai: Guji, 1978), ch. 3, p. 81. In his commentary on a passage in the *Sima fa*, Liu Yin (1302–1355 A.D.) refers to the practice of destroying the camp and explains that it demonstrated the army's resolve on death. See *Sima fa zhijie*, ch. 5, p. 56a. At one point in his campaigns against Liu Bang, Xiang Yu (232–202 B.C.) also sank his boats, destroyed his utensils, and burned his camp "in order to demonstrate that the soldiers must die and should have no thought of returning." See *Shi ji*, ch. 7, p. 307. This idea was also written into the Qin law code. If a man died in battle any ranks and honors he had earned were given to his descendants, but if he returned alive from a defeat he would be punished. See *Shuihudi Qin mu zhujian* (Beijing: Wenwu, 1978), p. 146.

40. *Zuo zhuan zhu*, Lord Ai year 2, pp. 1613–15. Other references to the use of these "oaths" in the army appear in *Sima fa zhijie*, ch. 2, pp. 19b–20a; ch. 4, p. 51a.

41. *Zuo zhuan zhu*, Lord Xi year 33, p. 499; Lord Xuan year 14, p. 752; Lord Cheng year 3, pp. 813–14; *Wei Liaozi zhijie*, ch. 3, p. 62b; ch. 5, pp. 11a–12a.

42. *Zuo zhuan zhu*, Lord Cheng year 2, p. 804; year 3, p. 813.

43. *Zuo zhuan zhu*, Lord Xuan year 12, p. 744.

44. *Lü Shih chun qiu jishi*, ch. 7, p. 402; ch. 15, pp. 917–918. Although the practice apparently died out in imperial China, it continued among various peoples at the borders of China. Thus the barbarian ruler Helianpopo (381–425 A.D.) built a *jing guan* from the skulls of the tens of thousands he had slain and called it the "Skull Tower." See *Taiping yulan*, compiled by Li Fang et al. (Taipei: Shangwu, 1935), ch. 335, p. 8a. The bodies of the soldiers of the Chinese army that unsuccessfully invaded Korea during the Sui dynasty were also gathered into a great collective tomb. See Liu Xu et al., *Jiu Tang shu* (Beijing: Zhonghua, 1975), ch. 3, p. 41; ch. 149a, p. 5321.

45. *Zuo zhuan zhu*, Lord Yin year 5, p. 42; Lord Huan year 2, p. 91; year 16, p. 145; Lord Xi year 28, p. 471; Lord Cheng year 7, p. 832—here the phrase "not call the army to order" indicates that they were beaten; Lord Xiang year 3, p. 925; *Gongyang zhuan zhushu*, annotated by Xu Yan, in *Shisan jing zhushu*, vol. 7 (Taipei: Yiwen, 1976), Lord Zhuang year 8, ch. 7, p. 1b; *Guliang zhuan zhushu*, Lord Zhuang year 8, ch. 5, p. 11a.

46. *Zuo zhuan zhu*, Lord Xi year 19, p. 381; year 28, pp. 471–72; year 33, p. 503; Lord Cheng year 2, p. 794—here some prisoners were "presented" to be killed, but apparently not at the ancestral temple; Lord Xiang year 8, p. 958; year 10, pp. 977–78—in this passage the commentator quotes several Zhou bronzes that mention the presentation of prisoners; Lord Zhao year 10, p. 1318; year 17, p. 1390; Lord Ai year 7, p. 1643; *Mao shi zhengyi*, ch. 16.4, p. 15a. The presentation of prisoners is also depicted on a bronze cowrie shell container cover from Shizhaishan. See Yi Xuezhong, "Qi shang renwu diaoshang kaoshi," pp. 433–34.

47. *Zuo zhuan zhu*, Lord Zhuang year 31, p. 249—this passage asserts that presentations of the spoils were to go only to the Zhou king and only if they were taken in battle with non-Chinese, but this rule was regularly violated; Lord Xi year 21, p. 389; year 28, pp. 463, 471; Lord Xuan year 15, p. 765; year 16, p. 768; Lord Cheng year 2, pp. 809–10; year 3, p. 813; year 9, p. 844; year 16, p. 894; Lord Xiang year 25, p. 1104; Lord Zhao year 10, p. 1318—in this case the prisoners presented were sacrificed; year 17, p. 1390; Lord Ding year 6, p. 1557; Lord Ai year 7, p. 1643.

48. *Zuo zhuan zhu*, Lord Xiang year 10, p. 979; Lord Ai year 14, p. 1682.

49. *Yi Zhou shu*, annotated by Kong Chao, in *Han Wei congshu*, vol. 1 (Taipei: Xinxing, 1977), ch. 4, pp. 2a–3a, 9a–11b; *Di wang shiji*, quoted in *Taiping yulan*, ch. 84, pp. 8a–b; *Tian wen shuzheng*, annotated by Wen Yiduo (Beijing: Sanlian, 1980), pp. 94, 109—for the argument that this second passage pertains to the "sacrifice" of King Zhou by King Wu, see Jiang Liangfu, *Qu Yuan fu jiaozhu* (Beijing: Renmin Wenxue, 1957) pp. 360–61; Guo Moruo, *Qu Yuan fu jin yi* (Beijing: Renmin Wenxue, 1981), p. 104; *Xunzi jijie*, annotated by Wang Xianqian, in *Xinbian zhuzi jicheng*, vol. 2 (Taipei: Shijie, 1974), ch. 12, p. 219; ch. 15, p. 260; *Mozi jiangu*, annotated by Sun Yirang, in *Xinbian zhuzi jicheng*, vol. 6 (Taipei: Shijie, 1974), ch. 8, p. 153; *Shi ji*, ch. 3, p. 108; ch. 4, p. 124; ch. 32, p. 1480; ch. 128, p. 3234; *Shizi*, ch. 2, p. 13a.

50. *Zuo zhuan zhu*, Lord Xi year 19, pp. 380, 381–82; Lord Cheng year 2, pp. 801–02; Lord Zhao year 10, p. 1318; year 11, p. 1327; *Mozi jiangu*, ch. 6, p. 107.

51. For a statistical analysis of the distribution of human sacrifice in archeological sites, see Huang Zhanyue, "Wo guo de gudai renxun he rensheng," *Kaogu* 1974 (3): 153–63. Various examples are discussed in Cheng Tek'un, *Archeology in China*, vol. 3, *Chou China* (Cambridge: W. Heffer & Sons, 1963), pp. 46–47, 58–59, 72–73, 77, 79, 132; K. C. Chang, *The Archeology of Ancient China*, 3rd ed. rev. (New Haven, Yale University, 1977), pp. 299–300; Li Xueqin, *Eastern Zhou and Qin Civilizations*, trans. K. C. Chang (New Haven: Yale University, 1985), pp. 475–76; Yang, *Zhanguo shi*, pp. 168–69; Gu Derong, "Zhongguo gudai de renxun renshengzhe de shenfen tanxi," *Zhongguo shi yanjiu* 1982 (2): 112–23; Shanxisheng Wenwu Gongzuo Weiyuanhui, "Houma Zhanguo nuli xunzang mu de fajue," *Wenwu* 1972 (1): 63–67.

52. Yi, "Qi shang renwu diaoxiang," pp. 413–37; Yi Xuezhong, "Jinning Shizhaishan shier hao mu zhu bei qi shang renwu diaoxiang kaoshi," *Kaogu Xuebao* 1988 (1): 37–49.

53. The character *huo*, which meant "beings captured for sacrifice" and was applied to prisoners, was also homophonous with the word that referred to the heads or ears of slain enemies presented in the temples (*huo* 馘), and the two words were used as mutual glosses by commentators. See Gu Jiegang, "*Yi Zhou shu* 'Shi fu pian,'" p. 6, note 3.

54. *Zuo zhuan zhu*, Lord Xi year 33, pp. 499–500; Lord Cheng year 3, p. 813; Lord Zhao year 5, p. 1271; Lord Ding year 4, p. 1535.

55. *Zuo zhuan zhu*, Lord Zhuang year 12, p. 192; Lord Xiang year 15, p. 1023; year 19, p. 1051; *Li ji jijie*, ch. 9, p. 3; *Tian wen shuzheng*, pp. 101–02, 107; *Di wang shiji*, quoted in *Taiping yulan*, ch. 381, p. 3b; *Beitang shu chao*, compiled by Yu Shinan, (Taipei: Xinxing, 1971), ch. 41, pp. 5b–6a; *Jing fa*, p. 61; *Shi ji*, ch. 83, p. 2463.

56. For a Warring States passage that identifies sacrifice with capital punishment, see *Shizi*, ch. 1, p. 21b. On the manner in which certain forms

of capital punishment can take on the form of a religious sacrifice, see Louis Gernet, "Some Connections between Punishment and Religion in Ancient Greece," and "Capital Punishment," in *The Anthropology of Ancient Greece*, trans. John Hamilton, S.J. and Blaise Nagy (Baltimore: Johns Hopkins University, 1981), pp. 240–76.

57. *Lun yu zhengyi*, ch. 19, pp. 354–56. On this passage as the organizing principle of the *Chun qiu*, see Gu Donggao, *Chun qiu da shi biao*, "Du *Chun qiu* ou bi," in *Huang Qing jingjie xubian*, ed. Wang Xianqian (Nanqing Shuyuan, 1888), *ce* 67, p. 4; Shu Shicheng, "Kongzi 'Chun qiu,'" in *Zhongguo shixue shi lunwen ji*, vol. 1, ed. Wu Ze (Shanghai: Renmin, 1980), p. 39.

58. The model of the "segmented state" derives from Aidan Southall's classic study of the Alur society in East Central Africa. These states are characterized by: 1) territorial sovereignty which is limited and relative, forming a series of zones in which authority is greatest near the center and recedes towards the periphery, 2) a central government with numerous peripheral foci of authority over which the center exercises limited control, 3) an administrative staff at the center which is repeated on a reduced scale at the peripheral foci, 4) a central authority which "monopolizes" force only in its own vicinity, while the peripheral foci also wield legitimate force on a reduced scale, 5) peripheral foci arranged into a multi-level hierarchy in which intermediate authorities stand in the same relation to lower ones as the central state does to the intermediate, so that structures and powers are repeated at each level in a reduced form. See Aidan Southall, *Alur Society* (Cambridge: W. Heffer & Sons, 1956), pp. 248–49.

59. *Zuo zhuan zhu*, Lord Zhao year 16, pp. 1378–79. On the ritual exchange of meat from sacrifices at the various temples and its relation to combat, see Yu Yueh, *Chaxiangshi jing shuo*, in *Biji sibian*, vols. 4–5 (Taipei: Guangwen, 1971), ch. 15, pp. 16a–17a.

60. *Zuo zhuan zhu*, Lord Zhuang year 10, p. 182; Lord Zhao year 4, p. 1249; Lord Ai year 13, p. 1677.

61. *Zhou li zhengyi*, ch. 34, pp. 10a–11a; *Zuo zhuan zhu*, Lord Xi year 24, p. 427; Lord Ding year 14, p. 1593.

62. *Zuo zhuan zhu*, Lord Xi year 9, p. 326; Lord Cheng year 13, p. 860; *Shi ji*, ch. 4, p. 160; ch. 5, pp. 203–04; ch. 68, p. 2232; ch. 69, p. 2250; *Guanzi jiaozheng*, ch. 8, p. 126. On the institution of the hegemony see Sidney Rosen, "Changing Conceptions of the Hegemon in Pre-Ch'in China," in *Ancient China: Studies in Early Civilization*, ed. David Roy and Tsuen-hsuin Tsien (Hong Kong: Chinese University, 1978), pp. 99–114; Lü Simian, *Xian Qin shi* (Shanghai: Kaiming, 1941), pp. 165–83.

63. *Zuo zhuan zhu*, Lord Min year 2, p. 271.

64. *Mengzi zhengyi*, ch. 12, p. 492.

65. *Zuo zhuan zhu*, Lord Cheng year 13, p. 861.

66. Tong Shuye, *Chun qiu Zuo zhuan yanjiu* (Shanghai: Renmin, 1980), pp. 310–12, 345–46.

67. *Zuo zhuan zhu*, Lord Yin year 5, p. 46; Lord Huan year 2, p. 94; Lord Xiang year 14, p. 1016; *Zhou li zhengyi*, ch. 44, p. 14b; *Gongyang zhuan zhushu*, Lord Yin year 3, ch. 3, p. 7b; *Xunzi jijie*, ch. 13, pp. 233, 239–40, 249; *Zhuangzi jishi*, annotated by Guo Qingfan (Taipei: Shijie, 1974), ch. 33, p. 465; *Guo yu*, ch. 18, pp. 564–65, 567; *Shizi*, ch. 2, p. 31b. The *Guo yu*, unlike all the other texts, grants commoners the right to sacrifice to their ancestors and thus to participate in the lowest level of ritual. The "Qu li" chapter of the *Li ji* contains many additional examples of such lists. Moreover, the *Zuo zhuan* describes a hierarchy of the permissable length of city walls based on the level of the lord of the town, but it is unlikely that the *shi* had towns of their own. See *Zuo zhuan zhu*, Lord Yin year 1, p. 11. Finally, the same book also distinguishes nobles from commoners by the type of armor they are allowed to wear, but it gives no gradations within the nobility. See *Zuo zhuan zhu*, Lord Xiang year 3, p. 925.

68. Yu Weichao and Gao Ming, "Zhoudai yong ding zhidu yanjiu," *Beijing Daxue xuebao, zhexue shehui kexue ban* 1978 (1): 84–98; 1978 (2): 84–97; [Zou Heng], *Shang Zhou kaogu* (Beijing: Wenwu, 1979), pp. 203–13, 262–69; Chen Gongrou, "Shisang li, Jixi li zhong suo jizai de sangzang zhidu," *Kaogu xuebao* 1956 (4): 67–84; Shen Wenzhuo, "Dui 'Shisang li, Jixi li zhong suo jizai de sangzang zhidu' jidian yanjiu," *Kaogu xuebao* 1958 (2): 29–38; Guo Baojun, *Shanbiaozhen yu Liulige* (Beijing: Kexue, 1959), pt. 1, sec. 2; Du Naisong, "Cong lieding zhidu kan ke ji fu li de fandong xing," *Kaogu* 1976 (1): 17–21; Li Xueqin, *Eastern Zhou and Qin Civilizations*, pp. 460–64.

69. *Zuo zhuan zhu*, Lord Huan year 2, p. 94; Lord Min year 2, p. 273; Lord Xuan year 12, p. 722; Lord Xiang year 9, p. 966; year 14, p. 1016; Lord Ding year 8, p. 1567; Lord Ai year 2, p. 1614; *Zhou li zhengyi*, ch. 2, p. 11a; ch. 25, pp. 1a–2b. One passage in the *Zuo zhuan* explicitly identifies the "petty people" as those who labor at agriculture to support their superiors. See *Zuo zhuan zhu*, Lord Xiang year 13, p. 1000.

70. *Li ji jijie*, ch. 2, p. 131.

71. *Yi li zhengyi*, annotated by Hu Peihui (Shanghai: Zhonghua, 1934), ch. 1, pp. 18–19; *Li ji jijie*, ch. 7, pp. 55–56.

72. *Kongzi jia yu*, annotated by Wang Su, in *Xinbian zhuzi jicheng*, vol. 2 (Taipei: Shijie, 1974), ch. 8, pp. 78–79; Ban Gu, *Han shu* (Beijing: Zhonghua, 1962), ch. 30, p. 1710.

73. *Mao shi zhengyi*, ch. 12.2, pp. 6a–b; ch. 20.4, p. 8b; *Shang shu zhengyi*, ch. 12, p. 17a—in this passage the "minister-nobles" are explicitly contrasted with the "common people"; ch. 18, p. 25b; *Zuo zhuan zhu*, Lord Yin year 3, p.

26; year 8, p. 58; Lord Xi year 5, p. 308; Lord Xiang year 25, p. 1106; Lord Ding year 1, p. 1526; year 4, p. 1540; Lord Ai year 16, p. 1701.

74. Li Xiaoding, ed., *Jiagu wenzi jishi* (Nanyang: Zhongyang Yanjiuyuan Lishi Yuyan Yanjiusuo, 1965), vol. 1, pp. 159–61; Kang Yin, *Wenzi yuanliu qianshuo* (Beijing: Rongbaozhai, 1979), pp. 412–14; Tōdō Akiyasu, *Kanji gogen jiten* (Tokyo: Gakutōsha, 1967), pp. 105–06; Katō, *Kanji no kigen*, pp. 451–52. Alternative explanations appear in Zhou Fagao et al., eds., *Jinwen gulin* (Hong Kong: Chinese University, 1974), vol. 1, pp. 300–10.

75. See the works cited in the preceding note for examples. Also *Lü Shi chun qiu jishi*, ch. 21, p. 1462; *Shi ji*, ch. 30, p. 1442; *Mengzi zhengyi*, ch. 6, p. 256; *Xunzi jijie*, ch. 3, p. 48.

76. On the tension in ancient China between affiliation based on cult and that based on biological descent, see Marcel Granet, *The Religion of the Chinese People*, trans. Maurice Freedman (New York: Harper & Row, 1975), pp. 80–90.

77. *Shang shu zhengyi*, ch. 11, pp. 12a–b; *Xunzi jijie*, ch. 15, p. 259; *Shi ji*, ch. 3, pp. 105, 107–08; ch. 4, pp. 121, 122.

78. *Zuo zhuan zhu*, Lord Xi year 33, p. 499; Lord Huan year 2, p. 128; *Gongyang zhuan zhushu*, Lord Zhuang year 12, ch. 7, pp. 13b–14a; *Zuo zhuan zhu*, Lord Zhuang years 11–12, pp. 189–91; Lord Xuan year 4, pp. 677–78; Lord Xiang year 14, pp. 1010–11.

79. Itō Michiharu, *Chūgoku kodai ōchō no keisei* (Tokyo: Sōbunsha, 1975), pp. 172–246; Zhao Guangxian, *Zhou dai shehui bianxi* (Beijing: Renmin, 1980), pp. 99–122; Sun Yao, *Chun qiu shidai zhi shizu*, 2nd ed. (Shanghai: Zhonghua, 1936), pp. 1–45.

80. *Zuo zhuan zhu*, Lord Xiang year 11, p. 986.

81. *Zuo zhuan zhu*, Lord Xuan years 17–18, pp. 771–77.

82. *Zuo zhuan zhu*, Lord Wen year 6, pp. 544–45, 552–53.

83. In 594 B.C. the chief minister of Jin executed the ruler's elder sister, and the ruler sought to lead an attack against him, but the rest of the court refused to participate—*Zuo zhuan zhu*, Lord Xuan year 15, pp. 762–65. In 563 B.C. Zi Si, the chief minister of Zheng, controlled the issuing of weapons at the ancestral temple, and he personally stripped a warrior of the prisoners he had won in battle for violations of ritual—Lord Xiang year 10, pp. 980–81. In 555 B.C. the king of Chu sought to launch an expedition, but the chief minister overruled him—Lord Xiang year 18, p. 1041. In 554 B.C. Zi Kang, the chief minister of Zheng, controlled the court and commanded the army—Lord Xiang year 18, p. 1050. In 546 B.C. Ning Jia, the chief minister of Wei, controlled all the affairs of government until assassinated by the titular ruler—Lord Xiang year 27, p. 1127. In 545 B.C. all the business of the court of Qi was conducted at

the residence of the chief minister Qing Feng—Lord Xiang year 28, p. 1145. In 506 B.C. the ruler of Wei ordered the official in charge of the state altars to lead an armed expedition intended to seal a covenant, but the official refused because he held his office as a hereditary trust and could not leave the capital—Lord Ding year 4, p. 1535.

84. On records in bronzes of nobles leading their own detachments in the royal Zhou army, see Shanxisheng Wenwu Guanli Weiyuanhui, *Qingtong qi tushi* (Beijing: Wenwu, 1960), p. 24 and plate #78. On the *fu* as an allotment of troops from the lineage to the state and other references to "private armies" of the nobility, see *Zuo zhuan zhu*, Lord Yin year 4, p. 36; Lord Xi year 28, p. 457; Lord Wen year 2, p. 521; year 12, p. 591; Lord Cheng year 2, p. 789; year 7, p. 834; year 16, p. 885; Lord Xiang year 4, p. 935; year 22, p. 1065; year 25, pp. 1104, 1106–07; year 27, p. 1137; year 28, p. 1148; year 30, pp. 1175, 1176; Lord Zhao year 5, pp. 1261, 1269—this passage refers to the size of the *fu* of a lineage to show its power; year 12, p. 1340; year 16, pp. 1375–79; year 24, p. 1451; year 26, p. 1475; Lord Ding year 4, p. 1544; Lord Ai year 6, p. 1634; year 7, p. 1644 (2); year 13, p. 1676.

85. *Zuo zhuan zhu*, Lord Xi year 28, pp. 456–59; Lord Wen year 2, p. 521; year 12, pp. 589–91; Lord Xuan year 12, pp. 722–37; Lord Cheng year 16, pp. 882–84; Lord Xiang year 3, p. 929; year 10, p. 982; year 14, p. 1009.

86. *Zuo zhuan zhu*, Lord Ding year 4, p. 1542 states, "From the accession of King Zhao [of Chu in 515 B.C.] the army of Wu invaded every year." But the text contains no mention of any invasion by Wu in the years 514, 513, or 509 B.C. As for the frequency of campaigns, the states of Zheng, Chu, Jin, Qi, Lu, and Song each figure in more than one hundred campaigns, while the powerful but more distant Qin, Wu, and Yue appear relatively infrequently. This clearly reflects not the actual number of campaigns but the limits of knowledge or interest on the part of the compilers.

87. *Zuo zhuan zhu*, Lord Xi year 7, p. 445.

88. *Zuo zhuan zhu*, Lord Xuan year 12, p. 726.

89. *Zuo zhuan zhu*, Lord Cheng year 16, p. 882.

90. *Zuo zhuan zhu*, Lord Xiang year 3, p. 929. At two later points in the text men of Jin justify raising armies by the need to maintain their exalted position among the states. See Lord Zhao year 13, pp. 1353, 1356.

91. Rebecca Zerby Byrne, "Harmony and Violence in Classical China: A Study of the Battles in the 'Tso-chuan'" (Ph.D. dissertation, University of Chicago, 1974), pp. 216–22. This study regrettably covers only the period up to 606 B.C., but my own examination of the subsequent text suggests that her conclusions are valid for the work as a whole.

92. Marcel Granet, *Chinese Civilization*, trans. K. E. Innes and M. R. Brailsford (London: Routledge & Kegan Paul, 1930), pp. 263–70.

93. *Zuo zhuan zhu*, Lord Zhao year 5, p. 1267.

94. *Zuo zhuan zhu*, Lord Zhao year 22, p. 1433; Lord Huan year 11, p. 131—in this passage a commander refused to wait for reinforcements before attacking because it would be dishonorable; Lord Xi year 33, p. 504; Lord Wen year 12, p. 591; Lord Cheng year 2, pp. 786–87; year 16, p. 882; Lord Xiang year 10, p. 982; year 23, p. 1084—this passage concerns two men who went out on their own to issue a challenge, encountered the entire enemy army, but decided that honor impelled them to fight.

95. *Zuo zhuan zhu*, Lord Xi year 8, p. 322; year 22, p. 398.

96. See notes 88 and 94. For the execution see *Zuo zhuan zhu*, Lord Xi year 33, p. 504.

97. *Zuo zhuan zhu*, Lord Huan year 8, p. 122. See also *Mao shi zhengyi*, ch. 16.4, p. 11a. The commentary quotes a fragment of the *Di wang shiji* saying: "Tai Gong said, 'I have heard that the former kings attacked those who rebelled, not those who obeyed; they attacked the difficult and not the easy.'"

98. *Zuo zhuan zhu*, Lord Xi year 26, p. 439; year 33, p. 495; Lord Wen year 10, p. 577; Lord Xuan year 12, pp. 735, 736; Lord Zhao year 5, p. 1271.

99. *Zuo zhuan zhu*, Lord Zhuang year 11, pp. 186–87; Lord Xi year 15, p. 356; year 28, pp. 459–60; year 33, p. 504; Lord Wen year 12, p. 592; Lord Cheng year 2, pp. 790–91; Lord Xiang year 23, p. 1084; year 28, p. 1149—this last occurs in a civil war; *Gongyang zhuan zhushu*, Lord Xuan year 12, ch. 16, p. 8b.

100. *Zuo zhuan zhu*, Lord Xi year 26, p. 439; Lord Wen year 7, p. 560; Lord Xuan year 12, p. 718—here faked mourning persuaded an invading army to withdraw; Lord Xiang year 4, p. 932; year 19, p. 1049; *Sima fa zhijie*, ch. 1, p. 5a. It is significant that just as mourning and warfare were mutually exclusive, so were mourning and sacrifice. See *Li ji jijie*, ch. 1, p. 68; ch. 2, p. 10; ch. 7, pp. 41–42; *Zhou li zhengyi*, ch. 70, pp. 6a–7b.

101. *Zuo zhuan zhu*, Lord Zhuang year 28, pp. 241–42; Lord Xi year 26, p. 439; Lord Wen year 14, p. 604; Lord Ai year 7, p. 1643. The last example is a case in which this stricture was ignored over strenuous objections.

102. *Zuo zhuan zhu*, Lord Xi year 22, pp. 397–98; Lord Cheng year 12, p. 592; Lord Ding year 4, p. 1547. In these last two cases men explicitly argue that to attack an enemy in straits is cowardly. On the principle of not beginning until both sides have given a signal, see *Zuo zhuan zhu*, Lord Zhuang year 10, p. 183.

103. *Zuo zhuan zhu*, Lord Xi year 33, p. 499; Lord Xuan year 14, p. 752; Lord Cheng year 3, pp. 813–14; *Wei Liaozi zhijie*, ch. 2, p. 27a.

104. For a sampling of these wars in English see Henri Maspero, *China in*

Antiquity, trans. Frank A. Kierman, Jr. (n.p.: University of Massachusetts, 1978), pp. 190–91, 203–08, 212–17, 225–36, 243–46.

105. On vengeance in ritualist theory and imperial law, see Michael Dalby, "Revenge and Law in Traditional China," *The American Journal of Legal History* 25 (1981): 267–307; Makino Tatsumi, *Chūgoku kazoku kenkyū*, in *Makino Tatsumi chosaku zenshū*, vol. 2 (Tokyo: Ochanomizu, 1980), pp. 3–59; Nishida Taiichirō, "Fukushū to keibatsu," in *Chūgoku keihō shi kenkyū* (Tokyo: Iwanami, 1974), pp. 95–120.

106. *Mozi jiangu*, ch. 12, p. 265. On the translation of this passage see A. C. Graham, "The Background of the Mencian Theory of Human Nature," in *Studies in Chinese Philosophy and Philosophical Literature* (Singapore: Institute of East Asian Philosophies, 1986), p. 36. On the origins of the Confucian stress on ritual out of fear of vengeance or feuds, see note 93.

107. *Gongyang zhuan zhushu*, Lord Zhuang year 12, ch. 7, pp. 13b–14b; *Zuo zhuan zhu*, Lord Zhuang years 11–12, pp. 189–92. I have followed the more detailed and colorful account from the *Gongyang*.

108. *Zuo zhuan zhu*, Lord Xuan year 4, pp. 677–78; Lord Xiang year 12, pp. 1010–12. For another case of a ruler murdered for a perceived insult, see Lord Xuan year 10, pp. 707–08.

109. *Zuo zhuan zhu*, Lord Xiang years 7–8, pp. 953–55.

110. *Zuo zhuan zhu*, Lord Wen year 1, pp. 513–15; Lord Xiang year 26, p. 1111.

111. *Zuo zhuan zhu*, Lord Wen year 2, pp. 519–21.

112. *Zuo zhuan zhu*, Lord Xiang year 27, p. 1127.

113. *Zuo zhuan zhu*, Lord Ding year 13, pp. 1589–90.

114. *Zuo zhuan zhu*, Lord Xiang year 28, pp. 1145–49. This story is particularly interesting in that it depicts the chief minister's lineage surrounding their temple with armed troops while holding a sacrifice even before they knew of the imminent civil war. This suggests that in this society the noble lineages lived constantly surrounded by their armed bands, like the warring families of a late medieval Italian city-state. For further evidence of this see *Zuo zhuan zhu*, Lord Zhao year 17, pp. 1389–90.

115. *Zuo zhuan zhu*, Lord Wen year 6, pp. 552–53; Lord Zhao year 26, p. 1472.

116. *Zuo zhuan zhu*, Lord Yin year 11, pp. 72–73; Lord Xuan year 2, p. 652; Lord Xiang year 26, p. 1115; Lord Wen year 2, pp. 519–21.

117. *Zuo zhuan zhu*, Lord Wen year 18, pp. 629–30.

118. *Zuo zhuan zhu*, Lord Wen year 6, pp. 544–45, 552–53. For another

example of disdaining to exact revenge upon the descendants of an enemy, see *Zuo zhuan zhu*, Lord Ding year 4, pp. 1546–47; Lord Zhao year 4, p. 1366.

119. *Zuo zhuan zhu*, Lord Zhao year 1, pp. 1211–12. Leaping on and off a chariot in full armor was a considerable feat and formed a major element in the training of warriors. See Lan Yongwei, *Chun qiu shiqi de bubing* (Beijing: Zhonghua, 1979), p. 219.

120. *Mao shi zhengyi*, ch. 5.2, pp. 7b–8b; pp. 13a–16b; ch. 5.3, pp. 9b–11b; ch. 6.3, pp. 6a–14b; ch. 9.3, pp. 14a–15a; ch. 10.2; ch. 10.3; ch. 16.2, pp. 1a–10a; ch. 18.3, pp. 1a–10b; ch. 18.5, pp. 1a–6b; Akatsuka, "A New Study of the *Shih-ku Wen*," pp. 85–87.

121. Takeuchi Teruo, "A Study of the Meaning of *Jen* Advocated by Confucius," *Acta Asiatica* 9 (1965): 57–77.

122. William Hung et al., eds., *Harvard-Yenching Institute Sinological Index Series Supplement #11: Combined Concordances to Ch'un-Ch'iu, Kung-yang, Ku-liang, and Tso-chuan* (Taipei: Chengwen, 1966 reprint), pp. 1545–53.

123. *Lü Shih chun qiu jishi*, ch. 12, pp. 633–34.

124. *Huainanzi*, compiled under the auspices of Liu An, in *Xinbian zhuzi jicheng*, vol. 7 (Taipei: Shijie, 1974), ch. 13, p. 215.

125. Huan Tan, *Xin lun*, quoted in *Shi ji*, ch. 5, p. 204.

126. *Xunzi jijie*, ch. 19, pp. 333, 340; *Gongyang zhuan zhushu*, Lord Huan year 3, ch. 4, p. 9b; *Guliang zhuan zhushu*, Lord Yin year 8, ch. 2, pp. 9a–b. The Qing scholar Jiang Yong (1681–1762 A.D.) argued that the institution of blood covenants began with Chi You, the mythic creator of weapons and warfare. This will be discussed in Chapter Five.

127. For evidence of related practices during the Shang dynasty, see Lin Yun, "Jiaguwen zhong de Shangdai fangguo lianmeng," in *Guwenzi yanjiu*, no. 6 (Beijing: Zhonghua, 1981), pp. 67–92. On their use in the Western Zhou, see *Mao shi zhengyi*, ch. 12.3, p. 11b; *Zuo zhuan zhu*, Lord Xi year 5, p. 308; year 9, p. 327; year 26, p. 440.

128. *Guliang zhuan zhushu*, Lord Zhuang year 29, ch. 6, p. 1a. One passage in the *Zuo zhuan* describes the covenants as one of the "great services" of the state. See Lord Ai year 13, p. 1677. The Han Confucian Dong Zhongshu (179–104 B.C.) argued, "It is better to have no covenants than to have a covenant, but there are covenants which can be called good. It is better to have no wars than to have a war, but there are wars which can be called righteous." This passage linked covenants to wars, expressed disapproval of both, but acknowledged they could play a positive social role. *Chun qiu fan lu yizheng*, annotated by Su Yu (Taipei: Heluo, 1975), ch. 2, p. 4a.

129. *Zuo zhuan zhu*, Lord Xiang year 9, pp. 968–69, 971; *Li ji jijie*, ch. 2, p. 33—"When they bind trust it is called an 'oath,' and in the presence of a

sacrifice it is called a 'covenant.'" *Zhou li zhengyi*, ch. 69, p. 1a; *Shuo wen jie zi zhu*, ch. 7a, p. 27a; *Zuo zhuan zhu*, Lord Xi year 25, p. 435; Lord Xiang year 26, p. 1118. On simple oaths, see *Zuo zhuan zhu*, Lord Yin year 1, p. 14; Lord Xuan year 17, p. 772; Lord Cheng year 11, p. 853; Lord Zhao year 6, p. 1279. On the gods as enforcers of covenants, see *Zuo zhuan zhu*, Lord Cheng year 9, p. 843; Lord Ai year 12, p. 1671.

130. For the argument that blood covenants began only after Lord Huan, see *Gongyang zhuan zhushu*, Lord Huan year 3, ch. 4, p. 9b; *Guliang zhuan zhushu*, Lord Yin year 8, ch. 2, pp. 9a–b; *Mengzi zhengyi*, ch. 12, p. 497. For references to covenants under the Western Zhou and Lord Huan see note 127.

131. *Zuo zhuan zhu*, Lord Zhao year 1, p. 1202.

132. *Zuo zhuan zhu*, Lord Zhao year 6, pp. 1278–79; Lord Xiang year 26, p. 1118.

133. On the evidence from Houma, see Shanxisheng Wenwu Gongzuodui Weiyuanhui, eds., *Houma mengshu* (Shanghai: Wenwu, 1976); Shanxisheng Wenwu Gongzuodui Weiyuanhui, "'Houma mengshu' de faxian, fajue yu zhengli qingkuang," *Wenwu* 1975 (5): 7–11; Shanxisheng Wenwu Gongzuodui Weiyuanhui, "'Houma mengshu' zhushi si zhong," *Wenwu* 1975 (5): 20–26; Zhang Han, "Houma Dongzhou yizhi faxian Jinguo zhu shu wenzi," *Wenwu* 1966 (2): 1–3; Zhang Han, "Houma mengshu congkao," *Wenwu* 1975 (5): 12–19; Zhang Han, "Houma mengshu congkao xu," in *Guwenzi yanjiu*, no. 1 (Beijing: Zhonghua, 1979), pp. 78–102; Guo Moruo, "Houma mengshu shitan," *Wenwu* 1966 (2): 4–6; Guo Moruo, "Chutu wenwu er san shi 'Xin chu Houma mengshu shiwen,'" *Wenwu* 1972 (3): 4–7; Guo Moruo, "Taodu, Nuwa, Jialing," *Wenwu* 1973 (1): 5–6; Chen Mengjia, "Dongzhou mengshi yu chutu zaishu," *Kaogu* 1966 (5): 271–79; Tao Zhenggang and Wang Kelin, "Houma Dongzhou mengshi yizhi," *Wenwu* 1972 (3): 27–37, 71; Tang Lan, "Houma chutu Jinguo Zhao Jia zhi meng zaishu xin shi," *Wenwu* 1972 (8): 31–35, 58; Zhu Dexi and Qiu Xigui, "Guanyu Houma mengshu de jidian bushi," *Wenwu* 1972 (8): 36–38, 48; Li Yumin, "Wo dui Houma mengshu de kanfa," *Kaogu* 1973 (3): 185–91; Gao Ming, "Houma zaimeng zhu kao," in *Guwenzi yanjiu*, no. 1 (Beijing: Zhonghua, 1979), pp. 103–15; Huang Shengzhang, "Guanyu Houma mengshu de zhuyao wenti," *Zhongyuan wenwu* 1981 (2): 27–33; Wei Jin and Jin Wen, "'Houma mengshu' he Chun qiu houqi Jinguo de jieji douzheng," *Wenwu* 1975 (5): 1–6, 94; Takahashi Yasuichirō, "Chūgoku kodai no seibun to meibun," *Kōnan kokubun* 19 (1982): 169–82.

134. *Zuo zhuan zhu*, Lord Cheng year 11, p. 854; Lord Zhao year 1, p. 1204; *Zhou li zhengyi*, ch. 11, pp. 7a–9a; ch. 72, p. 8b; *Houma mengshu*, pp. 13–21.

135. The digging of the pit and its use, as well as the smearing of the blood, are described in the cases cited previously, and the layout of the pits has been reconstructed at Houma. Additional references to the smearing of blood are *Zuo zhuan zhu*, Lord Xiang year 9, p. 971; Lord Zhuang year 32, p. 253;

Lord Ding year 4, p. 1547—these last two used human blood; *Guanzi jiaozheng*, ch. 8, p. 126. On the cursing of violators, see *Zuo zhuan zhu*, Lord Xiang year 11, p. 990. On the left ear of the animal, see *Zuo zhuan zhu*, Lord Ding year 27, p. 1566; Lord Ai year 17, p. 1711.

136. *Zuo zhuan zhu*, Lord Xi year 5, p. 308; year 26, p. 440; Lord Xiang year 11, p. 993. *Zuo zhuan zhu*, Lord Xiang year 10, p. 984 and *Zhou li zhengyi*, ch. 51, pp. 11a–b indicate that lineages as well as states had some form of archives for preserving the texts of old covenants.

137. See the passages cited in note 135.

138. *Zuo zhuan zhu*, Lord Yin year 11, p. 76; Lord Xuan year 2, p. 663; Lord Xiang year 11, p. 990; Lord Ding year 6, p. 1559. The malediction is also mentioned in the *Shi jing*. See *Mao shi zhengyi*, ch. 12.3, pp. 17a–18b.

139. For an interesting presentation of the social uses of the covenant, see W. A. C. H. Dobson, "Some Legal Instruments of Ancient China: *Ming* and *Meng*," in *Wen-lin: Studies in the Chinese Humanities*, ed. Chow Tse-tsung (Madison, Wis.: University of Wisconsin, 1968), pp. 269–82. Professor Dobson's theory that the covenant originated among the common people, however, is completely unsubstantiated.

140. For secondary works on the role of covenants in international relations, see the various titles listed in the editor's note on Dobson, "Legal Instruments," p. 270. See also Liu Baiji, *Chun qiu huimeng zhengzhi* (Taipei: Zhonghua Congshu, 1963).

141. *Zuo zhuan zhu*, Lord Wen year 6, p. 547; Lord Cheng year 2, p. 798; year 3, p. 815; year 8, p. 837; Lord Xiang year 9, p. 969; year 23, p. 1077 (2); year 26, pp. 1117, 1125; year 27, pp. 1129, 1133; year 31, pp. 1186, 1187; Lord Zhao year 1, pp. 1201, 1207; year 2, p. 1231; year 4, p. 1247; year 5, p. 1270; year 7, p. 1290; year 11, p. 1325; year 13, p. 1362; year 23, p. 1442 (2); year 24, p. 1450; year 25, p. 1459; year 29, p. 1504; year 32, p. 1517; Lord Ai year 1, p. 1607; *Shi ji*, ch. 14, p. 509.

142. *Zuo zhuan zhu*, Lord Yin year 8, p. 59; Lord Xi year 28, p. 452; Lord Zhao year 1, pp. 1206–07.

143. *Zuo zhuan zhu*, Lord Xiang year 11, pp. 989–90.

144. *Zuo zhuan zhu*, Lord Huan year 11, p. 132; Lord Xiang year 13, p. 1012; year 19, p. 1048; year 24, p. 1084; year 26, p. 1118; year 27, p. 1128; year 28, p. 1146; year 29, p. 1168; year 30, pp. 1173, 1176, 1177; Lord Zhao year 1, p. 1215; year 4, pp. 1253, 1257–58; year 20, p. 1412; year 26, p. 1475; Lord Ding year 5, p. 1553; year 6, p. 1559; year 14, p. 1595; Lord Ai year 2, p. 1610; year 26, pp. 1730–31.

145. *Zhou li zhengyi*, ch. 51, pp. 2a–b; ch. 69, pp. 1a–3b; *Mozi jiangu*, ch. 8, pp. 144–45.

146. These city-states are not to be confused with the Greek *poleis*. The term refers simply to the geographic range of the political unit and does not imply democratic or popular rule. On the character of the Eastern Zhou states, see Tong Shuye, *Chun qiu shi* (Shanghai: Kaiming, 1946), pp. 82–84; Tong Shuye, *Chun qiu Zuo zhuan yanjiu*, pp. 177–84, 366–68; Du Zhengsheng, *Zhou dai chengbang* (Taipei: Lianjing, 1979); Miyazaki Ichisada, "Chūgoku jōdai wa hōkensei ka toshi kokka ka," in *Ajia shi kenkyū*, vol. 3 (Kyoto: Dōshōsha, 1957), pp. 63–86; Miyazaki Ichisada, "Chūgoku ni okeru shuraku keitai no hensen ni tsuite," in *Ajia shi ronkō*, vol. 2 (Tokyo: Asahi Shinbun, 1978), pp. 3–30; Miyazaki Ichisada, "Chūgoku jōdai no toshi kokka to sono bōchi," in *Ajia shi ronkō*, vol. 2, pp. 31–55; Kaizuka Shigeki, *Chūgoku no kodai kokka*, in *Kaizuka Shigeki chosaku shū*, vol. 1 (Tokyo: Chūō Kōron, 1978), pp. 255–382; Kaizuka Shigeki, "Chūgoku kodai toshi kokka no seikaku," in *Kaizuka Shigeki chosaku shū*, vol. 2, pp. 119–32; Kimura Masao, *Chūgoku kodai teikoku no keisai— toku ni sono seiritsu no kiso jōken* (Tokyo: Fumeitō, 1967), pp. 60–81; Nemoto Makoto, *Chūgoku dentō shakai to sono hō shisō* (Tokyo: Tōkyō Tetsugaku Kenkyūsho, 1980), pp. 117–72; Masubuchi Tatsuo, *Chūgoku kodai no shakai to kokka* (Tokyo: Kōbundō, 1962), pp. 421–35; Itō Michiharu, *Chūgoku kodai ōchō no keisei*, pp. 172–224.

Mainland Chinese scholars have also examined the question of city-states in ancient China, but they have been too obsessed with the Greek model to come to terms with the Chinese case. See Lin Zhichun, "Kong Meng shu zhong fanying de gudai Zhongguo chengshi guojia zhidu," *Lishi yanjiu* 1980 (3): 123–32; Ri Zhi, "Cong *Chun qiu* cheng ren zhi li zailun Yazhou gudai minzhu zhengzhi," *Lishi yanjiu* 1981 (1): 3–17; Lü Shaowang, "Zhongguo gudai bu cunzai chengbang zhidu," *Zhonguo shi yanjiu* 1983 (4): 91–105.

On the nature and status of the inhabitants of the capital, see Tong Shuye, *Chun qiu Zuo zhuan yanjiu*, pp. 36–38, 132–46, 371–72; Kaizuka Shigeki, "Chūgoku kodai toshi ni okeru minkai no seido," in *Kaizuka Shigeki chosaku shū*, vol. 2, pp. 95–118; Masubuchi Tatsuo, "Shunjū Sengoku jidai no shakai to kokka," in *Iwanami kōza sekai rekishi*, vol. 4 (Tokyo: Iwanami, 1970), pp. 139–79.

147. On the role of the capital's inhabitants in the army, see, for example, *Zuo zhuan zhu*, Lord Min year 2, p. 265; Lord Xiang year 30, p. 1176; Lord Ding year 12, p. 1587. On the expulsion or murder of princes or unpopular ministers, see Lord Xi year 28, p. 452; Lord Wen year 7, p. 558; year 16, p. 622; year 18, p. 633; Lord Xiang year 19, p. 1050; year 31, p. 1189; Lord Zhao year 23, p. 1444; Lord Ai year 11, p. 1661; year 16, p. 1704; year 26, p. 1731. On the rulers' fear of the wrath of the people, see Lord Xiang year 10, p. 981; Lord Zhao year 13, p. 1347; year 26, p. 1472; Lord Ai year 25, p. 1726. On actions performed to quiet the populace, see Lord Wen year 18, p. 643; Lord Cheng year 15, p. 876; Lord Xiang year 15, p. 1022; Lord Zhao year 13, p. 1348; year 22, p. 1434.

148. On the urban populace in civil wars, see the citations in the preceding note and Lord Zhuang year 20, p. 220; Lord Cheng year 13, pp. 866–67;

year 15, p. 875; Lord Xiang year 10, pp. 979–81; year 17, p. 1032; year 26, p. 1113; Lord Zhao year 5, p. 1262; year 10, pp. 1316–17; Lord Ding year 12, pp. 1586–87; year 13, pp. 1590–91; Lord Ai year 6, p. 1634. On playing a role in deciding the succession to the throne, see Lord Wen year 18, p. 633; Lord Xiang year 31, p. 1189; Lord Zhao year 14, p. 1365. On trying to win the support of the capital populace through displays of generosity, see Lord Wen year 16, p. 620; Lord Xiang year 29, p. 1157; Lord Zhao year 3, p. 1235; year 25, p. 1463.

149. *Zuo zhuan zhu*, Lord Xi year 15, pp. 359–61; Lord Ding year 8, p. 1567; Lord Ai year 6, p. 1607. Because they could be assembled at court the urban populace was also called the "court populace." See Lord Xi year 19, p. 378.

150. For example, *Zuo zhuan zhu*, Lord Xi year 28, pp. 469–70; Lord Cheng year 13, p. 866; Lord Xiang year 25, p. 1099; year 30, p. 1176; Lord Zhao year 20, p. 1412; Lord Ding year 6, p. 1559; Lord Ai year 6, p. 1637. On the basis of several passages in the *Zhou li* and the texts cited in the preceding notes, Kaizuka Shigeki argued that the city-states of ancient China had a "popular assembly" reminiscent of the one in democratic Athens. This assembly, known as the "outer court," was gathered when the state faced a crisis, when a new ruler was installed, or when the ruler desired to move the capital. See Kaizuka, "Chūgoku kodai toshi ni okeru minkai no seido," pp. 98–110. There is no evidence for such an assembly as a regular practice in any reliable early text, and it is likely that the authors of the *Zhou li* had mistaken an ad hoc, emergency procedure for a normative institution. Nevertheless, this mistake reflects the historical fact that the capital's populace played an important and sometimes decisive role in pre-imperial China's political order, and their support was regularly sought by anyone who wished to rule.

151. *Zuo zhuan zhu*, Lord Xuan year 4, pp. 679–82, 684; year 13, p. 752; Lord Cheng year 7, pp. 833–34; Lord Zhao year 28, pp. 1491–93. On the use of the term *mie zu* in the *Zuo zhuan*, see Ogura Yoshihiko, *Chūgoku kodai seiji shisō kenkyū* (Tokyo: Aoki, 1970), pp. 189–94. See also *Houma mengshu*, pp. 73–74.

Chapter Two

1. The term "warring state" was applied in pre-imperial texts to each of the seven great, territorial states that had divided the Chinese world between them by the late fifth century B.C. The use of the term "Warring States" to describe the period was coined in the Han. See Yang, *Zhanguo shi*, pp. 1–4.

2. Professor Robin Yates has done considerable work on this topic and will be discussing it in some detail in a major monograph.

3. On the changing relation of chariots and infantry in the Spring and Autumn armies, see Lan, *Chun qiu shiqi de bubing*.

4. The Qing dynasty commentator Jiang Yong (1681–1762 A.D.) collected passages from the *Zuo zhuan* and other texts to demonstrate that in the early Eastern Zhou farmers outside the capital did not give military service. See *Qun jing bu yi* (Shuyetang edition, 1792), ch. 2, pp. 7a–9b. For modern studies of the separation of the capital and its hinterland, and the exclusion of the latter from military service, see Yang Kuan, *Gu shi xin tan* (Beijing: Zhonghua, 1965), pp. 135–65; He Ziquan, "Zhou dai tudi zhidu he ta de yanbian," *Lishi yanjiu* 1964 (3): 156–59; Kaizuka, *Chūgoku no kodai kokka*, pp. 162–253; Du, *Zhou dai chengbang*, pp. 21–122; Li Ling, "Zhongguo gudai jumin zuzhi de liang da leixing ji qi bu tong laiyuan—Chun qiu Zhanguo shiqi Qiguo jumin zuzhi shitan," *Wen shi* 28 (March, 1987), pp. 59–75; Ying Yongchen, "Lun Chun qiu shidai Luguo he Jinguo de shehui tedian jian ji rujia he fajia chansheng de lishi beijing," *Lishi yanjiu* 1964 (1): 156–62.

One passage in the *Zuo zhuan* refers to an army that built dwellings and planted crops in order to maintain a protracted siege, which suggests that the army included some peasants and artisans who probably served as porters and laborers. The fact that the seasonal hunts were timed to avoid interfering with the agricultural season also suggests that farmers participated in these as well. See *Zuo zhuan zhu*, Lord Xuan year 15, p. 761; Lord Yin year 5, pp. 42–43. However, since an army could safely remain in the field over a growing season, the percentage of peasants accompanying the army could not have been great, and it is likely that most of them were *guo ren* or *shi* who worked fields in the vicinity of the capital. The solemn declaration cited in Chapter One also included farmers, artisans, merchants, and even slaves in the army, but this speech is attributed to 493 B.C. and hence postdates the reforms that extended service to new elements of the population.

5. Jiang, *Qun jing bu yi*, ch. 2, p. 7b; Okazaki Fumio, "'San goku go hi' no sei ni tsuite," in *Haneda Hakushi shōju kinen tōyōshi ronsō* (Kyoto: Tōyōshi Kenkyūkai, 1950), pp. 211–23.

6. *Guanzi jiaozheng*, ch. 8, pp. 123–24. A similar but less detailed account of Guan Zhong's reforms appears in *Guo yu*, ch. 6, pp. 224–32. This passage also stipulates that the units of five families which formed the military squads of five men should sacrifice and mourn their dead together. Less systematic discussions of the identification of civil government and military organization in the *Guanzi* appear in ch. 1, p. 10; ch. 2, p. 28; ch. 3, p. 39; ch. 8, p. 125; ch. 9, p. 143.

7. Du Zhengsheng, "Zhou dai fengjian jieti hou de junzheng xin zhixu: bianhu qimin de yanjiu zhi er," *Zhongyang Yanjiuyuan Yuyan Lishi Yanjiusuo jikan* 55:1 (1984): 78–79.

8. *Zuo zhuan zhu*, Lord Xi year 15, pp. 360–63. A virtually identical account appears in *Guo yu*, ch. 9, p. 330.

9. For the relevant characters and the passage from the *Zhou li*, see *Shuo wen jie zi zhu*, ch. 2a, pp. 37a–b.

10. Yu, *Chaxiangshi jing shuo*, ch. 14, pp. 16b–17a.

11. See, for example, Yang Kuan, *Shang Yang bianfa* (Shanghai: Renmin, 1955), pp. 38, 42–43; Zhu Shaohou, "'Ming tian' qianlun," in *Zhongguo gudai shi luncong*, no. 1 (Fujian: Renmin, 1981), p. 158; Wu Hui, "Shi lun Chun qiu shiqi de shehui xingzhi wenti," in *Zhongguo shehui jingji shi luncong*, no. 1 (Shanxi: Renmin, 1981), pp. 116–19; Han Lianqi, "Chun qiu Zhanguo shidai tudi suoyouzhi de yanhua he nongcun gongshe de jieti," in *Lishi luncong*, no. 2 (Ji'nan: Qilu, 1981), pp. 150–52; Xiong Tieji and Wang Ruiming, "Qin dai de fengjian tudi suoyouzhi," in *Yunmeng Qin jian yanjiu* (Beijing: Zhonghua, 1981), pp. 76–77; Zhang Jinguang, "Shi lun Qin zi Shang Yang bianfa hou de tudi zhidu," *Zhongguo shi yanjiu* 1983 (2): 30, 40.

12. *Shuo wen jie zi zhu*, ch. 4b, pp. 5b–6a.

13. *Mengzi zhengyi*, ch. 7, pp. 306–07.

14. On the application of the term "*shou* field" to the well-field system, see *Han shu*, ch. 24a, pp. 1119–20. On its use in the Qin code, see *Shuihudi Qin mu zhujian* (Beijing: Wenwu, 1978), pp. 27–28. For a discussion of "*shou* fields" under the Qin, see Zhang Jinguang, "Shi lun Qin zi Shang Yang bianfa hou de tudi zhidu," pp. 28–31. See also Wang Yuquan, "Yuantian jie," *Lishi yanjiu* 1957 (4): 79–87.

15. *Han shu*, ch. 28b, p. 1641.

16. For a detailed discussion of the links of Shang Yang's reforms to the old Jin institutions as modified in the state of Wei by Li Ke, see Koga Noboru, *Kan Chōanjō to senpaku kenkyōteiri seido* (Tokyo: Yūsankaku, 1980), pp. 411–35. On the "*yuan* fields" in Qin, see Kusuyama Shūsaku, "Shō Yō no enten ni tsuite," *Tōhōgaku* 46 (1973): 70–87.

One of the previously unknown chapters of the *Sunzi* military treatise discovered at Linyi states that Zhao, another successor state of Jin, had replaced the one-hundred-pace acre with one of 240 paces. This was one of the reforms carried out in Qin by Shang Yang, which strengthens the ties between the *yuan* fields of Jin state and the land system of Qin. See *Shiyi jia zhu Sunzi* (Shanghai: Guji, 1978), p. 495.

17. *Guanzi jiaozheng*, ch. 18, p. 303; *Li ji jijie*, ch. 4, p. 74; ch. 10, p. 2; Gu Yanwu (1613–1682 A.D.), *Yuanchaoben ri zhi lu* (Taipei: Pingping, 1975), ch. 8, p. 178.

18. *Zuo zhuan zhu*, Lord Ai year 17, p. 1710. See also *Lü Shi chun qiu jishi*, ch. 25, p. 1681.

19. *Zuo zhuan zhu*, Lord Xuan year 11, pp. 714–15.

20. *Zuo zhuan zhu*, Lord Xuan year 15, p. 766; Lord Cheng year 1, p. 783. On these reforms, see Satō Taketoshi, "Shunjū jidai Rokoku no fusei sei kaikaku ni kansuru ichi kōsatsu," in *Chūgoku kodai no shakai to bunka* (Tokyo: Tōkyō Daigaku, 1957), pp. 1–24.

21. On *qiu* as a unit of population, see *Sima fa*, quoted in *Mao shi zheng-yi*, ch. 13.2, p. 8a; *Zhou li zhengyi*, ch. 20, p. 8a; *Sunzi zhijie*, annotated by Liu Yin, in *Mingben wujing qi shu zhijie*, vol. 1 (Taipei: Shi Di Jiaoyu, 1972), ch. 1, p. 17a; *Mengzi zhengyi*, ch. 14, p. 573; *Zhuangzi jijie*, ch. 7, pp. 173–74. On its use in place names, see Du, *Zhou dai chengbang*, p. 141.

22. *Zuo zhuan zhu*, Lord Xiang year 30, pp. 1181–82; Lord Zhao year 4, p. 1254. For the same account with some textual variants, see *Lü Shi chun qiu jishi*, ch. 16, p. 989.

23. *Zuo zhuan zhu*, Lord Xiang year 25, pp. 1106–07.

24. *Zuo zhuan zhu*, Lord Zhao year 12, p. 1340; year 13, p. 1353.

25. In 714 B.C. the Rong attacked the capital of Zheng, and the lord of Zheng worried over the ability of his chariot army to deal with the Rong infantry. At the battle of An in 589 B.C. the Di contributed an infantry army to the Jin forces. See *Zuo zhuan zhu*, Lord Yin year 9, p. 65; Lord Cheng year 2, p. 795.

26. *Zuo zhuan zhu*, Lord Zhao year 1, pp. 1215–16.

27. On the rise of infantry armies in general, see Lan, *Chun qiu shiqi de bubing*. On the invention of the crossbow, probably in the state of Chu, see Jerry Norman and Mei Tsu-lin, "The Austroasiatics in Ancient South China: Some Lexical Evidence," *Monumenta Serica* 32 (1976): 293–94; Gao Zhixi, "Ji Changsha Changde chutu nuji de Zhanguo mu—jian tan youguan nuji gongshi de jige wenti," *Wenwu* 1964 (6): 33–45; Noel Barnard and Sato Tamotsu, *Metal-lurgical Remains of Ancient China* (Tokyo: Nichiōsha, 1975), pp. 116–17; Hayashi Minao, *Chūgoku Yin Shū jidai no buki* (Kyoto: Kyōto Daigaku Jinbun Kagaku Kenkyūsho, 1972), pp. 301–20; Yang Hong, *Zhongguo gu bingqi lun-cong* (Beijing: Wenwu, 1980), pp. 135–39. On the development and spread of the sword and of fittings for cavalry, see Yang, *Zhongguo gu bingqi luncong*, pp. 94–104, 115–30; Hayashi, *Chūgoku Yin Shū jidai no buki*, pp. 199–236. On the proliferation of iron weapons and armor and of lamellar armor, see Yang, *Zhongguo gu bingqi luncong*, pp. 1–35; Albert Dien, "A Study of Early Chinese Armor" (Paper delivered at "China's Past Unearthed: the Reconciliation of the New Discoveries and the Historical Records of the Early Imperial Period," San Francisco, March 26–28, 1980); Hayashi, *Chūgoku Yin Shū jidai no buki*, pp. 395–415.

28. Hsu, *Ancient China in Transition*, pp. 65–68.

29. On the relation of the *xian* to military recruitment, see Yang, *Zhan-guo shi*, pp. 209–13, 229–33.

30. Kimura, *Chūgoku kodai teikoku no keisei*; Kimura Masao, *Chūgoku nōmin hanran no kenkyū* (Tokyo: Tōkyō Daigaku, 1979), pp. 3–116.

31. The most important studies are Yang, *Shang Yang bianfa*; Koga, *Kan Chōanjō*; Moriya Mitsuo, *Chūgoku kodai no kazoku to kokka* (Kyoto: Tōyōshi

272 NOTESNOTES

Kenkyūkai, 1968), pp. 3–138; Nishijima, *Chūgoku kodai teikoku no keisei to kōzō*. This last focuses on Han institutions, but these were successors to those created in Qin, and discussions of Shang Yang's reforms and Qin institutions are scattered throughout the text. Lin Jianming, *Qin shi gao* (Shanghai: Renmin, 1981), pp. 172–233 contains a good discussion that does not get bogged down in the numerous disputes produced by the paucity of evidence and abundance of researchers.

32. A. F. P. Hulsewe has published a complete, annotated translation of the legal and administrative texts, and this translation includes a discussion of the published versions of the primary sources and a good bibliography of the secondary literature. See *Remnants of Ch'in Law* (Leiden: E. J. Brill, 1985).

33. *Shi ji*, ch. 68, pp. 2230, 2232. Other fragmentary references to the reforms appear in *Shi ji*, ch. 5, p. 203; ch. 83, p. 2461; *Xunzi jijie*, ch. 10, p. 181; *Han Feizi jishi*, annotated by Chen Qiyou (Shanghai: Renmin, 1974), ch. 17, p. 907; *Han shu*, ch. 23, p. 1096; ch. 24a, p. 1126; ch. 28b, p. 1641. The *Shang Jun shu*, although not actually written by Shang Yang, is a product of his followers and contains much material about the reforms.

34. Households in Qin had first been linked together into military units of five in 375 B.C. See *Shi ji*, ch. 6, p. 289. The reiteration of this reform in 356 B.C. indicates that opposition from powerful families or the capital populace had blocked its introduction. There is abundant evidence of these units of five and their legal and military uses in the Qin strips from Shuihudi. See *Shuihudi Qin mu zhujian*, pp. 143, 146, 159, 192, 193, 194, 217, 271.

35. *Shang Jun shu zhuyi*, annotated by Gao Heng (Beijing: Zhonghua, 1974), ch. 19, pp. 406–07; *Wei Liaozi zhijie*, ch. 5, pp. 25b–26a.

36. Yang, *Zhanguo shi*, pp. 234–42.

37. In addition to the passages cited above, the system of ranks for military merit forms the primary topic of Chapter Nineteen of the *Shang Jun shu* and of one of the eighteen sections of the Qin laws found at Yunmeng. On the use of titles to redeem relatives and the awarding of posthumous titles to descendants see *Shuihudi Qin mu zhujian*, pp. 93, 146.

For modern studies of the ranks in Qin see Gao Min, "Cong Yunmeng Qin jian kan ci jue zhidu," in *Yunmeng Qin jian chutan*, 2nd ed. rev. (Henan: Renmin, 1981), pp. 155–69; Yu Haoliang and Yu Junming, "Qin jian suo fanying junshi zhidu," in *Yunmeng Qin jian yanjiu*, pp. 163–68; Moriya, *Chūgoku kodai no kazoku to kokka*, pp. 3–69, 111–90; Koga, *Kan Chōanjō*, pp. 325–410. On their continuation under the Han, see Nishijima, *Chūgoku kodai teikoku no keisei to kōzō*; Kamada Shigeo, "Seikan shakusei," in *Kandai shi kenkyū*, 2nd ed. rev. (Tokyo: Kawada Shobō, 1948), pp. 33–62.

38. Masubuchi, *Chūgoku kodai no shakai to kokka*, pp. 421–48; Li Jiahao, "Xian Qin wenzi zhong de 'xian,'" *Wen shi* 28 (March, 1987), pp. 49–58; Yang, *Zhanguo shi*, pp. 209–13, 230–32.

39. Prior to the twelfth century A.D. Chinese historians and commentators agreed that these were a grid of paths set up by Shang Yang. The Song scholar Zhu Xi (1130–1200 A.D.), however, sought to demonstrate that the *qian* and *mo* were actually paths that had divided the fields in the "well-field" system supposedly employed by the Zhou and earlier dynasties, and that Shang Yang's reform had been the destruction of these paths in order to facilitate the free sale of land. This interpretation was universally accepted until World War II. Since that time a series of Japanese scholars have revived the original explanation, demonstrating that references to *qian* and *mo* first appeared only in the Warring States period and continued well into the Three Kingdoms. See Kimura Masao, "'Senpaku' ni tsuite," *Shichō* 12:2 (March, 1943): 1–72; Moriya, *Chūgoku kodai no kazoku to kokka*, pp. 86–110; Koga, *Kan Chōanjō*, pp. 92–108. In recent years, perhaps spurred by clear references in the Shuihudi strips to *qian* and *mo* as legally-decreed dividers in the fields, Chinese historians have also begun to reject Zhu Xi and recognize that Shang Yang created the *qian* and *mo*. See Zhang Jinguang, "Shi lun Qin zi Shang Yang bianfa hou de tudi zhidu," pp. 31–34; Li Jiemin, "'Kai qian mo' bianzheng," *Wen shi* 11 (March, 1981): 47–60; Gao Min, "Cong Yunmeng Qin jian kan Qin de tudi zhidu," in *Yunmeng Qin jian chutan*, pp. 133–54.

40. *Shi ji*, ch. 5, p. 203. The geographic range of the reform was discussed by the Qing scholar Yu Zhengxie (1775–1840 A.D.) in *Gui si lei gao* (Taipei: Shijie, 1965), ch. 3, p. 97. For the study of topographic maps, see Frank Leeming, "Official Landscapes in Traditional China," *Journal of the Economic and Social History of the Orient* 23 (1980): 153–204. Mr. Leeming suggests that the grids reflect the lingering traces of the old Zhou "well-fields." This conclusion is quite implausible, since the notion that the well-fields formed a grid originated only with Mencius, and his model was probably an idealization of Warring States practice. Moreover, the Zhou state lacked the centralized power and administrative capacities to reshape the countryside of China on such a scale. Once the meaning of *qian-mo* is understood, and it is recognized that Shang Yang, probably copying a model from the successor states of Jin, created this network of paths throughout Qin state, then the origins of the patterns observed by Mr. Leeming become clear.

For evidence of *qian-mo* in Jin, see the fragment of the *Fengsu tongyi* preserved in the commentary to *Shi ji*, ch. 5, p. 204. See also Koga, *Kan Chōanjō*, pp. 98–99, for a discussion of the significance of this fragment.

41. That the area of land marked out by the *qian* and *mo* was the amount that could be worked by one man is suggested by the fact that the law penalized households where several adult males lived together. This clearly aimed at dividing households in order to maximize both the land in cultivation and the number of men providing taxes and service.

42. On the twin realms of the state and the household and their complicated relationship of mutual opposition and mutual reinforcement in imperial China, see Ogata Isamu, *Chūgoku kodai no "ie" to kokka* (Tokyo: Iwanami, 1979).

43. *Shang Jun shu zhuyi*, ch. 3, p. 56.

44. *Han Feizi jishi*, ch. 4, p. 239; ch. 5, p. 269; ch. 11, pp. 617, 619, 659; ch. 17, p. 899; ch. 18, pp. 948, 973; ch. 19, p. 1076. Han Fei echoes or anticipates the *Shang Jun shu* in insisting that the only true services of the state were warfare and agriculture, and that all honors should be obtained through those activities.

45. See, for example, *Guanzi jiaozheng*, ch. 8, p. 125; *Huainanzi*, ch. 15, p. 257; *Taiping yulan*, ch. 339, p. 2b.

46. The major expositions of this theory appear in the syncretistic *Lü Shi chun qiu* and the Confucian "Yue ling," but it appeared in a wide range of texts, including the Qin legal code. See Yang, *Zhanguo shi*, pp. 62–64.

47. *Xunzi jijie*, ch. 10, pp. 176–77. For a defence of this passage as the orthodox Confucian position, see *Han shu*, ch. 23, p. 1085.

48. *Shang Jun shu zhuyi*, ch. 10, p. 238; ch. 11, p. 248; *Han Feizi jishi*, ch. 19, pp. 1066–67.

49. See, for example, *Zuo zhuan zhu*, Lord Wen year 7, p. 563; Lord Xiang year 26, pp. 1117, 1125; year 27, pp. 1135–36; Lord Zhao year 1, pp. 1201–02, 1205–07; year 11, p. 1325.

50. In the *Zuo zhuan* several passages identify *de* as a power that commanded through the act of preserving life, and contrasted it with "punishments" or "strength." See Lord Yin year 11, p. 76; Lord Xi year 4, p. 292; year 9, p. 327; year 15, p. 366; year 25, p. 434; Lord Xuan year 11, p. 711; year 12, p. 722; Lord Cheng year 8, p. 837; year 16, pp. 880, 891; year 17, p. 903. In these passages *de* and force were linked together as two complementary poles of action necessary to attain the hegemony. In other passages *de* was a general potency including both charismatic power and armed force. The hegemon showed his life-giving potency by sparing those who submitted, but he punished with force any who opposed him. See Lord Xi year 1, p. 278; year 30, p. 483; Lord Wen year 7, p. 563; Lord Xiang year 26, p. 1117; year 27, p. 1136. Many of the references to *de* appear when a lord launched an expedition against another state, defeated it, but then spared it because it submitted. See Lord Yin year 11, pp. 74–76; Lord Xi year 15, p. 366; Lord Cheng year 16, pp. 891–92; Lord Xuan year 12, p. 722; Lord Xiang year 26, p. 1117. Other passages describe the practice of sparing states that submit, but do note use the term *de*. See Lord Huan year 8, pp. 121–22; Lord Xi year 6, p. 314; Lord Xuan year 12, pp. 718–21; Lord Zhao year 13, p. 1361.

51. That the hegemon came to be viewed as a kind of monarch is shown by the fact that he assumed the duty of the Zhou king to sacrifice to the ancestors of earlier ruling houses. See *Zuo zhuan zhu*, Lord Zhao year 7, p. 1290. For the argument that the hegemon's potency and not the covenant was the basis of the league's unity, see *Zuo zhuan zhu*, Lord Cheng year 9, pp. 842–43; Lord Xiang year 27, p. 1133.

52. On interstate alliances as bonds, see *Zhanguo ce*, ch. 3, pp. 81, 87; ch. 12, p. 427; ch. 14, p. 505; ch. 15, p. 524; ch. 22, p. 796; ch. 24, pp. 854, 879; ch. 25, p. 900; ch. 26, p. 942; *Shi ji*, ch. 6, p. 235 (4); ch. 39, p. 1650; ch. 46, p. 1884; ch. 69, pp. 2249, 2256, 2261, 2262, 2263; ch. 70, pp. 2280 (3), 2285, 2287 (4), 2292, 2296, 2301, 2304; ch. 78, p. 2393; ch. 81, p. 2442 (2); *Zhuangzi jijie*, ch. 7, p. 169; *Mengzi zhengyi*, ch. 12, p. 504. On the master or senior of a bond, see *Shi ji*, ch. 8, pp. 365, 376; ch. 69, p. 2261; ch. 70, p. 2304. The *Sunzi* argued that any state which claimed to be seeking peaceful relations without offering a bond was plotting treachery. See *Sunzi zhijie*, ch. 2, p. 42a.

53. *Shi ji*, ch. 64, pp. 2157–59; ch. 65, pp. 2161–62.

54. *Wuzi zhijie*, ch. 2, pp. 36b–37b. On bonds as a central feature in accounts of the careers of commanders, see *Shi ji*, ch. 25, p. 1241—this passage explicitly identifies the bonds as the later and "degenerate" form of the oaths and proclamations of antiquity; ch. 27, p. 2074; ch. 64, pp. 2157–58; ch. 65, pp. 1261–62; ch. 81, pp. 2441, 2447, 2449, 2450; ch. 82, p. 2454; *Han shu*, ch. 79, p. 3298; *Hou Han shu*, ch. 19, p. 718; ch. 69, p. 2249; ch. 79, p. 2961; Chen Shou, *Sanguo zhi* (Beijing: Zhonghua, 1959), ch. 14, p. 432; ch. 28, p. 759.

55. *Shi ji*, ch. 70, p. 2299; ch. 76, p. 2366; ch. 122, p. 3143; *Lü Shi chun qiu jishi*, ch. 19, p. 1257; *Zuo zhuan zhu*, Lord Xiang year 10, p. 984; *Zhou li zhengyi*, ch. 51, pp. 2a–b; ch. 69, p. 3a.

56. On the "Tong yue," see Utsunomiya Kiyoyoshi, *Kandai shakai keizai shi kenkyū* (Tokyo: Kōbundō, 1955), pp. 256–374. An English translation and commentary appears in C. Martin Wilbur, *Slavery in China During the Former Han Dynasty* (New York: Russell & Russell, 1943), pp. 382–92. For examples of bonds as contracts to purchase grave sites, see Luo Zhenyu, *Zhensongtang ji gu yiwen*, in *Luo Xuetang Xiansheng quanji chubian*, vol. 13 (Taipei: Wenhua, 1968), ch. 15, pp. 26b–27a, 30a; Lu Bo, "Handai Xu Sheng maidijuan jianjie," *Wenwu* 1972 (5): 62. On the use of *yue* in loan agreements, see *Shi ji*, ch. 75, pp. 2360, 2361. For a general study of business contracts in early China, see Zhang Chuanxi, *Qin Han wenti yanjiu* (Beijing: Beijing Daxue, 1985), pp. 140–208.

57. *Shi ji*, ch. 6, p. 235; ch. 7, pp. 309–10; ch. 9, p. 400; ch. 69, p. 2249; ch. 70, p. 2285; ch. 76, p. 2366; ch. 85, p. 2515; ch. 86, p. 2529; *Han shu*, ch. 16, p. 527; ch. 40, p. 2047; Chang Qu, *Huayang guo zhi* (Taipei: Zhonghua, 1966), ch. 4, p. 5a; *Hou Han shu*, ch. 28a, pp. 966, 969, 970, note 3. Xun Kuang linked together "bonds, covenants, and oaths" as a single category. See *Xunzi jijie*, ch. 6, p. 129.

58. *Shi ji*, ch. 69, p. 2249.

59. *Zhou li zhengyi*, ch. 51, pp. 2a, 2b; ch. 69, p. 3a. This text also refers to documents which stipulated the service obligations of communities and those which recorded legal cases and decisions as *yao* (要). See ch. 21, p. 1b; ch. 56, pp. 18a–b; ch. 67, p. 7b. The reconstructed pronunciation of this character is *iog, so it was homophonous with the character for "bond" (*yue* 約 *iog) and

was used interchangeably with it. For such a substitution in two versions of the same sentence, see *Shi ji*, ch. 8, p. 352 and *Han shu*, ch. 1, p. 23. Sometimes the two characters appeared as a synonym compound. See *Shi ji*, ch. 69, p. 2249. For other examples of their substitution, see *Lun yu zhengyi*, ch. 17, p. 308; *Zuo zhuan zhu*, Lord Xiang year 11, p. 984; Lord Ai year 14, p. 1682—this passage distinguishes *yao/yue* from covenants as two levels of oath; *Xunzi jijie*, ch. 2, p. 42 (commentary by Yu Yueh); *Gongyang zhuan zhushu*, Lord Zhuang year 15, ch. 7, p. 17a (commentary by He Xiu); *Shi ji*, ch. 75, pp. 2360, 2361; *Han shu*, ch. 22, p. 1049 (commentary by Yan Shigu); *Hou Han shu*, ch. 19, p. 718; ch. 69, p. 2249; ch. 79, p. 2961; *Sanguo zhi*, ch. 14, p. 432; ch. 28, p. 759; *Huayang guo zhi*, ch. 4, p. 5a.

60. *Wen xuan*, compiled by Xiao Tong (Taipei: Zhengzhong, 1971), ch. 3, p. 24a. The text does not refer to *yue* but to *gao shi* (詁誓). However, as the commentator notes, the description of these *gao shi* is the same as that applied to the *yue* proclaimed by Sun Wu in the *Shi ji*. In addition, Sima Qian clearly links *gao shi* with *yue*. See *Shi ji*, ch. 64, p. 2161; ch. 25, p. 1241.

61. *Zhuangzi jijie*, ch. 8, p. 190; *Shi ji*, ch. 68, p. 2232.

62. *Shi ji*, ch. 8, pp. 356, 362, 365, 376.

63. On the "bond of the three regulations," see *Shi ji*, ch. 8, p. 322; *Han shu*, ch. 23, p. 1096; Wang Fu, *Qian fu lun jian* (Beijing: Zhonghua, 1979), ch. 5, p. 224. On Xiao He and Cao Can, see *Shi ji*, ch. 53, p. 2014; ch. 54, p. 2029.

64. *Shi ji*, ch. 9, p. 400; ch. 57, p. 2077; ch. 58, p. 2090; *Han shu*, ch. 40, p. 2047; *Hou Han shu*, ch. 1b, p. 83; ch. 11, p. 470; ch. 61, p. 2021.

65. *Shi ji*, ch. 120, p. 3107.

66. *Shi ji*, ch. 27, p. 2074; ch. 81, pp. 2249, 2250; *Han shu*, ch. 67, p. 2910.

67. *Han shu*, ch. 89, p. 3462; *Hou Han shu*, ch. 76, p. 2466.

68. *Hou Han shu*, ch. 11, p. 478.

69. *Sanguo zhi*, ch. 11, p. 341; Fang Xuanling et al., *Jin shu* (Beijing: Zhonghua, 1974), ch. 88, p. 2283.

70. *Shi ji*, ch. 129, pp. 3279, 3280.

71. Han Lianqi, "Lun Chun Qiu shidai falü zhidu de yanbian," *Zhongguo shi yanjiu* 1983 (4): 3–12.

72. *Shuo wen jie zi zhu*, ch. 3a, p. 13b; *Han shu*, ch. 76, p. 3211; *Hou Han shu*, ch. 19, p. 718.

73. *Li ji jijie*, ch. 2, p. 33. See also *Zhanguo ce*, ch. 3, p. 81.

74. *Lun yu zhengyi*, ch. 6, p. 130; ch. 9, p. 182; ch. 15, p. 274. See also *Zuo zhuan zhu*, Lord Yin year 3, p. 27.

75. *Lü Shi chun qiu jishi*, ch. 14, p. 739. See also *Shizi*, ch. 2, p. 6a; *Guanzi jiaozheng*, ch. 4, p. 65; *Li ji jijie*, ch. 10, p. 16: "The greatest potency requires no agents. The greatest Way requires no vessel. The greatest faith requires no bonds."

76. *Xunzi jijie*, ch. 7, pp. 131, 133; *Mengzi zhengyi*, ch. 12, p. 504.

77. *Zhuangzi jijie*, ch. 2, p. 36; ch. 3, p. 54; ch. 4, p. 102.

78. *Xunzi jijie*, ch. 16, pp. 276 (2), 279, 280.

79. *Mao shi zhengyi*, ch. 10.2, p. 10a; ch. 11.2, p. 6b; ch. 20.3, p. 10a.

80. *Shuo wen jie zi zhu*, ch. 13a, p. 8a. The character here translated "bundle" often appears with the character *yue* in a compound which is used interchangeably with *yue* in isolation.

81. *Mao shi zhengyi*, ch. 1.3, pp. 4b–7b, 7b–10a; ch. 1.5, pp. 8a–10b—on this ode there is a lengthy epistolary discussion in Gu Jiegang, ed., *Gu shi bian* (reprint ed., Shanghai: Guji, 1982), vol. 3, pp. 510–73; ch. 3.1, pp. 9b–11b; ch. 4.1, pp. 9a–10b; ch. 4.4, pp. 7b–8a; ch. 5.2; pp. 1a–5b; ch. 6.2, pp. 1a–4a; ch. 7.1, pp. 4b–6b; ch. 8.3, pp. 3a–5b; ch. 14.2, pp. 13b–16b; ch. 15.2, pp. 12a–18b.

82. *Mao shi zhengyi*, ch. 6.2, p. 1b.

83. *Mao shi houjian*, annotated by Hu Chenggong (Qiushitang edition, 1837), ch. 1, pp. 49b–50a; ch. 2, pp. 49a–52b; ch. 22, pp. 39b–40a.

84. Marcel Granet, *Festivals and Songs of Ancient China*, trans. E. D. Edwards (London: George Routledge & Sons, 1932), pp. 62–63, 92–94, 115–16, 118–19, 129; Matsumoto Masaaki, "Shikyo renai shi ni okeru 'sai shin' no hyōgen ni tsuite," *Kumamoto Daigaku hōbun ronsō* 1 (June, 1950): 93–111.

85. Itō Seiji, "Yakusoku kō," *Shigaku* 30:4 (1958): 39–53. Itō cites two stories from the *Zuo zhuan* which involve bundled reeds, but these stories have no relation to the use of bundles in marriage ritual. However, his other literary references do show the practice. See *Huayang guo zhi*, ch. 4, p. 5a; Liu Jingshu, *Yi yuan*, in *Xue jin tao yuan* (Shanghai: Shangwu, n.d.), *tao* 31, *ce* 151, ch. 8, p. 4a.

86. *Lie xian zhuan*, attributed to Liu Xiang, in *Zhengtong Daozang*, vol. 8 (Taipei: Yiwen, 1962), p. 6116; *Yunmeng Shuihudi Qin mu* (Beijing: Wenwu, 1981), plate 135, strips 829–828 verso. The former example, like those from the medieval *zhi guai* stories cited by Itō, involves the seduction of "fairy" women and demons. The ties of this sympathetic plant magic with illicit sex and folk sorcery suggest why records of "binding" do not appear in the Confucian ritual manuals but only in the *Shi jing*—with their great antiquity and cultivated "rusticity"—as well as early vernacular fiction and works describing folk customs.

87. Donald Harper, "A Chinese Demonography of the Third Century B.C.," *Harvard Journal of Asiatic Studies* 45 (1985): 470–79. For the use of *jie* in

place of *yue*, see *Shi ji*, ch. 81, p. 2439. *Jie* was also the standard verb applied to the sealing of a covenant.

88. *Zhuangzi jijie*, ch. 3, p. 54; *Guanzi jiaozheng*, ch. 4, p. 65.

89. *Shi ji*, ch. 86, p. 2519.

90. *Shi ji*, ch. 44, p. 1840. See also *Hou Han shu*, ch. 28a, p. 956: "An official binds a prince with talent and cunning wisdom, just as a woman seeks a master through the way of seduction [or 'flattery']." Also *Mengzi zhengyi*, ch. 9, p. 363.

91. *Lun yu zhengyi*, ch. 21, p. 389.

92. *Han Feizi jishi*, ch. 3, p. 187; *Zhanguo ce*, ch. 3, p. 125. For other stories in which ministers are compared to wives or concubines, see *Zhanguo ce*, ch. 3, p. 129; ch. 22, p. 804; ch. 29, pp. 1049, 1074.

93. *Shang shu zhengyi*, ch. 11, pp. 12a–b; *Xunzi jijie*, ch. 15, p. 259. These charges were linked with the accusation that his fondness for women led him to abandon the sacrifices to his ancestors. See Chapter One, note 77. It is noteworthy that King Wu made a point of decapitating the two favorite wives of King Zhou, and of hanging their heads from his banners along with that of their husband. See Chapter One, note 49.

94. *Shi ji*, ch. 75, p. 2353. See also *Zhanguo ce*, ch. 11, p. 404.

95. *Shi ji*, ch. 76, pp. 2365–66. See also *Guo yu*, ch. 6, p. 223.

96. *Hou Han shu*, ch. 62, p. 2052. See also *Li ji jijie*, ch. 9, p. 7: "The ministers assist their prince's mandate; the wives assist their husbands."

97. Arthur Waley argued that the strange way that sex was mixed with politics in the *Li sao* indicated that the poet *was* demented. Cited in Laurence A. Schneider, *A Madman of Ch'u: The Chinese Myth of Loyalty and Dissent* (Berkeley: University of California, 1980), p. 33.

98. Masubuchi, *Chūgoku kodai no shakai to kokka*, pp. 49–186. See also Kaizuka, *Chūgoku no kodai kokka*, pp. 343–82.

99. Guo Moruo, *Liang Zhou jinwenci daxi kaoshi* (Tokyo: Bunkyodo, 1935), pp. 96b–99b; 121a–122b.

100. *Guo yu*, ch. 1, p. 24.

101. Yang, *Zhanguo shi*, pp. 83–84.

102. *Zuo zhuan zhu*, Lord Wen year 14, pp. 602–03.

103. Kaizuka, *Chūgoku no kodai kokka*, pp. 364–67. As Kaizuka has pointed out, Lord Wen was the son of a Di woman, married two Di wives, and lived for twelve years among the Di. Stories in the *Guo yu* and *Zuo zhuan* show

that the Di were noted for their loyalty to the person of their ruler. Thus it is possible that the rise of personalist ties in Jin, where the tendency was most pronounced, was influenced by values and patterns of behavior learned from non-Zhou peoples.

104. *Zuo zhuan zhu*, Lord Xiang year 21, pp. 1059, 1063; year 23, pp. 1073–76; Lord Zhao year 3, p. 1235; *Shi ji*, ch. 46, pp. 1881–83; *Han Feizi jishi*, ch. 13, pp. 716–17.

105. Masubuchi, *Chūgoku kodai no shakai to kokka*, pp. 187–231.

106. *Shi ji*, ch. 86, pp. 2519, 2521.

107. *Shi ji*, ch. 86; ch. 94, pp. 2648–49. See also *Lü Shi chun qiu jishi*, ch. 19, pp. 1257–58.

108. *Zhanguo ce*, ch. 22, p. 777; ch. 33, p. 1185.

109. Masubuchi, *Chūgoku kodai no shakai to kokka*, pp. 147–86. Cho-yun Hsu, as part of his argument for the crucial importance of the development of commerce to the Warring States transition, cites several passages in which Han Fei argues that the relation between ruler and minister was a simple exchange of service for pay in the name of mutual profit. See Hsu, *Ancient China in Transition*, pp. 152–53. These statements must be understood in the light of Han Fei's programmatic attempt to reduce the art of rulership to the giving of rewards and punishments. Considering the full range of metaphor, homily, poetry, commentary, and political argument cited above, they can be regarded as neither typical nor influential.

110. *Xunzi jijie*, ch. 13, pp. 233, 245, 246, 250–51. See also *Li ji jijie*, ch. 12, pp. 71–72.

111. Granet, *The Religion of the Chinese People*, p. 114.

112. *Lü Shi chun qiu jishi*, ch. 11, pp. 588–89.

113. On the relation of the "wandering swordsmen" to the new ethic of service, see Masubuchi, *Chūgoku kodai no shakai to kokka*, pp. 49–136. For general studies of the phenomenon of *you xia*, see Miyazaki Ichisada, "Yūkyō ni tsuite," in *Ajia shi kenkyū*, vol. 1, pp. 131–50—this essay explains the translation of *xia* as "swordsmen"; James J. Y. Liu, *The Chinese Knight Errant* (London: Routledge & Kegan Paul, 1967); T'ung-tsu Ch'ü, *Han Social Structure* (Seattle: University of Washington, 1972), pp. 161, 188–98, 232, 245–47; Lao Gan, "Lun Handai de you xia," in *Lao Gan xueshu lunwen ji* (Taipei: Yiwen, 1976), vol. 2, pp. 1021–36; Tao Xisheng, *Bianshi yu you xia* (Shanghai: Shangwu, 1933).

114. *Han Feizi jishi*, ch. 19, pp. 1057, 1058, 1091, 1095 (2); *Shi ji*, ch. 124, pp. 3181, 3184.

115. *Shi ji*, ch. 124, p. 3181.

116. Hihara Toshikuni, *Shunjū Kuyōden no kenkyū* (Tokyo: Sōbunsha, 1976), pp. 72–98.

117. *Gongyang zhuan zhushu*, Lord Xuan year 2, ch. 15, p. 6b; Lord Xuan year 6, ch. 15, pp. 10a–14b.

118. *Gongyang zhuan zhushu*, Lord Yin year 11, ch. 3, pp. 16b–17b. The statement that a man who is not avenged has no retainers or sons also appears in the writings of Dong Zhongshu. See *Chun qiu fan lu yizheng*, ch. 1, p. 26b.

119. That many Chinese identified revenge as part of, or the precondition to, funerary rites is shown by the fact that in several historical cases an avenger deferred the formal interment of the victim until vengeance had been attained. See *Shi ji*, ch. 124, pp. 3185–86; *Hou Han shu*, ch. 31, pp. 1107–09.

120. *Gongyang zhuan zhushu*, Lord Zhuang year 4, ch. 6, pp. 10b–12b. A second passage in the *Gongyang* also praises war for the sake of vengeance. The *Chun qiu* stated that the army of Lu suffered a grievous defeat at Ganshi, and the *Gongyang* asked why the chronicle did not follow its usual practice of not mentioning the defeats of Lu. It explained that the defeat was recorded here because the battle was fought for revenge, and so the chronicle will "boast" even of a defeat. See Lord Zhuang year 9, ch. 7, pp. 5a–b.

121. *Gongyang zhuan zhushu*, Lord Yin year 2, ch. 2, pp. 2a–3b; Lord Xi year 1, ch. 10, pp. 1a–1b; year 2, ch. 10, pp. 6b–7a; year 12, ch. 11, pp. 9a–b; Lord Zhao year 9, ch. 22, pp. 14b–15a; Lord Ai year 8, ch. 27, pp. 14b–15a.

122. *Gongyang zhuan zhushu*, Lord Huan year 18, ch. 5, pp. 18b–19a; Lord Zhuang year 1, ch. 6, pp. 1a–2b. After echoing Mencius's famous dictum that there were no "righteous wars" in the *Chun qiu*, Dong Zhongshu acknowledged that the chronicle glorified war for revenge. He explained this contradiction by arguing that two exceptions did not overthrow a general truth. But he accepted the proposition that wars to avenge a wrong were correct and obligatory. See *Chun qiu fan lu yizheng*, ch. 2, pp. 3a–b.

123. This idea appears in a later passage in which Lord Zhuang of Lu was criticized for hunting with Lord Xiang of Qi, the man who killed his father. Indeed he was criticized for even thinking of his mother, who fled to Qi. See *Gongyang zhuan zhushu*, Lord Zhuang year 1, ch. 6, pp. 1a–3a; Lord Zhuang year 4, pp. 13b–14a.

124. On the many accounts of Wu Zixu, see David Johnson, "Epic and History in Early China: The Matter of Wu Tzu-hsü," *Journal of Asian Studies* 40.2 (February, 1981): 255–71; David Johnson, "The Wu Tzu-hsü *Pien-wen* and its Sources: Parts I and II," *Harvard Journal of Asiatic Studies* 40.1 (June, 1980): 119–51; 40.2 (December, 1980): 465–505.

125. *Gongyang zhuan zhushu*, Lord Ding year 4, ch. 25, pp. 15a–16b.

126. *Gongyang zhuan zhushu*, Lord Ding year 4, ch. 25, pp. 16a–b. In spite of the Han government's attempt to outlaw revenge, this passage was still

accepted as authoritative in the great scriptural conference organized by the Eastern Han government in the White Tiger Hall. See *Bohutong de lun*, ch. 1, p. 48a.

127. Some of the elements of reciprocity as a general theory of society and human relationships in China are sketched in Lien-sheng Yang, "The Concept of 'Bao' as a Basis for Social Relationships in China," in *Chinese Thought and Institutions*, ed. John K. Fairbank (Chicago: University of Chicago, 1957), pp. 291–309.

128. Makino, *Chūgoku kazoku kenkyū*, vol. 2, pp. 4–15; Michael Dalby, "Revenge and the Law," pp. 270–75.

129. *Li ji jijie*, ch. 1, p. 79; ch. 2, p. 89.

130. *Bohutong de lun*, ch. 1, pp. 47b–48a. A slight variant of these formulas apears in He Xiu's commentary on the *Gongyang*. See *Gongyang zhuan zhushu*, Lord Zhuang year 4, ch. 6, p. 13b.

131. *Zhou li zhengyi*, ch. 26, p. 8b.

132. Xun Yue, *Shen jian*, in *Han Wei congshu*, vol. 1 (Taipei: Xinxing, 1977), ch. 2, pp. 6a–7a.

133. Michael Dalby, "Revenge and the Law," pp. 279–80 (citing Chen Ziang), p. 286 (citing Han Yu); T'ung-tsu Ch'ü, *Law and Society in Traditional China* (Paris: Mouton & Co., 1961), p. 86 (citing Emperor Xuanzong).

134. Alvin Cohen, "The Avenging Ghost: Moral Judgement in Chinese Historical Texts" (Ph.D. dissertation, University of California at Berkeley, 1971); Alvin Cohen, "Avenging Ghosts and Moral Judgement in Ancient Chinese Historiography: Three Examples from *Shih-chi*," in *Legend, Lore and Religions in China: Essays in Honor of Wolfram Eberhard on His Seventieth Birthday*, ed. Sarah Allan and Alvin P. Cohen (San Francisco: Chinese Materials Center, 1979), pp. 97–108; Alvin Cohen, *Tales of Vengeful Souls: A Sixth Century Collection of Chinese Avenging Ghost Stories* (Taipei: Variétés Sinologiques, 1982).

135. *Zhuangzi jijie*, ch. 6, p. 160—this passage explicitly links execution by ghosts with that by men; *Zuo zhuan zhu*, Lord Zhao year 7, pp. 1289–90.

136. Cohen, "The Avenging Ghost," pp. 88–90; Cohen, "Avenging Ghosts and Moral Judgements," pp. 99–102, 107–08.

137. *Shi ji*, ch. 124 and *Han shu*, ch. 92 are devoted entirely to men who became famous through the regular pursuit of vengeance. Additional references to officials who assisted in the pursuit of vengeance or to people who hired "retainers" from among the ranks of professional avengers appear in *Han shu*, ch. 67, p. 2192; ch. 83, p. 3407; *Hou Han shu*, ch. 11, pp. 467, 476, 477; ch. 14, p. 564; ch. 29, p. 1027; ch. 31, pp. 1097, 1108; ch. 42, p. 1427; ch. 43, pp. 1458–59; ch. 45, pp. 1536–37; ch. 77, p. 2498; *Taiping yulan*, ch. 460, pp. 2b–3a;

Yuan Hong, *Hou Han ji* (Shanghai: Shangwu, 1929), ch. 1, p. 13a; *Huayang guo zhi*, ch. 10c, p. 8b. The large associations of professional assassins and their ties to officialdom are described in *Han shu*, ch. 90, pp. 3673–74; *Qian fu lun jian*, ch. 5, p. 183. The prevalence of such professional avengers is suggested by the fact that Sima Qian states that the reason men acted as wandering swordsmen to wreak vengeance for others without regard for the legal prohibitions was for the sake of money. See *Shi ji*, ch. 129, p. 3271.

138. *Han shu*, ch. 72, p. 3088.

139. *Hou Han shu*, ch. 28a, p. 958.

140. *Hou Han shu*, ch. 67, p. 2184.

141. *Shi ji*, ch. 124, p. 3183.

142. For cases in which avengers were not arrested or immediately released, see *Shi ji*, ch. 100, p. 2733; ch. 118, p. 3076; *Han shu*, ch. 83, p. 3407; *Hou Han shu*, ch. 41, p. 1407—in this case he was only temporarily released to bury his mother; ch. 43, pp. 1458–59; ch. 44, p. 1409; ch. 67, p. 2217; ch. 68, p. 2230; ch. 84, pp. 2796–97; *Taiping yulan*, ch. 439, pp. 2a–b; ch. 465, p. 2b—this was only a temporary release to allow him to return home to father a child; ch. 481, p. 5b; ch. 482, p. 5b; ch. 598, p. 5b; ch. 818, p. 2a; ch. 882, p. 5b; Liu Zhen et al., *Dongguan Han ji* (Taipei: Zhonghua, n.d.), ch. 11, p. 3b; *Huayang guo zhi*, ch. 10b, p. 7a; ch. 10c, pp. 10b, 12a–b.

On the high degree of independence of local officials, particularly at the level of the commandery, see Yan Gengwang, *Zhongguo difang xingzheng zhidu shi*, Zhongyang Yanjiuyuan Lishi Yuyan Yanjiusuo zhuankan, no. 45 (Taipei, 1974), vol. 1, pp. 3–4. This problem was noted as particularly severe by Cui Shi in the late Eastern Han: "Now those who control provinces and commanderies themselves disobey imperial decrees. They act according to their own ideas, and no matter what the decrees seek to prohibit, even if they are written in extreme styles of sincere compassion or scolding rebuke, [the officials] repeatedly discard them and do not repent. Therefore in the villages they say, 'The written [commands] of the provinces and prefectures are [carried out] like lightning; imperial decrees are merely hung on the wall.'" See *Taiping yulan*, ch. 496, p. 4b.

143. *Shi ji*, ch. 100, p. 2733—tells of a slave who was freed and then given office because he avenged his master; *Han shu*, ch. 67, pp. 2912–13—this tells of a man who in his youth regularly associated with "swordsmen" and engaged in vengeance. He was recommended for office by a local official but blocked by the objections of an official at court; *Hou Han shu*, ch. 26, p. 912; ch. 29, p. 1027; ch. 67, pp. 2200–01—this avenger was originally appointed to the imperial university and ultimately given office; ch. 68, p. 2229; ch. 77, p. 2498; ch. 81, p. 3684; *Dongguan Han ji*, ch. 16, pp. 12b–13a—this man was given an exemption from corvee duties for attempting to wreak vengeance on a local official who abused him. His resort to vengeance is attributed to the fact that he learned

from the *Chun qiu* that revenge was righteous; *Taiping yulan*, ch. 482, p. 4a; *Huayang guo zhi*, ch. 10c, pp. 4a, 10b.

144. *Han shu*, ch. 67, pp. 2912–13; ch. 92, p. 3715—this passage tells of a man who became well known in his youth for the rigor with which he observed mourning for his father and then went on to avenge an uncle. This progression was treated as natural and even admirable; *Hou Han shu*, ch. 26, p. 912; ch. 31, pp. 1107–09; ch. 43, pp. 1458–59; ch. 44, p. 1409; ch. 53, p. 1751; ch. 67, p. 2217; ch. 68, p. 2230; ch. 83, p. 2761; ch. 84, pp. 2796–97; *Taiping yulan*, ch. 439, pp. 2a–b; ch. 440, pp. 2b–3a; ch. 441, pp. 8b–9a; ch. 460, pp. 2b–3a; ch. 481, p. 5b—here the avenger is praised for his "filiality"; *Dongguan Han ji*, ch. 11, p. 3b; ch. 16, pp. 12b–13a; *Huayang guo zhi*, ch. 10b, p. 7a.

145. *Hou Han shu*, ch. 84, pp. 2796–97; *Taiping yulan*, ch. 439, pp. 2a–b; ch. 440, pp. 2b–3a; *Huayang guo zhi*, ch. 10c, pp. 12a–b. The depictions of filial sons or daughters at the Wu family shrines include an illustration of Ding Lan. For his story, see Gan Bao, *Sou shen ji* (Beijing: Zhonghua, 1979), p. 249.

146. *Hou Han shu*, ch. 44, pp. 1502–03.

147. *Jin shu*, ch. 30, p. 925.

148. *Hou Han shu*, ch. 14, p. 564; ch. 31, pp. 1107–09; ch. 52, p. 1722; *Taiping yulan*, ch. 481, pp. 3b–4a; *Huayang guo zhi*, ch. 10c, pp. 4a, 12a–b.

149. *Qian fu lun jian*, ch. 5, pp. 173–97, esp. p. 183; *Han shu*, ch. 90, pp. 3673–74. On the role and frequency of amnesties in ancient China and the early empires, see Brian E. McKnight, *The Quality of Mercy: Amnesties and Traditional Chinese Justice* (Honolulu: University of Hawaii, 1981), pp. 1–36.

150. For a short sketch of mutual implication in Qin law as shown in old texts and the newly-discovered Qin code, see Liu Hainian, "Qin lü xingfa kaoxi," in *Yunmeng Qin jian yanjiu* (Beijing: Zhonghua, 1981), pp. 201–03. A more extensive treatment in English appears in Robin Yates, "Social Status in the Ch'in: Evidence from the Yun-meng Legal Documents. Part One: Commoners," *Harvard Journal of Asiatic Studies* 47:1 (June, 1987): 223–27. On its survival in Han law, see A. F. P. Hulsewe, *Remnants of Han Law* (Leiden: E. J. Brill, 1955), pp. 112–24.

151. On the use of the range of collective punishments to reconstruct the legal definition of a family in Qin and Han China, see Moriya, *Chūgoku kodai no kazoku to kokka*, pp. 297–415; Utsunomiya, *Kandai shakai keizai shi kenkyū*, pp. 405–72; Makino, *Chūgoku kazoku kenkyū*, vol. 1, pp. 143–50; Satake Yasuhiko, "Chūgoku kodai no kazoku to kazokuteki chitsujo," *Jinbun gakuhō* 141 (1980): 1–61; Satake Yasuhiko, "Shinkoku no kazoku to Shō Yō no bungirei," *Shirin* 62:1 (January, 1980): 1–29; Ōta Yukio, "Shō Yō henpō no saikentō hosei," *Rekishigaku kenkyū* 483 (August, 1980): 13–24, 46; Matsuzaki Tsuneko, "Suikochi Shin kan yori mita Shin no kazoku to kokka," in *Chūgoku kodai shi kenkyū*, no. 5 (Tokyo: Yūsankaku, 1983), pp. 269–89.

152. On this practice, see Ogura, *Chūgoku kodai no seiji shisō kenkyū*, pp. 164–89; *Mozi jiangu*, ch. 15, pp. 356, 358; Masubuchi, *Chūgoku kodai no shakai to kokka*, pp. 187–231, esp. pp. 220–31; Nishijima, *Chūgoku kodai teikoku no keisei to kōzō*, pp. 102–04. For a general study of the political use of hostages in China, see Lien-sheng Yang, "Hostages in Chinese History," in *Studies in Chinese Institutional History* (Cambridge, Ma.: Harvard University, 1961), pp. 43–57.

153. Du Zhengsheng, "Bianhu qimin de chuxian ji qi lishi yiyi: bianhu qimin de yanjiu zhi yi," *Zhongyang Yanjiuyuan Lishi Yuyan Yanjiusuo jikan* 54:3 (1983): 77–111.

154. *Han shu*, ch. 92, p. 3128; *Hou Han shu*, ch. 14, p. 564; ch. 26, p. 912; ch. 28, p. 958; ch. 31, pp. 1107–09; ch. 76, p. 2472; *Taiping yulan*, ch. 598, p. 5b; *Lie nü zhuan*, compiled by Liu Xiang (Taipei: Zhonghua, n.d.), ch. 5, pp. 11a–b. These stories of relatives offering themselves to an avenger in exchange for the life of the offender find an echo in the short-lived, Eastern Han practice of allowing people to take punishments in lieu of their kin. See *Hou Han shu*, ch. 48, pp. 1610–11; *Taiping yulan*, ch. 416, pp. 2b–3a; *Huayang guo zhi*, ch. 10c, p. 10b. References to an "avenging family" appear in *Shi ji*, ch. 124, p. 3187; *Han shu*, ch. 26, p. 912; ch. 84, pp. 2796–97; *Taiping yulan*, ch. 439, pp. 2a–b; *Lie nü zhuan*, ch. 5, pp. 11a–b. In addition to people becoming the targets of revenge because of their relatives' offenses, there were also cases in which the offense of a slave led to a master's murder. See *Han shu*, ch. 92, p. 3717; *Hou Han shu*, ch. 40, p. 1386.

155. *Shi ji*, ch. 68, p. 2230; Hulsewe, *Remnants of Ch'in Law*, p. 145.

156. *Shang Jun shu zhuyi*, ch. 5, pp. 140–41.

157. On the authoritarian character of law in China, where law was equated with the command of the ruler or dynastic founder, and was based ultimately on the conquest that established each dynasty, see Nemoto, *Chūgoku dentō shakai to sono hō shisō*, pp. 98–100.

Chapter Three

1. John Keegan, *The Mask of Command* (New York: Viking, 1987).

2. On the correlation of the rise of mass armies with the development of professional officers, see Maury D. Feld, "Mass Armies and the Professional Soldier," in *The Structure of Violence: Armed Forces as Social Systems* (Beverly Hills: Sage Publications, 1977), pp. 141–68.

3. On evidence for the development of military specialization from military texts, see Robin Yates, "New Light on Ancient Chinese Military Texts: The Development of Military Specialization," *T'oung Pao* 74:4–5 (1988): 212–48.

4. The only systematic discussion of early Chinese military thought is Christopher Rand, "The Role of Military Thought in Early Chinese Intellectual

History" (Ph.D. dissertation, Harvard University, 1977). His bibliography lists many studies of specific texts or problems.

5. An incorrect prediction in a previously-lost chapter of the *Sunzi* discovered at Linyi shows that the book was probably written between 453 and 403 B.C. On this find, see Shandongsheng Bowuguan Linyi Wenwuzu, "Shandong Linyi Xi Han mu faxian *Sunzi* bingfa he *Sun Bin bingfa* zhujian jianbao," *Wenwu* 1974 (2): 15–26; Xu Di, "Lue tan Yinqueshan Han mu chutu de gudai bing shu canjian," *Wenwu* 1974 (2): 27–31; Zhan Libo, "Lue tan Linyi Han mu zhujian *Sunzi* bingfa," *Wenwu* 1974 (3): 13–19; Wei Rulin, "Dalu Han mu chutu *Sunzi* bingfa canjian shiwen zhi yanjiu," *Huaxue yuekan* 49 (January 21, 1976): 38–46. On the evidence from this find for dating the *Sunzi*, see Tay Lien-soo (Zheng Liangshu), "Lun *Sunzi* de zuocheng shidai," in *Zhujian boshu lunwenji* (Beijing: Zhonghua, 1982), pp. 68–71; Wu Shuping, "Cong Linyi Han mu zhujian 'Wu wen' kan Sun Wu de fajia sixiang," *Wenwu* 1975 (4): 6–7; Li Ling, "Guanyu Yinqueshan jianben *Sunzi* yanjiu de shangque—*Sunzi* zhuzuo shidai he zuozhe de chongyi," *Wen shi* 7 (December, 1979): 23–34. Since the *Lun yu* was probably begun sometime after the death of Confucius in 479 B.C. and the *Mozi* at the end of the fifth century, the *Sunzi* would be one of the earliest books attributed to an individual and associated with a specific "school" or doctrine.

6. *Huang Di xuannü zhanfa*, quoted in *Taiping yulan*, ch. 15, p. 9b. For other versions of the same story, see *Taiping yulan*, ch. 79, p. 3b—in this version he receives a military tally, the insignia of a general's office, rather than a treatise; ch. 694, p. 4a; ch. 763, pp. 6a–b; ch. 872, p. 11b.

7. Gao Cheng, *Shiwu jiyuan*, in *Xi yin xian congshu* (Hongdao shuyuan edition, 1846), *tao* 11, *ce* 81, ch. 9, p. 44b.

8. *Shi ji*, ch. 55, pp. 2033–49.

9. Chi You was in various texts either the creator of warfare or a horned beast who butted men and whom no man could oppose. See Chapter Five. Xiang Yu was famous for his size and strength and was able single-handedly to battle and slay dozens of opponents. He is the classic case in Chinese history of a commander who won every battle but lost the war due to failures of policy.

10. *Shi ji*, ch. 55, pp. 2034, 2040, 2042.

11. *Shi ji*, ch. 55, pp. 2048, 2049. Sima Zhen identified Master Red Pine as the rain master in the time of the Divine Husbandman. The earliest known source for this identification dates to the late Western Han. Liu Xiang, *Lie xian zhuan*, in *Zhengtong daozang*, vol. 8, p. 6111. Another work attributed to Liu Xiang identifies him as the teacher of the legendary Emperor Gao. See Liu Xiang, *Xin xu*, in *Han Wei congshu*, vol. 1 (Taipei: Xinxing, 1977), ch. 5, p. 1a. He is also described in *Sou shen ji*, pp. 1–2. For a survey, see Zhao Yi, *Gai yu congkao* (Taipei: Huashi, 1975), ch. 39, p. 21a.

12. Chen Yinglue, *Guiguzi shenji bingfa* (Taipei: Xin Dongli Zazhi She, 1972), p. 13; Kaguraoka Masatoshi, "Sonshi to Rōshi," *Tōhō shūkyō* 37 (April,

1971): 39–50; Rand, "The Role of Military Thought," p. 91, note 7; pp. 93–94, note 18; Yuan Zhouzang, *Laozi shenshi ji qi bingxue* (Taipei: Shangwu, 1977).

13. *Zhanguo ce*, ch. 3, pp. 78–91; *Shi ji*, ch. 69, pp. 2241–61.

14. On the legends of Tai Gong, see Sarah Allan, "The Identities of Taigong Wang in Zhou and Han Literature," *Monumenta Serica* 30 (1972–73): 57–99. On the link of Tai Gong with the Yellow Emperor as the founders of military thought, see *Shiwu jiyuan*, ch. 9, p. 45a. On the identification of the book received by Su Qin, see *Shi ji*, ch. 69, p. 2242.

15. On the identification of the practice of persuasion with combat, see Chen, *Guiguzi shenji bingfa*; Chen Yinglue, *Guiguzi douzhi mijue* (Tainan: Xin Dongli Zazhi She, 1972); Lin Gengdong, *Guiguzi douzhi miji* (Tainan: Zhengye, 1975); Rand, "The Role of Military Thought," pp. 72–74, 90; Satō Hitoshi, "Kikokushi ni tsuite," *Tetsugaku nenpō* 18 (1955): 276–95. On Su Qin's study with the author of *Guiguzi*, see *Shi ji*, ch. 69, p. 2241. For the dating of the *Guiguzi*, see Liang Jiabin, "*Guiguzi* kao," *Dalu zazhi* 10.4 (February 28, 1955): 12–15; Yu Yan, *Guiguzi xin zhu* (Shanghai: Shangwu, 1937); Zhao Tiehan, "*Guiguzi* kaobian," *Dalu zazhi* 14.5 (March 15, 1957): 3–7; 14.6 (March 31, 1957): 20–25. That several sections of the text were later additions is demonstrated in G. Haloun, "Legalist Fragments, Part 1: Kuan-tsi 55 and Related Texts," *Asia Major* 2 (1951–52): 85–120. However, the additions discussed were based on actual Warring States passages.

On Su Qin's identification of persuasion and diplomacy as a form of war, see *Zhanguo ce*, ch. 12, pp. 427–46. It is also significant that all of Su Qin's counsels of political strategy were based on the manipulation of military power. Each began with an analysis of the number of troops, geographic position, and martial temper of the state whose ruler he was addressing, and then showed how a particular alliance would strengthen that state against its rivals. See *Shi ji*, ch. 69, pp. 2242–61; *Zhanguo ce*, ch. 8, pp. 337–42; ch. 14, pp. 500–03; ch. 19, pp. 635–42, 643–48; ch. 22, pp. 787–91; ch. 26, pp. 930–33; ch. 29, pp. 1044–45.

16. *Shi ji*, ch. 65, pp. 2162–65.

17. Feng Menglong, *Dong Zhou lieguo zhi*, revised by Cai Yuanfang (Taipei: Sanmin, 1976), ch. 87–89, pp. 631–46. In an earlier fictional version of the rivalry between Sun Bin and Pang Juan it was a *celestial* text that was revealed by the author of *Guiguzi*. See "Sun Pang douzhi yanyi," in *Baihua Zhongguo gudian xiaoshuo daxi* (Taipei: Heluo, 1980), pp. 1–166. In a Yuan dynasty play on the subject, the revelation of the text did not occur as an incident, but the text was mentioned several times in a manner which shows that the author assumed that his audience knew the story of the divinely-revealed text. See "Maling dao," in *Yuan qu xuan*, compiled by Zang Jinshu (Beijing: Zhonghua, 1958), vol. 2, pp. 737, 743, 747, 750.

18. Henri Maspero, "Le roman de Sou Ts'in," in *Études Asiatiques publiées a l'occasion du vingtcinquième anniversaire de l'École Francaise d'Extrême-*

Orient (Paris: G. van Oest, 1925), vol. 2, pp. 127–41; Maspero, "Le roman historique dans la littérature Chinoise de l'Antiquité," in *Mélanges posthumes* (Paris: Presses Universitaires de France, 1950), vol. 3, pp. 55–62; J. I. Crump, trans., *Chan-kuo Ts'e* (London: Oxford University, 1970), pp. 13–15.

19. *Sun Bin bingfa*, annotated by Yinqueshan Han Mu Zhujian Zhengli Xiaozu (Beijing: Wenwu, 1980), p. 67.

20. *Sima fa zhijie*, ch. 3, pp. 31b, 32a; *Wei Liaozi zhijie*, ch. 1, p. 19b; ch. 2, p. 24b.

21. *Wuzi zhijie*, ch. 5, pp. 53a–b. A similar parable on the superiority of unity over strength or numbers is told in *Wei Liaozi zhijie*, ch. 1, p. 11a.

22. *Sunzi zhijie*, ch. 1, p. 2a; ch. 2, p. 19a. See also *Sunzi zhijie*, 'ch. 2, pp. 5b–6a; ch. 3, p. 65a; *Sun Bin bingfa*, pp. 112–13.

23. *Wei Liaozi zhijie*, ch. 1, pp. 7b–8a, 10b–11a, 19b, 22b; ch. 2, pp. 24a–25b, 36a, 39b, 44a; ch. 3, pp. 3b–4b. On the total unity of troops as the decisive factor in battle, see ch. 2, pp. 24a, 29a; ch. 3, pp. 43a, 61a; ch. 4, p. 6a; ch. 5, pp. 22b, 28a. The identity in the treatment of the commander and his men is also stressed in *Tai Gong liu tao zhijie*, ch. 3, pp. 68a–70a; *Wuzi zhijie*, ch. 1, p. 6a; *Sima fa zhijie*, ch. 4, p. 51b; *Zhanguo ce*, ch. 11, p. 404. The theme also appears in accounts of campaigns in this period.

24. *Sunzi zhijie*, ch. 3, pp. 65a–66b.

25. *Wuzi zhijie*, ch. 4, pp. 39a–b.

26. *Sunzi zhijie*, ch. 3, p. 63a; *Sima fa zhijie*, ch. 3, p. 38.

27. *Wei Liaozi zhijie*, ch. 1, p. 10b; ch. 2, pp. 25a–b, 26a–b, 37b, 39b, 63a; ch. 5, pp. 14a, 22b; *Sun Bin bingfa*, p. 54; *Sima fa zhijie*, ch. 4, pp. 45b–46a.

28. *Sunzi zhijie*, ch. 3, pp. 56a–59b; 61b–63b; *Wuzi zhijie*, ch. 3, p. 30a. See also the parable cited above about the condemned bandit and his pursuers.

29. The most famous example, which became a model in later writings on warfare, was Han Xin's maneuvering at the battle of Jingxing. See *Shi ji*, ch. 92, pp. 2615–16. See also Kierman, "Phases and Modes," pp. 56–62. A more extended and systematic campaign of psychological manipulation by Tian Dan is described in *Shi ji*, ch. 82, pp. 2454–55.

30. *Sun Bin bingfa*, p. 107. The importance of decisiveness is also asserted in *Wei Liaozi zhijie*, ch. 3, p. 30a; *Tai Gong liu tao zhijie*, ch. 3, p. 76a; *Hou Han shu*, ch. 28a, p. 963.

31. Lan, *Chun qiu shiqi de bubing*, pp. 184–86, 207–08.

32. Maury D. Feld, "Military Discipline as a Social Force," in *The Structure of Violence*, pp. 13–30.

33. *Zhou yi zhengyi*, ch. 7, pp. 34a–b; *Shuo wen jie zi zhu*, ch. 8a, p. 18b; *Xunzi jijie*, ch. 18, p. 312; *Sima fa*, quoted in Du You, *Tong dian* (Taipei: Xinxing, 1963), ch. 148, p. 776b; *Yi Zhou shu*, ch. 1, p. 5b; ch. 3, p. 14b; *Zhou li zhengyi*, ch. 54, p. 5a; *Zhou li zhushu*, annotated by Jia Gongyan et al., in *Shisan jing zhushu*, vol. 3 (Taipei: Yiwen, 1976), ch. 11, p. 3a.

34. *Sima fa zhijie*, ch. 1, pp. 21a–b, 30b, 37b; *Wuzi*, quoted in *Tong dian*, ch. 149, p. 779c; *Sun Bin bingfa*, pp. 41, 49; *Tai Gong liu tao*, quoted in *Taiping yulan*, ch. 339, p. 2a; *Yi Zhou shu*, quoted in *Taiping yulan*, ch. 301, p. 2a; *Shi ji*, ch. 71, p. 2308.

35. See the last four citations in the preceding note.

36. Guo, *Shanbiaozhen*, pp. 20–22; plate 47, no. 2; plate 48, no. 2.

37. Lan, *Chun qiu shiqi de bubing*, pp. 123–28, 161–84.

38. *Sunzi zhijie*, ch. 2, p. 19b; *Sima fa zhijie*, ch. 1, pp. 24a, 43a, 46b; *Tai Gong Liu tao zhijie*, ch. 4, pp. 51a–53a; *Han Feizi jishi*, ch. 11, p. 654; *Huainanzi*, ch. 11, p. 186.

39. *Sima fa zhijie*, ch. 1, p. 50a.

40. On this pattern as a feature of mass armies, see Maury D. Feld, "Information and Authority: The Structure of Military Organization," in *The Structure of Violence*, pp. 71–84.

41. *Sunzi zhijie*, ch. 1, pp. 1b, 26a. Although this work does not list the troops as one of the five principal factors, it does append them as a subsidiary factor. See ch. 1, pp. 5a–b.

42. "Whenever you raise an army, the commander is its life [or 'fate']."—*Tai Gong liu tao zhijie*, ch. 3, p. 53b. "Therefore military action is the great service of the state, the Way of survival or destruction, and its fate lies in the commander."—*Tai Gong liu tao zhijie*, ch. 3, p. 60b. "Therefore the commander is the Ruler of Fate of the people. If he is regulated the three armies will be regulated, and if he is chaotic the three armies will be chaotic. If you obtain a talented general then the troops will be strong, and the state will flourish. If you do not obtain a talented general then the troops will be weak, and the state will perish."—*Tai Gong liu tao zhijie*, ch. 3, p. 82a.

43. *Wuzi zhijie*, ch. 4, pp. 40a–b.

44. *Sunzi zhijie*, ch. 1, pp. 21a, 24a.

45. *Wei Liaozi zhijie*, ch. 2, p. 22b.

46. See, for example, *Heguanzi*, annotated by Lu Dian (Taipei: Shijie, 1962), ch. 3, pp. 3a, 4b; *Sunzi zhijie*, ch. 2, p. 34a; *Wei Liaozi zhijie*, ch. 1, pp. 8b, 15a; ch. 5, p. 18b; *Tai Gong liu tao zhijie*, ch. 3, p. 60b; *Sun Bin bingfa*, p. 65; *Shi ji*, ch. 69, pp. 2244, 2245; *Zhanguo ce*, ch. 19, p. 636. These all refer to toppling an army and capturing/killing the commander. *Sunzi zhijie*, ch. 3, p.

73a and *Sun Bin bingfa*, pp. 89, 90 refer to victory as "killing the commander," while *Sunzi zhijie*, ch. 2, p. 15a says "capturing the commander." *Sun Bin bingfa*, p. 97 refers to an army that "although strong cannot protect its commander." *Wei Liaozi zhijie*, ch. 2, p. 28a refers to "weighing the enemy and examining their commander."

47. *Zhanguo ce*, ch. 22, pp. 784–85. See also *Sima fa zhijie*, ch. 4, p. 49a—"A victory of the three armies is a victory of one man."

48. *Sunzi zhijie*, ch. 3, pp. 49a–51b.

49. *Sima fa zhijie*, ch. 4, p. 51a.

50. *Wei Liaozi zhijie*, ch. 3, p. 62b; ch. 5, pp. 11a–12a.

51. *Heguanzi jie*, ch. 3, pp. 4a–5a.

52. *Sunzi zhijie*, ch. 1, pp. 34b, 39b, 40a; ch. 3, p. 66b.

53. *Wei Liaozi zhijie*, ch. 1, pp. 7a–b, 13a, 20b; ch. 2, pp. 43a, 46a; ch. 5, p. 14b. The image of water as that which is weakest and most yielding but can conquer that which is heavy and solid plays a prominent role in the *Dao de jing*. See *Laozi dao de jing zhu*, ch. 2, sect. 43, p. 27; sect. 78, p. 46.

54. *Sun Bin bingfa*, pp. 122–23.

55. *Sunzi zhijie*, ch. 3, pp. 52b–53a; *Wuzi zhijie*, ch. 3, pp. 28b–29a.

56. In the eighth century A.D. the revelation of the *Huang Di yinfu jing* to Li Quan was also made by a woman. See Christopher Rand, "Li Ch'üan and Chinese Military Thought," *Harvard Journal of Asiatic Studies* 39:1 (June, 1979), p. 120, note 33.

57. *Shi ji*, ch. 65, pp. 2161–62.

58. *Wuzi zhijie*, ch. 1, p. 18b.

59. *Sun Bin bingfa*, p. 97.

60. *Sunzi zhijie*, ch. 2, pp. 33a–34a, 45a–b; ch. 3, pp. 49b–50a. A similar but more extended list of the types of men who threaten the commander appears in *Tai Gong liu tao zhijie*, ch. 3, pp. 59b–60a.

61. *Wei Liaozi zhijie*, ch. 1, pp. 8a–b.

62. *Wei Liaozi zhijie*, ch. 1, pp. 8b–9a; ch. 2, pp. 27a, 46b; ch. 3, pp. 60b–61a; ch. 4, pp. 5b, 7a; ch. 5, pp. 11a, 16a, 23a.

63. *Sunzi zhijie*, ch. 1, p. 12a.

64. *Wei Liaozi zhijie*, ch. 2, p. 45a. This story found a later echo in the famous statement by Xiang Yu that the sword was not worthy of study because it was only useful to oppose a single man, and he desired to know how to oppose 10,000 men. So he chose to study military treatises. See *Shi ji*, ch. 7, pp. 295–96.

On the historical background of this later quotation, see Lao Gan, "'Shi ji Xiang Yu benji' zhong de 'xue shu' he 'xue jian' de jieshi," in *Lao Gan xueshu lunwen ji* (Taipei: Yiwen, 1976), vol. 2, pp. 895–906.

65. *Sunzi zhijie*, ch. 1, pp. 1b–6a, 12a.

66. *Sunzi zhijie*, ch. 1, pp. 33a–34a. See also ch. 2, pp. 8b–11a. Later in the text the author describes "the Way of knowing victory," and this passage reiterates that victory can and should be "known" before battle takes place: "Therefore there are five [ways] to know victory. He who fights when he knows he will win and does not fight when he knows he will not win will always be victorious.... These five are the Way of knowing victory. Therefore if you know yourself and the enemy you will be in no peril though you fight a hundred battles. If you do not know the enemy though you know yourself, then you will win half your battles and lose half. If you do not know the enemy or yourself, then you will invariably lose every battle." *Sunzi zhijie*, ch. 1, pp. 27a–29a. See also ch. 3, pp. 54a–55a.

67. *Sunzi zhijie*, ch. 1, pp. 29b–30a. See also ch. 2, pp. 7a, 32b.

68. *Sunzi zhijie*, ch. 1, pp. 31a–32b. See also ch. 2, p. 12a.

69. *Sunzi zhijie*, ch. 1, pp. 20a–23b.

70. *Wei Liaozi zhijie*, ch. 1, pp. 5b–6a, 15b–16a, 17a; ch. 2, pp. 27b–28a, 30b; *Tai Gong liu tao zhijie*, ch. 2, p. 36b; ch. 3, pp. 74a–75b; *Sun Bin bingfa*, pp. 97, 100, 104.

71. Some of these terms have been discussed in Rand, "The Role of Military Thought," pp. 69–85 and Roger T. Ames, *The Art of Rulership: A Study in Ancient Chinese Political Thought* (Honolulu: University of Hawaii, 1983), pp. 63–72. My discussion incorporates their analyses.

72. *Sunzi zhijie*, ch. 1, pp. 37a, 40a. The *shi* of an army is also compared to water in ch. 2, p. 12b. A similar passage says that by means of his "dispositions" the commander can give his men the power of pent-up water roaring through a gorge—ch. 1, p. 34b. D. C. Lau and Roger Ames have used this similarity to suggest that *shi* and *xing* could be synonyms. One might also argue that the two were distinct but closely related, since the disposition and maneuvering of troops were the primary means by which a commander dictated the *shi* of the battle. This close link is reflected in the common use of the compound *xing shi* to refer to tactics in general.

73. *Sun Bin bingfa*, pp. 54, 96.

74. *Sunzi zhijie*, ch. 1, pp. 38b, 39a.

75. *Wei Liaozi zhijie*, ch. 1, p. 25b refers to the "balance of fear and shame" which will determine victory. Ch. 3, p. 51a refers to the "balance of the master and the servant." Ch. 5, p. 19a refers to the "balance of inner and outer." *Sima fa zhijie*, ch. 3, p. 35b writes "Big and small, hard and yielding, threes

and fives [numbers of men in a unit], many and few, any opposed pairs are called the balances [*quan*] of warfare." Ch. 4, pp. 45b–46a discusses the role of determining the balance between the soldiers' thoughts of victory and their fear. Ch. 4, p. 49a asserts that warfare consists in the balancing (*quan*) of the fundamental and the peripheral.

76. *Sima fa zhijie*, ch. 1, p. 3b opposes *quan* with *zheng*, the "normative" or "regular" which was opposed with *qi*, "the extraordinary." *Quan* is identified with combat, while *zheng* is identified with statecraft and the desires of the people. In *Wuzi zhijie*, ch. 1, p. 11b *quan* appears along with *zha* (詐 "deception" or "treachery") at the bottom of a list of five means of bringing people to submission. It is identified with war and stands in opposition to "social rectitude" which brings order through ritual. Ch. 4, p. 40a says that one uses *quan* to respond to the formations of the opposing commander. *Tai Gong liu tao zhijie*, ch. 3, p. 56b speaks of "officers of *quan*" who were in charge of performing the "extraordinary" and the "deceptive." At the time of Wang Mang, Feng Yan stated, "I have heard that to achieve completion through according with principle is greatness according to the Way; to go against principle and achieve merit is what is exalted in *quan*." See *Hou Han shu*, ch. 28a, p. 962. See also p. 963, the passage from the *Gongyang* quoted on p. 964, note 3, and p. 968.

77. *Sun Bin bingfa*, pp. 119–20.

78. *Sima fa zhijie*, ch. 3, p. 32a. The next sentence states, "All fighting is courage." Warfare was defined as the assessments and maneuvers performed by the commander, while the actual fighting was placed in a lower category.

Another passage in the same book speaks of a two-fold Way of destroying all inauspicious occurrences (or "doubt and superstition"). One way is through "social rectitude," and the other is through "expedient assessment." From the description of these two ways, it is clear that the first refers to proper rule, while the second signifies warfare. So this passage also defines warfare as "expedient assessment." See *Sima fa zhijie*, ch. 3, p. 38b.

79. *Sun Bin bingfa*, p. 65.

80. *Wei Liaozi zhijie*, ch. 1, p. 24b; ch. 2, pp. 23a, 28a, 30b; ch. 3, pp. 59a, 61a.

81. *Sunzi zhijie*, ch. 1, pp. 7a–b.

82. *Zhou yi zhengyi*, annotated by Kong Yingda, in *Shisan jing zhushu*, vol. 1 (Taipei: Yiwen, 1976), ch. 8, pp. 13a–b. The character *ji* is also used in this sense in two parables in the *Zhuangzi*. See *Zhuangzi jijie*, ch. 7, pp. 49–51; ch. 18, pp. 112–14. During a discussion of the relation of "punishments" and "potency," the Mawangdui Huang-Lao manuscript states, "The reversals of the seasons are the pivots." See *Jing fa*, p. 65. The *Shang shu da zhuan* describes *ji* as the most minute changes that produce great movements. See *Shang shu da zhuan jijiao*, annotated by Chen Shouqi, in *Huang Qing jingjie xubian* (Nanqing Shuyuan, 1888), *ce* 354–56, ch. 1, p. 4a. At the end of the Western Han, Feng

292 NOTES

Yan used the phrase "changes of the myriad pivots" to describe the totality of natural processes, and he cited the *Shang shu* as his authority. See *Hou Han shu*, ch. 28a, p. 965.

The *Dao de jing* also argues that the Way of the sage is to deal with things before they occur, to catch them at the moment of beginning. See *Laozi dao de jing zhu*, ch. 2, sect. 64, p. 39.

83. *Guanzi jiaozheng*, ch. 3, p. 41. This quoted portion does not actually use the word *ji*, but earlier in the chapter the author refers to the "*ji* of security or danger," and shortly before the section quoted he writes, "Seize the *ji* and hold true to the essentials, then the enemy will be unable to measure [your strength]." See ch. 3, pp. 37, 40.

84. *Sunzi zhijie*, ch. 1, pp. 37a–b.

85. *Sun Bin bingfa*, pp. 64–65. The *Dao de jing* suggests that the drawn bow is the image of the Way, because it symbolizes the process of reversal. See *Laozi dao de jing zhu*, ch. 2, sect. 77, p. 45. Since the *ji* are the loci of reversal these statements are closely related.

86. "In warfare if you see a good [opportunity] but are laggard, if the critical moment arrives and you remain in doubt, if you simply eliminate errors but cannot settle [on a course], then you have ceased to follow the Way."—*Sun Bin bingfa*, p. 104. See also p. 107, where "decisiveness" based on "knowing victory" is one of the virtues of the commander. "Therefore it is said, 'Have no fear and no hesitation. Of all the harmful actions in employing troops, hesitation is the greatest.'"—*Tai Gong liu tao zhijie*, ch. 3, p. 76a. This same homily is quoted in *Wuzi zhijie*, ch. 3, p. 30a. "The general is the mind and the troops the limbs. If the mind moves with total resolve, then the limbs will inevitably be strong. If the mind moves with doubt or hesitation, then the limbs will disobey. If the general does not rule as the mind, then the troops will not move as the limbs. If you then are able to win it is mere good fortune; it is not the merit of expedient assessment."—*Wei Liaozi zhijie*, ch. 2, p. 24b. "Resolve early and settle first. If your calculations are not first settled and your worries resolved early, then the advances and retreats will be unsettled. If doubts appear then defeat is certain."—ch. 4, p. 6b. For related passages, see *Sima fa zhijie*, ch. 3, p. 38a; ch. 4, pp. 51b, 54b. In the story of Gongshu Cuo cited earlier, he also identified his contribution as recognizing the moment of opportunity and then drumming the troops to attack. See *Zhanguo ce*, ch. 22, p. 784.

87. *Wei Liaozi zhijie*, ch. 2, p. 38a. See also *Hou Han shu*, ch. 28a, p. 963—"The decisive man is the master of cunning wisdom; the man who hesitates is the servant of circumstance."

88. See Peter A. Boodberg, "The Art of War in Ancient China: A Study Based Upon the *Dialogues of Li, Duke of Wei*" (Ph.D. dissertation, University of California at Berkeley, 1930), pp. xi–xvii; Samuel B. Griffith, trans., *Sun-tzu: The Art of War* (London: Oxford University, 1963), pp. 39–40; Rand, "The Role of Military Thought," pp. 76–79; Benjamin E. Wallacker, "Two Concepts

in Early Chinese Military Thought," *Language* 42.2 (1966): 295–99. On *qi* as a general term for military action, see *Laozi dao de jing zhu*, ch. 2, sect. 57, p. 34.

89. *Sunzi zhijie*, ch. 1, pp. 36a–37a. My reading of the first line does not follow that suggested by most Chinese commentators since Cao Cao. These writers suggest that the passage means one "engages" the enemy with "normative" forces and then defeats him with "extraordinary" ones. The image they invoke is the battle of Changping, which resembles Hannibal's famous victory at Cannae. The normative forces engage the enemy head on and trick him into committing his troops, then the extraordinary forces attack on his flanks and rear to destroy him. However, as the author of a Song dynasty treatise pointed out, this reading produces a contradiction between the beginning of the passage and the end. If one assumes that an army is divided into normative and extraordinary forces as fixed categories, then how could they give birth to one another, form an endless cycle, and totally exhaust all the possible permutations of maneuver? So he suggested that the first reference to "normative" and "extraordinary" uses them in the same manner as does the *Dao de jing* when it argues that one rules a state through the normative but engages in war through the extraordinary. The army was constituted as a social body through the normative rules, but victory in the field was won through extraordinary maneuvers. See *Tang Taizong Li Weigong wendui zhijie*, annotated by Liu Yin, in *Mingben wujing qi shu zhijie*, vol. 2 (Taipei: Shi Di Jiaoyu, 1972), ch. 1, pp. 4b, 8a–11b. As will be shown in the following analysis, this second level of opposition between the normative and the extraordinary played a major role in the military treatises.

90. *Sun Bin bingfa*, p. 122.

91. *Sunzi zhijie*, ch. 1, pp. 8a–12a.

92. *Laozi dao de jing zhu*, ch. 1, sect. 36, pp. 20–21; ch. 2, sect. 41, p. 26; sect. 45, p. 28; sect. 69, p. 42.

93. *Laozi dao de jing zhu*, ch. 2, sect. 39, p. 25. See also *Sima fa zhijie*, ch. 2, p. 16a: "The social rectitude of the officers and commoners must be received from their parents and corrected [*zheng*] by the ruler."

The same idea, without specific reference to the polarity of *zheng* and *qi*, appears in *Guanzi jiaozheng*, ch. 6, pp. 91–92, 95–96; ch. 9, p. 145. These sections, however, disparage the value of *qi* and emphasize *zheng*. In this they represent those who sought to deny the independence of the commander.

94. *Laozi dao de jing zhu*, ch. 2, sect. 57, p. 34; sect. 58, p. 35; sect. 74, p. 44.

95. "So there are three means by which the ruler may harm the army. If he insists that the army advance or retreat without knowing whether or not it ought to, this is called 'haltering the army.' If without knowing the role of the army he identifies the regulating [*zheng*] of the army [with that of the state], then the soldiers will be confused. If without knowing [the use of] expedient assessments in the army he identifies the employment of men in the army [with that in the state], then the soldiers will be in doubt."—*Sunzi zhijie*, ch. 1, pp.

26a–27a. "If the general is capable and the ruler does not control him, then he will conquer."—ch. 1, p. 28a. "There are roads you should not follow, armies you should not attack, cities you should not storm, territory you should not fight over, and commands from the ruler that should not be obeyed."—ch. 2, pp. 28b–30b. "Therefore if the Way of warfare reveals that victory is inevitable and the ruler says, 'Do not fight,' you should fight. If the Way of warfare reveals that you will not win and the ruler says, 'Fight,' then you should not fight."—ch. 3, p. 52a.

For commentaries which give explanations, expansions, and historical applications of these passages, see *Shiyi jia zhu Sunzi*, pp. 70–73, 76–77, 202–03, 260–61. Particularly good is Du You. "In ruling a state you emphasize rituals and social rectitude, but in military actions you emphasize expedient assessments and deceit. The formations and power of circumstances are always different, so there is no constant, moral teaching. But the ruler does not know these changes, and if he uses the same regulations for the army and the state, then the soldiers will be in doubt and confused, and they will not know how to act. So the *Bing jing* says, 'In the state use good faith; in the army use deceit.'" *Sun Bin bingfa*, p. 54 also insists that for the ruler to control the commander leads to defeat.

96. *Tai Gong liu tao zhijie*, ch. 3, pp. 64a–66a. This last sentence also appears as the description of the commander in *Wei Liaozi zhijie*, ch. 2, pp. 42a–b. For a less detailed account of a similar ceremony, see *Wei Liaozi zhijie*, ch. 4, pp. 7b–8a. On this ceremony as described in Han sources, see Ōba Osamu, *Shin Kan hōsei shi no kenkyū* (Tokyo: Sōbunsha, 1984), pp. 365–70.

97. *Shang shu da zhuan jijiao*, ch. 1, p. 7b. On the legal powers and duties of the general in the Western Han, see Ōba, *Hōsei shi*, pp. 357–409.

98. "Fine weapons are inauspicious tools and are hated by creatures. Therefore he who has the Way does not rely on them. When the noble man is in the state he honors the left. When he uses troops he honors the right. Weapons are inauspicious tools and not the tools of the noble man. When forced to use them, it is best to be calm and unemotional. He does not regard it as praiseworthy to triumph, for to do so is to delight in killing men. One who delights in killing men cannot succeed under Heaven. In auspicious affairs you exalt the left. In inauspicious affairs you exalt the right. A subordinate commander stands on the left, while the supreme commander stands on the right. This means that [military affairs] are treated according to the rituals of mourning. You should approach the killing of a multitude in sorrow, so a victory in war is treated according to the rituals of mourning."—*Laozi dao de jing zhu*, ch. 1, sect. 31, p. 18.

The inauspicious character of those who slay many men and destroy states was also suggested in *Zuo zhuan zhu*, Lord Cheng year 2, pp. 803–04, as well as in the popular belief that families which served as commanders for generations would accumulate misfortune. See *Shi ji*, ch. 73, p. 2341. Finally, the description of the general as an "officer of death" in *Wei Liaozi zhijie*, ch. 2, pp. 42a–b also echoes this passage.

"Of old the bearing [including ritual and attire] of the state did not enter the army, and the bearing of the army did not enter the state. If the bearing of the army enters the state then the people's potency will decline, but if the bearing of the state enters the army, the potency of the people will be weak. So in the state the language is cultured and the speech harmonious. In the court they are respectful and obedient. They cultivate themselves in order to wait on others and do not approach unless summoned. If not asked they will not speak. They approach slowly and withdraw quickly. In the army they resist and stand firm. In the columns they pursue and do battle to the end. Those in armor do not bow, and military chariots do not follow the ritual of drivers in the state. Those on the city's walls do not run, and in matters of peril one does not employ the order of age [to rank men]."—*Sima fa zhijie*, ch. 2, pp. 24b–25a. See also ch. 2, pp. 16b–18a for a related passage.

99. See the cases cited in *Shiyi jia zhu Sunzi*, pp. 70–73, 76–77, 202–03, 260–61. On the legal separation of the army from the state under the Han, see *Han shu*, ch. 67, p. 2910.

100. *Lun yu zhengyi*, ch. 19, p. 354.

101. *Lun yu zhengyi*, ch. 16, p. 299; ch. 10, p. 191.

102. *Yanzi chun qiu jishi*, annotated by Wu Zeyu (Beijing: Zhonghua, 1962), ch. 3, pp. 177–78.

103. *Mengzi zhengyi*, ch. 14, p. 566.

104. *Mengzi zhengyi*, ch. 4, pp. 148–50.

105. The putative author of the text, Wu Qi, was said to have studied with a disciple of Confucius. See *Shi ji*, ch. 65, p. 2165. On Confucian elements in the text, see *Wuzi jin zhu jin yi*, annotated by Fu Shaojie (Taipei: Shangwu, 1976), pp. 10–12.

106. *Wuzi zhijie*, ch. 1, pp. 5a, 10b–11b, 12a, 13a, 14a; ch. 2, pp. 20b–21a; ch. 3, pp. 28a, 28b, 30b, 32b.

107. *Han shu*, ch. 23, p. 1085. "Heroic officers accorded with its inherent tendencies to aid [the world of] that time. They devised expedient assessments and deceits to topple one another. Wu state had Sun Wu, Qi had Sun Bin, Wei had Wu Qi, and Qin had Shang Yang. They all slew the enemy, achieved victories, and handed down writings [on the military art]. . . . For generations they battled for achievements and benefits, and the travelling persuaders [rhetoricians] regarded Sun and Wu as their masters. At this time only Sun Qing was illumined in the Way of kings, and he criticized them." The two surnames "Xun" and "Sun" were homophonous in the Warring States and Han periods, and in some texts Xun Kuang is called Sun Kuang. See, for example, *Han shu*, ch. 36, p. 1972. "Qing" was simply a title of respect, and Xun Kuang was sometimes called Xun Qing. See *Shi ji*, ch. 74, p. 2348.

108. *Shang Jun shu zhuyi*, ch. 10, p. 238; ch. 11, p. 248.

109. *Han Feizi jishi*, ch. 19, pp. 1066–67.

110. *Shi ji*, ch. 6, p. 255.

111. See Harry Joyner, "The Recruitment, Organization, and Control of Former Han Military Leadership" (M.A. thesis, University of Chicago, 1978); Ōba, *Hōsei shi*, pp. 374–409.

112. George Orwell, *Collected Essays, Journalism, and Letters of George Orwell*, ed. Sonia Orwell and Ian Anges (New York: Harcourt Brace Jovanovich, 1968), vol. 3, pp. 199–200.

Chapter Four

1. On the origins and nature of correlative thought, see Marcel Granet, *La pensée chinoise* (Paris: La Renaissance de Livre, 1934); A. C. Graham, *Yin-Yang and the Nature of Correlative Thinking*, Institute of East Asian Philosophies Occasional Paper and Monograph Series no. 6 (Singapore, 1986).

2. *Shang shu da zhuan jijiao*, ch. 1, p. 3a.

3. Derk Bodde, "The Chinese Cosmic Magic Known as Watching for the Ethers," in *Studica Serica Bernhard Karlgren Dedicata*, ed. Soren Egerod and Else Glahn (Copenhagen: Ejnar Munksgaard, 1959), pp. 14–35; Joseph Needham, *Science and Civilization in China*, Vol. 4: *Physics and Physical Technology*, Part 1: *Physics* (Cambridge: Cambridge University, 1962), pp. 186–92.

4. *Shi ji*, ch. 130, p. 3305; ch. 25, pp. 1239–42.

5. *Han shu*, ch. 30, pp. 1757, 1759, 1760, 1762.

6. A. F. P. Hulsewe, "Watching the Vapors: an Ancient Chinese Technique of Prognostication," *Nachrichten der Gesellschaft für Natur und Volkerkunde Ostasiens* 125 (1979): 40–49. For historical examples of its use, see *Mozi jiangu*, ch. 15, p. 359; *Hou Han shu*, ch. 12, p. 504; ch. 69, p. 2246.

7. *Shi ji*, ch. 27, p. 1343.

8. See Michael Loewe, "The Han View of Comets," *Bulletin of the Museum of Far Eastern Antiquities* 52 (1980): 2–31.

9. Derk Bodde, *Festivals in Classical China: New Year and Other Annual Observances During the Han Dynasty, 206 B.C.–A.D. 220* (Princeton: Princeton University, 1975).

10. Quoted in *Han shu buzhu*, annotated by Wang Xianqian, in *Ershiwu shi*, vol. 4 (Taipei: Yiwen, 1956 [?]), ch. 30, p. 6a.

11. *Han shu*, ch. 30, p. 1761.

12. *Shi ji*, ch. 111, p. 2939.

13. *Xi jing za ji*, attributed to Ge Hong, in *Han Wei congshu*, vol. 1 (Taipei: Xinxing, 1977), ch. 2, p. 6a; Fu Xuan, "Tan qi fu," quoted in a commentary to Liu Yiqing, *Shi shuo xin yu jiaojian*, annotated by Yang Yong (Hong Kong: Dazhong, 1969), ch. 21, p. 537. The former attributes the invention of chess to Jia Jun in the time of Emperor Wu (r. 140–86 B.C.), while the latter attributes it to the later Liu Xiang. The invention of chess in the time of Emperor Wu is also mentioned in the preface to the "Tan qi jing" quoted in *Taiping yulan*, ch. 755, p. 2a. This work, however, attributes the invention to Dong Fangshuo, who copied the game from the immortals. It also says that chess remained a palace secret until Changan fell to the Red Eyebrows. Clearly none of these are historically accurate accounts.

14. *Zhanguo ce*, ch. 8, p. 337.

15. On the social character of these games, see Yang, *Zhanguo shi*, pp. 514–15. On the tendency to violence of the wastrel youths, see Masubuchi, *Chūgoku kodai no shakai to kokka*, pp. 69–71.

16. Masamitsu, retainer of the Asukai clan, "Shūkiku shinan daisei," in *Zatsugei sōsho* (Tokyo: Kokusho Kankō Kai, 1915), vol. 190, p. 145.

17. *Jing fa*, p. 61. The character here translated "kick" most closely resembles a character meaning "grasp," and the commentators read it as "kick" solely because of the reference to the ball. However, several early texts contain stories in which leather balls, usually filled with blood, were used as archery targets, and at least one passage suggests that in some cases archery targets were "grasped" by men who thus themselves became potential targets. See Yang, *Gu shi xin tan*, pp. 334–37; *Hou Han shu*, ch. 15, p. 550; *Han Feizi jishi*, ch. 8, p. 456. It is possible that Chi You's stomach was used as such a target. However, this introduces several problems. First, the records of shooting stuffed leather balls all say that the ball was hung from a tower, not "grasped" by men. Second, the practice of stuffing balls as targets was always a form of "voodoo" against a living foe. Third, such a reading would reduplicate the archery contest that was already mentioned. Consequently, in the light of the statements of Liu Xiang and Masamitsu, it is still most likely that the text refers to kickball.

18. *Quan shanggu Sandai Qin Han Sanguo Liuchao wen*, compiled by Yan Kejun (Beijing: Zhonghua, 1958), vol. 2, ch. 98, p. 3b.

19. *Han shu*, ch. 97a, p. 3938.

20. Sima Guang et al., *Zizhi tongjian* (Hong Kong: Zhonghua, 1971), ch. 72, p. 2285; *Wen xuan*, ch. 11, p. 31a.

21. *Wen xuan*, ch. 11, p. 31a. A passage in the *Sanfu huang tu* shows that this pattern of steps and level was also a feature of Han palace design. See *Jiaozheng Sanfu huang tu*, annotated by Zhang Zongxiang (Shanghai: Gudian, 1958), ch. 2, p. 14. Thus the kickball stadium and the palace were both regarded as models or microcosms of the entire state.

22. Edward H. Schafer, "Hunting Parks and Animal Enclosures in Ancient China," *Journal of the Economic and Social History of the Orient* 11 (1968): 318–43.

23. *Wen xuan*, ch. 8, pp. 5b–6b. Translated in Burton Watson, *Chinese Rhyme-Prose* (New York: Columbia University, 1971), pp. 41–42.

24. *Lü Shi chun qiu jishi*, ch. 8, p. 441; *Shi ji*, ch. 6, pp. 245, 252—these passages quote the stone inscriptions erected by Qin Shihuang to proclaim his achievements; *Shizi*, ch. 2, p. 12a; *Wen xuan*, ch. 3, pp. 29a, 30a, 32a; Jia Yi, quoted in *Han shu*, ch. 48, p. 2253; *Shang shu da zhuan jijiao*, ch. 1, pp. 11a–b.

25. *Zhou li zhengyi*, ch. 58, pp. 18b, 22b; *Zuo zhuan zhu*, Lord Zhao year 29, pp. 1500–02; *Shi ji*, ch. 2, p. 66; ch. 5, p. 173.

26. *Shi ji*, ch. 3, p. 105; *Taiping yulan*, ch. 891, p. 4b.

27. *Mu Tianzi zhuan*, quoted in *Taiping yulan*, ch. 197, p. 6a; ch. 891, p. 4a.

28. K. C. Chang, "Changing Relationships of Man and Animal in Shang and Chou Myths and Art," in *Early Chinese Civilization: Anthropological Perspectives* (Cambridge, Ma.: Harvard University, 1976), pp. 174–96. On myths of battles between men and animals as an element in the "shamanic" hunting complex and their later development, see Walter Burkert, *Structure and History in Greek Mythology and Ritual* (Berkeley: University of California, 1979), pp. 78–98.

29. *Mao shi zhengyi*, ch. 4.2, p. 10a.

30. Zhongguo Lishi Ditu Ji Bianji Zu, eds., *Zhongguo lishi ditu ji* (Shanghai: Zhonghua Ditu Xueshe, 1975), vol. 1, maps 20–21, 27–28, 37–38; *Han shu*, ch. 28a, pp. 1556, 1557 (commentary).

31. *Lun yu zhengyi*, ch. 7, p. 140; *Mengzi zhengyi*, ch. 14, p. 581.

32. *Di wang shiji jicun*, compiled by Xu Zongyuan (Beijing: Zhonghua, 1964), p. 105.

33. Huaiyinshi Bowuguan, "Huaiyin Gaozhuang Zhanguo mu," *Kaogu xuebao* 1988 (2): 209 (figure 22), 211 (figure 25).

34. See reproductions in Hayashi, *Chūgoku Yin Shū jidai no buki*, p. 431.

35. *Wen xuan*, ch. 7, p. 20a; ch. 8, p. 9b; ch. 34, p. 9a.

36. *Han shu*, ch. 10, p. 327; *Wen xuan*, ch. 9, pp. 1b–2a.

37. The Weiyang palace at Changan contained nine pens for wild beasts and one for boars. See *Jiaozheng Sanfu huangtu*, ch. 6, p. 50. On the Jianzhang

palace, see *Shi ji*, ch. 26, p. 1402; *Taiping yulan*, ch. 197, p. 5b. On the evidence for the officials in charge of animals, see Chen Zhi, *Han shu xin zheng* (Tianjin: Renmin, 1979), pp. 297–98; *Shi ji*, ch. 102, p. 2752. On hunting by riders in even the smaller pens, see Ying Shao, *Fengsu tongyi jiaoshi*, annotated by Wu Shuping (Tianjin: Renmin, 1980), ch. 2, p. 74.

38. *Han shu*, ch. 97b, p. 4005.

39. Carl W. Bishop, "The Ritual Bullfight," *China Journal of Science and Arts* 3 (1925): 630–37; Edward A. Armstrong, "Chinese Bull Ritual and its Affinities," *Folk-lore* 56 (1945): 200–07; Richard Rudolph, "Bull Grappling in Early Chinese Reliefs," *Archeology* 13 (Winter, 1960): 241–45; Wolfram Eberhard, *The Local Cultures of South and East China*, trans. Alide Eberhard (Leiden: E. J. Brill, 1968), pp. 183–88; Bodde, *Festivals in Classical China*, pp. 201–09.

40. *Han shu*, ch. 68, p. 2940. For an account of cockfights imagined as a form of combat, see *Zhuangzi jijie*, ch. 5, pp. 118–19.

41. Guan Tianxiang, "Liangshan Han mu," *Wenwu cankao ziliao* 1955 (5): 46 (figure 3); Wang Sili, "Shandong Feicheng Han mu huaxiang shi mu diaocha," *Wenwu cankao ziliao* 1958 (4): 35; Henansheng Wenwuju Wenwu Gongzuodui, "Nanyang Han dai shike mu," *Wenwu cankao ziliao* 1958 (10): 39 (figures in middle and lower panels); Anhuisheng Wenwu Guanli Weiyuanhui, "Dingyuanxian Bawangzhuang gu huaxiang shi mu," *Wenwu* 1959 (12): 44 (figure 2); Henansheng Wenhuaju Wenwu Gongzuodui, "Henan Nanyang Yangguansi Han huaxiang shi mu fajue," *Kaogu* 1963 (1): 114 (figure 4), 119 (figure 1), 122 (figure 1); Hunansheng Bowuguan, "Changsha Shazitang Xi Han mu fajue jianbao," *Wenwu* 1963 (2): 16 (description only); Nanjing Bowuyuan, "Jiangsu Lianyungangshi Haizhou Wangtuanzhuang Han mu kuo mu," *Kaogu* 1963 (6): 288 (figure 2); Wang Baoxiang, "Henan Xinye chutu de Han dai huaxiang zhuan," *Kaogu* 1964 (2): 92 (figure 5); Lü Pin and Zhou Dao, "Henan Xinye chutu de Han dai huaxiang zhuan," *Kaogu* 1965 (1): 19 (figures 1, 3); Nanyangshi Wenwu Guanli Weiyuanhui, "Henan Nanyangshi faxian Han mu," *Kaogu* 1966 (2): 110 (figure 1); Zhengzhoushi Bowuguan, "Zhengzhou Xintongqiao Han dai huaxiang kongxin zhuan mu," *Wenwu* 1972 (10): 47 (figure 13), 48 (figures 3, 23); Henansheng Bowuguan, "Jiyuan Sijiangou san zuo Han mu de fajue," *Wenwu* 1973 (2): 51 (figure 9); Henansheng Bowuguan, "Nanyang Han huaxiang shi gai shu," *Wenwu* 1973 (6): 21 (figures 2, 3); Nanjing Bowuyuan, "Jiangsu Xuyi Dongyang Han mu," *Kaogu* 1979 (5): 415 (description only. Photo is in the set at the back of the issue—p. 4, figure 4.); Nanyang Diqu Wenwudui, "Tanghe Han Yuping Dayin Feng Jun ruren huaxiang shi mu," *Kaogu xuebao* 1980 (2): 250 (figure 17, panel 1), 251 (figure 21, panel 1); Nanyangshi Bowuguan and Fangchengxian Wenhuaguan, "Henan Fangcheng Dongguan Han huaxiang shi mu," *Wenwu* 1980 (3): p. 72 (figure 8); William Watson, *The Dynastic Art of China* (New York: Harry N. Abrams, 1981), part 2, plate 309.

42. *Han shu*, ch. 54, p. 2450; *Shi ji*, ch. 121, p. 3123.

43. *Han shu*, ch. 63, p. 2760.

44. *Shi ji*, ch. 1, p. 3; *Liezi jishi*, annotated by Yang Bojun (Beijing: Zhonghua, 1979), ch. 2, pp. 83–86. The Yellow Emperor's role as a commander of animal troops is also suggested by the titles of the tunes for the drum composed to commemorate his victory over Chi You. See *Gui zang*, in *Yuhan Shan fang jiyi shu* (Changsha, 1884), ch. 1, p. 31b.

45. *Da Dai li ji*, attributed to Dai De, in *Han Wei congshu*, vol. 1 (Taipei: Xinxing, 1977), ch. 11, pp. 3b–4a. For the argument that combat was natural since anger impelled men to fight, see also *Huainanzi*, ch. 8, p. 123. For the argument that weapons were natural and coeval with man, see *Lü Shi chun qiu jishi*, ch. 7, p. 383; *Taiping yulan*, ch. 339, p. 5b.

46. *Sun Bin bingfa*, p. 64. A similar but expanded version of this argument appears in *Huainanzi*, ch. 15, p. 1.

47. *Han Feizi jishi*, ch. 12, p. 682; *Guo yu*, ch. 15, pp. 496–97.

48. *Lü Shi chun qiu jishi*, ch. 10, p. 516; *Li ji jijie*, ch. 5, p. 448; *Huainanzi*, ch. 5, p. 81.

49. *Han shu*, ch. 23, p. 1085.

50. *Da gong bao*, March 11, 1957.

51. *Shu yi ji*, attributed to Ren Fang, in *Han Wei congshu*, vol. 2 (Taipei: Xinxing, 1977), ch. 1, pp. 2a–b.

52. *Taiping yulan*, ch. 755, p. 5b.

53. *Han shu*, ch. 6, p. 194, note 2. In this note Ying Shao, a late Eastern Han commentator still interpreted the phrase as a "matching of strength." The two later commentators, however, treated it as a generic term. See also *Hou Han shu*, ch. 79, p. 2963; Ma Duanlin, *Wenxian tongkao* (Taipei: Xinxing, 1963), ch. 147, p. 2.

Nevertheless, even in the Age of Disunion and the Tang, *jue di* continued to be used like *jue li* as the name of a wrestling match and military training ritual. Thus in the "Yue zhi" of the *Wei shu* the *jue di* appeared in a list of the "miscellaneous performances" immediately after performances with the "five weapons." See Wei Shou, *Wei shu* (Beijing: Zhonghua, 1974), ch. 109, p. 2828. The roughly contemporary *Loyang qielan ji* described two powerful warriors who were able to throw their weapons remarkable distances, and the emperor loved to match them in *jue di*. See Yang Xuanzhi, *Loyang qielan ji jiaoshi*, annotated by Zhou Zumo (Hong Kong: Zhonghua, 1976), ch. 5, p. 179. A late Tang diarist recorded that during the Guangqi reign period an army commander on expedition held a banquet, and at the end of the music and performances he commanded a *jue di*. This was described as a "matching of strength" in which the victor had to topple his opponent. See "Yutang xianhua," in *Shuo fu* (Weiwanshan Tang, 1647), *tao* 11, *ce* 48, pp. 4a–b. A gloss on *jue li* in one work explained that at the end of festivities the guests would form two teams—literally "armies"—and have powerful warriors grapple with one another in a match of strength. Clearly this referred to the same event as the *jue di* in the "Yutang xianhua." See Hu Zhenheng, *Tang yin gui qian* (Shanghai: Gudian Wenxue, 1957), ch. 14, p. 131. A fragment of a "Rhyme-prose on the *jue di*" mentioned various maneuvers used by wrestlers and said of the competitors, "There are none who are not mighty warriors." In another story the phrase "one who does *jue di*" was used to suggest a man's great strength. See Wang Dingbao, *Tang zhi yan* (Shanghai: Guji, 1978), ch. 10, p. 113; ch. 3, pp. 30–31. In the reign of Emperor Wen of the Tang (827–840 A.D.) there were references to matches under the name of *xiang pu* (相撲), a name better known in the West in its Japanese reading, *sumo*. See Zhao Lin, *Yin hua lu*, in *Biji xiaoshuo daquan*, vol. 1 (Taipei: Xinxing, 1962), ch. 1, p. 72. According to Song texts, this *xiang pu* was simply an alternative name for *jue di*. See Wu Zimu, *Meng liang lu*, in *Biji xiaoshuo daquan*, vol. 1, ch. 20, p. 6b.

54. *Wen xuan*, ch. 2, pp. 24b–26a. On lifting tripods as a demonstration of strength, see Yang, *Zhanguo shi*, pp. 521–23. The word I have translated here as "ax" is *yue* (越), homophonous and interchangeable with *yue* (鉞). The ax was the weapon of the thunder god that allowed him to command dragons and storms, so the spells invoked in these performances were based on those of the thunder god's ax. See Mori Yasutarō, *Kōtei densetsu: kodai Chūgoku shinwa no kenkyū* (Kyoto: Kyōto Joshi Daigaku Jinbun Gakkai, 1970), pp. 171–72.

55. *Xi jing za ji*, ch. 3, pp. 1a–b.

56. Lester Bilsky, *The State Religion of Ancient China*, especially pp. 14–16, 58–60, 66, 126–27, 162–69, 183–90, 235–46, 274–76, 297–308, 318–24.

57. Michael Loewe, *Chinese Ideas of Life and Death: Faith, Myth and Reason in the Han Period* (London: George Allen & Unwin, 1982), pp. 127–58; Howard J. Wechsler, *Offerings of Jade and Silk: Ritual and Symbol in the Legitimation of the T'ang Dynasty* (New Haven: Yale University, 1985), pp. 225–35.

Chapter Five

1. On the manner in which traditional tales act as a ". . . palimpsest on which generation after generation has engraved its own layer of messages. . ." see Wendy Doniger O'Flaherty, *Women, Androgynes, and Other Mythical Beasts* (Chicago: University of Chicago, 1980), p. 4.

2. Burkert, *Structure and History in Greek Mythology and Ritual*, p. 23; Georges Dumezil, *The Destiny of the Warrior*, trans. Alf Hiltebeitel (Chicago: University of Chicago, 1970), pp. 1–2; G. S. Kirk, *Myth: Its Meaning & Functions in Ancient & Other Cultures* (Berkeley: University of California, 1970), pp. 31–41, 252–61. Kirk defines myths as traditional tales that in addition to telling a

story also have an "operative, iterative, and validatory" function and a "speculative and explanatory" function. Claude Levi-Strauss makes a similar point when he emphasizes the two aspects of time in mythic narrative. "On the one hand, a myth always refers to events alleged to have taken place long ago. But what gives the myth an operational value is that the specific pattern described is timeless; it explains the present and the past as well as the future." See "The Structural Study of Myth," in *Structural Anthropology*, trans. Claire Jacobson and Brooke Grundfest Schoepf (New York: Basic Books, 1963), p. 209.

3. Qi Sihe, "Huang Di de zhi qi gushi," in *Zhongguo shi tanyan* (Beijing: Zhonghua, 1981), pp. 201–17.

4. Sarah Allan, *The Heir and the Sage: Dynastic Legend in Early China* (San Francisco: Chinese Materials Center, 1981). For a discussion of the pivotal role of the distinction between public/state and private/family in ancient China, see Ogata, *Chūgoku kodai no "ie" to kokka*. On the role of the myth of Yao and Shun in the ritual of dynastic change during the Age of Disunion, see Miyakawa Hisayuki, "Zenjō ni yoru ōchō kakumei no kenkyū," in *Rikuchō shi kenkyū: seiji shakai hen* (Kyoto: Heirakuji, 1964), pp. 73–172.

5. William B. Boltz, "Kung Kung and the Flood: Reverse Euhemerism in the Yao Tien," *T'oung Pao* 67 (1981): 141–53.

6. Gu Jiegang, ed., *Gu shi bian*, vols. 1–5 (Beijing, 1926–35), vols. 6–7 (Shanghai, 1938–41); Gu Jiegang and Yang Xiangkui, *San huang kao*, Yenching Journal of Chinese Studies Monograph Series no. 8 (Beijing, 1936); Henri Maspero, "Légendes mythologiques dans le Chou King," *Journal Asiatique* 204 (1924): 1–100; Bernhard Karlgren, "Legends and Cults in Ancient China," *Bulletin of the Museum of Far Eastern Antiquities* 18 (1946): 199–365; Derk Bodde, "Myths of Ancient China," in *Mythologies of the Ancient World*, ed. Samuel Noah Kramer (Garden City, N.Y.: Doubleday, 1961), pp. 367–408; K. C. Chang, "A Classification of Shang and Chou Myths," in *Early Chinese Civilization: Anthropological Perspectives* (Cambridge, Ma.: Harvard University, 1976), pp. 149–73; Allan, *The Heir and the Sage*; Sarah Allan, "Sons of Suns: Myth and Totemism in Early China," *Bulletin of the School of Oriental and African Studies* 44:2 (1981): 290–326; Boltz, "Kung Kung."

7. Gu Jiegang, "Yu Qian Xuantong Xiansheng lun gu shi shu," in *Gu shi bian* (Shanghai: Guji, 1982 reprint), vol. 1, pp. 63–64; Gu Jiegang, "Taolun gu shi da Liu Hu er xiansheng," in *Gu shi bian*, vol. 1, pp. 118–27; Laurence A. Schneider, *Ku Chieh-kang and China's New History: Nationalism and the Quest for Alternative Traditions* (Berkeley: University of California, 1971), pp. 223–30; Wolfram Eberhard, *Lokalkulturen im Alten China* (Leiden: E. J. Brill, 1942); Yinshun Fashi, *Zhongguo gudai minzu shenhua yu wenhua zhi yanjiu* (Taipei: Huagang, 1975).

8. *Shi ji*, ch. 1, p. 46.

9. *Han shu*, ch. 30, p. 1728.

10. A. C. Graham, "The *Nung-chia* 'School of the Tillers' and the Origins of Peasant Utopianism in China," *Bulletin of the School of Oriental and African Studies* 42 (1979): 66–100; Oshima Riichi, "Shin Nō to nōkasha ryū," in *Haneda Hakushi shōju kinen tōyōshi ronsō* (Kyoto: Tōyōshi Kenkyūkai, 1950), pp. 353–81.

11. *Shi ji*, ch. 74, pp. 2346–47; ch. 28, pp. 1368–69; Tu Wei-ming, "The Thought of Huang-Lao: A Reflection on the Lao Tzu and Huang Ti Texts in the Silk Manuscripts of Ma Wang-tui," *Journal of Asian Studies* 39:1 (November, 1979): 95–109; Kanaya Osamu, *Shin Kan shisō shi kenkyū* (Kyoto: Heirakuji, 1981), pp. 113–226; Guo Moruo, "Jixia Huang-Lao xuepai de pipan," in *Shi pipan shu* (Beijing: Kexue, 1956), pp. 152–84; Gu Jiegang, *Qin Han de fangshi yu rusheng* (Shanghai: Shangwu, 1955 reprint); Chen Pan, "Zhanguo Qin Han jian fangshi kaolun," *Zhongyang Yanjiuyuan Lishi Yuyan Yanjiusuo jikan* 17 (1948): 7–57; Kenneth S. Dewoskin, trans., *Doctors, Diviners, and Magicians of Ancient China: Biographies of Fang-shi* (New York: Columbia University, 1983); Ngo Van Xuyet, *Divination, magie et politique dans la Chine ancienne* (Paris: Presses Universitaires de France, 1976).

12. Xu Zhongshu, "Chen Hou si qi kaoshi," *Zhongyang Yanjiuyuan Lishi Yuyan Yanjiusuo jikan* 3–4 (1934): 498–504; Ding Shan, "You Chen Hou Yinzi dun ming Huang Di lun wu di," *Zhongyang Yanjiuyuan Lishi Yuyan Yanjiusuo jikan* 3–4 (1934): 536; Yang Kuan, "Zhongguo shanggu shi daolun," in *Gu shi bian*, vol. 7, pp. 189–93; Chen Pan, "Huang Di shiji yanbian kao," *Guoli Zhongshan Daxue Yuyan Lishi Yanjiusuo zhoukan* 3 (1928): 921–35; Lin, *Qin shi gao*, pp. 14–20.

13. *Shang Jun shu zhuyi*, ch. 7, pp. 182–83; ch. 14, pp. 296–97; ch. 18, pp. 374–76; *Guanzi jiaozheng*, ch. 11, p. 174; *Han Feizi jishi*, ch. 19, p. 1040.

14. *Mozi jiangu*, ch. 3, pp. 44, 47. On the need for rulers to fix language in order to standardize moral judgements, see also *Xunzi jijie*, ch. 16, pp. 275–76, 279–80. On theories in ancient China of the relation of language to political power and social order, see J. G. A. Pocock, "Ritual, Language, Power: An Essay on the Apparent Political Meanings of Ancient Chinese Philosophy," in *Politics, Language, and Time: Essays on Political Thought and History* (New York: Atheneum, 1973), pp. 42–79.

15. The *Dao de jing* does not actually refer to the former kings, but it repeatedly invokes a primal unity that was destroyed by the introduction of various technologies and social virtues. Thus the historical separation of men from animals through the invention of new techniques and the development of social virtues was a fundamental presupposition of the work. See *Laozi dao de jing zhu*, ch. 1, sect. 18, p. 10; sect. 32, pp. 18–19; ch. 2, sect. 38, p. 23; sect. 80, pp. 46–47. See also *Zhuangzi jijie*, ch. 3, pp. 57–58; ch. 8, pp. 194–98. These passages appear in the so-called "primitivist" chapters. See A. C. Graham, "How Much of *Chuang Tzu* Did Chuang Tzu Write?" *Journal of the American Academy of Religion: Thematic Issue* 47 (September, 1979): 459–501; Graham, "The *Nung-chia*," pp. 87–91.

16. This passage and the philosophical terms involved are discussed in Graham, "The Mencian Theory of Human Nature," pp. 59–63.

17. *Mengzi zhengyi*, ch. 5, p. 219. A modified version of this "creation" appears in ch. 6, pp. 263–65.

18. *Xunzi jijie*, ch. 5, p. 104.

19. *Xunzi jijie*, ch. 1, p. 7. On men without duty becoming beasts, see also *Zuo zhuan zhu*, Lord Wen year 17, p. 626.

20. *Xunzi jijie*, ch. 3, p. 50.

21. *Mao shi zhengyi*, ch. 8.2, pp. 7a–10b; *Sima fa zhijie*, ch. 1, p. 14b; *Zhou li zhengyi*, ch. 55, p. 6b.

22. *Liezi jishi*, ch. 8, p. 241; Yang Xiong, *Yangzi fa yan*, in *Xinbian zhuzi jicheng*, vol. 2 (Taipei: Shijie, 1974), ch. 11, p. 35.

23. *Zuo zhuan zhu*, Lord Xi year 29, p. 477.

24. *Zuo zhuan zhu*, Lord Xi year 2, pp. 393–94.

25. *Zuo zhuan zhu*, Lord Xuan year 4, p. 629; Lord Cheng year 28, p. 1493. The prevalence of this belief is shown by the fact that it appeared in more than one state and was the topic of a proverb. The proverb refers to the wolf child's *ye xin* (野心), which would usually mean insatiable ambition, but since these were considered to be humans with an animal nature it would be better to translate the phrase according to its literal sense of a wild, uncivilized, and hence inhuman heart.

This idea could be related to the popular belief attested in later Chinese society that male children born on the fifth day of the fifth month would have their souls stolen by owls and consequently kill their fathers or both parents. See Eberhard, *The Local Cultures of South and East China*, pp. 153–59.

26. Dumezil, *The Destiny of the Warrior*, pp. 139–47; James Redfield, *Nature and Culture in the Iliad: The Tragedy of Hector* (Chicago: University of Chicago, 1975), pp. 192–200.

27. *Mao shi zhengyi*, ch. 6.3, p. 10a; *Zuo zhuan zhu*, Lord Zhuang year 10, pp. 183–84; Lord Xiang year 10, p. 975; *Han shu*, ch. 76, p. 3214. This identification of warriors with tigers existed at all levels of the Chinese population, as is shown by the fact that the soldiers of the "Red Eyebrow" peasant army, which played a major role in the overthrow of Wang Mang's Xin dynasty, called themselves "savage tigers." See *Hou Han shu*, ch. 11, p. 477.

28. *Wuzi zhijie*, ch. 2, p. 20b; Han Ying, *Han Shi wai zhuan*, in *Han Wei congshu*, vol. 1 (Taipei: Xinxing, 1977), ch. 8, p. 8a.

29. *Zuo zhuan zhu*, Lord Xi year 33, p. 499; Lord Xuan year 12, p. 729; *Guo yu*, ch. 10, p. 344.

30. *Zuo zhuan zhu*, Lord Zhuang year 12, p. 192; Lord Xiang year 15, p. 1023; year 19, p. 1051; *Shi ji*, ch. 83, pp. 2462–63; ch. 106, p. 2835; *Jing fa*, p. 61.

31. *Zuo zhuan zhu*, Lord Xiang year 4, pp. 935–39.

32. *Zuo zhuan zhu*, Lord Min year 2, pp. 265–66.

33. *Shi ji*, ch. 1, pp. 1–9.

34. Burton Watson, *Early Chinese Literature* (New York: Columbia University, 1961), p. 95.

35. In trying to make sense of the narrative, most Chinese commentators have sought to reduce the number of adversaries to two through the identification of the Fiery Emperor with the Divine Husbandman or Chi You. These attempts, however, have proved unsatisfactory. See Liang Yusheng, *Shi ji zhi yi* (Beijing: Zhonghua, 1981), vol. 1, p. 3; Cui Shu, *Kao xin lu* (Taipei: Shijie, 1968), "Supplement on High Antiquity," ch. 2, pp. 1–5.

36. Li Daoyuan, *Shui jing zhu* (Taipei: Shijie, 1974), ch. 31, pp. 402–03. From commentaries quoted in a Song history we know that in the Tang dynasty several places claimed to be the old site of these wells, and men offered sacrifices there at temples dedicated to the Divine Husbandman. See Luo Bi, *Lu shi*, in *Siku quanshu zhenben jiu ji*, vols. 101–08 (Taipei: Shangwu, 1979), ch. 12, pp. 1b–2a.

37. *Shizi*, ch. 2, p. 5b; *Yi Zhou shu*, quoted in Luo Bi, *Lu shi*, ch. 12, p. 2b.

38. Ying, *Fengsu tongyi jiaoshi*, ch. 1, p. 11.

39. The *Huainanzi* states that prior to the Divine Husbandman men ate grass as their vegetable, drank water, picked wild fruit, and ate the raw meat of shellfish. See *Huainanzi*, ch. 19, p. 331. The *Bohutong* says that before the Divine Husbandman men ate the raw flesh of wild beasts and birds. See *Bohutong de lun*, ch. 1, p. 9b. The early Han writer Lu Jia wrote that before the Divine Husbandman men ate flesh, drank blood, and wore the skins of animals. See *Xin yu*, in *Xinbian zhuzi jicheng*, vol. 2 (Taipei: Shijie, 1974), ch. 1, p. 1. This same vision of the condition of humanity before the sages—eating meat, drinking blood, and wearing skins—appears in the *Li ji*. See *Li ji jijie*, ch. 6, p. 35. For a similar description of the state of men in high antiquity without specific reference to the Divine Husbandman, see *Han Feizi jishi*, ch. 19, p. 1040.

40. The definition of the aristocracy as "meat-eaters" and the role of drinking blood in covenants were both discussed in Chapter One. The nobles were also often metonymically called "the fox furs" (*hu qiu* 狐裘) because they wore animal skins. See *Zuo zhuan zhu*, Lord Xi year 5, p. 304; Lord Xiang year 4, p. 940; year 14, p. 1015; Lord Ai year 17, p. 1706.

41. Marcel Detienne, *Dionysos Slain*, trans. Mireille Muellner and Leonard Muellner (Baltimore: Johns Hopkins University, 1979), pp. 27–28. On the centrality of this mythic opposition between the hunter and agriculture in American civilization, see Slotkin, *Regeneration Through Violence*.

42. As to his refinement of clothing, there are no textual accounts. I can only point out that in later illustrations, such as the Ming dynasty *San cai tu hua*, he appeared dressed in a garment woven from leaves. In this we see perhaps the vegetal garments that replaced animal skins.

43. *Zhanguo ce*, ch. 19, p. 663; *Huainanzi*, ch. 13, p. 215; *Zhuangzi jijie*, ch. 8, p. 195.

44. *Lü Shi chun qiu jishi*, ch. 12, pp. 633–34.

45. One text quotes the famous Warring States diplomat Su Qin to the effect that the Divine Husbandman engaged in warfare, but the context of the statement suggests that it is not to be accepted as accurate. It appears in Su Qin's unsuccessful attempt to persuade the Lord of Qin to conquer the Chinese world through force and declare himself to be emperor. Within the context of the complete story of Su Qin as presented in the *Shi ji* and *Zhanguo ce*, this persuasion is unique in three ways. It is the only speech given before the discovery of the "magical" text that transformed his career, it is his only unsuccessful persuasion, and it is the only speech in which he advocated reliance on naked force as the route to power. Since this first persuasion was his only failure and took place prior to the momentous "conversion" that led to his triumphant career, it is likely that its contents were intended to demonstrate the weaknesses of fact and argument underlying Su Qin's initial rebuff. The mistaken advocacy of brute force was associated with the mistaken insistence that all rulers, even the Divine Husbandman, engaged in warfare.

46. For an excellent treatment of the development of the theme of the mythic opposition between the Divine Husbandman and the Yellow Emperor as competing models of rule, see Graham, "The *Nung-chia*," pp. 94–100.

47. Chen Mengjia, "Shang dai de shenhua yu wushu," *Yanjing xuebao* 20 (1936): 563–66; Edward H. Schafer, "Ritual Exposure in Ancient China," *Harvard Journal of Asiatic Studies* 14 (1951): 130–84; Sarah Allan, "Drought, Human Sacrifice and the Mandate of Heaven in a Lost Text from the *Shang shu*," *Bulletin of the School of Oriental and African Studies* 47:3 (1984): 523–39. For evidence of the practice under the Shang dynasty, see Qiu Xigui, "Shuo buci de 'fen wuwang' yu 'zuo tulong,'" in *Jiaguwen yu Yinshang shi*, ed. Hu Houxuan (Shanghai: Guji, 1983), pp. 21–35; Peter Glum, "Rain Magic at Anyang?" *Bulletin of the Museum of Far Eastern Antiquities* 54 (1982): 241–65.

48. *Shi ji*, ch. 28, pp. 1364, 1401.

49. Jia Yi, *Jiazi xin shu jiaoshi*, annotated by Qi Yuzhang (Taipei: Qi Yuzhang, 1974), ch. 1, p. 172; ch. 2, p. 207; *Di wang shiji*, quoted in *Taiping yulan*, ch. 79, p. 1b; *Guo yu*, ch. 10, p. 356.

50. *Lü Shi chun qiu jishi*, ch. 7, p. 383.

51. *Huainanzi*, ch. 15, p. 1; *Shi ji*, ch. 25, p. 1241.

52. The Wind Monarch was linked to the Yellow Emperor in many texts and in one Han text was explicitly named as the Emperor's teacher. See *Qian fu lun jian*, ch. 1, p. 1. There was also a book entitled *The Yellow Emperor's Canon of the Wind*. See *Taiping yulan*, ch. 9, p. 8b. The cloud titles and army were first mentioned in the *Zuo zhuan*. See *Zuo zhuan zhu*, Lord Zhao year 17, p. 1386.

53. For the observation that the Yellow Emperor had the face of a dragon, see Wang Chong, *Lun heng* (Shanghai: Renmin, 1974), ch. 3, p. 36; *Di wang shiji*, quoted in *Taiping yulan*, ch. 79, pp. 1b–2a; ch. 17, p. 4b. On the appearance of dragons as the sign of the imminent attainment of the Mandate by the Yellow Emperor, see *Shi ji*, ch. 28, p. 1366; *Lü Shi chun qiu jishi*, ch. 13, p. 677. The identity of the creatures mentioned in the above two passages is shown in *Shuo wen jie zi zhu*, ch. 13a, p. 54b. On the constellation Xianyuan as a dragon which ruled storms, see *Shi ji*, ch. 27, p. 1299; *Taiping yulan*, ch. 5, p. 4a; ch. 13, p. 3a; Qutanxida (Gotamasiddha?) et al., *Kaiyuan zhan jing*, in *Siku quanshu zhenben si ji*, vol. 172–81 (Taipei: Shangwu, 1973), ch. 66, pp. 11a, 12a. This last passage preserves a quotation from the Western Han astronomer Shi Shen, which states explicitly that the constellation was the "palace of the Yellow Emperor." On the departure of the Emperor on a dragon, see *Shi ji*, ch. 28, p. 1394.

54. See the *zhengyi* commentary on *Shi ji*, ch. 1, p. 2; *Di wang shiji*, quoted in *Taiping yulan*, ch. 79, pp. 1b–2a, 3a. On the principle of the "immaculate conception" of the sages, see Xu Shen and Zheng Xuan, *Bo wu jing yi yi*, in *Hou zhibuzuzhai congshu* (Chang Shubao Shi, 1884), *tao* 1, ch. 1, pp. 19a–b. For a study by a modern scholar, see Yasui Kōzan, *Isho no seiritsu to sono tenkai* (Tokyo: Kokusho Kankō, 1981), pp. 413–44.

55. The *Mu Tianzi zhuan* records that King Mu "ascended Mt. Kunlun in order to see the palace of the Yellow Emperor and pile a mound on the tomb of Fenglong." See *Mu Tianzi zhuan*, ch. 2, p. 1b. Fenglong, perhaps an onomatopoeia, appears in several Warring States and Han texts as an adjective describing storms, or as the proper name of a spirit of thunder and storms. Another text tells of a beast called *kui* "which caused the wind and rain when it entered the water, and made a sound like thunder. The Yellow Emperor captured it, made a drum of its skin, and beat it with the bone of the 'thunder beast.'" This produced a sound, presumably thunder, that overawed all under Heaven. See *Shan hai jing jiaozhu*, annotated by Yuan Ke (Shanghai: Guji, 1980), ch. 14, p. 361.

56. *Han Feizi jishi*, ch. 3, pp. 171–72.

57. *Zhi lin*, quoted in *Taiping yulan*, ch. 15, pp. 9a–b; *Di wang shiji*, quoted in *Taiping yulan*, ch. 15, p. 7a.

58. *Shan hai jing jiaozhu*, ch. 17, p. 430.

59. *Shan hai jing jiaozhu*, ch. 14, p. 359.

60. In his study on the Yellow Emperor, Mori Yasutarō points out that the Tian lineage, which usurped the throne of Qi in the fourth century B.C., claimed descent from the Yellow Emperor, while the Fiery Emperor was the putative ancestor of the Jiang surnamed lineage that had previously ruled Qi. He then suggests that the story of the battle and the very figure of the Yellow Emperor were invented by the Tian clan to provide a mythic sanction for their usurpation. See Mori, *Kōtei densetsu*, pp. 153–55, 169–70. While the Tian clan may have availed themselves of existing mythology to bolster their claims, the fabrication of such a story is implausible. First, an invented story known only to the Tian clan themselves would have lacked any persuasive authority. Second, creation for political purposes would not explain the existence of all the elements dealing with weapons of fire and water, drought and storm, and popular rituals of drought prevention related to the stories. Third, the record of the existence of the Yellow Emperor's cult in Qin in the fifth century B.C., evidence based on the surviving records of that state, shows that the cult of the Yellow Emperor existed long before the Tian usurpation. Indeed, to account for its links to both Qi and Qin, it must have existed in the Western Zhou, when the Qin rulers moved from Qi. Finally, the argument is based on a faulty reading of the bronze in which the Tian supposedly claimed the Yellow Emperor as an ancestor. The Tian did not claim physical descent from the Yellow Emperor, but "intellectual" descent, in the same way that the Confucians claimed "descent" from Yao and Shun. This is shown by the fact that they trace their "line" from the Yellow Emperor through the two hegemons, Lord Huan of Qi and Lord Wen of Jin. These two were not members of the same lineage, and in fact Lord Huan was the ancestor of the Tian's rivals. In this bronze the Yellow Emperor and the hegemons are invoked as the prototypes of a right to rule based on the proper use of force, the actual grounds that legitimated the Tian seizure of authority.

61. Chen Mengjia, "Shang dai de shenhua," pp. 512–15; Sun Zuoyun, "Chi You kao," *Zhong he yuekan* 4.2 (April, 1941): 31–35.

62. *Taiping yulan*, ch. 79, p. 3b; Ren, *Shu yi ji*, ch. 1, p. 2a; *Huainanzi*, ch. 4, p. 60. A commentary by Li Bo (699–761 A.D.) on a Tang dynasty biography of the Yellow Emperor suggests that this tradition stemmed from southerners' misperception of the flour products eaten by northerners. This explanation, however, appears anachronistic. See "Xianyuan ben ji," in *Zhengtong daozang* (Taipei: Yiwen, 1962), vol. 37, p. 31053a.

63. *Chun qiu fan lu yizheng*, ch. 74, pp. 9a–b. This sacrifice is described in an Eastern Han text, and it included the "exposure of the shaman." See Wei Hong, *Han jiu yi*, in *Index du Han-koan ts'i-tchong*, ed. Chen Tsu-lung (Paris: L'Institut des Hautes Études Chinoises de l'Université de Paris, 1962), supplement, ch. 2 , pp. 7a–b. On Dong Zhongshu building a model of a dragon as part of a rainmaking sacrifice, see Wang, *Lun heng*, ch. 16, p. 245.

64. *Shi ji*, ch. 28, p. 1367.

65. *Taiping yulan*, ch. 270, p. 1a (2); *Shi ji*, ch. 28, p. 1367; *Guanzi jiaozheng*, ch. 23, p. 382; *Shan hai jing jiaozhu*, ch. 17, p. 430; *Shizi*, ch. 2, p. 21a; *Lü Shi chun qiu jishi*, ch. 7, p. 383; *Da Dai li ji*, ch. 11, pp. 3b–4a.

66. Liu Mingshu, "Han Wuliangci huaxiang zhong Huang Di Chi You zhantu kao," *Zhongguo wenhua yanjiu huikan* 2 (September, 1942): 342–65; Bodde, *Festivals in Classical China*, pp. 121–22.

67. *Shi ji*, ch. 27, p. 1348.

68. *Shi ji*, ch. 28, p. 1378.

69. *Shi ji*, ch. 97, p. 2695. This reference to "Chi You's weapons" appears to have become a common expression for military success, for in the *Yan tie lun*, Sang Hongyang (152–80 B.C.) made the following defense of Emperor Wu's campaigns against the Xiongnu: "The Yellow Emperor achieved his task through war, and Tang and Wu completed their filiality through assaults. . . . The former emperors raised up dutiful troops to execute the violent and powerful. . . . Li Mu chased away the Xiongnu in order to expand the northern provinces. These are the acts of Tang and Wu, the weapons of Chi You." See Huan Kuan, *Yan tie lun*, in *Xinbian zhuzi jicheng*, vol. 2 (Taipei: Shijie, 1974), ch. 43, p. 46; ch. 52, p. 54.

70. *Hou Han shu*, ch. 24, p. 859.

71. *Shi ji*, ch. 27, p. 1335. On this comet in the divination manual found at Mawangdui, see Loewe, "The Han View of Comets," pp. 12–13.

72. Indeed, according to one text the famous Taoist scholar, Tao Hongjing (456–536 A.D.) made thirteen "spirit swords" for Emperor Wu of the Liang dynasty, and one of them bore the image of Chi You. See *Taiping yulan*, ch. 343, p. 9a. This indicates that Chi You survived into the sixth century A.D. as a cultic figure associated with weapons.

73. *Shan hai jing jiaozhu*, ch. 14, p. 361; *Taiping yulan*, ch. 13, p. 4. This page quotes numerous examples of describing thunder as a drum.

74. Bodde, *Festivals in Classical China*, pp. 45–220; William Boltz, "Philological Footnotes to the Han New Year Rites," *Journal of the American Oriental Society* 99 (1979): 423–39; Guan Donggui, "Zhongguo gudai de fengshouji ji qi yu 'linian' de guanxi," *Zhongyang Yanjiuyuan Lishi Yuyan Yanjiusuo jikan* 31 (1960): 191–270; Yang Jingshuang, "Fangxiangshi yu danuo," *Zhongyang Yanjiuyuan Lishi Yuyan Yanjiusuo jikan* 31 (1960): 123–65; Ikeda Suetoshi, "Sa rō kō—kodai Chūgoku no nōkō saishi," in *Chūgoku kodai shūkyō shi kenkyū* (Tokyo: Tōkai Daigaku, 1983), pp. 734–59.

75. On the basis of the lack of any phonetic link between the two words (reconstructed as *lap and *dz'ag) and the fact that textual evidence places the *Zha* at the beginning of winter in the tenth month and the *La* at the end of winter in the twelfth month, Derk Bodde argues that they were two separate festivals. However, he suggests that "in pre-imperial times the old year was

separated from the new by an indeterminate but extended period of time, punctuated perhaps by more than one ceremonial," and that the *Zha* and *La* were two coexisting foci of a common concern with the transition from the old to the new year. William Boltz, through a more systematic examination of the uses of the two festivals and a more wide-ranging analysis of their phonetic ties, has concluded that *Zha* and *La* were the earlier and later names respectively for the same festival. See Bodde, *Festivals in Classical China*, pp. 68–74; Boltz, "Philological Footnotes," pp. 426–30.

76. *Li ji jijie*, ch. 7, p. 47.

77. *Li ji jijie*, ch. 7, pp. 47–48. The ceremony of ritually exposing or burning a shaman to end a drought also entailed the wearing of white garments. See Schafer, "Ritual Exposure," pp. 136, 137, 138.

78. The Han dictionary *Shuo wen jie zi* stated that *zha* (蜡 *dzag) was the same as 胆 *tsag, and that both characters meant "maggot." See *Shuo wen jie zi zhu*, ch. 13a, p. 52b. Both these characters belong to a phonetic series which also includes 昔 *siak "anciently, former," 腊 *siak "dried meat, old meat (not fresh)," and 惜 *siak "to regret."

79. *Zhou li zhengyi*, ch. 70, pp. 6a–7b.

80. *Chun qiu fan lu yizheng*, ch. 16, p. 8a.

81. *Shi ji*, ch. 28, p. 1367.

82. *Shi ji*, ch. 1, p. 5.

83. *Li ji jijie*, ch. 11, p. 50.

84. *Hou Han shu, zhi* 5, p. 3130; ch. 10a, p. 424.

85. Ying, *Fengsu tongyi jiaoshi*, ch. 8, pp. 316–20. Earlier in the same work he quotes Deng Ping, one of the scholars responsible for the great calendrical reform of 104 B.C. "*La* is the means by which we send off the virtue of punishments [associated with the autumn and winter, when the punishing power of Heaven and the emperor was in the ascendant]." See p. 312. This explicitly links the *La* to the role of the *Zha* and ties them both to the *Zu* through the image of "sending off." *Quan shanggu Sandai Qin Han Sanguo Liuchao wen*, vol. 2, ch. 31, p. 2b.

86. *Taiping yulan*, ch. 736, p. 6a.

87. Cui Shi (d. ca. 170 A.D.) said that he was a son of the Yellow Emperor. See *Si min yue ling jishi*, annotated by Miao Qiyu and Wan Guoding (Beijing: Nongye, 1981), ch. 1, p. 1. Ying Shao said that he was a son of Gong Gong, and he glossed *Zu* as *zu* (徂 *tsag), a homophone meaning "to go" or "to die." See *Fengsu tongyi jiaoshi*, p. 318. For evidence that the former story became the standard version, see *Wen xuan*, ch. 20, p. 31b; ch. 28, p. 28b; Shen Yue, *Song shu* (Beijing: Zhonghua, 1974), ch. 12, p. 260.

88. In the fifth century A.D. Shen Yue wrote that there were two schools of thought on the origin of the *Zu* sacrifice. Some felt that it was made to an ancestor who had perished on the road. Others said that the ghosts of ancient ancestors, whose names had been lost and gravesites forgotten, had to wander the world and could receive no sacrifice from their families. On a selected day a sacrifice was made to all of them to keep them from doing harm to travelers. *Song shu*, ch. 12, p. 260.

89. Sun Zuoyun, "Ping 'Yinan gu huaxiang shi mu fajue baogao,'" *Kaogu tongxun* 1957 (6): 81–84; Bodde, *Festivals in Classical China*, pp. 75–85, 117–27.

90. *Zhou li zhengyi*, ch. 59, pp. 20a–21a; ch. 54, p. 13b.

91. *Wen xuan*, ch. 2, p. 19a. Another poem in the same anthology described Chi You guarding an imperial procession from demons. See *Wen xuan*, ch. 7, p. 2b. Xun Kuang, writing in the third century B.C., described exorcising shamans who preceded the king when he went out, and performed the travel sacrifices before his journeys. See *Xunzi jijie*, ch. 12, p. 223.

92. Ren, *Shu yi ji*, ch. 1, pp. 2a–b.

93. *Song shu*, ch. 12, p. 260.

94. Horned figures were found in tombs at Changsha as early as the 1920s. For a reproduction, see Ling Chunsheng, "Taidong tu she xiang ji qi zai Taipingyang qu de leiyuan," *Minzuxue Yanjiusuo jikan* 1956 (2): plate 14, no. 3a. For more recent finds, see Henansheng Wenhuaju Wenwu Gongzuodui, "Xinyang Changtaiguan di er hao Chu mu de fajue," *Kaogu tongxun* 1958 (11): 79–80; plates 5, 6; Hubeisheng Wenhuaju Wenwu Gongzuodui, "Hubei Jiangling san zuo Chu mu chutu dapi zhongyao wenwu," *Wenwu* 1966 (5): plate 20; Hubeisheng Jingzhou Diqu Bowuguan, "Jiangling Tianxingguan yi hao Chu mu," *Kaogu xuebao* 1982 (1): 104, plate 23, no. 7. On horned beasts in Tang tombs, see Hubeisheng Wenwu Gongzuodui, "Wuhan diqu yi yue dao ba yue gu muzang de fajue gaikuang," *Wenwu cankao ziliao*, 1957 (1): 70.

95. Zeng Zhaoyu, Jiang Baogeng, and Li Zhongyi, *Yinan gu huaxiang shi mu fajue baogao* (Shanghai: Wenhuabu Wenwu Guanliju, 1956), plates 32–33.

96. For example *Shi ji*, ch. 1, p. 1; ch. 2, p. 45. Sun Zuoyun argued that the Yellow Emperor was originally a bear totem. See "Chi You kao," pp. 39–40. Sarah Allan, in a private communication, has suggested that the character read as "bear" is a mistake for a similar character that identified a kind of dragon. However, this confusion must have taken place prior to the Warring States period to account for its appearance in early texts.

97. *Tian wen shuzheng*, p. 45. Other scholars think that this passage refers to Yu, who turned into a bear in some myths. The common animal associations of these sages may be related to a common origin in shamanistic practices, where the bear was a frequent spirit partner of the shaman.

98. *Shizi*, quoted in *Taiping yulan*, ch. 79, p. 6a.

99. The silk manuscript discovered at Mawangdui states that the Yellow Emperor made a statue of himself, and it had four faces. See *Jing fa*, p. 45. The *Lü Shi chun qiu* also mentioned the four faces of the Yellow Emperor. See *Lü Shi chun qiu jishi*, ch. 14, p. 740. Another text employed the "four ministers" explanation, but in this case they were called the "Yellow Emperor's four eyes." See *Di wang shiji*, quoted in *Taiping yulan*, ch. 79, p. 2a.

On four-eyed beings in ancient Chinese art, archeology, and mythology, see Yang, "Fangxiangshi yu danuo," pp. 132–38.

100. "Xianyuan ben ji," p. 30156b.

101. The story relates that the lord of Jin, having decided to replace his heir, sent him out in command of an army, but instead of the usual regalia of the commander he gave his son a parti-colored costume and a broken bronze disc. Asked to explain the meaning of these items, one man stated, "This is the clothing that the madmen use to expel [or 'curse']." See *Zuo zhuan zhu*, Lord Min year 2, p. 271; *Guo yu*, ch. 7, pp. 277–78. The "madmen" were the chief assistants of the exorcist, and the exorcist himself wore a parti-colored costume under his bearskin. The verb which I have translated as "expel" is *zu* (阻 *tsag), which several commentators gloss as *zu* (詛 *tsag "to curse"), but which was also homophonous with the now familiar *zu* (祖 *tsag) and Ying Shao's cognate gloss *zu* (徂 *tsiag). The original meaning of 阻 was "difficult" or "dangerous," and by extension "to avoid." The classic Chinese dictionary *Er ya* glossed it as *nan* (難). See *Er ya zhushu*, annotated by Xing Bing, in *Shisan jing zhushu*, vol. 8 (Taipei: Yiwen, 1976), ch. 2, p. 17a. This character means "difficult," but it also signified the great seasonal exorcism which was held at the *La*. Hence it is quite possible that the passage says, "This is the costume of the madmen at the *Zu*." If this reading is correct then the madmen participated in the *Zu*, and presumably so did their leader, the exorcist.

102. Jiang Shaoyuan, *Zhongguo gudai lüxing zhi yanjiu* (Shanghai: Shangwu, 1935), pp. 5–77.

103. *Lü Shi chun qiu jishi*, ch. 14, p. 816; Wang, *Lun heng*, ch. 1, p. 2.

104. *Huainanzi*, ch. 11, p. 284; ch. 19, p. 336; Wang, *Lun heng*, ch. 1, p. 2; ch. 18, p. 186; ch. 24, p. 233; *Lü Shi chun qiu jishi*, ch. 14, p. 816. The *Shuo wen* identifies her as "consort of an ancient emperor" and describes her as the "extreme of ugliness [*chou* 醜 *t'iog]." See *Shuo wen jie zi zhu*, ch. 12b, pp. 27a–b. The *Huainanzi* pairs her with another name that the *Shuo wen* defines as "ugly [*chou*] face." See *Huainanzi*, ch. 19, p. 336; *Shuo wen jie zhu*, ch. 8a, p. 36b.

105. *Huainanzi*, ch. 7, p. 104.

106. This spirit-mask, in the graphic variant 倛 *kieg, appeared as early as the *Shi jing*. See Bernhard Karlgren, *Grammata Serica Recensa* (1957; reprint ed., Stockholm: Museum of Far Eastern Antiquities, 1964), p. 250. To describe

the ugliness of Confucius, Xun Kuang said, "He looked like one wearing a spirit-mask [倛 *kieg]." See *Xunzi jijie*, ch. 3, p. 47. The Han commentator explained that the "spirit-mask" in this passage was identical with that of the exorcist. In his commentary on the *Zhou li*, the Eastern Han scholar Zheng Xuan (127–200 A.D.) explained that the exorcist was the same as the "spirit-mask" [魌 *kieg] of his own day. See *Zhou li zhengyi*, ch. 59, p. 20a. In a gloss on the character 魌 *kieg, Xu Shen said that it meant "ugly [*chou* 醜 *t'iog]," and he commented that in his day, the first century A.D., this "spirit-mask" was used to "chase away pestilences." This is a clear reference to the exorcist. He also discussed the graphic variant 魌 *kieg, which also had the meaning of "ugly." See *Shuo wen jie zi zhu*, ch. 9a, p. 14a; ch. 12b, p. 4b.

107. There is some secondary literature on the evidence in archeological finds and wall paintings of the use of masks in ancient China, and much of it centers on the mask of the exorcist. For example, see Yang Jingshuang, "Fangxiangshi yu danuo," pp. 125–32; Itō Seiji, "Kodai Chūgoku no saigi to kasō," *Shigaku* 30:1 (1957): 75–122; Chang Renxia, *Zhongguo gudian yishu* (Shanghai: Shanghai Chubanshe, 1954), pp. 82–104; Chang Renxia, *Dongfang yishu congtan* (Shanghai: Xin Wenyi, 1956), pp. 56–76. These articles and chapters contain references to the individual site reports.

108. See, for example, *Hou Han shu*, ch. 80b, p. 2632; *Wen xuan*, ch. 17, p. 1b; ch. 31, p. 20b.

In several cases the second character in the name, *you* (尤), had the sense of "extraordinary physical appearance." See *Zhuangzi jijie*, ch. 24, p. 161; *Zuo zhuan zhu*, Lord Xiang year 26, p. 1118; Lord Zhao year 28, p. 1493. In these cases it referred to beauty rather than ugliness, but it was a beauty that destroyed men. On this topic, see Glen Dudbridge, *The Tale of Li Wa* (Oxford: Ithaca, 1983), pp. 67–72.

109. On the primary role of the *wu* in securing rain, as well as carrying out the exorcisms, see Werner Eichorn, *Die alte chinesische Religion und das Staatskultwesen* (Leiden: E. J. Brill, 1976), pp. 17–19.

Memories of ritual encounters between the shamaness and the dragon are perhaps preserved in hexagram 54, "The Marrying Younger Daughter." This hexagram was the image of the concubine or secondary wife, and Mo Mu was the secondary wife of the Yellow Emperor. It is composed of the trigram ☳ on top and the trigram ☱ on the bottom. The former represents thunder, the dragon, dark yellow, the eldest son, or a great road. The latter represents a swamp, the youngest daughter, or the shamaness. See *Zhou yi zhengyi*, ch. 5, pp. 31b–34b; ch. 9, pp. 8a, 10a–b. The hexagram as a whole would thus stand as an image of the encounter or mating of the dragon and the shamaness. Since the Yellow Emperor had the features of a dragon, it was also the image of the encounter of the Yellow Emperor with Mo Mu, the shamaness and exorcist.

110. *Xunzi jijie*, ch. 12, p. 223.

111. Thus he led the Yellow Emperor's procession up Mt. Tai to play the clear *jiao* music, and in the *Guanzi* he appeared as one of the "six assistants"

through whom the Yellow Emperor was able to regulate both Heaven and Earth. The account of the creation of weapons in the same work also indicates that Chi You was originally a follower of the Yellow Emperor. See *Guanzi jiaozheng*, ch. 14, p. 242; ch. 23, p. 382. Again, a Han apocryphal text stated that after the battle of Zhuolu, Chi You became the Yellow Emperor's servant and used the weapons he had created to subdue the eight regions. See *Taiping yulan*, ch. 872, p. 11b.

112. Qiu, "Shuo buci de 'fen wuwang' yu 'zuo tulong,'" pp. 23–26.

113. Allan, "Drought, Human Sacrifice, and the Mandate of Heaven."

114. *Shi ji*, ch. 27, p. 1299.

115. In the Eastern Han exorcism, not only did the exorcist and his assistants wield spears and shields, but after cleansing the palace, the torches employed and, by extension, the baleful influences removed were carried off to the Luo River by the cavalry from the army camps near the capital. See *Hou Han shu*, *zhi* 5, p. 3128. By the fifth century A.D. under the Northern Wei, the exorcism at the *La* festival had become the occasion for a general military exercise and review. See *Wei shu*, ch. 108.4, p. 2810.

116. I equate the "Yellow Emperor" (*Huang Di* 黃帝), with the "Venerable Emperor" (*Huang Di* 皇帝). The two characters were homophonous and appeared as loan words for one another. See Yang, "Zhongguo gudai shi daolun," pp. 189–93. Pointing out that there is no evidence of a belief in the Yellow Emperor prior to the end of the fifth century B.C., he suggests that the name was originally *huang* (皇) and equates this figure with the God on High of the Shang. While equating *huang* (黃) with *huang* (皇) is solid, his assignment of priority to the latter cannot be maintained. See Mitarai Masaru, "On the Mythology of the Yellow Sovereign," in *East Asian Civilizations: New Attempts at Understanding Civilizations*, Vol. 2, *Nation and Mythology*, ed. Wolfram Eberhard, Krzysztof Gawlikowski, and Carl-Albrecht Seyschab (Bremen: Simon & Magiera, 1983), pp. 68–74. The new oracle bone evidence on the relation of the character *huang* (黃) to the ceremony of burning or exposing the shaman also suggests the priority of this graph, because it is linked to the actual role of the Yellow Emperor in myth and ritual.

117. The passages cited here appear in *Shang shu zhengyi*, ch. 19, pp. 17a–18b, 20a, 31b–32a.
   Noah Fehl has suggested that this account was put together from several independent literary traditions. See "Notes on the 'Lü Xing': Proposing a Documentary Theory," *The Chung Chi Journal* 9:1 (November, 1969): 10–36. While he makes some interesting suggestions, his argument suffers from the common weakness of all *quellenscheidung*. Although useful for tracing the multiple origins of various elements, it can offer no explanation of the coherence or meaning of the text for its ultimate authors or audience. Since the 'Lü Xing' had taken shape by the early Warring States period, one should seek the internal coherence and meaning that it had for the men of that time. See Matsumoto

Masaaki, *Shunjū Sengoku ni okeru Shōsho no tenkai* (Tokyo: Kazema, 1968), pp. 399–404.

118. Rene Girard, *Violence and the Sacred*, trans. Patrick Gregory (Baltimore: Johns Hopkins University, 1977) pp. 14–15.

119. Derk Bodde and Clarence Morris, *Law in Imperial China* (Philadelphia: University of Pennsylvania, 1967), pp. 12–15.

120. *Jing fa*, p. 1.

121. Wang, *Lun heng*, ch. 17, pp. 270–71.

122. *Shi ji*, ch. 2, p. 83.

123. *Shuo wen jie zi zhu*, ch. 4a, p. 35b.

124. On the evidence from the oracle inscriptions, see Akatsuka Kiyoshi, *Chūgoku kodai no shūkyō to bunka* (Tokyo: Kadokawa, 1977), pp. 105–22. *Hou Han shu*, ch. 87, p. 2876.

125. The *Bei shi* refers to a Qiang state called the "Red Goat State" because of a huge, fiery-colored goat that dwelt there. See Li Yanshou, *Bei shi* (Beijing: Zhonghua, 1974), ch. 96, p. 3191. A local history of Gansu tells of an "Earthen Goat Spirit Temple" supposedly founded during the Qin dynasty at a spot where Qin Shihuang encountered the spirits of two clay statues of goats. Cited in Yinshun Fashi, *Zhongguo gudai minzu shenhua zhi yanjiu*, p. 63.

126. *Hou Han shu*, ch. 87, p. 2869; *Shi ji*, ch. 36, p. 1585; *Guo yu*, ch. 16, p. 511.

127. *Gui zang*, ch. 1, p. 32b.

128. *Mozi jiangu*, ch. 8, pp. 144–45.

129. Shiratori Kiyoshi, *Nihon Chūgoku kodaihō no kenkyū: shinpan to seimei no kenkyū* (Shiratori Kiyoshi Sensei Shoju Kinenkai, 1972), pp. 111–64.

130. The three aspects correspond to the levels in a third century B.C. model of decline in the forms of human struggle. See *Han Feizi jishi*, ch. 18, p. 974; ch. 19, p. 1042. These passages state that in high antiquity men struggled through the Way, in later times through cunning wisdom, and in the present through force. As "the Way" refers to conduct guided by ritual and moral principle, "cunning wisdom" to the stratagems of the general or rhetorician, and "force" to the armies, these three levels of struggle tally with the three aspects of the innovations of the Yellow Emperor.

131. *Liezi jishi*, ch. 2, pp. 83–86. The Yellow Emperor's role as a commander of beasts is also suggested by the titles of the tunes for the drum composed to commemorate his victory over Chi You. See *Gui zang*, ch. 1, p. 31b.

132. Ge Hong, *Baopuzi nei pian jiaoshi*, annotated by Wang Ming (Beijing: Zhonghua, 1980), ch. 17, p. 287.

133. A man named Zhao Bing from Donghai Commandery also obtained these "ax spells" and was thereby able to command winds, storms, rivers, and tigers. See *Hou Han shu*, ch. 82b, pp. 2741–42.

On references to the "Yellow Lord" in later Taoism, see Donald Holzman, "Ts'ao Chih and the Immortals," *Asia Major*, Third Series 1:1 (1988): 53–54, note 130.

134. *Taiping yulan*, ch. 79, pp. 2b, 3a.

135. *Wen xuan*, ch. 14, p. 12a.

136. *Han shu*, ch. 30, pp. 1758–59.

137. *Taiping yulan*, ch. 79, p. 3b. Another version of this story contains the information that after the Yellow Emperor received the tally, Chi You became his servant and conquered the world for him. Yet another text tells the same story, save that the tally was sent not by a nameless celestial woman, but by the Queen Mother of the West. See *Taiping yulan*, ch. 872, p. 11b; ch. 736, pp. 6a–b; ch. 694, p. 4a.

138. *Lü Shi chun qiu jishi*, ch. 12, p. 648.

139. *Lü Shi chun qiu jishi*, ch. 5, pp. 284–85.

140. *Jing fa*: "Heaven has its seasons of life and death, while the state has its policies of life and death. To nourish life in accord with the propagating of Heaven is called 'culture' [*wen* 文]. To attack and cause things to die in accord with the killing of Heaven is called 'martiality' [*wu* 武]. When culture and martiality are used together, then all under Heaven will obey."—p. 13.

"For movement and quietude to accord with Heaven and Earth is called 'culture.' For killing. . . [character missing]. . . when the season is proper is called 'martiality.'"—p. 22.

"To kill at the peak of *yang* and propagate at the peak of *yin* is called 'going against the commands of *yin* and *yang*.'"—p. 23.

"To follow the seasons of Heaven and attack what Heaven would destroy is called 'martiality.'"—p. 24.

"To begin with culture and end with martiality is the Way of Heaven and Earth. That the four seasons have their proper measure is the ordering principle of Heaven and Earth. That the sun, moon, and constellations have their proper numerical periods is the rule of Heaven and Earth. That for three seasons there is completion and achievement and for one season punishment and killing is the Way of Heaven and Earth. . . . First established and then disposed, first propagated and then killed, the four seasons have their successive policies, and at the end they begin again. This is the ordering principle of government affairs."—p. 38.

"Without trammels or restraints correct them with punishments and virtuous potency. In spring and summer carry out virtuous potency; in fall and winter carry out punishments."—p. 49.

"The sage has no craft; he holds to the reversals of the seasons. In his benefactions and love of the people he shares the Way of Heaven. He holds himself correct to await Heaven and quiescent to await men; he does not abandon the punishments of Heaven nor break his covenants. In all decisions he matches the seasons of Heaven."—p. 50.

"To conflict is inauspicious, but without conflict there is no way to achieve merit. He who follows Heaven flourishes, and he who goes against Heaven perishes. . . . Heaven's virtuous potency is clear and brilliant, but without punishments it cannot function. Magnificent are the punishments of Heaven, but without virtuous potency they must be exhausted. Punishments and virtuous potency nourish each other; going in opposite directions they achieve completeness. Punishments are dark and virtuous potency light; punishments are *yin* and virtuous potency *yang*; punishments are hidden and virtuous potency manifest."—p. 53.

141. Marcel Granet, *Danses et légendes de la Chine ancienne* (1926; reprint ed., Paris: Presses Universitaires de France, 1959), vol. 1, pp. 212–97; Max Kaltenmark, "Religion and Politics in the China of the Tsin and the Han," *Diogenes* 34 (1961): 38.

142. Allan, "Drought, Human Sacrifice, and the Mandate of Heaven," pp. 530–34.

143. The manuscript actually contains two versions of the Yellow Emperor's victory over Chi You. However, the overarching structure of the two accounts is the same, and they vary only in the inclusion of more or less details on various points. Thus it is reasonable to treat them as a single account. See *Jing fa*, pp. 54–55, 60–62.

144. See *Gongyang zhuan zhushu*, Lord Xiang year 27, ch. 21, pp. 6a–b. The formula of the curse in this text and that used by the Yellow Emperor both employ the same verb, *shi* (視), in the special sense of "to imitate."

145. It is interesting that the Qing scholar Jiang Yong (1681–1762 A.D.) argued that the practice of swearing blood covenants began with Chi You. Although he probably assumed that this use of violence to bind good faith would have begun with the creator of violence, it seems that the covenant in fact mythically began with Chi You, in the sense that he was the prototype of the sacrifice that sanctified the oath. See Jiang, *Qun jing buyi*, ch. 12, p. 4b.

146. On the three days of seclusion and fasting, see *Li ji jijie*, ch. 4, p. 71; ch. 5, pp. 4, 27, 45; ch. 7, pp. 10, 72; ch. 12, pp. 45, 73; ch. 13, p. 10. These passages state that only after this period of purification and concentration could one have dealings with spirits and actually see the recipients of the sacrifice.

147. *Taiping yulan*, ch. 15, pp. 7a, 9a–b, 9b; ch. 79, p. 3b; ch. 694, p. 4a; ch. 736, pp. 6a–b; ch. 872, p. 11b.

148. The main sources of this story are *Zuo zhuan zhu*, Lord Xiang year 4, pp. 936–39; *Di wang shiji*, quoted in *Shi ji*, ch. 2, pp. 86–87. Various aspects of the story also appear in *Tian wen shuzheng*, pp. 54–59; *Li sao zuanyi*, anno-

tated by You Guoen (Beijing: Zhonghua, 1980), pp. 221–22; *Mengzi zhengyi*, ch. 8, p. 341; *Huainanzi*, ch. 14, p. 235; *Zuo zhuan zhu*, Lord Zhao year 28, p. 1493.

The act of feeding Yi to his son perhaps sought to avoid vengeance by forcing his participation in the "sacrifice," or perhaps it was intended to disqualify him from the succession. An echo of the practice may appear at *Shi ji*, ch. 7, pp. 327–28, where Xiang Yu threatened to boil the father of Liu Bang, and the latter requested to share the stew.

149. For cases of King Zhou feeding feudal lords to his court, see *Li ji jijie*, ch. 9, p. 3; *Di wang shiji*, quoted in *Taiping yulan*, ch. 381, p. 3b; *Beitang shu chao*, ch. 41, p. 5b; *Tian wen shuzheng*, pp. 100–01. On tricking King Wen into eating his own son, see *Di wang shiji*, quoted in *Shi ji*, ch. 3, p. 107; *Tian wen shuzheng*, p. 107.

150. See *Yi Zhou shu*, ch. 4, pp. 2a–3a, 11a–b; *Di wang shiji*, quoted in *Taiping yulan*, ch. 84, pp. 8a–b; *Tian wen shuzheng*, pp. 94, 109—for the argument that this second passage pertains to the story of Kings Zhou and Wu, see Jiang, *Qu Yuan fu jiaozhu*, pp. 360–61; Guo, *Qu Yuan fu jinyi*, p. 104; *Xunzi jijie*, ch. 12, p. 219; ch. 15, p. 260; *Mozi jiangu*, ch. 8, p. 153; *Shi ji*, ch. 4, p. 124; ch. 32, p. 1480; ch. 128, p. 3234.

151. *Shizi*, ch. 2, p. 13a.

152. *Zuo zhuan zhu*, Lord Xi year 19, p. 383; *Huainanzi*, ch. 15, p. 257.

153. *Mengzi zhengyi*, ch. 14, p. 565. For Gu's argument, see Gu, "*Yi Zhou shu* 'shi fu pian,'" pp. 1–2, 17–21, 24–31.

154. An example of the former response was the Song dynasty writer Su Shi (1036–1101 A.D.). See *Su Dongpo quan ji* (Taipei: Heluo, 1975), vol. 1, p. 581. An example of the latter was Liang Yusheng (1745–1819 A.D.). See *Shi ji zhi yi*, vol. 1, pp. 86–87.

155. On the ritual handling of the moral problems of dynastic transitions, see Wechsler, *Offerings of Jade and Silk*, especially Chapters Three and Four. On the "bad last ruler" see Arthur F. Wright, "Sui Yang-ti: Personality and Stereotype," in *The Confucian Persuasion*, ed. Arthur F. Wright (Stanford: Stanford University, 1960), pp. 47–76.

156. In his classic study of Zhou mythology, Bernhard Karlgren argued that most of the myths preserved in "free" Zhou texts were hero legends and nature myths linked with the hero cults devoted to the ancestors of the various noble lineages. See Karlgren, "Legends and Cults," p. 345. In contrast with this "heroic" mythology of the nobility, the tales of the sage-kings presented a "civilizing" mythology of empire.

Chapter Six

1. Paul Unschuld, *Medicine in China: A History of Ideas* (Berkeley: University of California, 1985), ch. 3.

2. Karlgren, *Grammata Serica Recensa*, p. 140, #517c.

3. Hiraoka Teikichi, *Kainanshi ni arawareta ki no kenkyū* (Tokyo: Kan Gi Bunka Gakkai, 1961), pp. 48, 191; Akatsuka Kiyoshi, "Chūgoku tetsugaku no hasseiteki jijitsu—gogyōkan no seiritsu o chūshin toshite," manuscript, p. 11; Akatsuka Kiyoshi, "Chūgoku kodai ni okeru kaze no shinkō to gogyō setsu," in *Nishō-gakusha Daigaku ronshū* (Tokyo: Nishō-gakusha Daigaku, 1977), pp. 52–91. The first is based on evidence from the *Huainanzi* and the *Lü Shi chun qiu*. The essays by Akatsuka are based primarily on oracle bones.

4. *Zhuangzi jijie*, ch. 1, p. 6; *Han shu*, ch. 21a, p. 959; Ying, *Fengsu tongyi jiaoshi*, ch. 8, p. 303; *Wen xuan*, ch. 13, p. 2a; ch. 25, p. 20b; ch. 45, p. 22b.

5. Chen Mengjia, *Yinxu buci zongshu* (Beijing: Kexue, 1956), p. 226.

6. *Zhuangzi jijie*, ch. 1, p. 1; ch. 4, pp. 105, 108.

7. Hu Houxuan, "Jiaguwen sifang fengming kaozheng," in *Jiaguxue Shang shi luncong chu ji* (Taipei: Datong, 1972), vol. 1, pp. 369–81; Yan Yiping, "Buci sifang feng xinyi," in *Jiagu wenzi yanjiu* (Taipei: Yiwen, 1976), pp. 173–85.

8. A later subdivision of the year into eight winds was made to serve other mathematical correlations, but it did not map gracefully onto the annual cycle, and it supplemented rather than replaced the four directional winds. See John S. Major, "Notes on the nomenclature of winds and directions in the early Han," *T'oung Pao* 65:1–3 (1979): 66–80.

9. *Huang Di suwen zhijie*, annotated by Gao Shizong (Shanghai: Kexue Jishu Wenxian, 1980), p. 36.

10. *Zhuangzi jijie*, ch. 14, p. 95; *Zuo zhuan zhu*, Lord Xi year 4, p. 289; *Shang shu zhengyi*, ch. 20, p. 8b. See also Chow Tse-tsung, "The Childbirth Myth and Ancient Chinese Medicine: A Study of Aspects of the *Wu* Tradition," in *Ancient China: Studies in Early Civilization*, ed. David T. Roy and Tsuen-hsuin Tsien (Hong Kong: Chinese University, 1978), p. 77.

11. *Zhou yi zhengyi*, ch. 5, p. 4b; *Taiping yulan*, ch. 9, p. 3a.

12. *Shi ji*, ch. 25, p. 1240.

13. *Han shu*, ch. 28b; p. 1640. A similar passage in the *Li ji* asserted that men have a constant nature, but that their emotions are inconstant. It associated the various emotions with types of music and described how the former kings harmonized men's vital *qi* and created proper social order through music. See *Li ji jijie*, ch. 10, pp. 39–41.

14. See, for example, *Li ji jijie*, ch. 10, pp. 38, 44; *Xunzi jijie*, ch. 14, p. 254 (2).

15. Ying, *Fengsu tongyi jiaoshi*, preface, p. 1.

16. *Mengzi zhengyi*, ch. 13, p. 550.

17. *Huainanzi*, ch. 4, p. 59.

18. *Wen xuan*, ch. 13, pp. 2b–4a. Translation from Watson, *Chinese Rhyme-Prose*, pp. 22–24.

19. For an excellent study of early Chinese music and its role in theories of cosmology and government, see Kenneth Dewoskin, *A Song for One or Two: Music and the Concept of Art in Early China*, Michigan Papers in Chinese Studies no. 42 (Ann Arbor: University of Michigan, 1982).

20. Gu Jiegang, "Lun *Shi jing* suolu quan wei yuege," in *Gu shi bian*, vol. 3b, pp. 608–57.

21. *Mao shi zhengyi*, ch. 18.3, p. 10b; *Shan hai jing jiaozhu*, ch. 11, pp. 395–96; ch. 18, p. 464; *Zuo zhuan zhu*, Lord Cheng year 9, p. 845.

22. *Zhuangzi jijie*, ch. 1, p. 6.

23. *Zuo zhuan zhu*, Lord Yin year 5, p. 46. On music as a means of ordering the winds for the sake of proper government, see also *Guo yu*, ch. 3, p. 128; ch. 14, p. 460.

24. *Li ji jijie*, ch. 10, p. 44.

25. *Shang shu da zhuan jijiao*, ch. 1, p. 11b.

26. *Guo yu*, ch. 14, p. 460.

27. *Han Feizi jishi*, ch. 3, pp. 170–72. The *Huainanzi* also wrote of the "music of perished states," referring to it as *feng*. See *Huainanzi*, ch. 9, p. 133.

28. *Zuo zhuan zhu*, Lord Xiang year 29, pp. 1161–65; *Shi ji*, ch. 31, pp. 1452–53. Another passage stated that Confucius was able to recognize King Wen in his music. See *Shi ji*, ch. 47, p. 1925.

29. *Shizi*, ch. 2, p. 32a.

30. *Liezi jishi*, ch. 5, p. 178.

31. *Shi ji*, ch. 47, pp. 1919–20, note 2, citing the *Qin cao*.

32. *Li ji jijie*, ch. 10, p. 24.

33. On the mythology of the phoenix, see Mori, *Kōtei densetsu*, pp. 89–122.

34. *Zhuangzi jijie*, ch. 6, p. 138.

35. *Zuo zhuan zhu*, Lord Zhao year 10, p. 1317.

36. *Lun yu zhengyi*, ch. 16, p. 359.

37. *Shang Jun shu zhuyi*, ch. 6, p. 163.

38. *Jing fa*, p. 54.

39. *Shizi*, ch. 2, p. 21b.

40. *Mengzi zhengyi*, ch. 3, pp. 111–19.

41. *Wei Liaozi zhijie*, ch. 1, pp. 15b, 16b.

42. *Wuzi zhijie*, ch. 2, p. 37b.

43. *Sun Bin bingfa*, p. 72.

44. *Sima fa zhijie*, ch. 3, p. 40a. See also ch. 4, p. 45a: "In warfare one can carry on a long fight through strength, but one conquers through *qi*."

45. *Sunzi zhijie*, ch. 2, p. 20b; *Zhanguo ce*, ch. 13, p. 467.

46. *Mengzi zhengyi*, ch. 3, pp. 115–16.

47. *Han Feizi jishi*, ch. 19, p. 1042. A similar passage is found in *Han Feizi jishi*, ch. 18, p. 974.

48. *Xunzi jijie*, ch. 12, p. 222.

49. Dai, *Da Dai li ji*, ch. 75, pp. 4a–5a. Wu Zixu likewise criticized King Fuchai of Wu for ignoring the advice of age and surrounding himself with reckless youth. See *Guo yu*, ch. 19, p. 602.

50. *Mozi jiangu*, ch. 11, p. 264.

51. *Shi ji*, ch. 47, p. 1926. See also *Mengzi zhengyi*, ch. 8, pp. 341–42.

52. *Yanzi chun qiu jishi*, ch. 2, pp. 164–70. For similar moral lessons, see *Yanzi chun qiu jishi*, ch. 1, p. 6; ch. 7, pp. 430–31.

53. *Wuzi zhijie*, ch. 4, p. 36a.

54. *Wuzi zhijie*, ch. 4, p. 37b.

55. *Li ji jijie*, ch. 12, p. 75; *Shang shu da zhuan jijiao*, ch. 2, pp. 1b–2a; *Huayang guo zhi*, ch. 1, p. 1b.

56. On the *wu* dance, see Lan Yongwei, *Chun qiu shiqi de bubing*, pp. 204–07.

57. *Li ji jijie*, ch. 10, pp. 46–47, 59–65, 71–72; *Xunzi jijie*, ch. 14, pp. 252–53.

58. *Zhou li zhengyi*, ch. 55, pp. 11b–14b. See also ch. 23, pp. 1a–7a. Xun Kuang stated explicitly that the drum was the "lord of music" and hence "like Heaven." See *Xunzi jijie*, ch. 14, pp. 255–56.

59. *Zuo zhuan zhu*, Lord Cheng year 2, pp. 791–92. The same idea underlies the account of an earlier engagement in the same campaign: "The lord

of Qi personally drummed the warriors to storm the wall, and in three days took Long."

An analogous phenomenon in modern times is the use of the *bombos* in Argentina. These kettle drums, three to four feet in diameter, were originally used at carnivals and then employed at soccer games to excite crowds and direct cheering. The Peronists introduced them into political rallies, and they are now used by all political parties to stir up crowds. An observer who witnessed their use in an attempt to sway voting for the dean of the engineering faculty at the University of Cordoba described their effect thus: "It was frightening. It gave me the feeling that we were at the mercy of blind forces." See Amos Elon, "Letter From Argentina," *The New Yorker*, 21 July 1986, p. 83. This use of pounding rhythms to stir up crowds and sweep them along "at the mercy of blind forces" is the role of the drums in accounts of battles in the *Zuo zhuan*.

60. *Zuo zhuan zhu*, Lord Zhuang year 10, p. 183. See also *Zuo zhuan zhu*, Lord Xi year 22, p. 398: "In the three armies you use what is beneficial; with bells and drums you use sound to [arouse] *qi*."

61. Liu Xi, *Shi ming* (Taipei: Shangwu, 1965), ch. 4, p. 15. Xun Kuang similarly asserted that proper music led to military strength and improper music to weakness. See *Xunzi jijie*, ch. 14, p. 253.

62. *Zuo zhuan zhu*, Lord Xiang year 18, p. 1043.

63. *Tai Gong liu tao zhijie*, ch. 1, pp. 82b–85a.

64. *Zhou li zhengyi*, ch. 45, pp. 1a–11a, esp. p. 11a.

65. *Mozi jiangu*, ch. 15, p. 339.

66. *Tai Gong liu tao zhijie*, ch. 1, pp. 85a–88a. The practice of using a special banner to prognosticate from the wind was associated with the Yellow Emperor and appears in works attributed to him. See *Taiping yulan*, ch. 339, p. 7a (2); ch. 338, p. 5a.

67. Manfred Porkert, *Theoretical Foundations of Chinese Medicine* (Cambridge, Ma.: MIT Press, 1978), pp. 13–19; Manfred Porkert, "Untersuchungen einiger philosophisch-wissenschaftlicher Grundbegriffe und Beziehungen im Chinesischen," *Zeitschrift der deutschen morgenländischen Gesellschaft* 110.2 (1961): 422–52; Manfred Porkert, "Wissenschaftliches Denken im alten China: Das System der energetischen Beziehungen," *Antaios* 2.6 (March, 1961): 532–51.

68. *Sunzi zhijie*, ch. 1, pp. 1b, 36a.

69. *Sunzi zhijie*, ch. 1, pp. 30b, 38a; ch. 2, p. 4a. The Ruler of Fate was a deity who determined the life spans of men. For other comparisons of the commander to this divinity, see *Sunzi zhijie*, ch. 1, p. 19b; *Tai Gong liu tao zhijie*, ch. 3, pp. 75a, 76b.

70. "He who has mastered military arts is like one hiding in the Earth or concealing himself in the depths of Heaven. He appears out of nothingness."— *Wei Liaozi zhijie*, ch. 1, p. 5a.

"Above the commander is not controlled by Heaven, below he is not controlled by Earth, and in the middle he is not controlled by man. He is broad, so that he cannot be provoked to anger. He is pure so that he cannot be controlled with material objects."—*Wei Liaozi zhijie*, ch. 1, p. 6b.

"The commander is the officer of death, so he is only employed when there is no alternative. He has no Heaven above him, no Earth beneath him, no ruler behind him, and no enemy in front of him. When this one man leads the army, then they are like wolves or tigers, like wind or rain, like thunder or lightning. Shattering like an earthquake, dark and mysterious like the primeval chaos, the whole human world is terrified."—*Wei Liaozi zhijie*, ch. 2, pp. 42a–b.

"The commander is the officer of cosmic principle, the master of the myriad objects. He is not partial to any individual, and because he is not partial he can regulate and command the myriad objects as he encounters them."—*Wei Liaozi zhijie*, ch. 2, p. 47a.

"Only one who knows the Way can give security to a great state, expand the power of a great state's king, or preserve intact the people of a great state. To know the Way means: above, to know the Way of Heaven; below, to know the Way of Earth; within, to obtain the minds of the people; outside, to know the predispositions of the enemy; in formations, to know the order of the Eight Formations. If he sees a victory then he will fight, if not then he will remain still. This is a king's commander."—*Sun Bin bingfa*, p. 59.

"It is the principle of Heaven and Earth that when something reaches the extreme it reverses. The sun and the moon reach fullness or a high point and then decline. The four seasons rise and fall in turn. The five phases [in sequence] conquer and lose. The myriad objects are born and die. The myriad living creatures are able and then fail. The power of circumstances and dispositions shift between surfeit and insufficiency. Thus any multitude that has form can be named, any multitude that can be named can be conquered. So the sage conquers each of the myriad objects with what will conquer it, and his victories are inexhaustible. Warfare is the mutual conquest of forms. No form cannot be conquered, but none knows the form that will conquer it. The transformations in forms and their conquests are coextensive with Heaven and Earth and hence inexhaustible. . . . Each form is conquered by what conquers it; you cannot conquer the myriad forms with a single form. That which rules the forms is single, but that which will conquer cannot be single. So one skilled in warfare perceives the enemy's strengths and thereby knows his weaknesses. He perceives his deficiencies and thereby knows his surpluses. He perceives his conquest just as he sees the sun and moon, and he dictates conquest just like water extinguishing a fire."—*Sun Bin bingfa*, pp. 121–22.

"The sage is illuminated in the movements of Heaven and Earth, so who can know his limits. He obeys the Way of *yin* and *yang* and follows their periods. He matches the swelling and shrinking of Heaven and Earth and thereby

achieves constancy. As to the lives and deaths of things, he follows the dispositions of Heaven and Earth."—*Tai Gong liu tao zhijie*, ch. 3, p. 75a.

"The general does not speak yet they defend; this is his structive force
[*shen*]. He does not see and yet perceives; this is his illumination. So if he knows
the Way of structive force and illumination none will be able to match him in the
field or establish a state against him."—*Tai Gong liu tao zhijie*, ch. 3, p. 76b.

"Of old, those who were skilled in battle raised up their armies in sequence. Their formations followed the Five Phases and their battles the five
sounds. Their commands reached the limits of Heaven and dwelt with the spirits
[*shen*]. Every sort of strategem was generated and completed, but through using
the one [Way] they were never exhausted. They took illumination as their model
and trod the subtle Way. At equilibrium they went beyond all advances or retreats and became a third to Heaven and Earth. . . . They avoided death to
attain life and moved with the seasons to seize victory. . . One who attains this
Way can command even men from the market place and move with the current,
soaring aloft with the Way. Soaring aloft they capture and firmly fixed they
defend. Inhaling and exhaling, standing and moving, changing with the
seasons."—*Heguanzi jie*, ch. 3, pp. 4a–5a.

71. *Jing fa*, pp. 1–3.

72. These phrases clearly echo descriptions of the commander's art in the
Sunzi. Thus its famous opening lines read: "Military action is the great service of
the state. It is the field of life and death, the way of survival and destruction [*cun
wang* 存亡]." See *Sunzi zhijie*, ch. 1, p. 1a. So when the author of the *Jing fa*
uses identical phrases to offer the ruler knowledge of the Way of life and death,
of how to "perish [*wang*] and yet survive [*cun*]," he clearly signals that he is
speaking of military strategy. Moreover, the ability to be cut apart and reunite,
or to die and return to life, is precisely the virtue that the *Sunzi* assigns to the
commander who is skilled in the extraordinary. See *Sunzi zhijie*, ch. 1, p. 36a.
The same phrases also appear in *Wei Liaozi zhijie*, ch. 5, p. 24a; *Tai Gong liu
tao zhijie*, ch. 3, p. 60b.

73. *Jing fa*, pp. 8, 22, 18–19, 33–35.

74. *Jing fa*, p. 12.

75. *Jing fa*, p. 8.

76. *Jing fa*, pp. 28–29.

77. *Jing fa*, pp. 41–42.

78. *Huainanzi*, ch. 9, p. 141. See also *Li ji jijie*, ch. 10, p. 44: "The eight
winds follow the pitchpipes and are not treacherous."

79. *Shang shu zhengyi*, ch. 4, p. 23b; ch. 11, p. 10a; *Mengzi zhengyi*, ch.
9, p. 381.

80. *Mengzi zhengyi*, ch. 13, p. 517; ch. 2, p. 89; ch. 3, p. 133; ch. 7,

p. 295; ch. 9, pp. 379–80. See also *Li ji zhengyi*, annotated by Kong Yingda et al., in *Shisan jing zhushu*, vol. 5 (Taipei: Yiwen, 1976), ch. 52, p. 1a.

81. Herbert Fingarette, *Confucius—the Secular as Sacred* (New York: Harper & Row, 1972).

82. *Zuo zhuan zhu*, Lord Huan year 6, pp. 111–12; Lord Zhuang year 10, pp. 182–83; year 14, pp. 196–97; year 32, pp. 251–53; Lord Xi year 5, pp. 309–10; year 15, p. 365; year 16, p. 369; year 19, pp. 381–82; year 21, p. 390; year 28, pp. 467–68; Lord Xuan year 15, pp. 762–63. The idea that social disorder could produce prodigies and natural disasters through the people's *qi* also appears in *Chun qiu fan lu yizheng*, ch. 17, p. 7b.

83. *Mengzi zhengyi*, ch. 1, p. 44; ch. 2, p. 90; ch. 3, p. 137; ch. 7, pp. 295–96; ch. 5, p. 194; ch. 8, p. 336.

84. *Mengzi zhengyi*, ch. 2, p. 90; ch. 6, p. 256.

85. *Xunzi jijie*, ch. 4, p. 76; ch. 5, p. 97 (2); ch. 6, pp. 117, 123; ch. 10, p. 188; ch. 12, p. 216.

86. *Mengzi zhengyi*, ch. 7, p. 309; ch. 8, p. 324; ch. 11, p. 441; ch. 13, pp. 527–28; *Xunzi jijie*, ch. 12, p. 214.

87. *Mengzi zhengyi*, ch. 5, pp. 218–19; ch. 7, pp. 286, 288–89; ch. 8, pp. 322, 350; ch. 11, pp. 465–67.

88. *Xunzi jijie*, ch. 15, pp. 265–67.

89. *Xunzi jijie*, ch. 5, p. 104; ch. 10, pp. 184, 185; ch. 12, p. 224; ch. 15, pp. 264–65; ch. 17, p. 296; *Mengzi zhengyi*, ch. 3, pp. 117–18; ch. 13, p. 528.

90. *Guanzi jiaozheng*, ch. 15, p. 285.

91. Carl von Clausewitz, *On War*, trans. Michael Howard and Peter Paret (Princeton: Princeton University, 1976), p. 89.

92. Frederic Wakeman, Jr., *The Fall of Imperial China* (New York: The Free Press, 1975), pp. 5–6.

93. *Xunzi jijie*, ch. 2, p. 44; ch. 3, pp. 50, 58–59; ch. 4, p. 82; ch. 5, pp. 96, 104–05; ch. 6, pp. 114, 115, 116, 118–19; ch. 12, p. 216 (2); ch. 13, pp. 231, 243; ch. 14, p. 255; ch. 16, p. 276.

Works Cited

Primary Sources

Bei shi 北史. Compiled by Li Yanshou 李延壽 (ca. 600–680 A.D.). Beijing: Zhonghua, 1974.

Beitang shu chao 北堂書抄. Compiled by Yu Shinan 虞世南 (558–638 A.D.). Taipei: Xinxing, 1971.

Bo wu jing yiyi 駁五經異義. Xu Shen 許慎 (d. ca. 120 A.D.) and Zheng Xuan 鄭玄 (127–200 A.D.). In *Hou zhibuzuzhai congshu* 後知不足齋叢書, *tao* 1, *ce* 1. Chang Shubao Shi 常熟鮑氏刊本, 1884.

Bohutong de lun 白虎通德論. Compiled by Ban Gu 班固 (32–92 A.D.) et al. In *Han Wei congshu* 漢魏叢書, vol. 1. Taipei: Xinxing, 1977.

Chun qiu fan lu yizheng 春秋繁露義証. Attributed to Dong Zhongshu 董仲舒 (179–104 B.C.). Annotated by Su Yu 蘇輿. Taipei: Heluo, 1975.

Chun qiu Gongyang zhuan zhushu 春秋公羊傳注疏. Annotated by Xu Yan 徐彥 (Tang dynasty). In *Shisan jing zhushu* 十三經注疏, vol. 7. Taipei: Yiwen, 1976.

Chun qiu Guliang zhuan zhushu 春秋穀梁傳注疏. Annotated by Yang Shixun 楊士勛 (Tang dynasty). In *Shisan jing zhushu*, vol. 7. Taipei: Yiwen, 1976.

Chun qiu Zuo zhuan zhu 春秋左傳注. Annotated by Yang Bojun 楊伯峻. Beijing: Zhonghua, 1981.

Cui, Shi 崔寔 (d. ca. 170 A.D.). *Simin yueling jishi* 四民月令集釋. Annotated by Miao Qiyu 繆啓愉 and Wan Guoding 禺國鼎. Beijing: Nongye, 1981.

Da Dai li ji 大戴禮記. Attributed to Dai De 戴德 (fl. 72 B.C.). In *Han Wei congshu*, vol. 1. Taipei: Xinxing, 1977.

327

Di wang shiji jicun 帝王世紀輯存. Compiled by Xu Zongyuan 徐宗元. Beijing: Zhonghua, 1964.

Dongguan Han ji 東觀漢記. Compiled by Liu Zhen 劉珍 (Second century A.D.). Taipei: Zhonghua, n.d.

Du, You 杜佑 (735–812 A.D.). *Tong dian* 通典. Taipei: Xinxing, 1963.

Er ya zhushu 爾雅注疏. Annotated by Xing Bing 邢昺 (932–1010 A.D.). In *Shisan jing zhushu*, vol. 8. Taipei: Yiwen, 1976.

Feng, Menglong 馮夢龍 (ca. 1574 – ca. 1645 A.D.). *Dong Zhou lieguo zhi* 東周列國志. Revised by Cai Yuanfang 蔡元放 (Seventeenth century A.D.). Taipei: Sanmin, 1976.

Gao, Cheng 高承 (Eleventh century A.D.). *Shiwu jiyuan* 事物記源. In *Xi yin xian congshu* 惜陰軒叢書, *tao* 11, *ce* 73–82. Hongdao Shuyuan 宏道書院, 1846.

Ge, Hong 葛洪 (ca. 280–342 A.D.). *Baopuzi nei pian jiaoshi* 抱樸子內篇校釋. Annotated by Wang Ming 王明. Beijing: Zhonghua, 1980.

Guanzi jiaozheng 管子校正. Annotated by Dai Wang 戴望 (1837–1873 A.D.). In *Xinbian zhuzi jicheng* 新編諸子集成, vol. 5. Taipei: Shijie, 1974.

Gui zang 歸藏, in *Yuhan Shan fang ji yi shu* 玉函山房輯佚書. Compiled by Ma Guohan 馬國翰 (1794–1857 A.D.). Changsha, 1883.

Guo yu 國語. Annotated by Shanghai Shifan Daxue Guji Zhengli Xiaozu 上海師範大學古籍整理小組. Shanghai: Guji, 1978.

Han Feizi jishi 韓非子集釋. Attributed to Han Fei 韓非 (d. 233 B.C.). Annotated by Chen Qiyou 陳奇猷. Shanghai: Renmin, 1974.

Han shu 漢書. Compiled by Ban Gu 班固 (32–92 A.D.). Beijing: Zhonghua, 1962.

Han shu buzhu 漢書補注. Annotated by Wang Xianqian 王先謙 (1842-1917 A.D.). In *Ershiwu shi* 二十五史, vols. 3–4. Taipei: Yiwen, 1956 [?].

Han Shi wai zhuan 韓氏外傳. Attributed to Han Ying 韓嬰 (f. 150 B.C.). In *Han Wei congshu*, vol. 1. Taipei: Xinxing, 1977.

Heguanzi jie 鶡冠子解. Annotated by Lu Dian 陸佃 (1042–1102 A.D.). Taipei: Shijie, 1962.

Hou Han shu 後漢書. Compiled by Fan Ye 范曄 (398–445 A.D.) et al. Beijing: Zhonghua, 1965.

Hu, Zhenheng 胡震亨 (fl. 1630 A.D.). *Tang yin gui qian* 唐音癸籤. Shanghai: Gudian Wenxue, 1957.

Huainanzi 淮南子. Compiled under the auspices of Liu An 劉安 (d. 122 B.C.). In *Xinbian zhuzi jicheng*, vol. 7. Taipei: Shijie, 1974.

Huang Di suwen zhijie 黃帝素問直解. Annotated by Gao Shizong 高士宗. Shanghai: Kexue Jishu Wenxian, 1980.

Huayang guo zhi 華陽國志. Attributed to Chang Qu 常璩 (fl. 347 A.D.). Taipei: Zhonghua, 1966.

Jiazi xin shu jiaoshi 賈子新書校釋. Attributed to Jia Yi 賈誼 (201–169 B.C.). Annotated by Qi Yuzhang 祁玉章. Taipei: Qi Yuzhang, 1974.

Jin shu 晉書. Compiled by Fang Xuanling 方玄齡 (578–648 A.D.) et al. Beijing: Zhonghua, 1974.

Jing fa 經法. Annotated by Mawangdui Han Mu Boshu Zhengli Xiaozu 馬王堆漢墓帛書整理小組. Beijing: Wenwu, 1976.

Kongzi jia yu 孔子家語. Annotated by Wang Su 王肅 (195–256 A.D.). In *Xinbian zhuzi jicheng*, vol. 2. Taipei: Shijie, 1974.

Laozi dao de jing zhu 老子道德經注. Annotated by Lu Deming 陸德明 (556–627 A.D.). In *Xinbian zhuzi jicheng*, vol. 3. Taipei: Shijie, 1974.

Li, Daoyuan 麗道元 (d. 527 A.D.). *Shui jing zhu* 水經注. Taipei: Shijie, 1974.

Li ji jijie 禮記集解. Annotated by Sun Xidan 孫希旦 (1736–1784 A.D.). Shanghai: Shangwu, 1936.

Li sao zuanyi 離騷纂義. Attributed to Qu Yuan 屈原 (d. ca. 300 B.C.). Annotated by You Guoen 游國恩. Beijing: Zhonghua, 1980.

Lie nü zhuan 列女傳. Attributed to Liu Xiang 劉向 (77–6 B.C.). Taipei: Zhonghua, n.d.

Lie xian zhuan 列仙傳. Attributed to Liu Xiang. In *Zhengtong daozang* 正統道藏, vol. 8. Taipei: Yiwen, 1962.

Liezi jishi 列子集釋. Annotated by Yang Bojun 楊伯峻. Beijing: Zhonghua, 1979.

Liu, Jingshu 劉敬叔 (Fifth century A.D.). *Yi yuan* 異苑. In *Xue jin tao yuan* 學津討原, *tao* 31, *ce* 131. Shanghai: Shangwu, n.d.

Liu, Xi 劉熙 (d. ca. 219 A.D.). *Shi ming* 釋名. Taipei: Shangwu, 1965.

Liu, Yiqing 劉義慶 (403–444 A.D.). *Shi shuo xin yu jiaojian* 世說新語校箋. Annotated by Yang Yong 楊勇. Hong Kong: Dazhong, 1969.

Lü Shi chun qiu jishi 呂氏春秋集釋. Compiled under the auspices of Lü Buwei 呂不韋 (290–235 B.C.). Annotated by Chen Qiyou 陳奇猷. Shanghai: Xuelin, 1984.

Lun yu zhengyi 論語正義. Attributed to Confucius 孔丘 (551–479 B.C.) and his disciples. Annotated by Liu Baonan 劉寶楠 (1791–1855 A.D.) and Liu Gongmian 劉恭冕 (1824–1883 A.D.). In *Xinbian zhuzi jicheng*, vol. 1. Taipei: Shijie, 1974.

Luo, Bi 羅泌 (d. ca. 1176 A.D.). *Lu shi* 路史. In *Siku quanshu zhenben jiu ji* 四庫全書珍本九集, vols. 101–08. Taipei: Shangwu, 1979.

Ma, Duanlin 馬端臨 (fl. 1273 A.D.). *Wenxian tongkao* 文獻通考. Taipei: Xinxing, 1963.

Mao shi zhengyi 毛氏正義. Annotated by Kong Yingda 孔穎達 (574–648 A.D.) et al. In *Shisan jing zhushu*, vol. 2. Taipei: Yiwen, 1976.

Mengzi zhengyi 孟子正義. Attributed to Mencius 孟軻 (ca. 372–ca. 289 B.C.) and his disciples. Annotated by Jiao Xun 焦盾 (1763–1820 A.D.). In *Xinbian zhuzi jicheng*, vol. 1. Taipei: Shijie, 1974.

Mozi jiangu 墨子間詁. Attributed to Mo Di 墨翟 (ca. 480–ca. 390 B.C.), his disciples, and later followers. Annotated by Sun Yirang 孫詒讓 (1848–1908 A.D.). In *Xinbian zhuzi jicheng*, vol. 6. Taipei: Shijie, 1974.

Mu Tianzi zhuan 穆天子傳. Attributed to Guo Pu 郭璞 (276–324 A.D.). In *Han Wei congshu*, vol. 1. Taipei: Xinxing, 1977.

Quan shanggu Sandai Qin Han Sanguo Liuchao wen 全上古三代秦漢三國

六朝文. Compiled by Yan Kejun 嚴可均 (1762–1843 A.D.). Beijing: Zhonghua, 1958.

Qutanxida 瞿曇悉達 [Gotamasiddha?] (Eighth century A.D.) et al. *Kaiyuan zhan jing* 開元占經. In *Siku quanshu zhenben si ji* 四庫全書珍本四集, vols. 172–81. Taipei: Shangwu, 1973.

Ren, Fang 任昉 (460–508 A.D.). *Shu yi ji* 述異記. In *Han Wei congshu*, vol. 2. Taipei: Xinxing, 1977.

(Jiaozheng) Sanfu huang tu 校正三輔黃圖. Annotated by Zhang Zongxiang 張宗祥. Shanghai: Gudian, 1958.

Sanguo zhi 三國志. Compiled by Chen Shou 陳壽 (233–297 A.D.). Beijing: Zhonghua, 1959.

Shan hai jing jiaozhu 山海經校注. Annotated by Yuan Ke 袁珂. Shanghai: Guji, 1980.

Shang Jun shu zhuyi 商君書注譯. Attributed to Shang Yang 商鞅 (390–338 B.C.), his disciples, and later followers. Annotated by Gao Heng 高亨. Beijing: Zhonghua, 1974.

Shang shu da zhuan jijiao 尚書大傳輯校. Annotated by Chen Shouqi 陳壽祺 (1771–1834 A.D.). In *Huang Qing jingjie xubian* 皇清經解續編, *ce* 354–56. Compiled by Wang Xianqian. Nanqing Shuyuan 南菁書院, 1888.

Shang shu zhengyi 尚書正義. Annotated by Kong Yingda et al. In *Shisan jing zhushu*, vol. 1. Taipei: Yiwen, 1976.

Shi ji 史記. Begun by Sima Tan 司馬談 (d. 112 B.C.) and primarily composed by Sima Qian 司馬遷 (ca. 145 – ca. 86 B.C.). Beijing: Zhonghua, 1959.

Shizi 尸子. Zhejiang Shuju 浙江書局, Huhailou edition 胡海樓刊本, 1877.

Shuihudi Qin mu zhujian 睡虎地秦墓竹簡. Annotated by Shuihudi Qin Mu Zhujian Zhengli Xiaozu 睡虎地秦墓竹簡整理小組. Beijing: Wenwu, 1978.

Shuo wen jie zi zhu 說文解字注. Compiled by Xu Shen 許慎 (d. ca. 120 A.D.). Annotated by Duan Yucai 段玉裁 (1735–1815 A.D.). Taipei: Yiwen, 1974.

Sima fa zhijie 司馬法直解. Annotated by Liu Yin 劉寅 (1302–1355 A.D.). In

Mingben wujing qi shu zhijie 明本武經七書直解, vol. 1. Taipei: Shi Di Jiaoyu, 1972.

Sima Guang 司馬光 (1019–1086 A.D.) et al. *Zi zhi tongjian* 資治通鑑. Hong Kong: Zhonghua, 1971.

Song shu 宋書. Compiled by Shen Yue 沈約 (441–513 A.D.). Beijing: Zhonghua, 1974.

Sou shen ji 搜神集. Compiled by Gan Bao 干寶 (fl. 317–350 A.D.). Beijing: Zhonghua, 1979.

Sun Bin bingfa 孫臏兵法. Annotated by Yinqueshan Han Mu Zhujian Zhengli Xiaozu 銀雀山漢墓竹簡整理小組. Beijing: Wenwu, 1975.

"Sun Pang douzhi yanyi" 孫龐鬥志寅義. In *Baihua Zhongguo gudian xiaoshuo daxi* 白話中國古典小說大係. Taipei: Heluo, 1980.

(Shiyi jia zhu) Sunzi 十一家注孫子. Shanghai: Guji, 1978.

Sunzi zhijie 孫子直解. Annotated by Liu Yin. In *Mingben wujing qi shu zhijie*, vol. 1. Taipei: Shi Di Jiaoyu, 1972.

Tai Gong liu tao zhijie 太公六韜直解. Annotated by Liu Yin. In *Mingben wujing qi shu zhijie*, vol. 2. Taipei: Shi Di Jiaoyu, 1972.

Taiping yulan 太平御覽. Compiled by Li Fang 李昉 (925–996 A.D.) et al. Taipei: Shangwu, 1935.

Tang Taizong Li Weigong wendui zhijie 唐太宗李衛公問對直解. Annotated by Liu Yin. In *Mingben wujing qi shu zhijie*, vols. 1–2. Taipei: Shi Di Jiaoyu, 1972.

Tian wen shuzheng 天問疏證. Annotated by Wen Yiduo 聞一多. Beijing: Sanlian, 1980.

Wang, Chong 王充 (27–ca. 100 A.D.). *Lun heng* 論衡. Shanghai: Renmin, 1974.

Wang, Dingbao 王定保 (ca. 870–955 A.D.). *Tang zhe yan* 唐摭言. Shanghai: Guji, 1978.

Wang, Fu 王符 (90–165 A.D.). *Qian fu lun jian* 潛夫論箋. Annotated by Wang

Jipei 王繼培 (b. 1775 A.D., *jinshi* in 1805) and Peng Duo 彭鐸. Beijing: Zhonghua, 1979.

Wei, Hong 衛宏 (fl. 25–57 A.D.). *Han jiu yi* 漢舊儀. In *Index du Hankoan ts'i-chong* 漢官七種通檢. Edited by Chen Tsu-long 陳祚龍. Paris: L'Institut des Hautes Études Chinoises de l'Université de Paris, 1962.

Wei Liaozi zhijie 尉繚子直解. Annotated by Liu Yin. In *Mingben wujing qi shu zhijie*, vol. 2. Taipei: Shi Di Jiaoyu, 1972.

Wei shu 魏書. Compiled by Wei Shou 魏收 (502–572 A.D.). Beijing: Zhonghua, 1974.

Wen xuan 文選. Compiled by Xiao Tong 蕭統 (501–531 A.D.). Taipei: Zhengzhong, 1971.

Wuzi zhijie 吳子直解. Annotated by Liu Yin. In *Mingben wujing qi shu zhijie*, vol. 1. Taipei: Shi Di Jiaoyu, 1972.

Wu, Zimu 吳自牧 (ca. 1256–ca. 1334 A.D.). *Meng liang lu* 夢梁錄. In *Biji xiaoshuo daquan* 筆記小說大全, vol. 1. Taipei: Xinxing, 1962.

Xi jing za ji 西京雜紀. Attributed to Ge Hong. In *Han Wei congshu*, vol. 1. Taipei: Xinxing, 1977.

"Xianyuan ben ji" 軒轅本紀. In *Zhengtong daozang*, vol. 37. Taipei: Yiwen, 1962.

Xin yu 新語. Attributed to Lu Jia 陸賈 (Third–second centuries B.C.). In *Xinbian zhuzi jicheng*, vol. 2. Taipei: Shijie, 1974.

Xunzi jijie 荀子集解. Attributed to Xun Kuang 荀況 (313–238 B.C.) and his disciples. Annotated by Wang Xianqian. In *Xinbian zhuzi jicheng*, vol. 2. Taipei: Shijie, 1974.

Xun, Yue 荀悅 (148–209 A.D.). *Shen jian* 申鑒. In *Han Wei congshu*, vol. 2. Taipei: Xinxing, 1977.

Yan tie lun 鹽鐵論. Recorded by Huan Kuan 桓寬 (fl. 73 B.C.). In *Xinbian zhuzi jicheng*, vol. 2. Taipei: Shijie, 1974.

Yanzi chun qiu jishi 晏子春秋集釋. Annotated by Wu Zeyu 吳則虞. Beijing: Zhonghua, 1962.

Yang, Xiong 楊雄 (53 B.C.–18 A.D.). *Yangzi fa yan* 楊子法言. In *Xinbian zhuzi jicheng*, vol. 2. Taipei: Shijie, 1974.

Yang, Xuanzhi 楊衒之 (d. ca. 555 A.D.). *Loyang qielan ji jiaoshi* 洛陽伽藍記校釋. Annotated by Zhou Zumo 周祖謨. Hong Kong: Zhonghua, 1976.

Yi li zhengyi 儀禮正義. Annotated by Hu Peihui 胡培翬 (1782–1849 A.D.). Shanghai: Zhonghua, 1934.

Yi Zhou shu 逸周書. Annotated by Kong Chao 孔晁 (Third century A.D.). In *Han Wei congshu*, vol. 1. Taipei: Xinxing, 1977.

Ying, Shao 應劭 (d. ca. 206 A.D.). *Fengsu tongyi jiaoshi* 風俗通義校釋. Annotated by Wu Shuping 吳樹平. Tianjin: Renmin, 1980.

Yuan qu xuan 元曲選. Compiled by Zang Jinshu 藏晉叔 (fl. 1580–1616 A.D.). Beijing: Zhonghua, 1958.

"Yutang xianhua" 玉堂閒話. In *Shuo fu* 說郛, *tao* 11, *ce* 49. Weiwanshan Tang 委宛山堂, 1647.

Yuan, Hong 袁宏 (328–376 A.D.). *Hou Han ji* 後漢記. Shanghai: Shangwu, 1974.

Zhanguo ce 戰國策. Compiled by Liu Xiang. Shanghai: Guji, 1978.

Zhao, Lin 趙璘 (fl. 836–846 A.D.). *Yin hua lu* 因話錄. In *Biji xiaoshuo daquan*, vol. 1. Taipei: Xinxing, 1962.

Zhou li zhengyi 周禮正義. Annotated by Sun Yirang. Shanghai: Zhonghua, 1934.

Zhou li zhushu 周禮注疏. Annotated by Jia Gongyan 賈公彥 (Seventh century A.D.). In *Shisan jing zhushu*, vol. 3. Taipei: Yiwen, 1976.

Zhou yi zhengyi 周易正義. Annotated by Kong Yingda et al. In *Shisan jing zhushu*, vol. 1. Taipei: Yiwen, 1976.

Zhuangzi jijie 莊子集解. Annotated by Wang Xianqian. In *Xinbian zhuzi jicheng*, vol. 4. Taipei: Shijie, 1974.

Zhuangzi jishi 莊子集釋. Annotated by Guo Qingfan 享慶藩 (1844–1897 A.D.). Taipei: Shijie, 1974.

Secondary Works in Chinese and Japanese

Akatsuka, Kiyoshi 赤塚忠. "Chūgoku kodai ni okeru kaze no shinkō to gogyō setsu" 中國古代における風の信仰と五行說. In *Nishō-gakusha Daigaku ronshū* 二松學社大學論集. Tokyo: Nishō-gakusha Daigaku, 1977.

————. *Chūgoku kodai no shūkyō to bunka* 中國古代の宗教と文化. Tokyo: Kadokawa, 1977.

————. "Chūgoku tetsugaku no hasseiteki jijitsu—gogyōkan no seiritsu wo chūsin to shite" 中國哲學の發生的事実—五行観の成立お中心として. Undated manuscript.

Anhuisheng Wenwu Guanli Weiyuanhui 安徽省文物管理委員會. "Dingyuanxian Bawangzhuang gu huaxiang shi mu" 定遠縣壩王庄古畫像石墓. *Wenwu* 文物 1959 (12): 43–46.

Chang, Renxia 常任俠. *Dongfang yishu congtan* 東方藝術叢談. Shanghai: Xin Wenyi, 1956.

————. *Zhongguo gudian yishu* 中國古典藝術. Shanghai: Shanghai Chuban, 1954.

Chen, Gongrou 陳公柔. "Shisang li, Jixi li zhong suo jizai de sangzang zhidu" 士喪禮, 既夕禮中所記載的喪藏制度. *Kaogu xuebao* 考古学报 1956 (4): 67–84.

Chen, Mengjia 陳夢家. "Dong Zhou mengshi yu chutu zaishu" 東周盟誓與出土載書. *Kaogu* 考古 1966 (5): 271–79.

————. "Shang dai de shenhua yu wushu" 商代的神話與巫術. *Yanjing xuebao* 燕京學報 20 (1936): 485–576.

————. "Xi Zhou tongqi duan dai (5)" 西周銅器斷代. *Kaogu xuebao* 1956 (3): 105–27.

————. *Yinxu buci zongshu* 殷墟卜辭綜述. Beijing: Kexue, 1956.

Chen, Pan 陳槃. "Huang Di shiji yanbian kao" 黃帝事蹟演變考. *Guoli Zhongshan Daxue Yuyan Lishi Yanjiusuo zhoukan* 國立中山大學語言歷史研究所週刊 3 (1928): 921–35.

————. "Zhanguo Qin Han jian fangshi kaolun" 戰國秦漢間方士考論. *Zhong-*

yang Yanjiuyuan Lishi Yuyan Yanjiusuo jikan 中央研究院歷史語言研究所集刊 17 (1948): 7–57.

Chen, Yinglue 陳英略. *Guiguzi douzhi mijue* 鬼谷子鬥智秘訣. Taipei: Xin Dongli Zazhi She, 1972.

———. *Guiguzi shenji bingfa* 鬼谷子神機兵法. Taipei: Xin Dongli Zazhi She, 1972.

Chen, Zhi 陳直. *Han shu xin zheng* 漢書新証. Tianjin: Renmin, 1979.

Cui, Shu 崔述 (1740–1816 A.D.). *Kao xin lu* 考信錄. Taipei: Shijie, 1968.

Ding, Shan 丁山. "You Chen Hou Yinzi dun ming Huang Di lun wu di" 由陳侯因資鐓銘黃帝論五帝. *Zhongyang Yanjiuyuan Lishi Yuyan Yanjiusuo jikan* 3–4 (1934): 517–36.

Dong, Zuobin 董作賓 et al. *Xiaotun dierben: Yinxu wenzi: yibian*, part 2 小屯第二本:殷墟文字:乙編. Nanjing: Academia Sinica, 1949.

Du, Naisong 杜廼松. "Cong lieding zhidu kan ke ji fu li de fandong xing" 從列鼎制度看克己復禮的反動性. *Kaogu* 1976 (1): 17–21.

Du, Zhengsheng 杜正勝. "Bianhu qimin de chuxian ji qi lishi yiyi: bianhu qimin de yanjiu zhi yi" 編戶齊民的出現及其歷史義意:編戶齊民的研究之一. *Zhongyang Yanjiuyuan Lishi Yuyan Yanjiusuo jikan* 54:3 (1983): 77–111.

———. *Zhou dai chengbang* 周代城邦. Taipei: Lianjing, 1979.

———. "Zhou dai fengjian jieti hou de junzheng xin zhixu: bianhu qimin de yanjiu zhi er" 周代封建解體後的軍政新秩序:編戶齊民的研究之二. *Zhongyang Yanjiuyuan Lishi Yuyan Yanjiusuo jikan* 55:1 (1984): 73–113.

Gao, Min 高敏. *Yunmeng Qin jian chutan* 雲夢秦簡初探. 2nd ed. rev. Henan: Renmin, 1981.

Gao, Ming 高明. "Houma zaimeng zhu kao" 侯馬載盟主考. In *Guwenzi yanjiu* 古文字研究, no. 1. Beijing: Zhonghua, 1979.

Gao, Zhixi 高至喜. "Ji Changsha Changde chutu nuji de Zhanguo mu—jian tan youguan nuji gongshi de jige wenti" 記長沙常德出土弩機的戰國墓—兼談有關弩機弓矢的幾箇問題. *Wenwu* 1964 (6): 33–45.

Gu, Derong 顧德融. "Zhongguo gudai renxun renshengzhe de shenfen tanxi" 中國古代人殉人牲者的身分探析. *Zhongguo shi yanjiu* 中國史研究 1982 (2): 112–23.

Gu, Donggao 顧棟高. *Chun qiu da shi biao* 春秋大事表. In *Huang Qing jingjie xubian*, *ce* 67–133. Nanqing Shuyuan, 1888.

Gu, Jiegang 顧頡剛 et al., eds. *Gu shi bian* 古史辨. 1926–1941. Reprint. Shanghai: Guji, 1982.

———. "Lun *Shi jing* suo lu quan wei yuege" 論詩經所錄全為樂歌. In *Gu shi bian*, vol. 3. Shanghai: Guji, 1982.

———. *Qin Han de fangshi yu rusheng* 秦漢的方士與儒生. Reprint. Shanghai: Shangwu, 1955.

———. "Taolun gu shi da Liu Hu er xiansheng" 討論古史答劉胡二先生. In *Gu shi bian*, vol. 1. Shanghai: Guji, 1982.

———. "*Yi Zhou shu* 'Shi fu pian' jiaozhu xieding yu pinglun" 逸周書 世俘篇校注寫定與評論. *Wen shi* 文史 2 (April, 1963): 1–42.

———. "Yu Qian Xuantong Xiansheng lun gu shi shu" 與錢玄同先生論古史書. In *Gu shi bian*, vol. 1. Shanghai: Guji, 1982.

——— and Yang, Xiangkui 楊向奎. *San huang kao* 三皇考. Beijing: Yenching Journal of Chinese Studies Monograph Series no. 8, 1936.

Gu, Yanwu 顧炎武 (1613–1682 A.D.). *Yuanchaoben ri zhi lu* 原抄本日知錄. Taipei: Pingping, 1975.

Guan, Donggui 管東貴. "Zhongguo gudai de fengshouji ji qi yu 'linian' de guanxi" 中國古代的豐收祭及其與歷年的關係. *Zhongyang Yanjiuyuan Lishi Yuyan Yanjiusuo jikan* 31 (1960): 191–270.

Guan, Tianxiang 關天相 and Ji, Gang 冀剛. "Liangshan Han mu" 梁山漢墓. *Wenwu cankao ziliao* 文物參考資料 1955 (5): 38–39.

Guo, Baojun 郭寶鈞. *Shanbiaozhen yu Liulige* 山彪鎮與琉璃閣. Beijing: Kexue, 1959.

Guo, Moruo 郭沫若. *Buci tongzuan* 卜辭通纂. Tokyo: Bunkyodo, 1933.

———. "Chutu wenwu er san shi: xin chu Houma mengshu shiwen" 出土文物二三事：新出侯馬盟書釋文. *Wenwu* 1972 (3): 1–10.

———. "Houma mengshu shitan" 侯馬盟書試探. *Wenwu* 1966 (2): 4–6.

———. "Jixia Huang–Lao xuepai de pipan" 稷下黃老學派的批判. In *Shi pipan shu* 十批判書. Beijing: Kexue, 1956.

———. *Jiagu wenzi yanjiu* 甲骨文字研究. Shanghai: Dadong, 1931.

———. *Liang Zhou jinwenci daxi kaoshi* 兩周金文辭大系考釋. Tokyo: Bunkyodo, 1935.

———. *Qu Yuan fu jinyi* 屈原賦今譯. Beijing: Renmin Wenxue, 1981.

———. "Taodu, Nuwa, Jialing" 桃都, 女媧, 加陵. *Wenwu* 1973 (1): 2–6.

Han, Lianqi 韓連琪. "Chun qiu Zhanguo shidai tudi suoyouzhi de yanhua he nongcun gongshe de jieti" 春秋戰國時代土地所有制的演化和農村公社的解體. In *Lishi luncong* 歷史論叢, no. 2. Edited by Wang Zhongluo and Ge Mouchun. Ji'nan: Qilu, 1981.

———. "Lun Chun qiu shidai falü zhidu de yanbian" 論春秋時代法律制度的演變. *Zhongguo shi yanjiu* 1983 (4): 2–12.

Hayashi, Minao 林巳奈夫. *Chūgoku Yin Shū jidai no buki* 中國殷周時代の武器. Kyoto: Kyōto Daigaku Jinbun Kagaku Kenkyūsho, 1972.

He, Ziquan 何茲全. "Zhou dai tudi zhidu he ta de yanbian" 周代土地制度和它的演變. *Lishi yanjiu* 歷史研究 1964 (3): 145–62.

Henansheng Bowuguan 河南省博物館. "Jiyuan Sijiangou san zuo Han mu de fajue" 濟源泗澗溝三座漢墓的發掘. *Wenwu* 1973 (2): 46–53.

———. "Nanyang Han huaxiang shi gai shu" 南陽漢畫像石概述. *Wenwu* 1973 (6): 16–25.

Henansheng Wenhuaju Wenwu Gongzuodui 河南省文化局文物工作隊. "Nanyang Han dai shike mu" 南陽漢代石刻墓. *Wenwu cankao ziliao* 1958 (10): 239–62.

———. "Henan Nanyang Yangguansi Han huaxiang shi mu fajue" 河南南陽楊官寺漢畫像石墓發掘. *Kaogu xuebao* 1963 (1): 111–39.

———. "Xinyang Changtaiguan di er hao Chu mu de fajue" 信陽長台關第二號楚墓的發掘. *Kaogu tongxun* 1958 (11): 79–80.

Hihara, Toshikuni 日原利國. *Shunjū Kuyōden no kenkyū* 春秋公羊傳の研究. Tokyo: Sōbunsha, 1976.

Hiraoka, Teikichi 平剛禎吉. *Kainanshi ni arawareta ki no kenkyū* 淮南子に表れた氣の研究. Tokyo: Kan Gi Bunka Gakkai, 1961.

Hu, Chenggong 胡承珙 (1771–1832 A.D.). *Mao shi houjian* 毛詩後箋. Qiushitang 求是堂, 1837.

Hu, Houxuan 胡厚宣. "Jiaguwen sifang fengming kaozheng" 甲骨文四方風名考証. In *Jiaguxue Shang shi luncong chu ji* 甲骨學商史論叢初集, vol. 1. Taipei: Datong, 1972.

Huaiyinshi Bowuguan 淮陰市博物館. "Huaiyin Gaozhuang Zhanguo mu" 淮陰高庄戰國墓. *Kaogu xuebao* 1988 (2): 189–232.

Huang, Shengzhang 黃盛璋. "Guanyu Houma mengshu de zhuyao wenti" 關於侯馬盟書的主要問題. *Zhongyuan wenwu* 中原文物 1981 (2): 27–33.

Huang, Zhanyue 黃展岳. "Wo guo gudai de renxun he rensheng" 我國古代的人殉和人牲. *Kaogu* 1974 (3): 153–63.

Hubeisheng Jingzhou Diqu Bowuguan 湖北省荆州地區博物館. "Jiangling Tianxingguan yi hao Chu mu" 江陵天星觀一號楚墓. *Kaogu xuebao* 1982 (1): 71–116.

Hubeisheng Wenhuaju Wenwu Gongzuodui 湖北省文化局文物工作隊. "Hubei Jiangling san zuo Chu mu chutu dapi zhongyao wenwu" 湖北江陵三座楚墓出土大批重要文物. *Wenwu* 1966 (5): 33–55.

———. "Wuhan diqu yi yue dao ba yue gu muzang de fajue gaikuang" 武漢地區一月到八月古墓藏的發掘概況. *Wenwu cankao ziliao* 1957 (1): 69–70.

Hunansheng Bowuguan 湖南省博物館. "Changsha Shazitang Xi Han mu fajue jianbao" 長沙砂子塘西漢墓發掘簡報. *Wenwu* 1963 (2): 13–24.

Ikeda, Suetoshi 池田末利. "Sa rō kō—kodai Chūgoku no nōkō saishi" 蜡臘考—古代中國の農耕祭祀. In *Chūgoku kodai shūkyō shi kenkyū* 中國古代宗教史研究. Tokyo: Tōkai Daigaku, 1983.

Itō, Michiharu 伊藤道治. *Chūgoku kodai ōchō no keisei* 中國古代王朝の形成. Tokyo: Sōbunsha, 1975.

Itō, Seiji 伊藤清司. "Kodai Chūgoku no saigi to kasō" 古代中國の祭儀と假裝.
Shigaku 史學 30:1 (1957): 75–122.

———. "Yakusoku kō" 約束考. *Shigaku* 30:4 (1958): 39–53.

Jiang, Liangfu 姜亮夫. *Qu Yuan fu jiaoshi* 屈原賦校釋. Beijing: Renmin Wenxue, 1957.

Jiang, Shaoyuan 江紹源. *Zhongguo gudai lüxing zhi yanjiu* 中國古代旅行之
研究. Shanghai: Shangwu, 1935.

Jiang, Yong 江永 (1681–1762 A.D.). *Qun jing buyi* 群經補義. Shuyetang
書業堂, 1792.

Kaguraoka, Masatoshi 神樂岡昌俊. "Sonshi to Rōshi" 孫子と老子. *Tōhō
shūkyō* 東方宗教 37 (April, 1971): 39–50.

Kaizuka, Shigeki 貝塚茂樹. "Chūgoku kodai toshi kokka no seikaku"
中國古代都市國家の性格. In *Kaizuka Shigeki chosaku shū* 貝塚
茂樹著作集, vol. 2. Tokyo: Chūō Kōron, 1978.

———. "Chūgoku kodai toshi in okeru minkai no seido" 中國古代都市にお
ける民會の制度. In *Kaizuka Shigeki chosaku shū*, vol. 2. Tokyo:
Chūō Kōron, 1978.

———. *Chūgoku no kodai kokka* 中國の古代國家. In *Kaizuka Shigeki chosaku
shū*, vol. 1. Tokyo: Chūō Kōron, 1978.

Kamada, Shigeo 鎌田重雄. *Kandai shi kenkyū* 漢代史研究. 2nd ed. rev. Tokyo:
Kawada Shobō, 1949.

Kanaya, Osamu 金谷治. *Shin Kan shisō shi kenkyū* 秦漢思想史研究. 2nd ed.
rev. Kyoto: Heirakuji, 1981.

Kang, Yin 康殷. *Wenzi yuanliu qianshuo* 文字源流淺說. Beijing: Rongbaozhai,
1979.

Katō, Jōken 加藤常賢. *Kanji no kigen* 漢字の起源. Tokyo: Kadokawa, 1972.

Kimura, Masao 木村正雄. *Chūgoku kodai nōmin hanran no kenkyū* 中國古
代農民叛亂の研究. Tokyo: Tōkyō Daigaku, 1979.

———. *Chūgoku kodai teikoku no keisei—toku ni sono seiritsu no kiso jōken*
中國古代帝國の形成—特にその成立の基礎條件. Tokyo: Fumeitō,
1967.

————. "'Senpaku' ni tsuite" 阡陌について. *Shichō* 史潮 12:2 (March, 1945): 1–72.

Koga, Noboru 古賀登. *Kan Chōanjō to senpaku kenkyōteiri seido* 漢長安城と阡陌縣鄉亭理制度. Tokyo: Yūsankaku, 1980.

Kusuyama, Shūsaku 楠山修作. "Shō Yō enten ni tsuite" 商央爰田について. *Tōhōgaku* 東方學 46 (1973): 70–87.

Lan, Yongwei 藍永蔚. *Chun qiu shiqi de bubing* 春秋時期的步兵. Beijing: Zhonghua, 1979.

Lao, Gan 勞榦. "Lun Han dai de you xia" 論漢代的游俠. In *Lao Gan xueshu lunwen ji* 勞榦學術論文集, vol. 2. Taipei: Yiwen, 1976.

————. "'Shi ji Xiang Yu ben ji' zhong 'xue shu' he 'xue jian' de jieshi" '史記項羽本紀' 中的 '學書' 和 '學劍' 的解釋. In *Lao Gan xueshu lunwen ji*, vol. 2. Taipei: Yiwen, 1976.

Li, Jiahao 李家浩. "Xian Qin wenzi zhong de 'xian'" 先秦文字中的 '縣'. In *Wen shi* 28 (March, 1987): 49–58.

Li, Jiemin 李解民. "'Kai qianmo' bianzheng" '開阡陌' 辨正. *Wen shi* 11 (March, 1981): 47–60.

Li, Ling 李零. "Guanyu Yinqueshan jianben *Sunzi* yanjiu de shangque—*Sunzi* zhuzuo shidai he zuozhe de chongyi" 關於銀雀山簡本孫子的商榷—孫子著作時代和作者的重議. *Wen shi* 7 (December, 1979): 23–34.

————. "Zhongguo gudai jumin zuzhi de liang da leixing ji qi butong laiyuan" 中國古代居民組織的兩大類型及其不同的來源. *Wen shi* 28 (March, 1987): 59–75.

Li, Xiaoding 李孝定 et al., eds., *Jiagu wenzi jishi* 甲骨文字集釋. Nanyang: Zhongyang Yanjiuyuan Lishi Yuyan Yanjiusuo, 1965.

Li, Yumin 李裕民. "Wo dui Houma mengshu de kanfa" 我對侯馬盟書的看法. *Kaogu* 1973 (3): 185–91.

Liang, Jiabin 梁嘉彬. "*Guiguzi* kao" 鬼谷子考. *Dalu zazhi* 大陸雜志 10.4 (February 28, 1955): 12–15.

Liang, Yusheng 梁玉繩 (1745–1819 A.D.). *Shi ji zhi yi* 史記志疑. Beijing: Zhonghua, 1981.

Lin, Gengdong 林耕東. *Guiguzi douzhi miji* 鬼谷子鬥智祕笈. Tainan: Zheng-ye, 1975.

Lin, Jianming 林劍鳴. *Qin shi gao* 秦史稿. Shanghai: Renmin, 1981.

Lin, Yun 林沄. "Jiaguwen zhong de Shang dai fangguo lianmeng" 甲骨文中的商代方國聯盟. In *Guwenzi yanjiu*, no. 6. Beijing: Zhonghua, 1981.

Lin, Zhichun 林志純. "Kong Meng shu zhong suo fanying de gudai Zhongguo chengshi guojia zhidu" 孔孟書中所反映的古代中國城市國家制度. *Lishi yanjiu* 1980 (3): 122–32.

Ling, Chunsheng 凌純聲. "Taidong tu she ren xiang ji qi zai Taipingyang qu de leiyuan" 臺東吐舌人像及其在太平洋區的類綠. *Minzuxue Yanjiusuo jikan* 民族學研究所集刊 1956 (2): 137–52.

Liu, Baiji 劉伯驥. *Chun qiu huimeng zhengzhi* 春秋會盟政治. Taipei: Zhonghua Congshu, 1963.

Liu, Mingshu 劉銘恕. "Han Wuliangci huaxiang zhong Huang Di Chi You zhantu kao" 漢武梁祠畫像中黃帝蚩尤戰圖考. *Zhongguo wenhua yanjiu huikan* 中國文化研究彙刊 2 (September, 1942): 341–65.

Lu, Bo 魯波. "Han dai Xu Sheng maidi qian juan jianjie" 漢代徐勝買地鉛卷簡介. *Wenwu* 1972 (5): 60–62.

Lü, Pin 呂品 and Zhou, Dao 周到. "Henan Xinye chutu de Han dai huaxiang zhuan" 河南新野出土的漢代畫像磚. *Kaogu* 1965 (1): 17–20.

Lü, Shaowang 呂紹綱. "Zhongguo gudai bu cunzai chengbang zhidu" 中國古代不存在城邦制度. *Zhongguo shi yanjiu* 1983 (4): 91–105.

Lü, Simian 呂思勉. *Xian Qin shi* 先秦史. Shanghai: Kaiming, 1941.

Luo, Zhenyu 羅振玉. *Sandai ji jinwen cun* 三代吉金文存. In *Luo Xuetang Xiansheng quanji qibian* 羅學堂先生全集七編, vols. 17–20. Taipei: Wenhua, 1968.

———. *Zengding Yinxu wenzi shuqi kaoshi* 增訂殷墟文字書契考釋. In *Luo Xuetang Xiansheng quanji sanbian* 三編, vol. 2. Taipei: Wenhua, 1968.

———. *Zhengsongtang jigu yiwen* 貞松堂集古遺文. In *Luo Xuetang Xiansheng quanji chubian* 初編, vol. 13. Taipei: Wenhua, 1968.

Makino, Tatsumi 牧野巽. *Chūgoku kazoku kenkyū* 中國家族研究. In *Makino Tatsumi chosaku shū* 牧野巽著作集, vols. 1–2. Tokyo: Ochanomizu, 1980.

Masubuchi, Tatsuo 增淵龍夫. *Chūgoku kodai no shakai to kokka* 中國古代の社会と國家. Tokyo: Kōbundō, 1962.

———. "Shunjū Sengoku jidai no shakai to kokka" 春秋戰國時代の社会と國家. In *Iwanami kōza sekai rekishi* 岩波講座世界歷史, vol. 4. Tokyo: Iwanami, 1970.

Matsumoto, Masaaki 松本雅明. "Shikyo renai shi ni okeru saishin no hyōgen" 詩經戀愛詩における採薪の表現. *Kumamoto Daigaku hōbun ronsō* 熊本大學法文論叢 1 (June, 1950): 93–111.

———. *Shunjū Sengoku ni okeru Shōsho no tenkai* 春秋戰國における尚書の展開. Tokyo: Kazema, 1968.

Matsuzaki, Tsuneko 松崎つね子. "Suikochi Shin kan yori mita Shin no kazoku to kokka" 睡虎地秦簡よりみた秦の家族と国家. In *Chūgoku kodai shi kenkyū* 中國古代史研究, no. 5. Tokyo: Yūsankaku, 1983.

Miyakawa, Hisayuki 宮川尚志. *Rikuchō shi kenkyū: seiji shakai hen* 六朝史研究：政治社會篇. Kyoto: Heirakuji, 1964.

Miyazaki, Ichisada 宮崎市定. "Chūgoku jōdai no toshi kokka to sono bōchi" 中國上代の都市國家とその墓地. In *Ajia shi ronkō* アジア史論考, vol. 2. Tokyo: Asahi Shinbun, 1978.

———. "Chūgoku jōdai wa hōkensei ka toshi kokka ka" 中國上代は封建制か都市國家か. In *Ajia shi kenkyū* アジア史研究, vol. 3. Kyoto: Dōshōsha, 1957.

———. "Chūgoku ni okeru shuraku keitai no hensen ni tsuite" 中國における聚落形體の變遷について. In *Ajia shi ronkō*, vol. 2. Tokyo: Asahi Shinbun, 1978.

———. "Kodai Chūgoku fusei seido" 古代中國賦稅制度. In *Ajia shi kenkyū*, vol. 3. Kyoto: Dōshōsha, 1957.

———. "Yūkyō ni tsuite" 游俠について. In *Ajia shi kenkyū*, vol. 1. Kyoto: Dōshōsha, 1957.

Mori, Yasutarō 森安太郎. *Kōtei densetsu: kodai Chūgoku shinwa no kenkyū* 黃帝傳說：古代中國神話の研究. Kyoto: Kyōto Joshi Daigaku Jinbun Gakkai, 1970.

Moriya, Mitsuo 守屋美都雄. *Chūgoku kodai no kazoku to kokka* 中國古代 の家族と國家. Kyoto: Tōyōshi Kenkyūkai, 1968.

Nanjing Bowuyuan 南京博物院. "Jiangsu Lianyungangshi Haizhou Wangtuan-zhuang Han mu kuo mu" 江蘇連雲港市海州網疃庄漢木槨墓. *Kaogu* 1963 (6): 287–300.

———. "Jiangsu Xuyi Dongyang Han mu" 江蘇盱眙東陽漢墓. *Kaogu* 1975 (5): 412–26.

Nanyang Diqu Wenwudui 南陽地區文物隊. "Tanghe Han Yuping Dayi Feng Jun ruren huaxiang shi mu" 唐河漢郁平大伊馮君孺人畫像石墓. *Kaogu xuebao* 1980 (2): 239–62.

Nanyangshi Bowuguan 南陽市博物館. "Henan Fangcheng Dongguan Han huaxiang shi mu" 河南方城東關漢畫像石墓. *Wenwu* 1980 (3): 69–72.

Nanyangshi Wenwu Guanli Weiyuanhui 南陽市文物管理委員會. "Henan Nanyangshi faxian Han mu" 河南南陽市發現漢墓. *Kaogu* 1966 (2): 108–10.

Nemoto, Makoto 根本誠. *Chūgoku dentō shakai to sono hō shisō* 中國傳統 社會とその法思想. Tokyo: Tōyō Tetsugaku Kenkyūsho, 1980.

Nishida, Taiichirō 西田太一郎. *Chūgoku keihō shi kenkyū* 中國刑法史研究. Tokyo: Iwanami, 1974.

Nishijima, Sadao 西嶋定生. *Chūgoku kodai teikoku no keisei to kōzō—nijū tō shakusei no kenkyū* 中國古代帝國の形成と構造—二十等爵制の研究. Tokyo: Tōkyō Daigaku, 1961.

Ōba, Osamu 大庭脩. *Shin Kan hōsei shi no kenkyū* 秦漢法制史の研究. Tokyo: Sōbunsha, 1984.

Ogata, Isamu 尾形勇. *Chūgoku kodai no "ie" to kokka* 中國古代の家と國家. Tokyo: Iwanami, 1979.

Ogura, Yoshihiko 小倉芳彦. *Chūgoku kodai seiji shisō kenkyū* 中國古代政治 思想研究. Tokyo: Aoki, 1970.

Okazaki, Fumio 岡崎文夫. "'San goku go hi' no sei ni tsuite" '參國伍鄙' の制について. In *Haneda Hakushi shōju kinen tōyōshi ronsō* 羽田 博士頌壽記念東洋史論叢. Kyoto: Tōyōshi Kenkyūkai, 1950.

Oshima, Riichi 大島利一. "Shin Nō to nōkasha ryū" 神農と農家者流. In *Haneda Hakushi shōju kinen tōyōshi ronsō*. Kyoto: Tōyōshi Kenkyūkai, 1950.

Ōta, Yukio 太田幸夫. "Shō Yō henpō no saikentō hosei" 商央變法の再檢討補正. *Rekishigaku kenkyū* 歷史學研究 483 (August, 1980): 13–24, 46.

Qi, Sihe 齊思和. "Huang Di de zhi qi gushi" 黃帝的制器故事. In *Zhongguo shi tanyan* 中國史探研. Beijing: Zhonghua, 1981.

Qiu, Xigui 裘錫圭. "Shuo buci de 'fen wuwang' yu 'zuo tulong'" 說卜辭的'焚巫尫'與'作土龍.' In *Jiaguwen yu Yinshang shi* 甲骨文與殷商史. Edited by Hu Houxuan 胡厚宣. Shanghai: Guji, 1983.

Ri, Zhi 日知. "Cong Chun qiu cheng ren zhi li zai lun Yazhou gudai minzhu zhengzhi" 從春秋稱人之例再論亞洲古代民主政治. *Lishi yanjiu* 1981 (1): 3–17.

Sanaka, Sō 佐中壯. *Sengoku Sōsho kan no shinkō to gijutsu no kankei* 戰國宋初間の信仰と技術の關係. Kyoto: Kogakukan Daigaku, 1977.

Satake, Yasuhiko 佐竹靖彦. "Chūgoku kodai no kazoku to kazokuteki chitsujo" 中國古代の家族と家族的秩序. *Jinbun gakuhō* 人文學報 141 (1980): 1–61.

———. "Shinkoku no kazoku to Shō Yō no bungirei" 秦國の家族と商央の分異令. *Shirin* 史林 62:1 (January, 1980): 1–29.

Satō, Hitoshi 左藤仁. "*Kikokushi* ni tsuite" 鬼谷子について. *Tetsugaku nenpō* 哲學年報 18 (1955): 276–95.

Satō, Taketoshi 左藤武敏. "Shunjū jidai Rokoku no fusei sei kaikaku ni kansuru ichi kōsatsu" 春秋時代魯國の賦稅制改革に關する一考察. In *Chūgoku kodai no shakai to bunka* 中國古代の社會と文化. Tokyo: Tōkyō Daigaku, 1957.

Shandongsheng Bowuguan Linyi Wenwuzu 山東省博物館臨沂文物組. "Shandong Linyi Han mu faxian *Sunzi* bingfa he *Sun Bin bingfa* zhujian jianbao" 山東臨沂漢墓發現孫子兵法和孫臏兵法竹簡簡報. *Wenwu* 1974 (2): 15–26.

Shang, Chengzuo 商承祚. *Yinqi yicun* 殷契佚存. Nanjing: Jinling Daxue, 1933.

Shanxisheng Wenwu Gongzuo Weiyuanhui 山西省文物工作委員會. *Houma mengshu* 侯馬盟書. Shanghai: Wenwu, 1976.

———. "'Houma mengshu' de faxian, fajue yu zhengli qingkuang" '侯馬盟書' 的發現發掘與整理情況. *Wenwu* 1975 (5): 7–11.

———. "Houma Zhanguo nuli xunzang mu de fajue" 侯馬戰國奴隸殉藏墓的發掘. *Wenwu* 1972 (1): 63–67.

———. "'Houma mengshu' zhushi si zhong" '侯馬盟書' 注釋四種. *Wenwu* 1975 (5): 20–26.

Shanxisheng Wenwu Guanli Weiyuanhui 山西省文物管理委員會. *Qingtong qi tushi* 青銅器圖釋. Beijing: Wenwu, 1960.

Shen, Wenzhuo 沈文倬. "Dui 'Shisang li, Jixi li zhong suo jizai de sangzang zhidu' jidian yijian" 對 '士喪禮, 旣夕禮中所記載的喪藏制度' 幾點意見. *Kaogu xuebao* 1958 (2): 29–38.

Shiratori, Kiyoshi 白鳥清. *Nihon Chūgoku kodai hō no kenkyū: shinpan to seimei no kenkyu* 日本中國古代法の研究：神判と誓盟の研究. Tokyo: Shiratori Kiyoshi Sensei Shōju Kinenkai, 1972.

Shu, Shicheng 束世澂. "Kongzi 'Chun qiu'" 孔子 '春秋.' In *Zhongguo shixue shi lunwen ji* 中國史學史論文集, vol. 1. Edited by Wu Ze 吳澤. Shanghai: Renmin, 1980.

Sun, Yao 孫曜. *Chun qiu shidai zhi shizu* 春秋時代之世族. 2nd ed. Shanghai: Zhonghua, 1936.

Sun, Zuoyun 孫作雲. "Chi You kao" 蚩尤考. *Zhong he yuekan* 中和月刊 2.4 (April, 1941): 27–50; 2.5 (May, 1941): 36–57.

———. "Ping 'Yinan gu huaxiang shi mu fajue baogao'" 評 '沂南古畫像石墓發掘報告'. *Kaogu tongxun* 考古通訊 1957 (6): 77–87.

Takahashi, Yasuichirō 高橋安一郎. "Chūgoku kodai no seibun to meibun" 中國古代の誓文と盟文. *Kōnan kokubun* 甲南國文 19 (1982): 169–82.

Tang, Lan 唐蘭. *Guwenzixue daolun* 古文字學導論. 2nd ed. rev. Ji'nan: Qilu, 1981.

———. "Houma chutu Jinguo Zhao Jia zhi meng zaishu xin shi" 侯馬出土晉國赵嘉之盟載書新釋. *Wenwu* 1972 (8): 31–35, 58.

———. *Yinxu wenzi ji* 殷墟文字集. n.p., n.d. [1974?]. Unattributed photographic reprint of 1934 manuscript.

Tao, Xisheng 陶希聖. *Bianshi yu you xia* 辯士與游俠. Shanghai: Shangwu, 1933.

Tao, Zhenggang 陶正剛 and Wang, Kelin 王克林. "Houma Dong Zhou mengshi yizhi" 侯馬東周盟誓遺址. *Wenwu* 1972 (4): 27–37, 71.

Tay, Lien-soo (Zheng, Liangshu) 鄭良樹. *Zhujian boshu lunwenji* 竹簡帛書論文集. Beijing: Zhonghua, 1982.

Tōdō, Akiyasu 藤堂明保. *Kanji gogen jiten* 漢字語源辭典. Tokyo: Gakutōsha, 1967.

Tong, Shuye 童書業. *Chun qiu shi* 春秋史. Shanghai: Kaiming, 1946.

———. *Chun qiu Zuo zhuan yanjiu* 春秋左傳研究. Shanghai: Renmin, 1980.

Utsugi, Akira 宇都木章. "'Sha ni korosu' ni tsuite—*Shū ri* no sha no seido ni kansuru ichi kōsatsu '社に戮す' について―周禮の社の制度に關する一考察. In *Chūgoku kodai shi kenkyū* 中國古代史研究. Tokyo: Yoshikawa Kōbun, 1962.

Utsunomiya, Kiyoyoshi 宇都宮清吉. *Kandai shakai keizai shi kenkyū* 漢代社會經濟史研究. Tokyo: Kōbundō, 1955.

Wang, Baoxiang 王襃祥. "Henan Xinye chutu de Han dai huaxiang zhuan" 河南新野出土的漢代畫像磚. *Kaogu* 1962 (2): 90–93.

Wang, Guowei 王國維 (1877–1927 A.D.). *Guantang jilin* 觀堂集林. Taipei: Heluo, 1975.

Wang, Sili 王思禮. "Shandong Feicheng Han mu huaxiang shi mu diaocha" 山東肥城漢墓畫像石墓調查. *Wenwu cankao ziliao* 1958 (4): 34–36.

Wang, Yinglin 王應麟 (1223–1296 A.D.). *Kun xue ji wen* 困學紀聞. Taipei: Zhonghua, 1966.

Wang, Yuquan 王毓銓. "Yuantian jie" _ _田解. *Lishi yanjiu* 1957 (4): 79–87.

Wei, Jin 衛今 and Jin, Wen   . "'Houma mengshu' he Chun qiu houqi Jinguo de jieji douzheng" '侯馬盟書' 和春秋後期晋國階級鬥爭. *Wenwu* 1975 (5): 1–6, 94.

Wei, Rulin 委汝霖. "Dalu Han mu chutu *Sunzi* bingfa canjian shiwen zhi yanjiu" 大陸漢墓出土孫子兵法殘簡釋文之研究. *Huaxue yuekan* 化學月刊 49 (January, 1976): 38–46.

Wu, Hui 吳慧. "Shi lun Chun qiu shiqi de shehui xingzhi wenti" 試論春秋時期的社會性質問題. In *Zhongguo shehui jingji shi luncong* 中國社會經濟史論叢. Edited by Shanxisheng Shehui Kexue Yanjiusuo 山西省社會科學研究所. Shanxi: Renmin, 1981.

Wu, Shuping 吳樹平. "Cong Linyi Han mu zhujian 'Wu wen' kan Sun Wu de fajia sixiang" 從臨沂漢墓竹簡 '吳問' 看孫武的法家思想. *Wenwu* 1975 (4): 6–13.

Xiong, Tieji 熊鐵基 and Wang, Ruiming 王瑞明. "Qin dai de fengjian tudi suoyouzhi" 秦代的封建土地所有制. In *Yunmeng Qin jian yanjiu* 雲夢秦簡研究. Beijing: Zhonghua, 1981.

Xu, Di 許狄. "Lue tan Yinqueshan Han mu chutu bing shu canjian" 略談銀雀山漢墓出土兵書殘簡. *Wenwu* 1976 (2): 27–31.

Xu, Zhongshu 徐中舒. "Chen Hou si qi kaoshi" 陳侯四器考釋. *Zhongyang Yanjiuyuan Lishi Yuyan Yanjiusuo jikan* 3–4 (1934): 479–506.

Yan, Gengwang 嚴耕望. *Zhongguo difang xingzheng zhidu shi* 中國地方行政制度史. Zhongyang Yanjiuyuan Lishi Yuyan Yanjiusuo zhuankan 45. Taipei, 1974.

Yan, Yiping 嚴一萍. "Buci sifang feng xinyi" 卜辭四方風新義. In *Jiagu wenzi yanjiu* 甲骨文字研究. Taipei: Yiwen, 1976.

Yang, Hong 楊泓. *Zhongguo gu bingqi luncong* 中國古兵器論叢. Beijing: Wenwu, 1980.

Yang, Jingshuang 楊景霱. "Fangxiangshi yu danuo" 方相氏與大儺. *Zhongyang Yanjiuyuan Lishi Yuyan Yanjiusuo jikan* 31 (1960): 123–65.

Yang, Kuan 楊寬. *Gu shi xin tan* 古史新探. Beijing: Zhonghua, 1965.

———. *Shang Yang bianfa* 商央變法. Shanghai: Renmin, 1955.

———. *Zhanguo shi* 戰國史. 2nd ed. rev. Shanghai: Renmin, 1980.

———. "Zhongguo shanggu shi daolun" 中國上古史導論. In *Gu shi bian*, vol. 7. Shanghai: Guji, 1982.

Yang, Shuda 楊樹達. *Jiweiju xiaoxue shulin* 積微居小學述林. Beijing: Zhongguo Kexueyuan, 1954.

Yasui, Kōzan 安居香山. *Isho no seiritsu to sono tenkai* 偉書の成立とその展開. Tokyo: Kokusho Kankō, 1981.

Yi, Xuezhong 易學鍾. "Jinning Shizhaishan shier hao mu zhu bei qi shang renwu diaoxiang kaoshi" 晋寧石寨山十二號墓貯貝器上人物雕像考釋. *Kaogu xuebao* 1987 (4): 413–36.

———. "Jinning Shizhaishan yi hao mu zhu bei qi shang renwu diaoxiang kaoshi" 晋寧石寨山一號墓貯貝器上人物雕像考釋. *Kaogu xuebao* 1988 (1): 37–49.

Ying, Yongchen 應永深. "Lun Chun qiu shidai Luguo he Jinguo de shehui de tedian jian ji rujia he fajia chansheng de lishi beijing" 論春秋時代魯國和晋國的社會的特點兼及儒家和法家產生的歷史背景 *Lishi yanjiu* 1964 (1): 151–68.

Yinshun Fashi 印順法師 (Buddhist name). *Zhongguo gudai minzu shenhua yu wenhua zhi yanjiu* 中國古代民族神話與文化之研究. Taipei: Huagang, 1975.

Yu, Weichao 俞偉超 and Gao, Ming 高明. "Zhou dai yong ding zhidu yanjiu" 周代用鼎制度研究. *Beijing Daxue xuebao: zhexue shehui kexue ban* 北京大學學報:哲學社會科學版 1 (1978): 84–98; 2 (1978): 84–97.

Yu, Yan 俞棪. *Guiguzi xin zhu* 鬼谷子新注. Shanghai: Shangwu, 1937.

Yu, Yueh 俞樾 (1821–1907 A.D.). *Chaxiangshi jing shuo* 茶香室經說. In *Biji si bian* 筆記四編, vols. 4–5. Taipei: Guangwen, 1971.

Yu, Zhengxie 俞正燮 (1775–1840 A.D.). *Gui si lei gao* 癸巳類稿. Taipei: Shijie, 1965.

Yuan, Zhouzong 袁宙宗. *Laozi shenshi ji qi bingxue sixiang tanze* 老子身世及其兵學思想探賾. Taipei: Shangwu, 1977.

Yunmeng Qin jian yanjiu 雲夢秦簡研究. Beijing: Zhonghua, 1981.

Yunmeng Shuihudi Qin mu 雲夢睡虎地秦墓. Beijing: Wenwu, 1981.

Zeng, Zhaoyu 曾昭燏, Jiang, Baogeng 蔣寶庚, and Li, Zhongyi 黎忠義. *Yinan gu huaxiang shi mu fajue baogao* 沂南古畫像石墓發掘報告. Shanghai: Wenhuabu Wenwu Guanliju, 1956.

Zhan, Libo 詹立波. "Luetan Linyi Han mu zhujian *Sunzi* bingfa" 略談臨沂漢墓竹簡孫子兵法. *Wenwu* 1974 (12): 13–19.

Zhang, Chuanxi 張傳璽. *Qin Han wenti yanjiu* 秦漢問題研究. Beijing: Beijing Daxue, 1985.

Zhang, Jinguang 張金光. "Shi lun Qin zi Shang Yang bianfa hou de tudi zhidu" 試論秦自商央變法後的土地制度. *Zhongguo shi yanjiu* 1983 (2): 26–42.

Zhang, Han 張頷. "Houma Dong Zhou yizhi faxian Jinguo zhu shu wenzi" 侯馬東周遺址發現晉國朱書文字. *Wenwu* 1966 (2): 1–3.

———. "Houma mengshu congkao" 侯馬盟書叢考. *Wenwu* 1974 (5): 12–19.

———. "Houma mengshu congkao xu" 侯馬盟書叢考續. In *Guwenzi yanjiu*, no. 1. Beijing: Zhonghua, 1979.

Zhao, Guangxian 趙光賢. *Zhou dai shehui bianxi* 周代社會辨析. Beijing: Renmin, 1980.

Zhao, Tiehan 趙鐵寒. "*Guiguzi* kaobian" 鬼谷子考辨. *Dalu zazhi* 14.5 (March 15, 1957): 3–7; 14.6 (March 31, 1957): 20–25.

Zhao, Yi 趙翼. *Gai yu congkao* 陔餘叢考. Taipei: Huashi, 1975.

Zhengzhoushi Bowuguan 鄭州市博物館. "Zhengzhou Xintongqiao Han dai huaxiang kongxin zhuan mu" 鄭州新通橋漢代畫像空心磚墓. *Wenwu* 1972 (10): 41–48.

Zhongguo Lishi Ditu Ji Bianji Zu 中國歷史地圖集編輯組. *Zhongguo lishi ditu ji* 中國歷史地圖集. Shanghai: Zhonghua Ditu Xueshe, 1975.

Zhou, Fagao 周法高 et al., eds. *Jinwen gulin* 金文詁林. Hong Kong: Chinese University, 1975.

Zhu, Dexi 朱德熙 and Qiu, Xigui 裘錫圭. "Guanyu Houma mengshu de jidian bushi" 關於侯馬盟書的幾點補釋. *Wenwu* 1972 (8): 36–38, 48.

Zhu, Shaohou 朱紹侯. "'Ming tian' qianlun" '名田'淺論. In *Zhongguo gudai shi luncong* 中國古代史論叢, no. 1. Fujian: Renmin, 1981.

[Zou Heng] 鄒衡. *Shang Zhou kaogu* 商周考古. Beijing: Wenwu, 1979.

Secondary Works in Western Languages

Akatsuka, Kiyoshi. "A New Study of the *Shih-ku Wen*: the Ancient Letters Carved in Ten Drum-Type Stones." *Acta Asiatica* 4 (1963): 80–96.

Allan, Sarah. "Drought, Human Sacrifice and the Mandate of Heaven in a Lost Text from the *Shang Shu*." *Bulletin of the School of Oriental and African Studies* 47:3 (1984): 523–39.

———. *The Heir and the Sage: Dynastic Legend in Early China*. San Francisco: Chinese Materials Center, 1981.

———. "The Identities of Taigong Wang in Zhou and Han Literature." *Monumenta Serica* 30 (1972–73): 57–99.

———. "Sons of Suns: Myth and Totemism in Early China." *Bulletin of the School of Oriental and African Studies* 44:2 (1981): 290–326.

Ames, Roger T. *The Art of Rulership: A Study in Ancient Chinese Political Thought*. Honolulu: University of Hawaii, 1983.

Arendt, Hannah. "On Violence." In *Crises of the Republic*. New York: Harcourt Brace Jovanovich, 1972.

Armstrong, Edward A. "Chinese Bull Ritual and its Affinities." *Folk-lore* 56 (1945): 200–07.

Barnard, Noel and Sato, Tamotsu. *Metallurgical Remains of Ancient China*. Tokyo: Nichiōsha, 1975.

Bilsky, Lester James. *The State Religion of Ancient China*. Taipei: The Chinese Association for Folklore, 1975.

Bishop, Carl W. "The Ritual Bullfight." *China Journal of Science and Arts* 3 (1925): 630–37.

Blainey, Geoffrey. *The Causes of War*. New York: Free Press, 1973.

Bodde, Derk. "The Chinese Cosmic Magic Known as Watching for the Ethers." In *Studia Serica Bernhard Karlgren Dedicata*. Edited by Soren Egerod and Else Glahn. Copenhagen: Ejnar Munksgaard, 1959.

———. *Festivals in Classical China: New Year and Other Annual Observances*

During the Han Dynasty, 206 B.C.–A.D. 220. Princeton: Princeton University, 1975.

———. "Myths of Ancient China." In *Mythologies of the Ancient World.* Edited by Samuel Noah Kramer. Garden City, New York: Doubleday & Company, 1961.

——— and Morris, Clarence. *Law in Imperial China.* Philadelphia: University of Pennsylvania, 1967.

Boltz, William G. "Kung Kung and the Flood: Reverse Euhemerism in the *Yao tien.*" *T'oung Pao* 67 (1981): 141–53.

———. "Philological Footnotes to the Han New Year Rites." *Journal of the American Oriental Society* 99 (1979): 423–39.

Boodberg, Peter A. "The Art of War in Ancient China: A Study Based Upon the *Dialogues of Li, Duke of Wei.*" Ph.D. dissertation, University of California at Berkeley, 1930.

Burkert, Walter. *Homo Necans: The Anthropology of Ancient Greek Sacrificial Ritual and Myth.* Translated by Peter Bing. Berkeley: University of California, 1983.

———. *Structure and History in Greek Mythology.* Berkeley: University of California, 1979.

Byrne, Rebecca Zerby. "Harmony and Violence in Classical China: A Study of the Battles of the *Tso-chuan.*" Ph.D. dissertation, University of Chicago, 1974.

Chang, Kwang-chih. *The Archeology of Ancient China,* 3rd ed. rev. New Haven: Yale University, 1977.

———. *Art, Myth, and Ritual: The Path to Political Authority in Ancient China.* Cambridge, Ma.: Harvard University, 1983.

———. *Early Chinese Civilization: Anthropological Perspectives.* Cambridge, Ma.: Harvard University, 1976.

Cheng, Te-k'un. *Archeology in Ancient China,* Vol. 3: *Chou China.* Cambridge: W. Heffer & Sons, 1963.

Chow, Tse-tsung. "The Childbirth Myth and Ancient Chinese Medicine: A

Study of Aspects of the *Wu* Tradition." In *Ancient China: Studies in Early Civilization*. Edited by David T. Roy and Tsuen-hsuin Tsien. Hong Kong: Chinese University, 1978.

Ch'ü, T'ung-tsu. *Han Social Structure*. Seattle: University of Washington, 1972.

———. *Law and Society in Traditional China*. Paris: Mouton & Co., 1961.

Clausewitz, Carl von. *On War*. Translated by Michael Howard and Peter Paret. Princeton: Princeton University, 1976.

Cohen, Alvin. "The Avenging Ghost: Moral Judgement in Chinese Historical Texts." Ph.D. dissertation, University of California at Berkeley, 1971.

———. "Avenging Ghosts and Moral Judgement in Ancient Chinese Historiography: Three Examples from *Shih-chi*." In *Legend, Lore, and Religions in China: Essays in Honor of Wolfram Eberhard on His Seventieth Birthday*. Edited by Sarah Allan and Alvin P. Cohen. San Francisco: Chinese Materials Center, 1979.

———. *Tales of Vengeful Souls: A Sixth Century Collection of Avenging Ghost Stories*. Taipei: Variétés Sinologiques, 1982.

Dalby, Michael. "Revenge and the Law in Traditional China." *The American Journal of Legal History* 25 (1981): 267–307.

Deguy, Michel and Dupuy, Jean-Pierre, eds. *René Girard et le problème du mal*. Paris: Grasset, 1982.

De Heusch, Luc. *Le sacrifice dans les religions africaines*. Paris: Gallimard, 1986.

De Jouvenel, Bertrand. *Du Pouvoir*. Paris: Librarie Hachette, 1972.

Detienne, Marcel. *Dionysos Slain*. Translated by Mireille Muellner and Leonard Muellner. Baltimore: Johns Hopkins University, 1979.

———. "Pratiques culinaires et esprit de sacrifice." In *La cuisine du sacrifice en pays grec*. Edited by Marcel Detienne and Jean-Pierre Vernant. Paris: Gallimard, 1979.

Dewoskin, Kenneth S. *Doctors, Diviners, and Magicians of Ancient China: Biographies of Fang-shih*. New York: Columbia University, 1983.

———. *A Song for One or Two: Music and the Concept of Art in Early China*.

Michigan Papers in Chinese Studies no. 42. Ann Arbor, Michigan: University of Michigan Center for Chinese Studies, 1982.

Dien, Albert. "A Study of Early Chinese Armor." Paper presented at China's Past Unearthed: the Reconciliation of the New Discoveries and the Historical Records of the Early Imperial Period. San Francisco. March 26–28, 1980. Mimeographed.

Dobson, W. A. C. H. "Some Legal Instruments of Ancient China: The *Ming* and the *Meng*." In *Wen-lin: Studies in the Chinese Humanities*. Edited by Chow Tse-tsung. Madison, Wisconsin: University of Wisconsin, 1968.

Dudbridge, Glen. *The Tale of Li Wa*. London: Ithaca, 1983.

Dumezil, Georges. *The Destiny of the Warrior*. Translated by Alf Hiltebeitel. Chicago: University of Chicago, 1970.

Dumouchel, Paul, ed. *Violence et vérité*. Paris: Grasset, 1985.

Eberhard, Wolfram. *The Local Cultures of South and East China*. Translated by Alide Eberhard. Leiden: E. J. Brill, 1968.

———. *Lokalkulturen im Alten China*. Leiden: E. J. Brill, 1942.

Egan, Ronald. "Narratives in *Tso Chuan*." *Harvard Journal of Asiatic Studies* 37.2 (1977): 323–52.

Eichorn, Werner. *Die alte chinesische Religion und das Staatskultwesen*. Leiden: E. J. Brill, 1976.

Evans-Pritchard, E. E. *The Nuer*. Oxford: Clarendon Press, 1940.

Feld, Maury D. *The Structure of Violence: Armed Forces as Social Systems*. Beverly Hills, Ca.: Sage Publications, 1977.

Fehl, Noah Edward. "Notes on the 'Lü Xing': Proposing a Documentary Theory." *The Chung Chi Journal* 9:1 (November, 1961): 10–36.

Fingarette, Herbert. *Confucius—the Secular as Sacred*. New York: Harper & Row, 1972.

Fortes, M. and Evans-Pritchard, E. E., eds. *African Political Systems*. London: Oxford University, 1940.

Freud, Sigmund. *Civilization and its Discontents*. Translated by James Strachey. New York: W. W. Norton, 1961.

Gallie, W. B. *Philosophers of Peace and War*. Cambridge: Cambridge University, 1978.

Giddens, Anthony. *The Nation-State and Violence*. Berkeley: University of California, 1985.

Gernet, Louis. *The Anthropology of Ancient Greece*. Translated by John Hamilton, S.J. and Blaise Nagy. Baltimore: Johns Hopkins University, 1981.

Girard, René. *Le bouc émissaire*. Paris: Grasset, 1982.

———. *Des choses cachées depuis la fondation du monde*. Paris: Grasset, 1978.

———. *La route antique des hommes pervers*. Paris: Grasset, 1985.

———. *La violence et le sacré*. Paris: Grasset, 1972.

———. *Violence and the Sacred*. Translated by Patrick Gregory. Baltimore: Johns Hopkins University, 1977.

Glum, Peter. "Rain Magic at Anyang?" *Bulletin of the Museum of Far Eastern Antiquities* 54 (1982): 241–65.

Goldsmith, M. M. *Hobbes's Science of Politics*. New York: Columbia University, 1966.

Gough, Kathleen. "Nuer Kinship: A Re-examination." In *The Translation of Culture*. Edited by T. L. Beidelman. London: Tavistock, 1972.

Graham, A. C. "The Background of the Mencian Theory of Human Nature." In *Studies in Chinese Philosophy & Philosophical Literature*. Singapore: Institute of East Asian Philosophies, 1986.

———. "How Much of *Chuang Tzu* did Chuang Tzu Write?" *Journal of the American Academy of Religion: Thematic Issue* 47 (September, 1979): 459–501.

———. "The *Nung-chia* 'School of the Tillers' and the Origins of Peasant Utopianism in China." *Bulletin of the School of Oriental and African Studies* 42 (1971): 66–100.

————. *Yin-Yang and the Nature of Correlative Thinking*. The Institute of East Asian Philosophies Occasional Paper and Monograph Series no. 6. Singapore, 1986.

Granet, Marcel. *Chinese Civilization*. Translated by K. E. Innes and M. R. Brailsford. London: Routledge & Kegan Paul, 1930.

————. *Danses et légendes de la Chine ancienne*. 1926. Reprint (2 vols. in 1). Paris: Presses Universitaires de France, 1959.

————. *Festivals and Songs of Ancient China*. Translated by E. D. Edwards. London: George Routledge & Sons, 1932.

————. *La pensée chinoise*. Paris: La Renaissance du Livre, 1934.

————. *The Religion of the Chinese People*. Translated by Maurice Freedman. New York: Harper & Row, 1975.

Haloun, G. "Legalist Fragments—Part 1: *Kuan-tsi* 55 and Related Texts." *Asia Major*, o.s. 2 (1951–1952): 85–120.

Harper, Donald. "A Chinese Demonography of the Third Century B.C." *Harvard Journal of Asiatic Studies* 45 (1985): 459–98.

Havelock, Eric. "War as a Way of Life in Classical Culture." In *Classical Values and the Modern World*. Edited by Etienne Gareau. Ottawa: University of Ottawa, 1972.

Holzman, Donald, "Ts'ao Chih and the Immortals." *Asia Major*, Third Series 1:1 (1988): 15–57.

Hsu, Cho-yun. *Ancient China in Transition: An Analysis of Social Mobility, 722–222 B.C.* Stanford: Stanford University, 1965.

Hulsewe, A. F. P. *Remnants of Ch'in Law*. Leiden: E. J. Brill, 1985.

————. *Remnants of Han Law*. Leiden: E. J. Brill, 1955.

————. "Watching the Vapors: an Ancient Chinese Technique of Prognostication." *Nachrichten der Gesellschaft für Natur und Volkerkunde Ostasiens* 125 (1979): 40–49.

Jacob, Margaret C. *The Newtonians and the English Revolution, 1689–1720*. Ithaca, New York: Cornell University, 1976.

Johnson, David. "Epic and History in Early China: The Matter of Wu Tzu-hsü." *Journal of Asian Studies* 40.2 (February, 1981): 255–71.

———. "The Wu Tzu-hsü *Pien-wen* and Its Sources: Parts I and II." *Harvard Journal of Asiatic Studies* 40.1 (June, 1980): 119–51; 40.2 (December, 1980): 465–505.

Karlgren, Bernhard. *Grammata Serica Recensa*. 1957. Reprint. Stockholm: Museum of Far Eastern Antiquities, 1964.

———. "Legends and Cults in Ancient China." *Bulletin of the Museum of Far Eastern Antiquities* 18 (1946): 199–365.

Keegan, John. *The Mask of Command*. New York: Viking, 1987.

Kierman, Frank A., Jr. "Phases and Modes of Combat in Early China." In *Chinese Ways in Warfare*. Edited by Frank A. Kierman, Jr. Cambridge, Ma.: Harvard University, 1974.

Kirk, G. S. *Myth: Its Meaning & Functions in Ancient & Other Cultures*. Berkeley: University of California, 1970.

Leeming, Frank. "Official Landscapes in Traditional China." *Journal of the Economic and Social History of the Orient* 23 (1980): 153–204.

Li, Xueqin. *Eastern Zhou and Qin Civilizations*. Translated by K. C. Chang. New Haven: Yale University, 1985.

Liu, James J. Y. *The Chinese Knight Errant*. London: Routledge & Kegan Paul, 1967.

Loewe, Michael. *Chinese Ideas of Life and Death: Faith, Myth and Reason in the Han Period (206 B.C. – A.D. 220)*. London: George Allen & Unwin, 1982.

———. "The Cult of the Dragon and the Invocation for Rain." In *Chinese Ideas About Nature and Society: Studies in Honour of Derk Bodde*. Edited by Charles LeBlanc and Susan Blader. Hong Kong: Hong Kong University, 1987.

———. "The Han View of Comets." *Bulletin of the Museum of Far Eastern Antiquities*. 52 (1980): 1–32.

McKnight, Brian E. *The Quality of Mercy: Amnesties and Traditional Chinese Justice*. Honolulu: University of Hawaii, 1981.

Major, John S. "Notes on the Nomenclature of Winds and Directions in the Early Han." *T'oung Pao* 65.1–3 (1979): 66–80.

Maspero, Henri. *China in Antiquity*. Translated by Frank A. Kierman, Jr. n.p.: University of Massachusetts, 1978.

———. "Légendes mythologiques dans le *Chou King*." *Journal Asiatique* 204 (1924): 1–100.

———. "Le roman historique dans la littérature chinoise de l'antiquité." In *Mélanges posthumes*, vol. 3. Paris: Presses Universitaires de France, 1950.

———. "Le roman de Sou Ts'in." In *Études Asiatiques publiées a l'occasion du vingt-cinquième anniversaire de l'École Francaise d'Extrême-Orient*, vol. 2. Paris: G. van Oest, 1925.

Mattos, Gilbert. "The Stone Drums of Ch'in." Ph.D. dissertation, University of Washington, 1973.

Middleton, John and Tait, David, eds. *Tribes Without Rulers*. London: Routledge & Kegan Paul, 1958.

Needham, Joseph. *Science and Civilization in China*, Vol. 4: *Physics and Physical Technology*, Part 1: *Physics*. Cambridge: Cambridge University, 1962.

Nock, Arthur Darby, ed. and trans. *Sallustius: Concerning the Gods and the Universe*. Cambridge: Cambridge University, 1926.

Norman, Jerry and Mei, Tsu-lin. "The Austroasiatics in Ancient South China: Some Lexical Evidence." *Monumenta Serica* 32 (1976): 274–301.

O'Flaherty, Wendy Doniger. *Women, Androgynes, and Other Mythical Beasts*. Chicago: University of Chicago, 1980.

Orwell, George. *The Collected Essays, Journalism, and Letters of George Orwell*. Edited by Sonia Orwell and Ian Anges. New York: Harcourt Brace Jovanovich, 1968.

Passerin d'Entreves, Alexander. *The Notion of the State*. Oxford: Clarendon Press, 1967.

Pocock, J. G. A. "Ritual, Language, Power: An Essay on the Apparent Political Meanings of Ancient Chinese Philosophy." In *Politics, Language, and Time: Essays on Political Thought and History*. New York: Atheneum, 1973.

Poggi, Gianfranco. *The Development of the Modern State: A Sociological Introduction*. Stanford: Stanford University, 1978.

Porkert, Manfred. *Theoretical Foundations of Chinese Medicine*. Cambridge, Ma.: MIT, 1978.

———. "Untersuchungen einiger philosophisch-wissenschaftlicher Grundbegriffe und Beziehungen in Chinesischen." *Zeitschrift der deutschen morgenländischer Gesellschaft* 110.2 (1961): 422–52.

———. "Wissenschaftliches Denken im alten China: Das System der energetischen Beziehungen." *Antaios* 2.6 (March, 1961): 532–51.

Rand, Christopher C. "Li Ch'üan and Chinese Military Thought." *Harvard Journal of Asiatic Studies* 39.1 (June, 1979): 107–37.

———. "The Role of Military Thought in Early Chinese Intellectual History." Ph.D. dissertation, Harvard University, 1977.

Redfield, James. *Nature and Culture in the Iliad: The Tragedy of Hector*. Chicago: University of Chicago, 1975.

Rosen, Sidney. "Changing Conceptions of the Hegemon in Pre-Ch'in China." In *Ancient China: Studies in Early Civilization*. Edited by David T. Roy and Tsuen-hsuin Tsien. Hong Kong: Chinese University, 1978.

Rudolph, Richard C. "Bull Grappling in Early Chinese Reliefs." *Archeology* 13 (Winter, 1960): 241–45.

Scarry, Elaine. *The Body in Pain: The Making and Unmaking of the World*. New York: Oxford University, 1985.

Schafer, Edward H. "Hunting Parks and Animal Enclosures in Ancient China." *Journal of the Economic and Social History of the Orient* 11 (1968): 318–43.

———. "Ritual Exposure in Ancient China." *Harvard Journal of Asiatic Studies* 14 (1951): 130–84.

Schmitt, Carl. *The Concept of the Political*. Translated by George Schwab. New Brunswick, New Jersey: Rutgers University, 1976.

Schneider, Laurence A. *Ku Chieh-kang and China's New History: Nationalism and the Search for Alternative Traditions*. Berkeley: University of California, 1971.

———. *A Madman of Ch'u: The Chinese Myth of Loyalty and Dissent*. Berkeley: University of California, 1980.

Segal, Charles. *Tragedy and Civilization: An Interpretation of Sophocles*. Cambridge, Ma.: Harvard University, 1981.

Slotkin, Richard. *Redemption Through Violence: The Mythology of the American Frontier, 1600–1860*. Middletown, Connecticut: Wesleyan University, 1973.

———. *The Fatal Environment: The Myth of the Frontier in the Age of Industrialization, 1800–1890*. New York: Atheneum, 1985.

Southall, Aidan. *Alur Society*. Cambridge: W. Heffer & Sons, 1956.

Spragens, T. A., Jr. *The Politics of Motion: the World of Thomas Hobbes*. London: Croom Helm, 1973.

Takeuchi, Teruo. "A Study of the Meaning of *Jen* Advocated by Confucius." *Acta Asiatica* 9 (1965): 57–77.

Tu, Wei-ming. "The Thought of Huang-Lao: A Reflection on the Lao Tzu and Huang Ti Texts in the Silk Manuscripts of Ma Wang-tui." *Journal of Asian Studies* 39.1 (November, 1979): 95–109.

Unschuld, Paul U. *Medicine in China: A History of Ideas*. Berkeley: University of California, 1985.

Valeri, Valerio. *Kingship and Sacrifice: Ritual and Society in Ancient Hawaii*. Translated by Paula Wissing. Chicago: University of Chicago, 1985.

Vermeule, Emily. *Aspects of Death in Early Greek Art and Poetry*. Berkeley: University of California, 1979.

Wallacker, Benjamin E. "Two Concepts in Early Chinese Military Thought." *Language* 42.2 (1966): 295–99.

Watson, Burton. *Early Chinese Literature*. New York: Columbia University, 1962.

Watson, William. *The Art of Dynastic China*. New York: Henry N. Abrams, 1981.

Weber, Max. "Politics as a Vocation." In *From Max Weber: Essays in Sociology*. Edited by H. H. Gerth and C. Wright Mills. New York: Oxford University, 1958.

Wechsler, Howard J. *Offerings of Jade and Silk: Ritual and Symbol in the Legitimation of the T'ang Dynasty*. New Haven: Yale University, 1985.

Wilbur, C. Martin. *Slavery in China During the Former Han Dynasty, 206 B.C.–3 A.D.* New York: Russell & Russell, 1943.

Wright, Arthur F. "Sui Yang-ti: Personality and Stereotype." In *The Confucian Persuasion*. Edited by Arthur F. Wright. Stanford: Stanford University, 1960.

Xuyet, Ngo Van. *Divination, magie et politique dans la Chine ancienne*. Paris: Presses Universitaires de France, 1976.

Yang, Lien-sheng. "The Concept of 'Pao' as a Basis for Social Relationships in China." In *Chinese Thought and Institutions*. Edited by John K. Fairbank. Chicago: University of Chicago, 1957.

―――. "Hostages in Chinese History." In *Studies in Chinese Institutional History*. Cambridge, Ma.: Harvard University, 1961.

Yates, Robin D. S. "New Light on Ancient Chinese Military Texts: The Development of Military Specialization." *T'oung Pao* 74:4–5 (1988): 212–48.

―――. "Social Status in the Ch'in: Evidence from the Yun-meng Legal Documents. Part One: Commoners." *Harvard Journal of Asiatic Studies* 47:1 (June, 1987): 197–237.

Index